FINANCIAL TIMES

MASTERING RISK

Volume 1: Concepts

executive editor

James Pickford

Executive editor James Pickford

Subeditor Ken Pottinger

FT Mastering designer Gabrielle Izen

Graphics Graham Parish

PEARSON EDUCATION LIMITED
Edinburgh Gate
Harlow CM20 2JE
Tel: +44 (0)1279 623623
Fax: +44 (0)1279 431059
Website: www.pearsoned.co.uk
Website: www.business-minds.com

First published in Great Britain in 2001

ISBN 978 0 273 65379 0

British Library Cataloguing in Publication Data
A CIP catalogue record for this book can be obtained from the British Library.

12

Typeset by Land and Unwin (Data Sciences) Limited, Bugbrooke
Printed and bound in Great Britain by Ashford Colour Press, Hampshire

The Publishers' policy is to use paper manufactured from sustainable forests.

Contents

Introduction vii

1 THE NATURE OF RISK 1

2 RISK MEASUREMENT 31

3 RISK STRATEGY 63

4 FINANCIAL RISK 97

5 OPERATIONAL RISK 131

6 REGULATION AND POLITICAL RISK 161

7 INSURANCE AND SYSTEMIC RISK 191

8 EMERGING ISSUES IN RISK 225

9 ENVIRONMENTAL RISK AND EXTREME EVENTS 251

10 RISK 21C 285

Subject index 317
Organization index 322
Name index 324

Introduction

The *Financial Times Mastering* series represents a rare and fruitful collaboration between journalistic and academic organizations. In this, the eighth book in the series, the *FT* and some of the world's leading business schools have come together to create a definitive guide to the study and control of risk in business. This book contains the collected articles from the series that appeared in the *FT* newspaper between April and July 2000.

Mastering Risk is published in two volumes. The first introduces the reader to the main concepts of the subject, including methods for identifying, assessing, and controlling risks, and the role that different parts of the organization should play in managing risk. The second volume examines the techniques of financial risk management in much greater detail. Together these volumes form an invaluable guide to a complex and fast-changing subject.

Mastering Risk: Concepts contains 50 articles written by world-class academics and international risk experts. Faculty members from many business school have taken part, including the Wharton School of the University of Pennsylvania; INSEAD, near Paris in France; London Business School; Harvard Business School; Templeton College, University of Oxford; and Columbia Business School in New York.

In a departure from previous series, *Mastering Risk* also includes a significant number of contributions from expert practitioners, such as Peter Bernstein, Nigel Turnbull and Stephen Thieke, as well as specialist writers from Barclays Bank, Glaxo Wellcome and RiskMetrics.

There are ten sections, each of which covers a core area or a field of emerging importance: the nature of risk; risk measurement; risk strategy; financial risk; operational risk; regulation and political risk; insurance and systemic risk; emerging issues in risk; environmental risk and extreme events; and a concluding section on 21st century risk.

Risks to business come in many different guises. Financial risks, such as currency fluctuations or unforeseen increases in basic costs, can overwhelm a company's delicate financial plans. Operational risks, such as health and safety issues, manufacturing stoppages or product faults, can threaten the viability of its operations. Companies are encountering new kinds of risk, including brand and reputation risks, and many are confronting the legal problems associated with e-commerce. Natural disasters, such as earthquake, tornado or flood, are the best-known class of risks – and often the most devastating.

Fortunately, there are means to protect against many of these risks. Managers might insure their companies against natural disasters and prepare for them by duplicating their vital systems in alternative locations. Derivatives enable companies to hedge against swings in currency, interest rates, and commodity prices. And with the arrival of the Chief Risk Officer, organizations can integrate their disparate risk policies for the benefit of the whole.

The writers in this book address these issues with rigorous analysis and argument, suggesting practical solutions and citing key examples from industry and finance. At the end of each article, readers may also find useful suggestions for further reading.

As with previous series, thanks is owed primarily to these contributors, who gave generously of their time and expertise, and endured the cut and thrust of the *FT* newspaper's editorial process.

Finally, regular readers of Mastering series in the *FT* newspaper will know that *Mastering Risk* is followed by *Mastering Management*, an extensive survey of the core concepts of management, from strategy and marketing to ethics and leadership. You can find out more about future Mastering series by visiting the associated website at www.ftmastering.com

James Pickford
Executive editor, FT Mastering

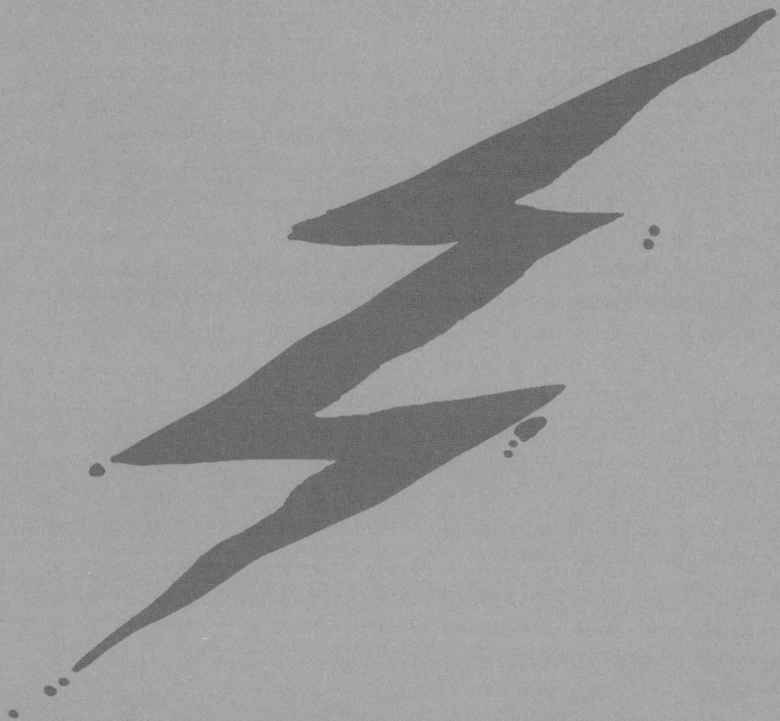

1

THE NATURE OF RISK

Contributors

Peter L. Bernstein is president of a New York-based consultancy to institutional investors and author of *Against the Gods: The Remarkable Story of Risk.*

Mark Butterworth is chairman of the Association of Insurance and Risk Managers (AIRMIC) and group insurance risk manager at the UK financial services group Prudential.

Anthony Carey was project director of the Internal Control Working Party of the Institute of Chartered Accountants in England and Wales. He is director of the Institute's Centre for Business Performance and secretary of its Corporate Governance Group.

Mark Fenton-O'Creevy is a lecturer in management at the Open University Business School and a consultant. His research interests include risk behavior, the effectiveness of employee involvement practices, and the management of organizational change.

Nigel Turnbull was chairman of the Internal Control Working Party of the Institute of Chartered Accountants in England and Wales. He is chairman of the Institute's Business Focus Group and a director of Lasmo.

Emma Soane is a research officer in organizational behavior at London Business School, an occupational psychologist, and consultant. Her research interests include decision making, risk, and personality.

René Stulz holds the Everett D. Reese Chair of Banking and Monetary Economics at the Fisher College of Business, Ohio State University. He was editor of the *Journal of Finance* for 12 years.

Contents

The enlightening struggle against uncertainty 5
Peter L. Bernstein
This article describes humankind's efforts to understand and control risk. The achievements have been impressive, but risk will never be vanquished – its ultimate source is human nature.

The boardroom imperative on internal control 10
Anthony Carey, Centre for Business Performance, Institute of Chartered Accountants in England and Wales
Nigel Turnbull, Business Focus Group, Institute of Chartered Accountants in England and Wales
Risk management should be a central part of a board's activities, not an annual exercise in satisfying regulatory requirements.

Diminishing the threats to shareholder wealth 15
René Stulz, Fisher College of Business, Ohio State University
Shareholders can protect themselves by diversification, but corporations can boost their market value by careful risk management strategies.

The emerging role of the risk manager 21
Mark Butterworth, Association of Insurance and Risk Managers
Is the risk manager a buyer of corporate insurance or a new type of strategic consultant?

The subjective perception of risk 25
Mark Fenton-O'Creevy, Open University Business School
Emma Soane, London Business School
Our perceptions of risk can be strongly influenced by psychological attributes.

Introduction

Mastering Risk provides a comprehensive guide to the most important concepts of risk management. The subject can be approached in many different ways, as the articles in this introductory chapter attest. First, it is important to realize that people have been managing risks for centuries – by principles that persevere even today in the calculation of insurance premiums. Peter Bernstein opens with a historical survey of humankind's efforts to control uncertainty – and sets limits on our ability to do so. Elsewhere in this section, authors examine why risk management has increased in importance, and describe the new role of the risk officer. Finally, they show how human subjectivity causes our standards of risk to vary according to our perceptions of loss and gain, control, and the decision-making process.

The enlightening struggle against uncertainty

by Peter L. Bernstein

The view that we can reach out to the future to bring it under control is one of the most audacious advances in the history of humanity. As the articles in this book will reveal, the subjects of risk management, risk measurement, and decision theory today command an extraordinary breadth and sophistication. The gods are still so unkind as to deny us knowledge of what the future holds, but we have made two giant strides: first, we now understand a great deal about the likelihood of unpleasant surprises; and, to a far greater extent, we are learning how to manage the consequences of unpleasant surprises when they do occur. Science has replaced seat-of-the-pants in many areas.

My goal here is twofold: first, to provide a brief narrative of how we got where we are; then, to offer a few thoughts on why we may not have traveled as far as many participants in the field would like us to believe. We now know an enormous amount. We are less attentive to assigning priorities to this great mass of wisdom.

It is difficult for us today to visualize a world in which no one knew the laws of probability, when no one had even heard of the Bell Curve that describes the way most variables distribute themselves around an average, or when people even had no sense of what "average" meant. For most of human history, however, tools for measuring risk were unknown because they were unnecessary. Economic activity consisted almost entirely of farming, fishing, and hunting. The single greatest variable was the weather – and we all know we can do nothing about the weather. Such techniques as sampling were either unknown or conducted in only the crudest manner, with no way of judging whether three rotten apples near the top of a barrel meant there were a lot more rotten apples below.

Human beings were never allowed to forget that they were helpless before the fates or the gods or whatever exogenous power struck their fancy. God's will, in an endless variety of formats, determined the future. The greatest of mathematicians among the Egyptians, the Assyrians, the Greeks, the Romans, and the scholars of the Middle Ages never considered risk measurement or risk management worth their time, keenly aware of uncertainty as they may have been. Even gambling – perhaps the second oldest profession in human history – was played by rules that seem idiotically arbitrary to anyone schooled in the simplest elements of probability.

The turning point came during the Renaissance and the Reformation, which brought about a transformation in the way people perceived the future. For the first time in history, men and women stood up and dared to think that they could control their fate.

It is no coincidence that economic life was changing at the same time. Stimulated by the discoveries of new sea routes around the world, the immense flows of gold and silver from the Americas, and the insatiable European hunger for Asian spices and textiles, what we now call globalization was causing almost as much interest and excitement as in modern times. Commerce and finance were spreading, technological change was occurring in agriculture and navigation, and gunpowder was changing warfare into an increasingly complex business. Innovation was gathering momentum in all these areas, but most notably in commerce, finance, and banking.

In 1654, at a time when many of these changes were in full bloom, one of the most influential intellectual innovations of all time occurred. The Chevalier de Méré, a French nobleman with a taste for both gambling and mathematics, challenged the great mathematician Blaise Pascal to resolve a puzzle that had been teasing mathematicians and gamblers for more than 150 years. How do you divide the stakes between two players in a game of chance if they stop the game before it is finished and one player is ahead of the other?

Nobody knew how to answer this question until Pascal and his colleague Pierre de Fermat suggested that these two players divvy up the stakes on the basis of the respective probability that each would win the game – and demonstrated for the first time how to calculate that probability. Even though Pascal and Fermat were responding to a puzzle in a game of chance, their innovation was an intellectual thunderclap.

The advancement of mathematics and finance moved forward at unprecedented speed. Insurance, whose entire functioning depends ultimately on the principles of probability, was almost certainly the most important force, since the rapid expansion in world trade was converting maritime insurance into one of the fastest-growing areas of economic activity. In addition, governments were eager to reduce their dependence on the great banking families of Italy and Germany and began to seek financing in the public markets. The financing instrument of choice was annuities that would repay the borrowings over the remaining lives of the lenders.

Building blocks

The theory of probability took hold like wildfire. In a little more than 50 years after 1654, in a whirlwind of innovation and discovery, a small group of mathematicians had developed the building blocks for just about all the tools of risk measurement we use today: statistical sampling and statistical significance, the application of probability to a wide range of practical problems from legal matters to engineering, and the first efforts to define the normal distribution and standard deviation. Soon giant advances in the uses of insurance were taking place, especially in the first systematic efforts to estimate life expectancies. Much of what followed, even such important contributions as options theory, were outgrowths of these elements of risk measurement.

After these advances, only three major components of the science of risk management remained to be discovered: utility, regression to the mean, and diversification. In 1738, the noted Swiss scientist and mathematician Daniel Bernoulli greatly enriched probability theory by introducing the first component – the notion of utility. This established a method for defining the value or attractiveness of different outcomes. His innovation showed that, when we make a decision, the consequences of different outcomes can often outweigh the probabilities that each will occur.

The second component is regression to the mean. It was discovered by Francis Galton, a Victorian-age explorer, amateur scientist, and first cousin of Charles Darwin. Broadly speaking, regression to the mean is the idea that everything returns to normal in the long run. Over time, there is an average to which extremes will always return. Galton's experiments in the late 1800s demonstrated this effect

Chronology of risk

■ **1654** French mathematicians Blaise Pascal and Pierre de Fermat analyze games of chance, providing for the first time a formal and mathematical basis for the theory of probability.

■ **1662** English merchant John Graunt publishes tables of births and deaths in London using innovative sampling methods. He estimates the population of London by the technique of statistical inference.

■ **1687** Edward Lloyd opens a coffee house in Tower Street, London. In 1696 he launches Lloyd's List, giving information on aspects of shipping from a network of European correspondents.

■ **1696** English mathematician and astronomer Edmund Halley shows how life tables can be used to price life insurance at different ages.

■ **1713** Swiss mathematician Jacob Bernoulli's "Law of Large Numbers" is published posthumously, showing how probabilities and statistical significance can be identified from limited information.

■ **1733** French mathematician Abraham de Moivre proposes the normal distribution, the pattern in which a series of variables distribute themselves around an average, from which he also derives the concept of standard deviation.

■ **1738** Jacob Bernoulli's nephew Daniel introduces the idea of utility: decisions relating to risk involve not only calculations of probability but also the value of the consequences to the risk taker.

■ **1885** English scientist Francis Galton discovers regression to the mean, the tendency of extremes to return to a normal or average.

■ **1944** In *Theory of Games and Economic Behavior*, US academics John von Neumann and Oskar Morgenstern apply the theory of games of strategy (in contrast to games of chance) to decision making in business and investing.

■ **1952** US economist Harry Markowitz demonstrates mathematically that risk and expected return are directly related, but that investors can reduce the variance of return on their investments by diversification without loss of expected return.

■ **1970** US academics Fischer Black and Myron Scholes publish a mathematical model for calculating the value of an option.

in heredity and suggested its status as a general statistical rule. Scientists who followed Galton showed that it also held sway in a vast range of situations, including weather patterns, stock markets, games of chance, frequencies of accident, and economic cycles.

The third piece of the jigsaw fell into place much later. In 1952, Harry Markowitz, a young graduate student at the University of Chicago, wrote an article that gave solid mathematical foundations to the strategy of diversification in investment. His work showed how investors and business managers could minimize the "variance of return" by carefully spreading their investments. In 1990, Markowitz was awarded the Nobel Prize for his theoretical and practical work on portfolio selection.

Thus a few powerful ideas provided the theoretical foundations for the noble edifice of modern risk management. My story has so far centered on the mathematical advances that underpinned efforts to control risk; yet I believe that the beating heart of risk analysis lies elsewhere. Mathematical innovations are only tools, mere instruments to be employed in the search for a more exciting objective. The more we stare at the jumble of equations and models, the more we lose sight of the mystery of life – which is what risk is all about. Knowing how risk management works is just the beginning. Knowing how and when to use these tools is the introduction to wisdom.

The seminal lesson on this subject comes from Pascal himself. In 1660, after he had retired to a monastery, he posed the question: "God is or God is not – which way should we incline?" He responded emphatically to his own question, saying: "Reason cannot answer." That is what life is all about: a sequence of problems to which there is no certain solution and where rational decisions are often impossible to define.

Pascal's next step was to differentiate between decision and belief. You cannot wake up one morning and decide, "Today I will believe in God," or "Today I will decide not to believe in God." You believe or you do not believe – that is in your gut, not your head. On the other hand, there is a decision you can make, which is how you behave in life. You can choose between acting as though God is or acting as though God is not, no matter how you believe.

The issue is in the consequences if your choice is wrong. Suppose you act as though God exists and lead a life of virtue and abstinence when in fact there is no God. You will have passed up some pleasant goodies in life, but there will also be rewards. On the other hand, suppose you act as though there is no God and lead a licentious and hedonistic life when in fact God does exist. You may have had lots of fun during the relatively brief duration of your lifetime, but you will spend eternity in Hell.

If you care about consequences, Pascal concludes, you must decide to act as though God exists, *regardless of your estimate of the probability that God exists.* By the time we find out whether God does or does not exist, it will be too late. The decision to act as though there is no God runs the risk of intolerable consequences.

The consequences of a bad outcome must always outweigh the expected probability of that outcome. "Bad outcomes" need not always be losses – they can also be opportunity costs. Suppose you are considering a modest investment in a cross-section of internet stocks. This is a risky bet, with a good chance that you will lose even though the smaller probability of winning could bring you a fortune. The consequences of not investing and being wrong are far more damaging than the consequences of investing and being wrong. When we place numbers on those kinds of calculations, we end up with what has come to be known as utility theory.

Strategy or chance

The star in the firmament of utility theory is John von Neumann, a quirky Hungarian and nuclear scientist who spent most of his active life at Princeton University in the US. He is perhaps best known for the theory he formulated in the 1930s concerning games of strategy, as distinct from games of chance. Von Neumann's key insight in the theory of games of strategy was to recognize that men and women are not Robinson Crusoes, each individual isolated from all other individuals. He brought decision theory into modern times by recognizing that the source of uncertainty was no longer to be found predominantly in nature and the weather – it lies instead in people. When decisions are made by intense interaction among all the players in the great game of life, maximizing one's objectives may no longer be possible. Real life is a sequence of compromises with our fellow human beings. That is not the case when throwing dice or betting on the roulette wheel, but it is true of bridge and poker.

As von Neumann and his Princeton collaborator Oskar Morgenstern point out in their masterpiece, *Theory of Games and Economic Behavior*, there is a profound distinction between a genuine economy and a Robinson Crusoe economy [italics added]: "Crusoe is confronted with a formal problem quite different from the one a participant in a social economy faces . . . [Crusoe] controls all the variables exclusively . . . to obtain maximum resulting satisfaction . . . In order to bring [the rules of the game] *into the sphere of combat and competition . . .* it is necessary to consider n-person games with $n \geq 2$ and thereby sacrifice the simple maximum aspect of the problem."

All economic systems, even the most primitive, depend on production and technology, but capitalism is about buying and selling – combat and competition – even more than it is about production and technology. Buying and selling mean human decisions. What will the customer decide? What will the supplier decide? What will the employee decide? What will the politicians decide? What happens when employees mess up, accidents occur on our property, our banks cut off our credit line, or the cost of our raw materials goes through the roof?

The decisions that each of us make as we ask ourselves these questions will in turn have an influence on how customers, suppliers, employees, politicians, and bankers will make choices in response. The most exquisite von Neumannism is the recognition that the value of your investment portfolio is not what some pundit estimates you might earn over the long run. The value of your portfolio is simply what other investors out there are going to be willing to pay you for your assets as the future unfolds. Markets are people, not accommodating machines.

Game theory teaches us that human beings create a complex jumble of uncertainties for one another. It is not enough to say that human nature never changes and let it go at that. Human beings learn from experience and from technology. Yesterday's response to a given set of circumstances is only a hint of what tomorrow's response to that set of circumstances will be – and in any case, today's circumstances will never reappear tomorrow precisely as they were today. So we really do not know what the future holds. Risk in our world is nothing more than uncertainty about the decisions that other human beings are going to make and how we can best respond to those decisions.

It is important to remember that uncertainty is our friend, not our adversary. For example, imagine what life would be if it were so orderly that everything – and I mean everything – regressed almost instantaneously to the mean, as Galton predicted, and that the mean itself was never changing. In such a stationary world, making decisions would be a waste of time. What is going to happen is going to happen regardless of the action we take. Life without uncertainty would be like a movie whose ending you always knew.

In such a world, you can forget about the outliers that make life exciting and are the source of the greatest profits to be earned in business and investing. Such a world is Nazism run wild. Free will – our most precious attribute as humans – would be meaningless, null and void. We would be God's prisoners rather than God's children.

I believe that the best of all worlds would be something close to the one we have, a world where the game of life is like bridge or poker rather than roulette. Outcomes are uncertain when the enemy is us, but we have some control over what is going to happen – or, at least, some control over the consequences of whatever other people choose to do.

Understanding that process is well worth the effort. That is what risk management is all about.

Summary

In this introduction to *Mastering Risk*, **Peter L. Bernstein** charts the extraordinary advances that humankind has made in seeking to control its own destiny. Controlling risk depends on understanding it, measuring it, and weighing its consequences. During most of history people have had no more than gut instinct and superstition to guide them when facing uncertainty. The first breakthrough came in 1654 when Blaise Pascal and Pierre de Fermat used mathematics to analyze a simple game of chance, and thus created the basis for probability theory. The discoveries that followed – including sampling techniques, utility, regression to the mean, and diversification – gave solid foundations to the insurance industry and catalyzed economic growth generally. Businesses could finally make rational assessments of risk and plan their operations accordingly. However, the immense sophistication of modern risk management techniques should not lead us to think we have wholly conquered risk – or that such a conquest will ever be possible. Human beings will continue to interact, make choices, and respond to those choices in unpredictable ways that are the ultimate sources of uncertainty. That is where the heart of risk management lies.

Suggested further reading

Bernstein, P. (1996) *Against the Gods: The Remarkable Story of Risk*, New York: Wiley.

Galton, F. (1869) *Hereditary Genius: An Inquiry into its Laws and Consequences*, London: Macmillan.

Hacking, I. (1975) *The Emergence of Probability: A Philosophical Study of Early Ideas about Probability, Induction and Statistical Inference*, London: Cambridge University Press.

Markowitz, H.M. (1952) "Portfolio Selection," *Journal of Finance*, 7(1): 77–91.

von Neumann, J. and Morgenstern, O. (1944) *Theory of Games and Economic Behavior*, Princeton, NJ: Princeton University Press.

The boardroom imperative on internal control

by Anthony Carey and Nigel Turnbull

Risk management should be an integral part of every business and not just an exercise in meeting regulatory requirements. Evaluating and controlling risks effectively will ensure that opportunities are not lost, competitive advantage is enhanced, and less management time is spent firefighting. The likely reduction in surprises and the increased ability to meet objectives will strengthen shareholder confidence in the corporate business process. In time, this should lead to a higher share price and a lower cost of capital.

The Turnbull report, prepared by a working party of the Institute of Chartered Accountants in England and Wales and endorsed by the Stock Exchange, seeks to reflect best business practice by adopting a risk-based approach to designing, operating, and maintaining a sound system of internal control. The guidance it offers comes in the form of a framework rather than a rulebook, and is planned so that each company can tailor the way it is applied to its specific circumstances. Thus, instead of specifying particular controls for all companies, the report calls on the boards of listed companies to identify risks that are significant to the fulfilment of corporate business objectives and to implement a sound internal control system to manage these effectively. To do this, the board needs to be clear about the company's objectives – not just about what it is doing today but about its long-term strategic aims.

The guidelines encourage the management of risk, not its elimination. In a competitive market economy, a company with a low risk appetite is unlikely to generate a high rate of return. Indeed, in some cases a board-level review of the company's significant risks may lead to the conclusion that more opportunities need to be seized and greater risks taken if the business is to succeed in the long run. However, directors and stakeholders must be aware that any risk management system can only provide reasonable assurance that a company's objectives will be met. The possibility of poorly judged decision making, human error, deliberate circumvention of controls, or unforeseen circumstances can never be ruled out.

Identifying risks

In determining the company's risk profile, the board should review information from senior managers on the significant risks it faces at group level. It should examine the kinds of risks it considers acceptable, the likelihood of their materializing, and the ability to reduce their impact if they do occur. It should also bear in mind the costs and benefits of particular controls.

A robust process for identifying and evaluating risks is the foundation of an effective control system. Companies need to consider all the types of risks they face, whether strategic, operational, financial, or related to compliance issues. In assessing their relative importance, a recent study showed that financial managers thought the principal risks were generally strategic and operational. Examples included the failure to manage major projects successfully, especially technological ones; the failure to be sufficiently innovative; problems arising from poor reputation or lackluster brand management; and difficulties with a lack of employee motivation.

When identifying risks, directors should be careful not just to select potential candidates from a generic matrix – the risks should be specific to the market sectors in which the business operates and to the company's circumstances at a given time. What are the possible obstacles standing in the way of the company achieving its business objectives? It will be helpful to look at how change, whether within the group or in the external business environment, is affecting the company's risk profile, as this can introduce new or increased risks.

It is important to consider problems or near misses that the company or its competitors have experienced recently, but managers should also address the types of risk that have yet to crystallize. Furthermore, consideration should be given to those business probity issues, including ones related to fraud, where the company might be especially vulnerable. With the development of global markets and worldwide brands, as well as the increased prominence of international pressure groups, many companies now find reputation risk a central cause of concern. In this context, environmental risks are substantial and growing for many sectors of business. These can lead to large direct costs, in terms of remedial expenditure and fines, and can severely damage corporate reputation.

Figure 1: How to prioritize risks

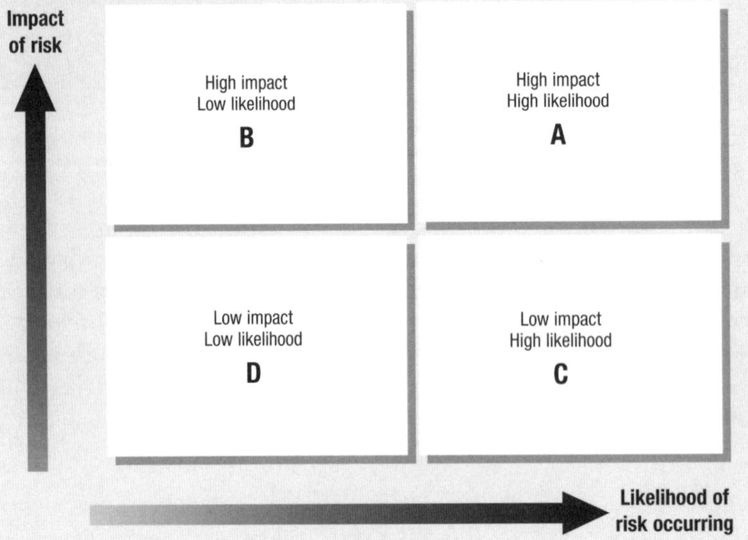

Some significant risks are most easily identified from a "bird's eye" view at senior group level, others from more detailed operational knowledge further down the organization. The challenge is to bring these two strands together. As companies develop risk management systems, they find they need a common language throughout the group to describe similar risks, and common categories to classify them, so that the cumulative exposure in any given area can be properly assessed.

Prioritizing risks

Once identified, risks must be prioritized. This can be done initially by examining the "gross" risks associated with an event or situation. A gross risk is the probability of an event or situation occurring coupled with an estimate of its impact (before taking account of the application of control strategies). The potential impact should be assessed not merely in direct financial terms, but more broadly by reference to the potential effect on the realization of corporate objectives.

Some organizations use two-by-two diagrams (*see* Figure 1) to divide up risks. Box A shows risks requiring immediate action; Box B, those for which a contingency plan is needed; Box C, those for which action should be considered; and Box D, those of lesser concern but nevertheless requiring periodic review. Risk assessment of this kind will to some extent be subjective and the degree of uncertainty that surrounds the estimation of the impact of different kinds of risk is unlikely to be uniform. These forces will affect any decisions about how to respond to particular risks.

An embedded control system

Once gross risks have been prioritized, the directors need to decide in each case their preferred control strategy for avoiding or mitigating these risks. They also need to identify those who are best placed to manage and account for them. Is it possible to design an early warning system? Such systems can identify problems

Corporate governance in the UK

When the London Stock Exchange published its Combined Code on Corporate Governance in summer 1998, the emphasis on control-related aspects of governance shifted from internal financial control to the broader concept of internal control. Principle D2 of the Code states that "the Board should maintain a sound system of internal control to safeguard shareholders' investment and the company's assets." A related Code provision says that the directors should conduct, at least annually, a review of the effectiveness of the group's system of internal control and should report to shareholders that they have done so.

The Turnbull report completed the construction of the current corporate governance infrastructure in the UK by providing implementation guidance on those aspects of the Code dealing with internal control and internal audit. It is fully effective for year-ends occurring on or after 23 December 2000 and transitional provisions are in force for those occurring up to that date.

The guidance calls on all listed companies incorporated in the UK to disclose whether their system of risk management accords with it, but it is for the market to decide how to respond to cases of departure from the guidance. The Combined Code superseded the Cadbury Code, published in 1992, which had indicated that directors should report on the effectiveness of the company's system of internal control, although the subsequent Rutteman report containing the implementation guidance on that occasion went on to focus principally on internal financial control.

before disaster strikes, when corrective action can still be taken. Once a control strategy has been agreed, the residual risk remaining in the business can be assessed.

There are various strategies for managing a given risk. These include accepting it; transferring it partially or fully to another party (such as through insurance or a joint venture); eliminating it by adopting an exit strategy; controlling it through building safeguards into the operational process; or ensuring that staff manage it.

The Turnbull report stresses that control should be embedded in the culture and processes of the business. It is better, therefore, to build appropriate mechanisms into existing management information systems than to develop entirely separate risk reporting models. Cumbersome risk databases can be a distraction from the primary goal of getting each person in the organization to be aware of, and manage, crucial risks related to the tasks that person performs. All employees have some responsibility for internal control. Collectively, they should have the necessary knowledge, skills, information, and authority to operate and monitor the internal control system. Communication between different levels of the organization and across departments plays a pivotal role in a successful risk management system.

The board's role

Continuous monitoring is a critical part of a sound control system but, as the Turnbull report stresses, the board cannot rely solely on this to discharge its responsibility for reviewing the effectiveness of the group's internal control system. It should also regularly receive and review reports on internal control from line managers and, if appropriate, from specialists in such areas as internal audit and health and safety. To ensure the board concentrates on the areas that will yield the best results, it should focus on the limited number of residual risks identified as being significant to the group.

In reviewing control issues, directors will want to consider whether they have sufficient timely and relevant information on the company's risks. For instance, do they have enough data on the company's position in the marketplace and, within the company, on employee skills and attitudes? Key risk indicators and the results of embedded monitoring should be regularly supplied to the board or designated committees. The chairperson should encourage a regular discussion of risk and control issues at board meetings. When there is a proposed acquisition, directors would be likely to want to know if a full risk analysis was part of the due diligence process. Similarly, a risk assessment should be included in the evaluation of proposed major capital investments.

Management reports to the board should provide a balanced assessment of the system of control for managing significant risk in the areas covered by them. Any control failings or weaknesses should be discussed in the context of their actual or potential consequences and corrective actions. At any given time, the board should be comfortable that it has an up-to-date picture of significant issues in the company's control environment.

The Turnbull report does not call on directors to discuss their main risks in the annual report. It does ask them to disclose, if this is the case, that there is an ongoing process for identifying, evaluating, and managing significant corporate risks, and that this process is regularly reviewed by the board and complies with the guidance. For insight into the extent of senior commitment to effective risk management, the board should also summarize its process for reviewing the effectiveness of internal control.

The Turnbull report sets out to promote a bespoke, rather than an off-the-peg, approach to risk management. If it is to achieve this goal, ownership must now pass from the working party that prepared the report to every listed company. These in turn must implement it in a way that reflects their own unique and continually changing conditions. If this happens, listed UK companies will be well prepared to meet the tough challenges of the twenty-first-century marketplace.

Summary

Risk management and internal control have moved firmly on to the boardroom agenda. Here, **Anthony Carey** and **Nigel Turnbull** argue that they should be an integral part of business and not a mere regulatory exercise. In the UK, the Turnbull report on internal control has provided companies with a framework for setting up robust systems of risk management. Directors should identify and evaluate the risks that are specific to the achievement of their company's objectives. In doing so, they should consider emerging types of risk such as those arising from branding and reputation as well as those in more traditional areas. Importantly, risk is not necessarily a bad thing; in fact, risk taking is an essential component of a competitive economy. Strategies for managing risk include acceptance, transfer, elimination, or control.

Suggested further reading

The Committee on the Financial Aspects of Corporate Governance (1992) *The Financial Aspects of Corporate Governance*, London: Gee (The Cadbury Code).

The Hampel committee (1998) *Committee on Corporate Governance: Final Report*, London: Gee.

Jones, M. and Sutherland, G. (1999) *Implementing Turnbull: A Boardroom Briefing*, London: ICAEW.

The Rutteman committee (1994) *Internal Control and Financial Reputation*, London: The Technical Department, ICAEW.

The Turnbull working party (1999) *Internal Control: Guidance for Directors on the Combined Code*, London: ICAEW (also at www.icaew.co.uk/internalcontrol).

Diminishing the threats to shareholder wealth

by René Stulz

The only reason a company ought to manage financial risks is that by doing so it makes its owners, the shareholders, better off. This article argues that a well-designed financial risk management policy achieves this. In particular, risk management increases the wealth of diversified shareholders.

It is not obvious that managing a company's risks should make shareholders better off. When we look at the range of risks a company faces, they can be divided into two categories: systematic risks and idiosyncratic risks. Systematic risks are common to many companies: they might include the risks of fluctuating business cycles. Idiosyncratic risks are specific to a company and might include the risk that its products malfunction or that its manufacturing plant burns down.

Investors choose to bear systematic risks because they expect to receive a higher return than if they were to invest in risk-free securities. This compensation – the risk premium – corresponds to the excess of a security's expected return over the short-maturity treasury-bill rate. In contrast, idiosyncratic risks disappear in diversified portfolios (over any period, some companies will have good news and others bad news). Therefore, investors earn no compensation for bearing idiosyncratic risks because they can get rid of them by diversifying across securities.

A company might reduce the volatility in its share price by reducing its idiosyncratic risks, but that does not mean that its share price will rise. Well-diversified shareholders did not notice these idiosyncratic risks before the company reduced them and will not reward the company for actions that they do not notice. In the long run, the argument goes, risk management cannot create wealth because it does not increase the company's expected cash flow – it just smooths out the ups and downs in cash flow.

If a company incurs costs to reduce its systematic risk, for example by diversifying into new activities to avoid damaging business cycles, shareholders equally have no reason to cheer, because they can always alter the amount of systematic risk they bear by changing their asset allocation. Investors can increase their exposure to the market, and hence their systematic risk, at the cost of typing a few instructions on their computer.

Since investors do not value shares more when they have less idiosyncratic risk and do not value changes in a company's systematic risks, how, then, can risk management create shareholder wealth?

The answer is that unexpectedly low cash flows have important indirect costs for companies. Remember that the value of a company's shares is based on the market's expectation of the company's future cash flows. An unexpectedly low cash flow could, for instance, bankrupt the company or place it in financial distress; this would cause its share price to fall by more than just the cash-flow shortfall.

To clarify the role of these indirect costs, consider the following experiment. Companies A and B are identical, except that company A has an idiosyncratic risk that company B does not have. For instance, both companies might have the same

A critical proposition

The Leverage Irrelevance Proposition plays a critical role in modern corporate finance. Proposed in the 1950s by Merton Miller and Franco Modigliani, it describes the relationship between a company's debt/equity ratio and its market value, defined as the sum of the market value of its debt and of its equity.

A good way to understand the proposition is to think of the company's cash flows as a pizza. Shareholders get some slices and debt holders get the others. As long as the size of the pizza stays the same, giving more slices to the shareholders because the company has more equity financing simply amounts to giving fewer slices to the debt holders. The size of the pizza – the underlying value of the company – remains unchanged.

projects, except that for company A the project has more extreme potential outcomes than for company B. Let us say that company A has a 50 percent chance of losing \$100m and a 50 percent chance of gaining \$100m in the near future. If one had to forecast the difference in cash flow between the companies in the near future, one would expect the difference to be zero, since a positive difference of \$100m is as likely as a negative difference of \$100m.

Assuming that shareholders can diversify this risk, it does not affect their expected return on the company's shares. If the only impact of the risk for company A is that it either loses \$100m or gains \$100m, capital markets would still value the two companies identically, even though company A carries additional risk.

One might think that a world in which company A is valued the same as company B does not exist, but such a world is precisely the one of the famed Modigliani–Miller Leverage Irrelevance Proposition, which is taught in introductory finance courses around the world (*see* box). A company's leverage is its ratio of debt to equity. The proposition states that the size of a company's leverage does not affect its value. In the context of our example, the impact of losing \$100m for company A would remain the same whether the company is highly levered or has no leverage. If the company loses \$100m, proponents of the proposition would argue, it could simply go to the capital markets and raise another \$100m.

The real world, however, does not work this way. Risks do have important indirect costs that managers must take into account when maximizing shareholder wealth. Once we identify these costs, we will know why risk management creates value and how companies should go about using risk management to capture that value for their shareholders.

The costs of risk

There are several reasons that the extra risk carried by company A creates indirect costs that reduce its value relative to company B. This article focuses on the most important ones.

Bankruptcy and distress costs

For a very large global company – with an equity capitalization exceeding \$100bn – a loss of \$100m has little impact. However, if \$100m is large compared with a company's equity capitalization, it is more likely to threaten the company with bankruptcy or financial distress.

Let us say that company A loses \$20m in bankruptcy costs if the loss of \$100m occurs. The markets value a company's shares based on their expectation of its future cash flows. If there is some possibility that a costly bankruptcy will occur in the future, the share price will fall to reflect the increase in expected bankruptcy costs (regardless of whether the company ultimately bears those bankruptcy costs or not). In our example, the risk of bankruptcy would decrease the value of company A relative to company B by roughly \$10m (which is the probability of bankruptcy multiplied by the bankruptcy cost, or 0.5 × \$20m). In this situation, any attempts by company A's managers to reduce risk will be applauded by its shareholders, because they would decrease the likelihood of bankruptcy costs and hence increase the share price.

More generally, companies can use risk management to avoid the costs of financial weakness. As companies become shakier, customers become reluctant to buy their products. Examples are Eastern Airlines in the early 1990s, once the eighth largest US carrier, and US carmaker Chrysler in the late 1970s, both of which faced an exodus of consumers when their survival was in doubt. Suppliers may also withhold their products because they might not get paid and workers may begin to look elsewhere for jobs. In industries where financial soundness is essential to conducting business, such as the financial services industry, companies can vanish almost overnight when credit risks become significant. This was illustrated in the late 1990s by bank runs in Indonesia and Russia.

Raising funds: costs and difficulties

Proponents of the Leverage Irrelevance Proposition might argue that companies can avoid bankruptcy and distress costs by raising funds on the stock or debt markets. They would claim that companies with convincing growth opportunities can always find new capital cheaply.

Sometimes a company's growth opportunities are so compelling that it can raise funds easily and at low cost. At other times, however, this is not possible. For instance, US savings and loan institutions were essentially locked out of the capital markets in the early 1990s because of regulatory uncertainty. During the Asian crisis, there were countless stories of companies that could not obtain capital for financing valuable exports. More recently, business-to-consumer internet companies have had difficulties in raising funds as market sentiment has turned against them.

One reason for this is that it is often difficult for managers to explain credibly growth opportunities to potential investors. In some cases, the nature of the growth opportunity is too complex. In others, they may fail because the markets worry that their desire to see the company grow clouds their judgment of those very opportunities. In any case, failure to find funding prevents a company from taking advantage of growth opportunities – and thereby benefitting shareholders – when it falls on hard times.

Stakeholders

Many managers, academics and policy makers argue that companies should not simply focus on maximizing the wealth of their shareholders, but should also be concerned with the welfare of stakeholders. If this entails taking money away from the owners of the company – the shareholders – and giving it to other individuals, it amounts to robbing the company's owners, which does not seem justifiable. However, it is important to remember that corporations maximize shareholder wealth by building valuable relationships with customers and employees. Without such relationships, companies pay more for services and receive less for their products.

Workers and customers often have claims against the company. A worker might be owed compensation in the future; a customer might hold a warranty. As a result, companies with more risk attached to them may have to pay more to hire workers. They may have to sell their products at a lower price to compete, since their warranties will be worth less than those from less risky companies.

But companies can reduce the risk attached to them through risk management. Since markets do not charge a premium for bearing risk that can be diversified, companies can reduce company-specific risk at no cost. If workers and customers charge the company for bearing its risk by requiring respectively higher wages and lower prices, the company is clearly better served by having capital markets bear its risk more cheaply.

Debt financing

Debt financing has both costs and benefits. Its costs are that it makes bankruptcy and distress more likely. Its benefits are threefold: debt confers tax benefits on companies; a greater concentration of shareholdings becomes possible because less equity is outstanding; and it forces management to disgorge cash flow that might otherwise be invested in low-return projects. Risk management decreases the cost of debt, since it makes it less likely that the company will experience distress or bankruptcy. As a result, reducing risk enables companies to benefit more from their existing debt financing and to increase levels of such financing.

Managerial incentives

It is now an accepted principle that a company's managers should benefit when they succeed in increasing shareholder wealth. Managers who receive a fixed wage, it is thought, have little incentive to worry about shareholders; they have nothing to gain financially from increasing shareholder wealth. Their compensation is risky when it is tied to stock price performance. Some of that risk can be controlled, but often it cannot. For instance, if a company's income depends on exchange rates, its managers' pay also depends on them. Managers cannot control exchange rates and are rarely skilled enough to forecast them. So, having their pay depend on exchange rates forces them to bear risks they can do nothing about. To get managers to bear such risks, their compensation has to be higher, otherwise they will tend to try to guarantee it by rejecting valuable but risky projects. Rather than pay them more or see them reject worthwhile projects, it makes sense to let managers eliminate risks that do not have to be taken to make the business succeed.

Undiversified shareholders

Companies often have large undiversified shareholders that play a critical leadership and monitoring role. Such shareholders increase the value of a company's equity through their efforts. Large undiversified shareholders have both the incentives (they make money) and the means (they control votes) to work to make the corporation better. Attracting such shareholders is valuable for corporations, but risk management can be critical in keeping them, because their lack of diversification means that they are affected adversely by the company's idiosyncratic risk.

A risk management strategy

It was argued above that cash flow problems have indirect costs for companies. Risk management can reduce the occurrence of such problems, but how should executives devise the best risk management strategy?

One approach is to calculate the debt rating that is consistent with maximizing value. Some types of companies lose lots of business opportunities because they have a low rating (for instance, a company that sells long-maturity financial products). For other types, a high rating is not as beneficial – such companies are better served with a lower rating because the costs of obtaining a higher rating do not make economic sense. Think of a new company with a highly risky but valuable R&D project. To obtain a higher rating, the company might have to give up its project, thereby abandoning what makes it valuable.

For a company that needs the higher rating, the threshold at which it must manage risk can easily be calculated. Suppose that a company knows that it will lose its desired rating if the probability of default over the year exceeds 1 percent, its default occurring when cash flow falls short by $100m. To keep its desired rating, the company therefore has to ensure that 99 percent of the time its cash-flow shortfall will be less than $100m. If this condition were not met, cash-flow risk would be excessive and managers would reduce the risk to preserve their rating.

One might be tempted to argue that the company would be better off eliminating the possibility of default. The difficulty with this view is that doing so is usually too expensive – the surest way of making default impossible is for the corporation to liquidate its assets and invest the proceeds in treasury bills. Rather, a company's risk management strategy should be designed to resolve as far as possible the trade-off between the benefits and costs of reducing the possibility of default and financial distress.

Companies might try to reduce their probability of default by raising more equity and keeping the proceeds as liquid assets that they can use to make up for cash-flow shortfalls. However, such a strategy is costly for a number of reasons. In particular, it reduces the company's ability to take advantage of the benefits of debt. Further, when a company stockpiles cash as an insurance policy, capital markets are often concerned that it could be used unproductively. For instance, there is evidence from academic research that cash-rich companies are more likely to make poor acquisitions.

Alternatively, companies can try to limit risk by changing the nature and scope of their operations. For instance, companies might diversify in order to stabilize their cash flow. Unfortunately, using operations to reduce risk is often extremely costly. Academic research has shown that diversified companies are typically worth less than specialized companies – there is a "diversification discount."

Using financial instruments can be a much cheaper way of managing risk. For instance, companies often use forward contracts to manage foreign exchange risk. A currency forward contract allows the company to sell a quantity of a specified foreign currency at a future date and at an agreed price. The transaction costs are often trivial and financial instruments can be tailored to eliminate more complex risks.

Yet there has been much concern that the use of financial instruments in risk management strategies can lead to losses such as those experienced by Metallgesellschaft, the German industrial company, Procter & Gamble, the consumer goods company, or Ashanti Goldfields, the Ghanaian mining corporation. Indeed, some companies have had poor risk management strategies, or have speculated and lost. However, it is important to understand that companies with competent managers and sound risk management strategies will, at times, lose on their derivatives positions.

Let us consider a simple example of a derivative – a forward contract. A British company expects to receive $10m from its customer in a year's time. It decides to hedge against changes in the dollar/sterling exchange rate by agreeing to sell the $10m in advance, for a fixed amount of sterling.

From the company's point of view it carries no risk, because the value of the hedged position after a year does not depend on the dollar/sterling exchange rate. However, if one makes the mistake of simply judging the performance of the forward contract after a year, roughly half the time the company will lose out and half the time it will win. If it happens to lose, headlines in the press might justifiably say that the company lost a large amount of money on derivatives. Yet these headlines would misrepresent the impact of the derivatives position on the company – in this case it used derivatives to eliminate the foreign exchange risk and succeeded in doing so.

Some derivatives losses, however, do deserve critical attention. Managers who lose on forward contracts half the time are doing their jobs properly, because they hedge systematically. Problems arise when managers make their own forecasts and use them as part of a hedging strategy. Corporate managers should not be in the business of speculating on foreign exchange, or more generally on financial prices and rates, when they do not have a comparative advantage in doing so. Financial markets are reasonably efficient – their inefficiencies certainly cannot justify the diversion of corporate attention from its primary focus.

Widget companies

Companies that implement a well-designed risk management strategy increase their shareholders' wealth. The criticism is often made that managers should forget about derivatives and financial instruments because they should focus on the company's operations. Managers of widget companies, it is said, should focus on producing better widgets, not on devising derivatives strategies. This criticism misses the point of risk management. Derivatives strategies and risk management are valuable precisely because they enable these managers to do a better job in producing widgets. Without risk management, they will occasionally see their strategies collapse because of risks that have nothing to do with the company's core abilities. By managing risks, they stand a much better chance of being able to implement their chosen strategy successfully.

Summary

In a truly frictionless economy, risk management is a pointless activity. Shareholders can adjust the risk profile of their portfolios by diversifying or shifting their assets. Healthy companies that suffer unwelcome financial shocks can always approach the capital markets for funding. Yet, as **René Stulz** argues, the world is a much more complex place than friction-free theoretical models admit. Adverse shocks to a company's cash flow typically create indirect costs. These costs might stem from the threat of expensive bankruptcy and financial distress, the difficulties of raising funds to finance corporate strategies or the consequences of these shocks to stakeholders. Risk management – particularly through the use of derivatives strategies – can help managers lessen these threats and thereby boost and sustain the value of the company.

The emerging role of the risk manager

by Mark Butterworth

Professional risk management is an important contributor to the corporate bottom line. As corporate governance demands develop, debate is growing as to whether the risk manager should sit on the board, perhaps as the "chief risk officer." Certainly, corporate governance increasingly requires boards to take responsibility for control processes and to review how these perform and are implemented. In effect, this raises the overall importance of risk management in the enterprise and will also have an impact on the cost of capital raised in equity markets.

What has driven the growth of risk management and what makes a good risk manager? Answers to these questions should help dispel any lingering notions that the risk manager is some kind of interloper in the corporate hierarchy.

Growth factors

The Risk and Insurance Management Society of the US and Canada (RIMS) is the world's largest association of corporate and public-sector risk managers. It recently celebrated its 50th anniversary. RIMS has been highly influential in promoting the cause of risk management. In the UK, the Association of Insurance and Risk Managers (AIRMIC) was set up in 1963.

With such long-established bodies of risk management practitioners, it might be supposed that the corporate risk manager's role is clearly recognized and equally well understood; regrettably not. Until recently, professional risk managers have been slow to define their tasks and impress their value on senior managers and workplace colleagues.

Developments in corporate governance requirements in recent years have changed this situation and raised levels of risk management awareness in boardrooms. Today, directors see regular risk analysis reports and annual assessments of risk performance. Greater public reporting of risk performance is turning the spotlight on directors' support for formal risk management practice. Good risk awareness and management will give organizations the confidence to take on new ventures, develop new products, and expand abroad. Indeed, risk assessment may well suggest that doing nothing (such as ignoring e-commerce trends) might be the most risky strategy of all.

Risk management has also extended into government. At the heart of the initiative to modernize UK government is a requirement for civil servants to adopt a new approach toward innovative and improved services. This implies taking some risk. The National Audit Office's response to the initiative (published in June 1999) was that it would support risk taking that had been well conceived and planned. An NAO study, published in summer 2000, examines risk taking and aims to disseminate good practice in business risk management. Government departments will then develop risk management frameworks.

Risk focus

Traditionally, "risk managers" in an organization spend much of their time administering the corporate risk financing program, comprising an array of conventional business insurance, self-funding, and perhaps a captive insurance company. Most AIRMIC members are drawn from an insurance background, although AIRMIC also includes many auditors, lawyers, and engineers. Insurance is not, however, the first line of defense to the presence of risk. Before insurance is purchased, companies should be satisfied that all reasonable measures are taken to reduce the likelihood of an event occurring and limiting the severity of losses when it does. Fraud prevention, property sprinkler protection, health and safety measures, contract management, and regulatory compliance are typical examples. Risk management has many parallels with quality management. An important feature of the former is the scenario analysis and the removal of causes of error that accompanies the process of learning after the event.

Risk managers tend to focus on operational risk (although there are certain specialist activities such as credit risk management in financial institutions) and contingency planning is an important feature of a broad response to risk. Contingency and crisis management planning includes incident management, public relations, relocation, and disaster recovery in many different scenarios, from product recall to loss of strategic staff or a major pollution incident.

Broad brief

Risk managers from an insurance background are imbued with loss prevention as a fundamental part of their role. They develop a finely honed "risk consciousness." This also applies to auditors, particularly where internal auditors have a broad brief that extends well beyond financial controls. This might seem unusual, as auditors tend to focus on compliance with accounting procedures or on specialties such as auditing IT development. Further, the primary role of the auditor, it is thought, is to audit, and their position outside the risk management framework gives them the independence they need. Treasury specialists need a strong risk management bias, essentially involving management of cash flow, capital, and foreign exchange.

With a deep understanding of their particular industry or market, risk managers can more easily identify relevant potential risks and can give focussed advice on controlling them to line managers. For example, in the construction industry risk managers must not only advise on physical protection such as fire prevention and worker safety but also contribute to contract negotiations where risk apportionment between the parties is critical. In banking, protection of IT facilities and fraud avoidance are very much part of the risk manager's role, and the task is carried out in close collaboration with the audit department. The banking industry is now looking in great detail at all operational risks and the implications for an "operational risk charge." The Global Association of Risk Professionals (GARP) has more than 10,000 members, concentrating almost entirely on risk issues in the financial institution sector. In transportation, risk issues are dominated by safety factors and risk management focus is on accident prevention.

Those who aspire to become risk managers generally need training in formal risk management practices. In the UK, probably the most widely recognized qualifications are associate or fellow of the Institute of Risk Management. Many practicing risk managers have emerged from a widening number of degree courses, such as the BA in risk management offered at Glasgow Caledonian University or the MSc in insurance and risk management from City University, London. The London School of Economics has a center for the analysis of risk and regulation. The best-equipped risk managers are those who combine formal risk management qualifications with an extensive understanding of their industry.

Risk managers will typically have certain interpersonal skills, such as a flair for working at many levels throughout the company, from line management to the board, and with outside parties such as lawyers, major investors, and business partners. In December 1999, AIRMIC surveyed members about their risk concerns. Reputation and brand value damage were high on the list, together with employee stress. Risk managers must work closely with marketing and finance departments in dealing with the first of these and with human resources departments and line managers over the second.

Effective risk management is all about getting business managers to assume ownership of the management of risks within their own areas, hence facilitation, training, and partnering skills are essential. Consulting skills are important where the role involves acting as an expert resource to corporate business divisions and departments.

A strong appreciation of finance and accounting is useful, since all risk effects will have an impact on the profit and loss account and the balance sheet. But this focus on finance as an important core skill may have been overemphasized. With much of the corporate governance work coming from the finance and accounting professions, the tendency is to interpret risk management purely as financial control measures. This has been further reinforced by the report of the UK's Turnbull committee, *Internal Control: Guidance for Directors on the Combined Code*, published in 1999. AIRMIC contributed to the consultation process, supporting the notion that guidance should cover the whole spectrum of business not just the more limited scope of internal financial control. In fact, the Turnbull guidelines go beyond internal controls and serve as a useful framework for company-wide risk management.

There has been much debate on whether the risk manager should be a board appointee – the chief risk officer. The implication is that risk management is of sufficient strategic importance that the company's risk management activities should be represented at the highest level. Some argue that the chief executive is in fact the single focal point for all risk issues in the enterprise; this view ignores the specific skills of qualified and experienced risk managers. Most chief executives would expect to have good risk management advice provided for them. The UK's various corporate governance reports and codes of recent years have been silent on the question of board representation for risk management, but this should not imply that there is no imperative for the board to include a risk director. Certainly, corporate governance requires boards to take ownership of control processes and regularly to review the controls on environment and performance. This means that the risk manager needs regular access to the board, probably through the finance director.

However, many organizations now call their risk manager "director of risk management," or ensure that the role encompasses other functions such as "director of compliance and risk management." A main board appointment in larger companies is not, as yet, common.

Reporting lines

In a review of the role of risk managers, Stephen Ward of the University of Southampton School of Management looked at the reporting lines for 30 risk managers in large organizations. Over two-thirds reported to the finance director. Others reported to the board through technical directors or the company secretary. In some cases, the risk manager reports to the head of internal audit or the treasurer. Ward notes that the risk management methodology in the organization is frequently operated through a risk forum or risk committee. Corporate governance requirements are encouraging companies to review the role of the audit committee and question whether the committee's brief should encompass risk management, or whether a separate committee, reporting to the board, should address risk.

As wider and more detailed public reporting of risk emerges after the implementation of the Turnbull guidelines, there will be greater appreciation of how companies position their risk management function, and their risk manager, within the organization. It is reasonable to expect that appointment of a risk director at board level will become more widespread.

The advantages are twofold: the risk director can communicate more effectively with the other directors; and the appointment signals very clearly to the rest of the company that the board regards risk management as sufficiently important to warrant a place at the highest level. Companies may also move to appoint at least one non-executive director with risk management skills to judge the effectiveness of the company's risk management framework.

It is an axiom of risk management that the more effective their performance, the less noticeable risk managers become – losses, control failures and similar occurrences are avoided and their absence is taken for granted. In order to win and maintain the board's support for their work, risk managers need to demonstrate clearly its value to the company.

Financial measurements for the value of risk management have been developed over the years, concentrated on reduction in the "cost of risk." Definitions of cost of risk have included elements such as insurance premium expenditure, self-insured losses, the overhead cost of the risk management department, consultant fees, loss prevention measures, and contingency planning expenses. Risk managers should also consider adding a percentage for general management time, particularly when a major incident requires senior management or board involvement. Added value can be demonstrated by comparing the total cost of risk on a year-by-year basis, or by linking it to turnover or capital employed. Data on the activities and achievements of other risk managers in comparable organizations should also be used to assess performance.

As corporate governance develops, it is reasonable to expect institutional shareholders to take a greater interest in risk management. Companies that can demonstrate an effective integrated risk management framework, which reduces the volatility of their financial performance, should expect to obtain capital at a lower cost. While stock exchange listing rules are an important force behind the growth of risk management, the longer-term motivation to commit to effective risk management practices in an organization will pay off in several ways, such as reductions in the cost of risk, reduced volatility in results, and greater shareholder (or stakeholder) confidence. But this will not emerge without a solid commitment by senior management to appointing professional risk managers charged with delivering these benefits.

Summary

Risk managers have existed since the 1960s, writes **Mark Butterworth**, yet perceptions of their role vary greatly. Traditionally seen as a corporate insurance buyer, the modern risk manager now exercises a variety of responsibilities ranging from health and safety, crisis management, and relocation planning to fraud prevention and reputation management. Regulatory changes and advances in risk management techniques have brought the role into sharper focus for senior managers and have raised the question of whether the growing importance of risk managers warrants their inclusion on the board of directors. Whatever the outcome of this debate, risk managers need to demonstrate loudly and clearly the commercial benefits they bring to the business.

Suggested further reading

Integrated Risk Management Special Interest Group (1999) *A Guide to Integrated Risk Management*, AIRMIC.
Shimpi, P.A. (ed.) (1999) *Integrating Corporate Risk Management*, Swiss Re New Markets.

The subjective perception of risk

by Mark Fenton-O'Creevy and Emma Soane

People make judgments about risk every day of their lives, epitomized by questions such as: "Should I pull out into the traffic now or wait until that car has passed?" "Will it really hurt my health if I fail to lose weight?" "Shall I buy that lottery ticket?" In some, relatively few, situations the possible outcomes are clear and the odds are calculable. In most cases, the probabilities are uncertain, the set of possible outcomes is unclear, and our perception of both is affected by a host of subjective factors. In the car example, one's perception of risk may be affected by a recent accident or a near miss; by whether one's baby is in the car; what mood one is in; confidence in one's driving ability (unfounded or otherwise); familiarity with the car one is driving, and so on. The perception of risk is a complex and subjective process.

This article outlines some of the important influences on risk perception, especially as it relates to financial risk. It draws on existing research on risk perception and the authors' own study (co-funded by the participating banks and the UK Economic and Social Research Council) into four of the world's leading investment banks between 1996 and 1999. With colleagues at London Business School, the authors interviewed 118 traders and 10 senior managers and gathered quantitative data on their performance and perceptions.

The result is a discussion of four important influences on risk perception: how one understands risk, how one perceives loss and gain, cognitive biases, and personality. It concludes with a review of the implications for management practice.

Understanding risk

In financial economic accounts, risk is generally regarded as a combination of the expected magnitude of loss or gain and the variability of that expected outcome. Human perception of risk works rather differently. Work by Paul Slovic of the University of Oregon and colleagues suggests there are two other important components of risk that influence our perceptions. These are the fear factor – how much we dread the potential outcome – and the control factor – the extent to which we are in control of events. When risks combine both dread and lack of control, for example in a nuclear accident, they are perceived as very great. It is, for instance, common to fear an accident more as a car passenger than as a driver, even when we acknowledge the other driver to be the more competent. The difference is the perception of control. In financial markets, both factors can be significant – fear and anticipation of loss frequently govern our actions. As one trader reported: "We (often) make decisions more because of the fear of losing than in the hope of winning."

There is also considerable variation in how individuals perceive risk. We discuss a number of important sources of this variation below.

Loss and gain

One major component of risk perception is how we perceive loss and gain. Loss and gain can take many forms. For example, some of the traders we interviewed emphasized the importance of reputation as well as financial gain. One trader explained: "Sometimes you should pull out of a trade and accept your loss; but a big loss is a big loss – if you double the loss it won't hurt your reputation much more. You weigh this against a small chance of recovering the trade and saving your reputation." Others emphasized a desire to win: "There was this guy on the other side of the trade and I just wanted his head on a stick."

Our perceptions of our current state of loss or gain influence the extent to which we seek or avoid risk. An important development in research concerning risk perception came from Daniel Kahneman and Amos Tversky. Their theory, known as Prospect Theory, was developed from observations that people tend to make different choices under different conditions. When people are in a position of gain, they become increasingly risk averse and unwilling to accept gambles because they wish to hold on to their gains. When people are in a position of loss and as losses increase, they become more risk seeking because they have nothing very much to lose. This asymmetry applies to financial loss and gain, but can also apply to less tangible factors such as reputation or the desire to maintain a positive mood.

However, there is an important complication here. What we perceive as loss and gain is not straightforward. We all have internal reference points that determine whether we perceive an outcome as a loss or gain. Traders who look as though they will make a £1m bonus may behave as if they are in a potential loss-making situation if they have been assuming they will make £2m and have just bought a country house on that assumption. Managers who have just made a major loss may behave as if they are in a position of gain if the loss is not as bad as expected. How others frame decisions and risk data for us can also have a significant effect. The decision people make when given a choice between two medical programs is strongly influenced, research shows, by whether outcome data are presented in terms of lives saved or number of deaths.

Reference points also shift over time. For example, some of the traders in this research, working in turbulent markets, reported that their managers expected them to lose money in such conditions. The traders therefore felt that just to break even would be perceived as a gain – their reference point was below zero, but would change when market conditions altered.

Generally, in the companies studied here, management controls worked effectively to guard against unrestrained risk taking in the domain of losses. The reverse is not, however, true for gains. The majority of traders interviewed for this research did as Prospect Theory would suggest: they became increasingly conservative as their gains grew. This was particularly influenced by their annual bonus target – as traders got close to, or reached, their annual target, many reduced their trading activities in order to reduce the risk of associated losses. In this situation, managers need to act to encourage appropriate risk taking if traders are to make optimal returns.

The effects of loss, gain, and the reference point discussed above can also operate at the group, or team, level. For example, a number of the trader-managers interviewed reported that there was a team approach to the level of acceptable risk taking. This group definition tended to be tacitly agreed by co-workers and in general fitted both the managers' and the traders' appetite for risk. The benefit of a collective approach to beliefs about risk and the reference point between loss and gain is that individuals are clear about what constitutes risk taking. There can, however, be a significant disadvantage. If an individual wishes to take more risk than they know is acceptable to their team, they are more likely to seek to conceal that risk. Such concealment can lead organizations into dangerous territory, as several "rogue trader" incidents have shown.

Economic and financial theories often assume that one makes optimal use of available information as a basis for rational decision making. In practice, research (and everyday experience) shows that human behavior departs significantly from that assumption.

Cognitive biases

Decision making about risk often departs from the prescriptively rational model. Cognitive biases are pervasive, systematic distortions of perception that influence much of our everyday thinking. Often these biases arise out of ways of thinking (heuristics) that act as short cuts to enable us to process information quickly or simplify complex situations. Such biases are positive in that they act as rules of thumb, enable us to reduce the time we spend processing information and make numerous judgments at high speed rather than deliberate over each element of the decision. However, when making complex decisions that do require careful consideration, we are often unaware of the heuristics we habitually use.

One common bias is that of retrievability, that which is more easily available or more easily recalled. People tend to give greater weight to such information. For example, many people perceive air travel to be more risky than car travel (despite evidence to the contrary). This is in part due to the greater proportion of air crashes that are reported in the press. This bias can also be important in trading decisions. Research by University of Chicago academics Werner De Bondt and Richard Thaler shows that a significant proportion of market volatility can be explained by overreaction to recent news. This applies to professional as well as to naive investors.

Another common bias is the confirmation bias. Having formed a hypothesis, most of us have a tendency to pay more attention to information that confirms our hypothesis than to information that contradicts it: this can lead to traders failing to cut their losses in a timely fashion. Risks fail to be perceived because information that gainsays the initial trading strategy is given insufficient weight.

A further important cognitive bias is the illusion of control. Control beliefs are an important aspect of risk perception. We all hold beliefs concerning the extent to which we are able to exert control over events in which we are involved and over tasks we undertake. Many of these beliefs are perfectly reasonable and arise out of experience. For example, I have a reasonable degree of confidence that when I press a light switch in my house the light will come on. However, there is a great deal of evidence that in some circumstances people systematically behave as if they were able to exert control in circumstances where this is impossible or highly unlikely. This tendency is known as the illusion of control. If I suffer from the illusion of control, this can mean I invest all my efforts in trying to change a situation when it would be more appropriate to focus on adapting to it. Further, when judging risks I am more likely to underestimate the risk I am taking, because I will believe (wrongly) that I can control the situation in such a way as to reduce such risk.

Illusion of control is more common in circumstances where there are cues often associated with skill-based tasks (such as an element of choice, familiarity with the stimulus, competition, and involvement in decisions). Stressful conditions, an exclusive focus on goals at the expense of reflection, and a high frequency of positive outcomes can also encourage illusion of control.

The authors' research has shown that traders in investment banks who suffer from the illusion of control are less effective at market analysis and manage risk less effectively. Consequently, they perform less well in profit terms. It is likely that this finding is equally relevant to a wide range of decision-making tasks where it is difficult to establish clear links between decisions and outcomes.

Personality and risk perception

Another important set of influences is one's own innate disposition. Personality comprises a largely inborn set of dispositions, feelings, biases, and characteristics that tend to be manifested in preferences, sensitivities, habits, and reactions. These preferences can underlie characteristic ways of perceiving the risk in one's environment and whether a situation is seen as an opportunity or a threat.

An important element of personality that relates to risk is sensation seeking. This aspect of personality comprises the four elements of thrill and adventure seeking, experience seeking, lack of inhibition, and susceptibility to boredom. Research studies have linked sensation seeking with a number of risk behaviors such as making risky financial decisions, taking large gambling bets, participation in dangerous sports, socially risky behavior, and reckless driving.

One of the reasons for the link between sensation seeking and risky behavior is the tendency to perceive risks as small. Any risk tends to be discounted because the possible gains, such as the excitement of watching a neck-and-neck finish to a race on which you have a large bet and a possible associated win, are great. The reverse is also true. People who do not have sensation-seeking tendencies and people who by nature experience emotions that are more negative often focus on the potential for loss. They believe that any possible gains are no compensation for the losses that taking a chance might entail.

Management of risk perception

Influences on the way one perceives risk are complex and pervasive. However, risk management can be significantly improved by taking adequate account of these influences.

First, one needs to consider one's own risk perceptions. What personal and organizational factors are shaping one's perceptions? Is one in a position of loss or gain? What reference points is one using to determine loss and gain? How is one's thinking about risk framed by the context? It is also valuable to be aware of one's own predispositions. Does one seek risk for its own sake or does one tend to be conservative in making decisions about risks?

Second, managers need to consider the influences on other key decision makers using the same checklist, by looking at the results of previous decisions and through discussion. Managers need to be alert to how others are using information and how they are thinking about loss and gain.

Research further suggests a number of more specific recommendations. It is as important to manage upside risk as it is to manage downside risk. It is, of course, important to control excessive risk taking, but managers need to be alert to conditions that may produce an excessively conservative approach to risk. In the trading situation and elsewhere, managers should be particularly alert to distortions in risk-taking behavior that may be produced by the annual bonus cycle and the way in which targets are set.

There are indications that the illusion of control may lead to poor risk management. Managers need to be aware of the conditions that encourage this bias. Reducing stress can help, as can creating opportunities for reflection and open debate about the extent to which outcomes are genuinely controllable. A management strategy that acknowledges the individualistic and variable nature of risk perception and enables the open discussion and reconciliation of such differences will increase the effectiveness of decision making.

Summary

Perception of risk is both complex and subjective, say **Mark Fenton-O'Creevy** and **Emma Soane**. Factors involved include an understanding of risk, a perception of loss and gain, cognitive biases, and personality. Keys to how individuals handle risk include the degree of fear they have of the potential outcome and their perceived control of events, illusory or otherwise. The implications for management practice are clear: it is vital to manage both the upside and downside of risk. Prospect Theory, by which individuals are held to make different choices under different conditions, suggests that when people are ahead they become increasingly risk averse, but when they are losing they are more risk disposed. This creates distinct decision-making advantages for those whose management strategy can take into account such individualistic and variable perceptions of risk.

Suggested further reading

Bazerman, M.H. (1997) *Judgment in Managerial Decision-Making*, 4th edn, New York: Wiley.

De Bondt, W.F.M. and Thaler, R.H. (1993) "Does the stock market overreact?" in Thaler, R.H. (ed.) *Advances in Behavioral Finance*, New York: Russell Sage Foundation.

Kahneman, D. and Tversky, A. (1979) "Prospect theory: an analysis of decision under risk," *Econometrica*, 47: 262–90.

Langer, E.J. (1975) "The illusion of control," *Journal of Personality and Social Psychology*, 32(2): 311–28.

Slovic, P., Fischhoff, B. and Lichtenstein, S. (1980) "Facts and fears: understanding perceived risk," in Schwing, R.C. and Albers, W.A. (eds) *Societal Risk Assessment: How Safe Is Safe Enough?*, New York: Plenum.

Soane, E., Fenton-O'Creevy, M., Nicholson, N. and Willman, P. (1998) "Psychological theory and financial institutions: individual and organisational influences on decision-making and behaviour," in Jameson, R. (ed.) *Operational Risk*, 159–72, Risk Publications in association with Arthur Andersen.

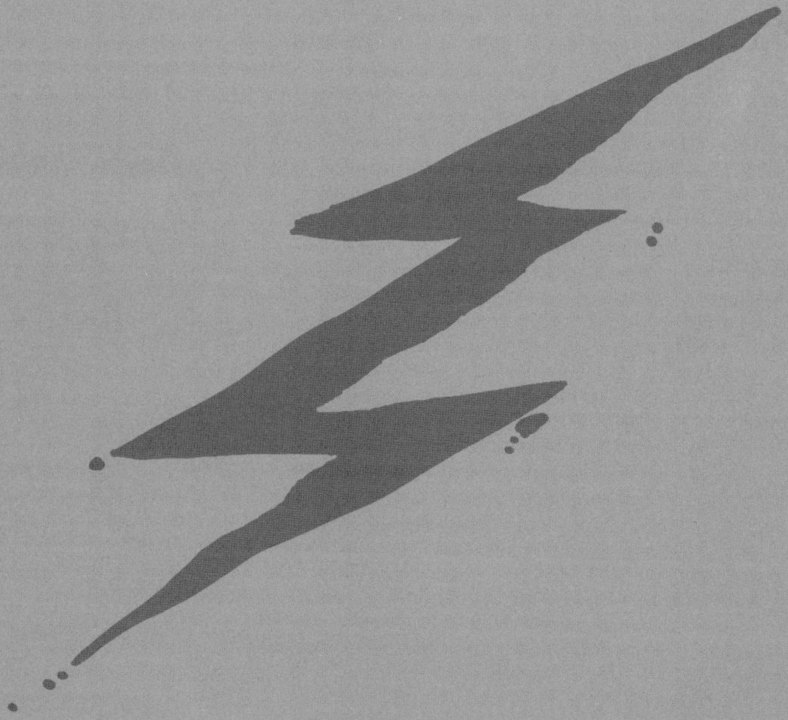

2

RISK MEASUREMENT

Contributors

Chris Lewin is chairman of the actuarial profession's Corporate Finance Committee. He was instrumental in the development of a framework for project risk known as RAMP (Risk Analysis and Management for Projects). Details can be found at www.ramprisk.com

Mike Hanley is strategic consultant to the Centre for the Analysis of Risk and Regulation at the London School of Economics and former editor of *International Risk Management*. This article is adapted from his management report, *Integrated Risk Management*, published by Informa.

Peter Schwartz is chairman of the Global Business Network and author of *The Art of the Long View*. He is former head of scenario planning at Royal Dutch/Shell.

Anil Gaba is a professor of decision sciences at INSEAD (located near Paris, France) and in Singapore. His research interests include risk analysis and decision making.

Kiriakos Vlahos is an assistant professor of decision science at London Business School. His research involves the development of flexible decision modeling frameworks for strategy analysis and scenario development.

Contents

Refining the art of the probable 35
Chris Lewin, Corporate Finance Committee for the actuarial profession
The rudimentary ideas of probability apply as much to games of chance as to complex share price movements. This article explains how to calculate simple probabilities.

The official future, self-delusion and the value of scenarios 42
Peter Schwartz, Global Business Network
Smart individuals and companies continue to take some very poor decisions. Managers who construct decision-making scenarios stand a better chance of recognizing underlying trends.

Tooling up for risky decisions 47
Kiriakos Vlahos, London Business School
A brief overview of some of the tools currently in use by companies grappling with different techniques for analyzing and managing risk.

Lowering exposure by spreading the risk 53
Mike Hanley, London School of Economics
Investors diversify to lower their exposure. Now, corporate risk managers are learning to adapt these techniques to their own world.

Quotas and contests in the battle for reward 57
Anil Gaba, INSEAD
Analysts are pondering how to harness increasingly pervasive winner-takes-all values for the individual and corporate good.

Introduction

If risk is to be controlled, it must first be measured, and the means for such measurement lie in mathematics. The theory of probability contains the principles that lie at the core of risk management, and forms the subject of the first article in this section. Elsewhere, authors examine how decision analysis can assist in major decisions, such as whether to develop a new product, and can specify the nature and extent of the downside when things go wrong. In addition, this section includes a presentation of scenario analysis from one of its early developers, and shows such analysis can highlight potential risks across a range of criteria.

Refining the art of the probable

by Chris Lewin

The Victorians produced many delightful parlor games for families to play during the long winter evenings. These included brightly colored table games, which were very popular in the pre-television era. Many of them involved an exciting element of chance in the movement of the pieces, the aim being to get to the end of a track first.

However, it was considered immoral for children to use dice, which were regarded as instruments of gambling. The games instead employed a multi-sided spinning top known as a teetotum. Each face was marked with a number, starting with 1 and ascending. These teetotums usually had 4, 6, 8, 10, or 12 sides.

Clearly, any defect in the manufacture of the teetotum, such as the spindle being off center, could affect the frequency with which certain numbers came up. However, if the teetotum was perfectly made (which was often not the case), one would expect that, if it were spun a large number of times, it would come to rest on each side with approximately equal frequency. Yet there is no guarantee of this result, and in practice one number often comes up more than the others do, just by chance.

Take a four-sided teetotum, marked with the numbers 1 to 4. If you spin it 100 times, you might expect to get about 25 instances of number 1, 25 of number 2, 25 of number 3, and 25 of number 4. If you were only spinning once, however, the chance of getting, say, a number 3 is 25%, or one in four. If you spun it four times in succession, the chance of getting a number 3 on all four occasions is 25% × 25% × 25% × 25%, or about 0.4%. In other words, if you spun it four times and then repeated this operation 1,000 times, you would expect that only about four of these 1,000 operations would yield four number 3s in a row.

In practice, if you only carried out the operation once and it produced a number 3 on all four occasions, you would be inclined to examine the teetotum carefully to see whether it had been carelessly (or deliberately) constructed so as to give a higher than 25% chance of yielding a number 3. Supposing, for example, we find that it is so lopsided that there is an 80% chance of getting a number 3 on a single spin. The chance of getting a number 3 four times in a row would then be 80% × 80% × 80% × 80%, or about 41%.

In other words, now that we are aware of the bias, we are not at all surprised that it gave the result that it did on four successive spins. Even if we had not been able to examine the teetotum, the fact that it had given four number 3s in succession would have made us feel that there was a high chance of it being lopsided, so that it would be more likely to give number 3 in future spins. Thus by looking at the frequency with which events happen when trials take place, we can sometimes infer something about the likelihood of those events happening in future.

However, we should beware of drawing the wrong conclusions. Let us return to the teetotum, assuming we have not examined it carefully. We realize that it may well not be perfectly made, but we have no prior knowledge about the extent of any bias. Suppose that we spin it 20 times and a number 3 comes up on four occasions.

What is our best estimate of the likelihood of a number 3 coming up on the next spin?

Many people would be tempted to say that their best estimate is 4 out of 20, that is, 20%. In fact, the correct answer is 5 out of 22, or around 22.7%. In general, if there is no prior knowledge of the probability with which an event will occur, and n successive independent trials result in m occurrences, then the probability of the event occurring in a future trial is not m/n, but $(m+1)/(n+2)$.

Sometimes we can work backwards from the results we obtain. Suppose that a friend spins a teetotum twice and tells us that it is accurately balanced and either a four-sided or a six-sided teetotum, but we cannot see which it is. What is the chance that it is a four-sided teetotum? At this stage, all we can say is that there is a 50% chance. Suppose the friend now says that he has spun it twice and on both occasions it came up with a number 3. What is now the chance that it is a four-sided teetotum?

Strangely enough, this innocuous piece of additional information has altered the chance. If it is a six-sided teetotum, the chance of getting the same number on the second spin as on the first is 1 in 6, or 16.7%. If it is a four-sided teetotum, it is 1 in 4, or 25%. By applying a technique known as Bayes's Theorem, we can say that the chance of it being a four-sided teetotum is 25% divided by (16.7% plus 25%), that is, 25/41.7, or 60%.

Thomas Bayes was a nonconformist minister whose famous essay on inverse probability was read to the Royal Society, Britain's senior scientific body, posthumously in 1763. To explain his theorem simply, suppose there are just two possible underlying situations, A and B, and that we seek the probability that A exists. We know beforehand that if A held good, there would be a probability p of seeing a specific effect occur, whereas if B held good there would be a probability q. Having now observed the effect taking place, the probability that the underlying situation is A is $p/(p+q)$. The theorem shows that the more information you collect about a situation, the more likely you are to be able to evaluate it correctly.

Suppose the friend now spins the teetotum again and once more it comes up as number 3. You are left to work out for yourself the revised chance that it is four-sided.

So far we have talked about chances and likelihood, which are part of the mathematical theory of probability. This theory is absolutely fundamental to the mastery of risk, yet risk involves not only the chance that an event will occur, but also the magnitude of the result if it occurs. However, what exactly do we mean by risk?

The meaning of risk

We often speak of the "risk of fraud" or the "risk of getting run over." Sometimes we use the word quantitatively; for example, we might say that there is a "20% risk of losing our money" in a particular investment. Alternatively, we might just say, "this investment carries a lot of risk." In these examples we are using the word "risk" in the sense of an undesirable outcome. This is often referred to as "downside risk." However, an investment might also have an upside potential. We can then use the word "risk" as a measure of the whole range of outcomes from the investment, both the upside and the downside outcomes.

Suppose that we were considering an investment in a Post Office Savings Account that would give us 5% interest. In other words, if we invested £100 now, we would have £105 in a year's time. Assuming we have absolute confidence in the British government's ability and willingness to pay us, we would say that the risk is nil; in other words, we know for certain what the outcome will be. It is a risk-free investment.

Stock market risk

If, on the other hand, we buy a share with the intention of selling it in a year's time, we have a whole range of possible outcomes in our mind. For share A, we might have detailed knowledge of the company and its markets and be confident that our return (assuming the general level of the market remains unchanged) will be within the range of +30% to –20%. For share B, we might feel less confident, though more optimistic, and expect the return to be within the range of +50% to –30%. We might then describe share B as more risky than share A.

A crude measure of riskiness would therefore be to look at the range of possible outcomes, considering both upside and downside. Share A has a range of 50%, whereas share B has a range of 80%. However, this does not really satisfy us as a good measure, because it does not tell us how likely we are in each case to get returns at different points within the range. It might be, for example, that for share B, we have greater confidence in the positive outcomes.

One of the factors that may have influenced us in arriving at our conclusion that share B has a wider range of outcomes over the next year than share A is that it has had a wider range of outcomes in the past. City share analysts use standard deviations as a measure of past variability. However, past experience is no sure guide to the future and we should not follow it slavishly.

What we really need, therefore, in considering our purchase of a single share is an assessment of how likely we are to get various possible outcomes from each share, so that we can make a judgment about which share we prefer. We might use a powerful technique called "scenario analysis," which focusses attention on selected scenarios that can be taken as representative of an underlying continuous distribution of future events.

The likelihoods of the various scenarios will be based on our own investigations and judgments, so they are only perceptions, which may not be very close to the true underlying position given perfect knowledge. However, they are the best we can do, and with all their imperfections may nevertheless provide a valuable aid to the selection process (*see* Table 1).

Table 1

	One year investment return	Share A	Share B
Scenario 1	+50%	-	15%
Scenario 2	+40%	-	10%
Scenario 3	+30%	10%	10%
Scenario 4	+20%	35%	10%
Scenario 5	+10%	25%	10%
Scenario 6	0	10%	10%
Scenario 7	-10%	10%	10%
Scenario 8	-20%	10%	10%
Scenario 9	-30%	-	15%
		100%	**100%**

Table 2

Profit per investment	Share A: Expected no. of investments having the given profit	Share A: Overall profit	Share B: Expected no. of investments having the given profit	Share B: Overall profit
£500	-	-	150	£75,000
£400	-	-	100	£40,000
£300	100	£30,000	100	£30,000
£200	350	£70,000	100	£20,000
£100	250	£25,000	100	£10,000
0	100	0	100	0
-£100	100	-£10,000	100	-£10,000
-£200	100	-£20,000	100	-£20,000
-£300	-	-	150	-£45,000
	1,000	**+£95,000**	**1,000**	**+£100,000**

If we invested in 1,000 different companies whose shares had the characteristics of share B, we could forecast that about 150 of these investments would give us +50%, 100 would give us +40%, 100 would give us +30%, and so on. Assuming each investment was £1,000, our overall profit would then be as shown in Table 2.

In this example, a portfolio consisting entirely of shares of type B is forecast to yield a higher overall profit than type A does. Although the range of returns is greater for type B, most portfolio investors would probably prefer this type because of the higher expected profit.

Why do we not say it would certainly be better for the portfolio investor to go for type B? The answer is that we have only been able to show in our table the expected number of investments having the given profit. We said, for example, that we could forecast that 150 of our 1,000 type B investments would give us +50%, but this ignores the risk of a different number having this outcome. Even if our perception of a 15% likelihood is entirely correct, perhaps only 130 of them or as many as 170 of them will have this outcome, or, if we were very unlucky, perhaps only 100 of them. In other words, we can envisage a whole distribution of possible overall outcomes, with various chances of occurrence.

The mathematical theory of probability shows that if you have (say) a 10% chance of a successful outcome and you make 1,000 independent trials, the number of successful outcomes will look rather like the curve illustrated in Figure 1. These bell-shaped curves are often found in practice, though the two sides of the bell are not always as symmetrical as they are here.

To return to our portfolio investor, this person might find it useful to do a whole series of simulations, using a computer, to examine more closely the possible overall profit from a £1m investment of £1,000 in each of 1,000 companies, using a technique known as stochastic modeling or Monte Carlo simulation, which attempts to calculate probabilities of outcomes. For a portfolio of shares of type A, the investor cannot be sure of getting exactly £95,000 – what will actually emerge is a range centered around £95,000 and following a bell-shaped curve. Similarly for type B, but the range will be centered around £100,000 with a wider dispersion. The investor might also examine mixed portfolios containing both types. Only then can the investor make a judgment, taking account of outliers in the distributions as well as the more likely results.

Figure 1: The Bell Curve

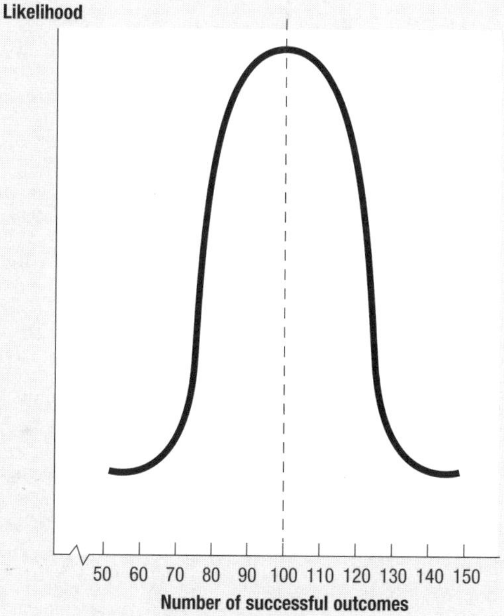

This is necessarily a much oversimplified discussion of a complex matter, and the actual techniques used by investment managers to control portfolio risk differ considerably from this in practice. Pension fund trustees carry out asset–liability modeling studies to determine how much risk is acceptable in their long-term strategic asset allocation. For a large fund, the investment activity is usually divided between several investment managers, whose contracts specify the extent to which the trustees are prepared to risk deviations from agreed benchmarks. Using a variety of risk controls, the investment managers then ensure that the portfolios they select will have only a very small risk of performing worse than the trustees have specified.

Risk of market movements

So far we have assumed that our investor wishes to be invested in shares and that it is merely a question of picking the right ones. A very important issue in practice, however, is judging the risk of being in or out of the share market at all.

Suppose that you are considering whether to be invested in shares over the next three months or to sell your existing holdings for cash with a view to reinvesting in three months' time. We shall assume that the total cost of selling and reinvesting is 4%, including bid–offer spreads, commissions, and so on. Let us assume that your assessment of the market is as in Table 3.

In this case, the risk of upward movement is the same as the risk of downward movement, so your "expected" return would be zero if you stayed in the market and –4% if you came out and reinvested in three months' time. The "expected" return means the average return you would expect to get if you were able to repeat this decision a very large number of times. Unfortunately, you do not have that luxury. There is only one period of the next three months! While it is true that you get four such opportunities a year, you would have to invest for many years before you could

Table 3

Market level in 3 months' time	Chance
30% higher	5%
20% higher	10%
10% higher	20%
Same	30%
10% lower	20%
20% lower	10%
30% lower	5%

be reasonably sure that the actual results were not being distorted by chance alone (just as spinning a four-sided teetotum 20 times would not necessarily produce five number 3s). Moreover, you know that your assessments are only your own perceptions – the true risks may be very different, due to factors outside your knowledge.

There is also a further factor to take into account. The "utility" to you of a loss may be greater than the utility of a gain of a similar amount. In other words, you might be much more upset at losing £10,000 than you would be pleased at gaining £10,000. We are all different in this regard. Some are risk takers and prepared to be philosophical when they lose. Others play for safety, possibly because their other resources are not great and they cannot afford to make a loss without it affecting their standard of living. If you put greater weight on losses than gains, you will switch into cash in the above situation, despite that option's lower expected value.

The worst dilemma for a risk-averse investor comes when the chances of a rise in the market are perceived to be higher than the chances of a fall, but the risk of a substantial fall is not so small as to be negligible. The use of derivatives to "insure" downside risk beyond a certain point might be considered, in return for giving up some of the upside, but in practice such contracts are not readily available for most investors and can be very expensive.

Reversion to the mean

In assessing the probabilities of how the stock market may move, one technique is to assume reversion to the mean (sometimes called regression to the mean). Suppose that historical statistics show that, for most of the time, fixed-interest bonds in a particular country have yielded about 4% per annum more than the dividend yields on equities, and that the difference is seldom outside the range 3% to 5%. If, at the present time, bonds yield 6% more than equities, the likelihood is that the position will revert fairly soon to the established pattern. This can be achieved either by a rise in the prices of bonds or by a fall in the prices of equities. If we feel that bond yields are about right, in relation to interest rates generally, we can attach quite a high probability to the likelihood of a fall in the equity market.

However, the technique will only work if the underlying situation remains unchanged. In nature, however extreme the weather during a particular week, we will normally find only quite small variations from one year to another if we take the year as a whole. If, however, global warming takes place, then we can expect to see a long-term trend in weather patterns. Similarly, if a country's economy changes, this could affect economic and stock market patterns, leading to the breakdown of established statistical relationships.

Assessing risk

Throughout this article we have assumed that the risks can be evaluated, at least approximately. However, this is often extremely difficult in practice. People find it hard to judge probabilities: in the UK, few people realize that if they buy a National Lottery ticket an hour before the draw, the risk of dying before the draw is greater than the chance of winning the jackpot! Past experience may be an unreliable guide, particularly if the underlying political or economic situation changes, and subjective judgment will always be necessary. Nevertheless, the techniques mentioned could still be usefully applied, using the best assessment of the magnitude of the risks and then testing the results for sensitivity to changes in these levels.

Life itself is risky. Every time we leave for work, we do not know for sure that we will arrive there safely. We still go to work, however, and accept the risk. People rightly take much bigger risks than this, and so do companies and even governments. The secret of mastering risks is to identify them, analyze them carefully, and mitigate downside risks as far as it is convenient and economical to do so. The remaining risks should be monitored and controlled, ensuring that contingency plans are in place should the risk event occur. Doing this methodically will increase the chances of success in any enterprise.

Summary

The rudimentary ideas of probability are simple and pervasive – they apply as much to games of chance as to complex movements in share prices. In this article, **Chris Lewin** explains how to calculate simple probabilities and shows how to make inferences from data using the theorem of inverse probability. He introduces the Bell Curve, the idea of utility and regression to the mean – in the light of the uncertainties that face a stock market investor.

Suggested further reading

Grimmett, G. and Stirzaker, D. (1982) *Probability and Random Processes*, Clarendon Press.
Kulkarni, V.G. (1995) *Modelling and Analysis of Stochastic Systems*, Thomson Science.

The official future, self-delusion and the value of scenarios

by Peter Schwartz

The current economic boom seems to have diminished the risks facing business. Yet the raft of success stories has diverted our attention from numerous individual strategic busts within the collective corporate boom. International Business Machines and US retailing giant Sears Roebuck each invested heavily in the US online service provider Prodigy, but instead of building a profitable internet company they each lost several billion dollars. In finance, US banks lost a great deal of capital in successive Latin American crises in the 1980s. The Nobel laureates at Long-Term Capital Management, the ill-fated hedge fund, lost billions in 1998 when they failed to consider scenarios that challenged key assumptions in their mathematical models. These massive failures remind us that very smart people and companies continue to make some very poor decisions.

In each case, the protagonists failed to ask themselves a vital question: what happens if we are wrong – very wrong? In other words, they badly misjudged the risks inherent in their decisions. This article describes a different way to approach these kinds of decisions and offers a new set of tools for managing risk in a capricious global marketplace.

There are two very different types of scenario planning. One is exploratory: trying to understand the contours of an unknown landscape – the future – mainly out of a general sense of interest. An exploratory approach may be helpful in seeking out potentially unforeseen risks, but is not always relevant for decision makers. The second class of scenarios, that relating to decision making, is far more important. This helps achieve a better understanding and managing of risk. This article focusses on this second use of scenarios.

Decision-making scenarios are not created in the abstract. We need to know who the decision makers are, since individuals base their decisions on perceptions as well as facts. People interpret facts and put them in context. Those interpretations and contexts are based on the decision makers' belief systems, psychological attitudes and worldviews.

The best way of finding this out is to ask a series of probing questions. Are the decision makers analytical and quantitative – an engineer or scientist, for example? Or are they intuitive and qualitative – perhaps historians, philosophers, or psychologists? Are they optimists or worriers? Are they systemic thinkers, always looking at the interactions of units, or more linear, following events in sequence? Do they have any political bias? Are they aristocrats and elitists or populists? Do they see lurking conspiracies or do they accept the logic of historical accidents? Are they blinded by their own ambitions and biases or are they eager to learn? Are they susceptible to herd mentality? These kinds of questions help account for the idiosyncrasies of decision makers and thus build the necessary foundations for developing good decision-making scenarios.

Subjective assessment

Companies assess the nature of strategic risk not as some objective reality but rather through the subjective viewpoints of the decision makers. While some risk assessment is amenable to straight factual analysis (usually when the risks are mainly technical), the risks we are most concerned with are those in which the decision maker themselves must observe and interpret the nature of risk. How might the variations in the subjective interpretations of individuals (and companies) affect their strategic decisions? Might one person aim too high and aspire to accomplish too much too quickly, or, conversely, shoot too low and expect to achieve too little?

Decision makers' cognitive maps may similarly bias their answers toward more "objective" questions. What are the nature of, and how great are, "killing risks"? How large might the losses be? How much room is there to maneuver? What is the balance between risk and reward? How large an insurance policy is needed against those risks? Decision makers' perceptions frame the way they think about these questions.

So how do decision makers evaluate risk in situations of great uncertainty? In large part, by engaging in collective self-delusion. They start out with a preferred scenario, the conventional wisdom, the accepted view or the "official future."

In scenario planning, it is important that planning staff who develop a set of possible futures for discussion ensure that the "official future" is included among them. Not until this initial scenario is called into question – through good research analysis and powerful new facts – will decision makers consider other possibilities among future options.

How do we identify and describe the "official future"? To do so, we must probe the decision makers' cognitive processes and the organizational and market environment in which they operate. A good approach is to engage crucial decision makers in a long interview and ask them a set of abstract questions intended to trigger spontaneous and expansive responses. There are five such questions, the first of which I call the "oracle" questions. If you could speak with an oracle, what questions would you ask about the future? Second, given the decision you face, what is the scenario for the best possible outcome? Third, what is the scenario for the worst possible outcome? Fourth, if you were retiring or leaving your company, what would you want your erstwhile colleagues to consider as your legacy? Finally, are there important barriers to change in your organization? These questions are designed to get decision makers to talk about what they believe, what they fear, what they hope for, how they see the nature of their organizations, what the limits and capabilities of those organizations are, and so on. The responses can be analyzed to see what natural categories various decision makers fall into and what shapes their real agenda. One can then present the findings to decision makers and test whether the perceived agendas of the individuals match the nominal agenda of the group.

Thus, the next stage in developing scenarios is to identify the primary decisions that managers face. Usually these center on the question: should we do something? This could involve building infrastructure, launching a product, starting a new business, or killing an old one. Scenarios are then constructed around the answer to that question by looking at the possible positive and negative outcomes. The key to each scenario is how it relates to the "should we" question.

African mining: scenarios in action

A major mining company had an option on a central African ore deposit of the type known in the industry as a "company maker," the kind of ore deposit found only once or twice every century. Unfortunately, this deposit sat in the middle of a war zone. The central question was, should the company continue to protect the option?

Clearly, it could not exercise the option and develop the site immediately. However, the option was up for renewal, and the company was going to have to pay several million dollars to preserve it. Faced with a difficult investment decision, the company chose scenario planning.

A new chief executive had just taken over the company and was skeptical of the chance of success, based on his experiences running businesses in Africa.

In the absence of the strong possibility of an improving political climate, he was unwilling to renew the option. So the significant analytical question was whether there were any plausible scenarios for a more orderly environment that would permit development of the ore deposit.

There were many paths to chaos – to some extent the country was already in chaos and it was not hard to see this continuing. But after doing its research, gathering reliable data, and engaging a number of credible experts in a series of scenario workshops, the planning team developed robust scenarios suggesting plausible paths to order. A scenario of a settlement imposed through the combined effort of the country's neighbors and the European powers seemed quite plausible.

There were some early signals that just such a process was under way. This demonstrated that while indeed there were paths to chaos, and probably more of them than to order, there were at least some credible paths to a more orderly environment that would support development. Crucially, there was a reasonable likelihood of big regrets if they let the option lapse. The chief executive changed his mind and renewed.

Mental maps

This process can best be illustrated by looking at a few examples. One of the most consequential strategic decisions in recent years was made by AT&T, the biggest US long-distance telephone company, in the late 1980s regarding the internet. At that time, the US government – in particular, the National Science Foundation (NSF) – loomed large in administrating the internet. The NSF wanted to withdraw from this role and offered to transfer the operation to AT&T at no cost. The US government thus offered AT&T a free monopoly on what in a single decade has become the increasingly dominant medium of communication. AT&T declined. How did this happen?

The answer lies in the unchallenged mental maps at the top of AT&T. The instinct of the significant decision makers was to see virtues in their current systems and flaws in the new technology. After all, they had designed and built the centrally switched network on which their services operated. Why would anyone want less efficient, lower-quality technology? Their technical experts only reinforced management prejudices. They thought that packet switching – the internet's fundamental technology – would not work. Furthermore, they believed that there would be little demand for internet-based services. Their technical experts concluded that the internet was insignificant for telephony and had no commercial significance in any other context.

If AT&T's decision makers had looked at alternative scenarios, they might have reached a different conclusion. On the issue of the technology and telephony, for example, they might have read the Huber Report for the US government, which explored how what would become the internet could restructure telephony. The report – rejected by some experts, hailed by others – was a credible document and

AT&T could have constructed a scenario in which the report's findings were correct. There was evidence, strong research and analysis available to them that could – and should – have led them to a scenario that would have challenged their technical judgments.

Second, AT&T ignored the considerable work that had already been done on the development of business-to-business electronic commerce. They might have explored, for example, how companies might restructure their activities, deliver new services, interact with each other in new ways, and create new demand for online business services. It required no great leap to project the efficiency improvements possible in this (now real) scenario.

AT&T planners might have provided the decision makers with two scenarios. One would have been the "official future," where centrally switched architecture remained dominant. They might also have developed an alternative in which new markets for internet services and new kinds of telephony challenged the then-dominant network architecture. Such a scenario would have at least given the decision makers a sense of the internet's potential, prompted them to take the decision more seriously, and perhaps have led to a very different conclusion.

Specific decisions

Not only are scenarios useful in making specific decisions, they also encourage decision makers to become much more sensitive to new signals of change. What has not been foreseen is unlikely to be seen in time. Scenarios can serve to train decision makers to recognize signals in a timely way. Even if AT&T had reached the same decision in light of the uncertainty, it might have chosen to cover against being wrong by developing router technology and online services. AT&T would then have been able to challenge both Cisco Systems, a computer networking company, and AOL, an internet service provider, early in the game, because by then the internet was becoming increasingly visible. It has to be worth speculating on the possibilities for a company combining the operations of AOL, Yahoo!, the web search engine pioneer, and Cisco under single control. AT&T got it badly wrong because it never seriously looked at alternative scenarios.

Another example shows how scenarios can provide a framework for thinking, a means of sifting through the information deluge for the facts of real consequence. Several years ago, a sophisticated technology company began looking at the future of some of its key technologies and its research and development strategies. In workshops designed to facilitate this process, discussions ranged over the potential of fuel cells, biotechnology extending human life, and nano-technology.

The participating group of senior technical executives mostly dismissed the potential of these new areas. However, they did develop multiple scenarios that looked at the interplay of technical developments and market acceptance. These addressed the possibility that there would be rapid advances in and early adoption of technology, or that technical progress might be slower or even that there could be real resistance in the marketplace. Each of these scenarios turned out to be perceptive in its own way and prepared the executives – despite their skepticism – for the early signals of change and to recognize their significance.

In the months that followed, members of the technical group reported that information on these scenarios had begun to leap out of the background. Articles from newspapers, journals and magazines on nano-technology, fuel cells, life extension, and genetically modified organisms emerged with increasing frequency.

Within a year, they had changed their views on the potential of these new technologies and successfully launched R&D efforts in two areas – ahead of competitors.

It might be argued that scenarios are unnecessary for such changes of mind and strategy. A straightforward discussion group flagging possible areas of technological advance could just as easily alert executives to the changes and produce precisely the same effects.

Yet scenarios differ in an important respect: their level of structure and detail. They gave these technical executives a familiar construct in which to fit and make sense of new data. Having considered the detailed, though hypothetical, consequences of the wide-scale adoption of these technologies, the group was able to make much more informed judgments about their real-world development. The scenario was a tool for enabling them to perceive new information in a timely way, to recognize important signals of change, and to understand the meaning of those changes for their organization. They were able to reassess the upside risks of the new technological opportunities.

Scenarios not only serve the immediate process of decision making but also lead to gradual changes in the perceptual models of the decision makers themselves. Decision makers can reconstruct their perceptions and change their minds, and ultimately change their agenda, even as they go forward. So scenarios can have their impact in the short term, in informing the immediate decision, as well as over time, as decision makers reframe their mental maps.

In conclusion, risk management scenarios show the decision maker their own perceptions of the risk environment. They thus provide a tool that links the perceptual context with the external environment. The stronger this link, the better placed we are to understand – and perhaps to improve on – a corporate record of spectacular successes and equally spectacular failures.

Summary

In the 1980s, US long-distance telephone operator AT&T turned down a free offer to take control of the internet. **Peter Schwartz** notes that smart individuals and companies continue to make some very poor decisions. Too often, for instance, they will assess risk through a lens of collective self-delusion. Decision-making groups often carry with them an "official future," an accepted view of the way things are and the way they will turn out to be. Scenario planning involves challenging that future by creating convincing and detailed alternatives. Even if no hypothesized future turns out to be correct, the planning process encourages a rare strategic focus and a proper assessment of the risks facing the company and its political, economic, or technological environment.

Suggested further reading

Fahey, F. and Randall. R. (eds) (1998) *Competitive Foresight Scenarios*, Wiley.
Ringland, G. (1998) *Managing for the Future*, Wiley.
Schwartz, P. (1991) *The Art of the Long View*, Doubleday.
van der Heijden, K. (1998) *The Art of Strategic Conversation*, Wiley.

Tooling up for risky decisions

by Kiriakos Vlahos

Betting on a single view of the future is a hazardous practice and most companies are now aware of the dangers of ignoring uncertainty. As a result, they have started to use a range of different approaches for analyzing and managing risk. Below is a brief overview of risk analysis tools available, followed by an introduction to decision analysis and an illustration of how it can support decision making.

Different decision situations involve varying degrees of complexity. Table 1 reflects two dimensions of complexity, the number of decision alternatives and the type of uncertainty. The simplest type of problem involves assessing a single project with a view to deciding whether or not to proceed. The dominant approach here is discounted cash flow, a favourite on all MBA finance courses, that uses a risk-adjusted discount factor to account for the uncertainties and is often complemented by simple sensitivity analysis, which involves asking "what if" questions in order to explore the impact of uncertain parameters. Recently, a number of academics and practitioners such as Lenos Trigeorgis, Thomas Copeland, and Phillip Keenan have criticized discounted cash flow analysis for its failure to account properly for uncertainty, project flexibilities, such as the ability to abandon, delay, or expand projects, and market information on traded securities and other financial instruments. When a number of discrete uncertainties (such as the win-or-lose legal case or the hit-or-miss search for oil reserves) and alternatives (whether to invest in a new product, outsource production, or carry out market research) are under consideration, scenarios, decision analysis, and real options can be used to analyze the problem.

This article outlines the technique of decision analysis; for information on real options and scenario planning, readers should consult respectively the articles by Jeffrey Reuer (Module 3) and Peter Schwartz's article in this module.

Finally, in situations where uncertainties are continuous distributions (such as market share), Monte Carlo simulation – defined in the box – can be used to derive the distribution of the project value. Monte Carlo simulation is also used to calculate the Value at Risk associated with trading operations, which is a statistical measure of possible losses, introduced and popularized by the investment bank JP Morgan.

Table 1: Overview of risk analysis techniques

Alternatives	Uncertainty: No	Uncertainty: Discrete	Uncertainty: Continuous
Project evaluation	DCF, sensitivity analysis	Scenarios, decision trees, real options	Monte Carlo simulation, real options
Portfolio problems	Optimization	Stochastic programming	Hard problems

The Monte Carlo simulation

Monte Carlo simulation is a technique named after the roulette wheels in Monte Carlo, viewed as devices for generating random numbers. It has been used in other scientific fields for a long time, but it was David Hertz of consulting firm McKinsey & Co. who suggested the use of Monte Carlo simulation for the evaluation of capital investments in an article published by the *Harvard Business Review* in 1979. The uncertainties affecting the success of a project are quantified using probability distributions. During the simulation, a large number of scenarios are generated by sampling these probability distributions and for each of them the project outcome is evaluated. The result of the analysis is the probability distribution of the outcome (for example NPV, IRR), which provides information about the expected value and range of possible outcomes and the downside risk of the project.

The decision problems facing a business unit are typically related to the allocation of a fixed budget to a large number of different projects. In other words, they are portfolio problems with decisions needed on which to support and which to kill. Simple versions of this problem, such as the mean-variance approach, introduced by Nobel laureate Harry Markowitz, can be solved by standard optimization techniques. This approach takes into account the mean return, the standard deviation, and the correlations of the returns of available projects to derive the portfolio of projects that minimizes risk for any given level of return. More complex problems involving multi-stage decision processes (for example balancing pension assets and liabilities over long planning horizons) require advanced modeling approaches such as stochastic programming, which are beyond the scope of this article.

Decision building blocks

Decision analysis is a normative approach to decision making with solid foundations in mathematics and statistics. Its building blocks are:

- visual tools for structuring multi-stage decision problems;
- probability theory for modeling uncertainty;
- utility theory for modeling risk preferences;
- extensions to decision problems with multiple conflicting objectives.

It is best to introduce decision analysis through an example. Pharmaceutical companies spend around 16 percent of their revenues on R&D. Basic research starts with the synthesis of chemical compounds. For every drug that reaches the market, more than 5,000 have been tested without success. One in every 400 of these chemical compounds enters pre-clinical trials, and of those one out of two is tested on humans (Phase I and Phase II trials). Of these drugs, one out of three enters Phase III clinical tests and, finally, one out of two of those is marketed. The whole process can take up to 10 years and costs on average between $100m and $200m per drug without counting the cost of failures, as discussed in R. Halliday's work in further reading. It is clear that the decision about which drugs to develop and test is not an easy one.

The decision tree shown in Figure 1 presents the process for developing a new drug that has passed pre-clinical testing and is ready to be tested on humans. In this figure, square nodes represent choices, circles represent uncertainties, and the sequence of nodes shows their timing. The tree depicts the multi-stage nature of the

Figure 1: Decision tree for new drug development

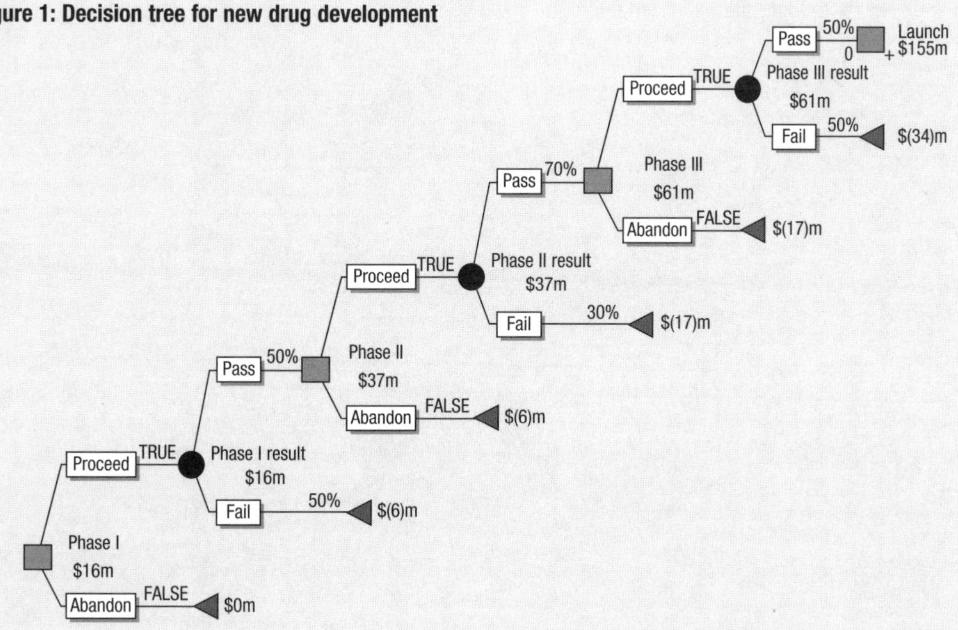

decision process from Phase I to launch. For example, the first decision is whether to proceed with Phase I testing or not. The outcome of the testing is uncertain and company experts estimate the probability of success for this drug to be 50 percent. If Phase I is successful, then the company needs to decide whether to proceed with Phase II and so on. The values on the leaves of the tree show the expected net present value (NPV) of cash flows associated with that outcome. For example, if the project fails Phase I, the estimated cost is $6m.

The part of the tree corresponding to the uncertainties after launch is shown in Figure 2. The model is a simplification of reality and only two major uncertainties are included, the market share of the drug and the price at which it is sold. Three scenarios for each uncertainty are included. The cash-flow calculations were carried out using a detailed spreadsheet model that covers 10 geographical regions and includes assumptions about penetration curves, product life cycle, market size and growth, and production and marketing costs. The NPV varies from $37m to $414m.

After mapping the problem into a decision tree, the next step of the analysis is to calculate the expected value of each alternative decision. In simple terms, the expected value is the average value that would result from performing the project a very large number of times. It can be found by working backwards from the leaf nodes to the start of the tree. For uncertainty nodes, the expected value is the sum of probability-weighted outcomes, and for decision nodes it is arrived at by selecting the branch with the highest expected value. In this case, the illustration of decision tree analysis was created using PrecisionTree, a software package that works as an Excel add-on and can be used with spreadsheets. The illustration indicates the best course of action at each decision node by showing "TRUE" in the corresponding branch. The expected value of each node is shown to the right of the node. In this example, the expected value of the whole tree is a positive $16m and the best initial

Figure 2: Uncertainties after launch

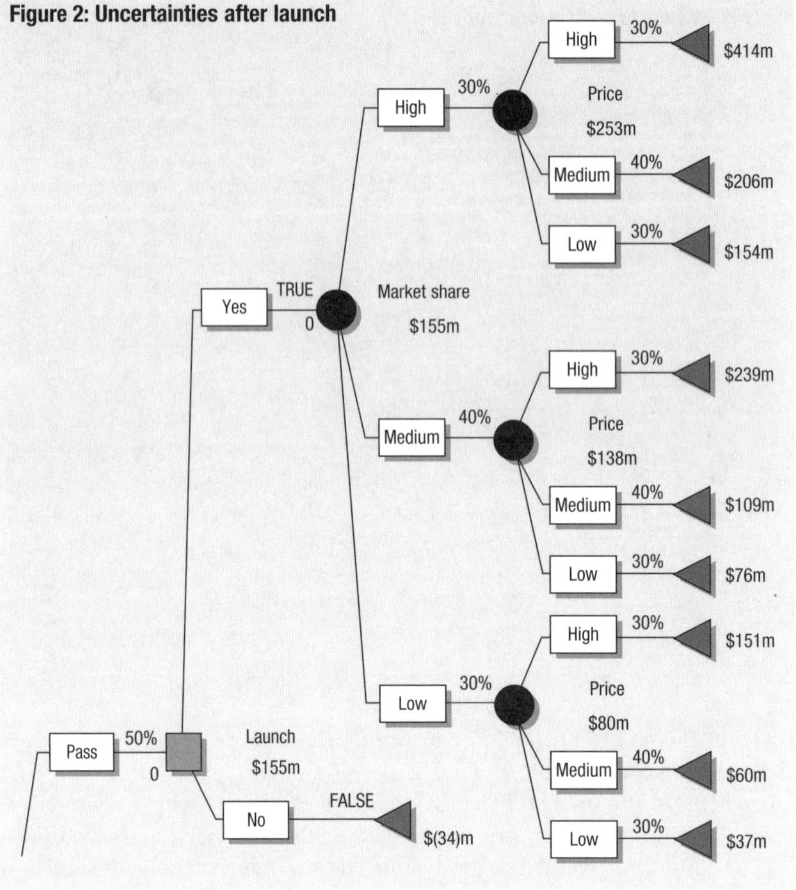

decision is to proceed with Phase I testing, since this has a higher expected value than the "Abandon" option.

The expected value hides a wide range of possible outcomes. As shown in Figure 3, the risk profile of the project (the probability distribution of outcomes) suggests that the most likely outcomes are negative. In fact, the probability of positive NPV is just 17.5 percent (roughly a one-in-six chance). Clearly, if a company were investing a large portion of its funds in this project, it would need to think twice. Large pharmaceutical companies that develop hundreds of similar drugs can afford to take the risk, but if the losses invite bankruptcy the downside needs careful examination.

At this point, utility theory comes into play. Traditional decision analysis models risk preferences using utility functions that map monetary outcomes to a measure of attractiveness. Figure 4 shows three different shapes of utility curves corresponding to risk-averse behavior, risk-neutral behavior, and risk-seeking behavior. In all three curves greater wealth corresponds to greater utility. But the risk-averse curve is concave because, as wealth increases, the incremental attractiveness of the same amount of money becomes smaller. This is intuitive: Bill Gates did not get the same kick out of making his fifth billion as he did from making his first. The risk-neutral curve is a straight line and a risk-seeking curve is convex (in technical terms, the second derivative is positive).

How do we integrate utility functions with decision trees? After assessing a utility

Figure 3: Risk profile for new drug

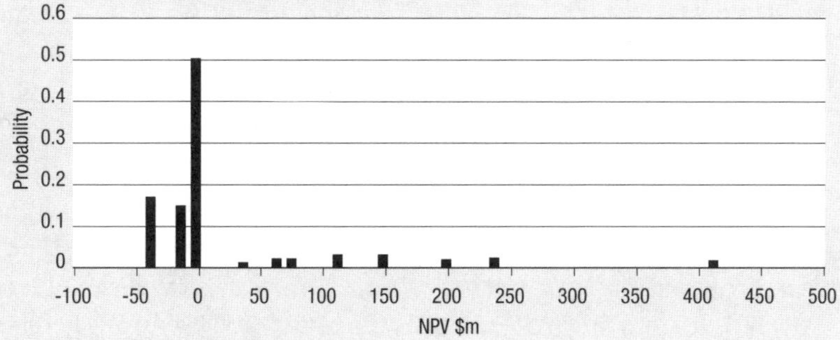

function that reflects our preferences, we just replace the monetary outcomes of the leaf nodes with their corresponding utilities. We then proceed to calculate expected utilities as normal. Note that if one is using a risk-averse utility function, the expected utility of a bet with 50 percent chance of winning $100 and 50 percent chance of losing $100 is less than the utility of a certain $0. A risk-seeking utility curve results in the reverse preference. Our earlier analysis using monetary values corresponds to risk-neutral behavior, assuming that the company is a large one and has a large and diversified R&D portfolio.

The benefits of decision tree analysis may be summarized as follows:

- The process of building a decision tree enhances our understanding of the problem and forces us to make all assumptions explicit.
- Decision trees are great tools for documenting and communicating one's thinking about uncertainty and risk and can increase the productivity of group meetings. They also help to generate new alternatives that can enhance the value of projects.
- The decision tree developed here would allow managers to monitor the progress of the project and revisit the analysis at each decision point or as soon as new information becomes available.
- The output of the analysis in terms of the expected NPV and the risk profile of the project could become inputs to the project portfolio selection process.

Figure 4: Utility functions

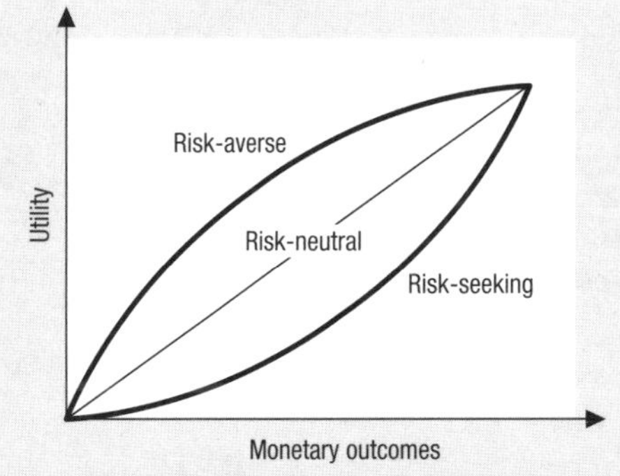

Decision analysis vs real options

The study of projects using real options is becoming increasingly popular among the financial community and promoted as a way of achieving project flexibility. Decision analysis and real options share much in common, but there are equally important differences. For each approach, the initial stages at which the problem is conceived and structured are identical. Often, real options analyses represent problems as decision trees; decision analysis is just as capable of representing project flexibilities as real options. The main advantage of option theory over decision analysis lies in its ability to incorporate market information, when such information exists, thus eliminating the need to assess probabilities (real options use "risk-neutral probabilities") and the discount rate or utility functions (real options use risk-neutral valuation). The last issue is a thorny problem in any type of project valuation.

On the other hand, real options have difficulty coping with so-called "private risks," that is, risks that cannot be hedged in the financial markets. It is also true that all projects, to varying extents, involve private risks. Depending on the relative importance of private risks versus market risks, one might choose between the two approaches or alternatively combine them, getting the best of both worlds.

A further benefit of decision analysis is its ability to incorporate and value information in the form of market research, advice from consulting firms, forecasting studies, and so on.

Decision analysis is a mature and proven approach to analyzing risk. Moreover, the recently explored integration with option theory (*see* box) has great potential. The commercial software tools available for decision analysis make the approach accessible to any manager with spreadsheet skills. But as with all other approaches, managers are well advised to keep it simple and combine it with a good deal of business sense.

Summary

Conscious of the dangers of ignoring uncertainty, companies are grappling with different techniques for analyzing and managing risk, says **Kiriakos Vlahos**. This article provides a brief overview of some of the tools currently in use, among which are scenarios, decision analysis, and real options. Focussing on decision analysis, the author examines its role in supporting decision making. For instance, decision trees – graphic representations of the issues at play – can be useful in documenting and communicating thinking about uncertainty and risk. They may also generate new ideas about choices and enhance project value. Real options for their part are becoming increasingly popular, but present shortcomings in dealing with private risks – those that cannot be hedged on financial markets.

Suggested further reading

Clemen, R. (1996) *Making Hard Decisions*, Duxbury.

Copeland, T.E. and Keenan, P.T. (1998) "How much is flexibility worth?" *The McKinsey Quarterly*, Number 2.

Halliday, R.G., Walker, S.R. and Lumley, C.E. (1992) "R&D philosophy and management in the world's leading pharmaceutical companies," *Journal of Pharmaceutical Medicine*, 2, 139–54.

Hertz, D. (1979) "Risk analysis in capital investment," *Harvard Business Review*, September–October.

PrecisionTree, Palisade Corp. 1997, www.palisade.com for details on the software analysis tool.

Raiffa, H. (1968) *Decision Analysis*, Addison-Wesley.

Smith, J.E. and Nau, R.F. (1995) "Valuing risky projects: option pricing theory and decision analysis," *Management Science*, 41, 795–816.

Trigeorgis, L. (1996) *Real Options*, Boston, MA: MIT Press.

Vlahos, K. (1997) "Taking the risk out of uncertainty" in *Mastering Management*, London: FT Pitman Publishing.

Lowering exposure by spreading the risk

by Mike Hanley

The modern mantra of corporate risk management is fast becoming: "A risk is a risk is a risk." Large, multinational companies are no longer prepared to approach risk management on a single risk-by-risk basis. It makes no sense for a manager to accept a potential \$50m loss in the organization's currency-trading activities and simultaneously hedge against a potential \$20m loss on a suburban office property.

Risk managers now realize that any particular risk can have consequences for many seemingly unconnected parts of the business – losses in one part of the business might be offset by gains elsewhere in the organization that result from that loss event. Just as financial investors can lower the risk in their investment portfolio by sensible diversification, so managers can benefit from continual review of their entire corporate project portfolio.

This kind of examination of a company's "risk portfolio" raises several questions. How do risks within the enterprise interact? Do natural hedges exist within the company that suggest a particular corporate structure? Does the "portfolio" effect of a multinational's business unit structure diversify risk sufficiently?

One example of this, reported in *The Economist*, concerns LVMH, the French luxury goods group. This company initially thought it would suffer a heavy loss after one of its Japanese warehouses was destroyed during the Kobe earthquake. In fact, a subsequent brandy-drinking binge by locals meant the loss was largely recovered. This suggests two things: first, that risks and rewards in one part of an organization affect risks and rewards in another; second, that they can sometimes be directly compared with each other in financial terms.

This is the driving force behind the creation of the portfolio theory of risk management. In the financial world, mathematicians have for years been developing techniques for looking at a portfolio of financial risks and analyzing the total risk exposure. Now corporate risk managers are seeking to adapt and apply these techniques from the financial world to their own, far more diversified, risk portfolios.

The problem is that if it is difficult to identify, quantify, model, and manage the risks of even the most uniform financial portfolio, how are risk managers expected to do so when their types of risk differ so radically? Financial managers have developed complex methodologies for attributing risk characteristics to individual instruments, positions, and portfolios. Yet, at best, such information gives only an indication of past performance and may or may not be a good indicator of the investment's future level of risk. The problem is multiplied as the number and complexity of risks grow.

Risk mapping is a technique for analyzing a company's portfolio of risks in a way that clarifies their links and their impact on each other. Risk mapping can help organizations:

- determine a company-wide "risk appetite" in a framework that can be applied across all operations;
- catalog their critical risks and ensure they are mitigated and managed;
- develop a dynamic financial model of the company that incorporates all the major risks affecting earnings.

However, applying quantification techniques to risks as diverse as political and social ones is tricky. A way is needed of looking at the individual risks one by one, then putting them on a scale and adding them up. In practice, this can be technically complex. Many risk management and risk-related consulting firms have developed proprietary methods for this. These fall into two broad categories – top-down and bottom-up techniques.

From top down

Top-down risk profiling or mapping looks at an organization from a corporate perspective, seeking to identify and analyze the risks that exist in each part of the company, extrapolating their impact on each other and the organization as a whole.

Top-down risk profiling broadly comprises five subprocesses:

- *Risk identification.* Risks are first identified by looking at the company as a whole; publicly available information is often valuable here. This information is then used in brainstorming sessions with key individuals, designed to identify the risks within the organization and produce raw information for the portfolio analysis.
- *Risk assessment.* The results of the risk identification process are then analyzed in terms of probability and severity. Information is often displayed on different matrices or axes representing different levels of frequency and severity for each risk. These attempt to give the results depth and meaning.
- *Risk profiling.* These results are then translated into a risk profile, arranging important risks into "risk families" ranging from high-probability, negligible outcomes to low-probability disasters. This profile can then be used to set risk-mitigation strategy priorities.
- *Risk quantification.* Risk families considered suitable for subsequent modeling can be fully assessed in a follow-up process, when actual losses and probabilities are estimated and distributions or confidence limits are added to these estimates. These estimates are typically based on the opinions of several experts combined with any valid loss data available.
- *Risk consolidation.* Risks analyzed at divisional or subsidiary level need to be aggregated to the corporate level. This can be a subjective risk-profiling analysis performed by a qualified team or, if sufficient quantification is possible, a mathematical process.

Once the risks are identified, the process moves to model their impact on the organization. The Monte Carlo simulation, which attempts to calculate probabilities of outcomes, is often used to develop probabilities for various loss scenarios. The picture that emerges from such simulations is used to develop strategies to protect the company from loss, or to redesign the corporation around a more appropriate risk profile. Organizations that promote top-down risk profiling include Zurich International, a financial services business, with its "Total Risk Profiling" brand

The risk mapping process

Techniques for mapping risk have several common features.

Risk identification. Risk identification seeks to pin down all risks facing the business, from stationery theft to fraud, liability, and fatality, without placing a value on these risks. In a top-down risk mapping process, risks are identified by examining publicly available information, conducting risk identification workshops with senior managers, or applying risk identification techniques to financial data. In a bottom-up process, workshops are held with middle and lower managers, with results aggregated up to board level.

Risk assessment. Once risks have been identified, each is assessed for its frequency and severity. For instance, office stationery may often be stolen, but this risk may not be considered serious. On the other hand, the explosion of an oil rig may not happen frequently, but its consequences can be extremely severe.

Risk consolidation. Once each risk has been identified and quantified, it can be placed on a risk map. Typically, this is a matrix with four quadrants, or a graph with two axes, representing levels of severity and levels of frequency. Each quadrant refers to a different category of risk, which needs to be handled differently (*see* Figure 1).

Risk portfolio management. The final step in risk mapping is the most difficult. It requires managers to take an unconventional look at their businesses. Corporations present certain value propositions to investors. These might say: "Invest in the tobacco industry's strong cash flows," "Invest in Hanson's ability to choose good projects," or "Invest in the strong potential of this e-commerce business." Risk portfolio management therefore demands that executives have a good understanding of their group's value proposition with respect to the risk and return from each and every one of their businesses. They must see the set of businesses as a portfolio of risks that amounts to the value offered by its shares. They must actively manage the company's return relative to the capital it places at risk to obtain that return.

Figure 1: Risk map – the classic approach

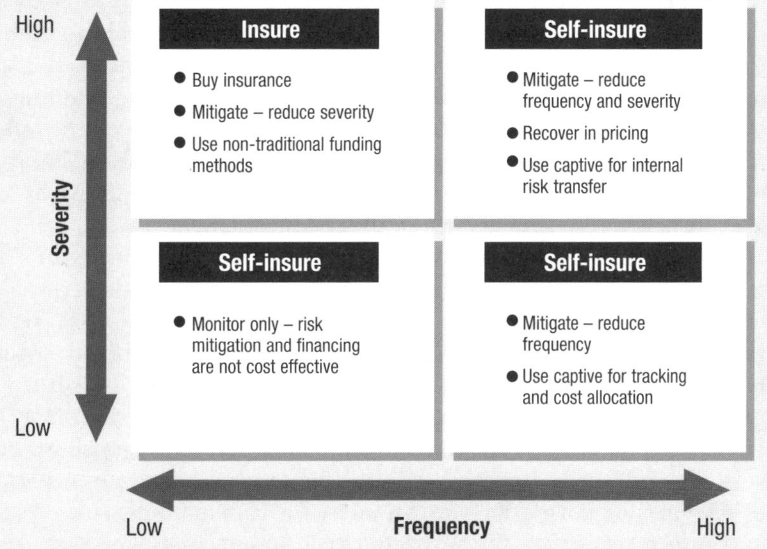

methodology, and PwC, the professional services firm, with its proprietary "ORCA (Objectives, Risk, Controls/Processes and Alignment)" technique.

From bottom up

Other firms promote what is called a bottom-up approach to risk mapping. Instead of viewing existing risks from a boardroom level, the method uses an intensive series of shopfloor focus groups to identify, discuss, and analyze risks. Workshops are organized with selected employees from the participating business units, during which facilitators, targetting specific objectives, use the consultant's control framework to review the controls in place. This data is summarized to produce a board-level picture, from which decisions about managing the risk portfolio can be made. Organizations that promote a bottom-up approach to risk mapping include KPMG, one of the Big Five accountancy firms, and Aon, the risk consultancy and reinsurers.

Another model of good risk management practice is known as dynamic financial analysis. A risk professional using this must first determine which external economic factors influence the enterprise. They will also need expert knowledge of the organization's major risk elements and their interaction. The problem with dynamic financial analysis, as with many such models, is that the quality of the conclusions rests entirely on the quality of the risk data and the ability of the assessment team to interpret it. Practitioners argue that just considering and setting up a dynamic financial analysis model for an organization can be as insightful and valuable as interpreting the actual results.

Assessing the portfolio approach

One selling point for the portfolio approach to risk management is that by tackling risks on an aggregate basis, managers gain a better understanding of what their business is about and how it works as an integrated whole. The approach provides a good basis for developing an innovative risk financing approach. It is one that takes into account the company's aggregate risk appetite and its ability to take different kinds of risk on to its books in different ways, such as captives, and transfer other types of risk off its books using other tools.

The portfolio approach can also assist a company to plan an efficient insurance program. It can avoid buying lots of high limits in different insurance lines by maximizing the value of its self-insured portion. After mapping risk, managers should study the portfolio and decide the most efficient way of retaining risk. Each risk has a point where it is no longer cheap to retain. Strategic risk financing seeks to determine both where that point is and the most efficient way to pass on the risks that lie beyond it. This applies to the risk portfolio as a whole.

Portfolio risk managing gives the company an opportunity to ask itself why it is managing risks at all. Companies where turnover exceeds several billion dollars do not expect to recover the losses caused by every accident or market swing affecting them. From the point of view of sound financial management, insurance only helps reduce the year-to-year volatility of their total risk cost by spreading risk over the course of several years. Risk management aims to increase the accuracy of forecasting and to give meaning to the company's strategic planning activities.

In the end, these activities dovetail: those who formulate corporate strategy come to rely on the information thrown up by the risk management process about current and future scenarios. With a sound risk management process, the strategists will better be able to respond convincingly when investors, customers, and regulators question their abilities to protect company assets and increase corporate value.

Summary

Just as financial investors use portfolio spread to lower their overall exposure in the markets, corporate risk managers are learning how to adapt these techniques to their own highly intricate world, writes **Mike Hanley**. This portfolio approach can give managers a better understanding of their businesses and help them build more efficient insurance programs. Risk is complex and managing it is only partially mitigated by systems such as risk mapping, a technique to track and quantify corporate risk interaction. Quantification, however, may not always be the most appropriate way of assessing political and social risk, among others. Therefore, risk management consultants have developed proprietary methods that apply either top-down or bottom-up approaches for scrutinizing risk portfolios. Sound risk management can also be useful to strategists who have to respond to investor or regulatory concerns on how to protect company assets.

Quotas and contests in the battle for reward

by Anil Gaba

The "winner-takes-all" phenomenon is an increasingly pervasive aspect of our lives. Examples include the race for developing and patenting a new internet-based product or service, the constant tussle among hundreds of mutual funds for a "top ten" ranking, tight contests between managers in a large organization over a few senior positions, and vying to be the star in entertainment or sports. Relative not absolute performance matters. Winning or being among the finest few brings disproportionately large rewards compared to losing.

For individuals and organizations, compensation is usually determined by contests or by quota-based performance schemes. The latter might be a quota-based payoff, a fixed salary, and a flat or a piece-rate bonus above a certain level of performance, offered to sales people or managers. It is increasingly rare to find compensation structures that do not include elements of contests or quotas.

Not surprisingly, such compensation schemes have attracted much attention from managers, economic researchers, and corporations. Most analysis has focussed on how to induce greater effort from participants in the compensation schemes.

The crucial assumption is that, for these people, effort is the only decision variable. It is argued that greater effort increases the participant's chances of success (winning in a contest or clearing a quota). It is acknowledged, however, that at a given level of effort, a participant's performance is likely to be affected by random fluctuations from exogenous factors that cannot be predicted and over which the participant has no control.

A typical individual model would assume that the individual is unable to alter random fluctuations in performance, but is able to shift them towards higher values by expending greater effort. In more formal terms, the individual can shift the mean of the probability distribution of individual performance to a higher level, but the dispersion or the variability remains unchanged.

Furthermore, it is common to assume that most individuals are risk averse and hence cannot be expected to perform risky activities. Such risk aversion implies a preference for the less risky option (for example, lower variability with the same mean or expected value).

All this ignores the point that, besides a decision on how much effort to expend, there is another key decision variable for an individual or an organization, and that is how much risk (variability or dispersion of the possible outcomes) to undertake in the performance. So risk in performance is often a choice and not a given destiny.

Consider as an example a sales person who, at a given level of effort, has the option of pursuing two different customers: one whose order will be worth \$250,000 and where the probability of obtaining the order is 0.8, and another whose order will be worth \$1m and where the probability of success is 0.2. Both options have the same expected value, but the second option is presumably more risky.

A manager in a promotion contest, or an internet-based company in a race to develop a new product, might have to consider whether to engage in an innovation with a low success probability and a high payoff, or in a more mediocre venture with a higher probability of success and lower payoff, where both require similar effort levels. Similarly, a fund manager has a band of choices involving volatility of performance, and so on. The issue then becomes how the risk behavior of individuals and organizations is affected by the way compensation is structured.

Quota-based compensation

For quota-based compensation, consider the following simple example. Suppose that a sales person draws a fixed salary of \$50,000 and a bonus of \$10,000 if sales exceed a certain level, say, Q. Further, suppose that the sales person has a choice of two strategies. By following Strategy A, sales will be anywhere between 21 and 30 units, each outcome being equally likely. But by following Strategy B, sales will be anywhere between 1 and 50 units, again each outcome being equally likely.

Clearly, both strategies have the same expected value or mean, but Strategy B is more risky. First, consider $Q = 27$, that is, the sales person will get a bonus if sales are 28 units or more. If the sales person opts for Strategy A, the probability of getting the bonus is $3/10 = 0.3$, whereas the probability of obtaining the bonus with Strategy B is $23/50 = 0.46$. Next, consider $Q = 23$, that is, the bonus is attained with sales of 24 units or more. Now, the sales person's probability of getting the bonus is 0.7 with Strategy A and 0.54 with Strategy B. It appears in this example that the sales person is better off choosing the high-risk option in the high-quota case and the low-risk option in the low-quota case.

This same phenomenon, under very general conditions, is discussed by Anil Gaba and Ajay Kalra (*see* further reading.) It is shown that the above holds for all possible variations of a quota-based compensation scheme used in real life and for all probability distributions. For example, sometimes a sales person gets a fixed salary and a piece-rate commission beyond the quota level rather than a flat bonus.

In general, higher levels of quota are more likely to induce participants to opt for greater risk in performance. Intuitively, when the quota is high, the greater risk (variability) in performance increases the upside potential by increasing the chances of exceeding the quota, and the greater downside risk is inconsequential since a fixed salary acts as the limitation from below. These propositions have also been tested in experimental studies, with results showing that the subjects' behavior is consistent with the propositions.

For space reasons, the above examples do not consider the simultaneous choice of effort and risk. Effort, for example, can be seen as a determinant of the mean of the performance distribution, which can be shifted to a higher level by expending greater effort. It is possible, then, to construct examples where a participant facing a high quota will opt for a high-risk and low-effort strategy rather than a low-risk and high-effort strategy.

The tradeoff is between the dislike of expending effort and the adoption of greater risk in performance. As the dislike for expending effort increases, one would expect a participant to be more likely to attempt to reach the quota by adopting greater risk in performance rather than by expending greater effort. Further, the choice of effort level by a participant is likely to be within tight bounds (there are only 24 hours in a day). After reaching the upper limitation in effort level, engaging in high-risk behavior might be the only way for a participant to increase the chances of attaining the quota. The point is that risk in performance remains a key decision variable and an important determinant of success.

The question of exactly how high or low the quota levels should be set by a company would depend on its operational context. Sales people, for example, might be induced to meet the short-term quota goal by adopting either a high-risk or a low-risk strategy.

However, the customer base that the sales force obtained in this way may not be the most desirable. For instance, with high-risk sales behavior, the company might end up with new but price-sensitive or brand-switching customers. On the other hand, with low-risk behavior, the company might never move beyond its existing customer base. A company should use the induced risk behavior of sales people to align their focus more to long-term corporate goals. Differentiating quota goals by, say, segment types (for example, new customers versus retaining existing customers) could be helpful.

Contest-based compensation

To illustrate the advantages of risk manipulation in a contest, consider the following simple contest among five people. Each contestant draws a number at random from one of three hats, which contain the following ranges of non-zero integer-valued numbers:

- Hat 1 contains numbers from –5 to 5
- Hat 2 contains numbers from –15 to 15
- Hat 3 contains numbers from –1,000 to 1,000.

Before any contestant draws a number from a hat, any previous numbers drawn are replaced. The player who draws the highest number wins and gets a reward. The remaining four contestants get no reward. All ties are resolved by randomization, such that in a tie each contestant has an equal chance of winning (that is, by tossing a coin or rolling a die).

The expected value of a draw from any of the hats is 0, but the variability is smallest for Hat 1 and largest for Hat 3. In comparative risk terms, it may be said that Hat 1 is the least risky and Hat 3 is the most risky.

Now, suppose that four of the contestants always draw from Hat 1 and the fifth contestant, say Sandy, has the opportunity to draw from one of the three hats. Consider the following variations for Sandy:

1 Sandy also draws from Hat 1. The probability of winning for any contestant, including Sandy, is 1/5 = 0.2.
2 Sandy draws from Hat 2. Her probability of winning is P {Sandy draws a number greater than 5} + P {Sandy draws a number between (and including) –5 and 5, and wins} = 1/3 + 1/3(1/5) = 0.4. The probability of winning for each of the other four contestants is 0.6/4 = 0.15. In shifting from Hat 1 to Hat 2, Sandy is able to increase her probability of winning by increasing risk.
3 Sandy draws from Hat 3. In this case, the probability of winning for Sandy is now close to 1/2 (0.4985, to be exact) and for each of the other four players it is close to 1/8. Also, note that if somehow Sandy could still further increase (symmetrically) the range of numbers in Hat 3, she would not improve her probability of winning beyond 0.5.

Of course, in shifting from Hat 1 to Hat 2 or Hat 3, Sandy will also increase her probability of obtaining the lowest number in the contest. However, whether she obtains the lowest number or the second highest is of no consequence, and what really matters is whether she can increase her probability of obtaining the highest number.

Consider yet another variation of the same contest. All five players draw from Hat 1 and the players with the top three numbers win, instead of only the player with the highest number, and each gets the same reward. The remaining two contestants lose and do not get any reward. The probability of winning for any one player is simply 3/5 = 0.6. Now, suppose, once again, that Sandy draws from Hat 2 while the other four players draw from Hat 1. In this case, by shifting from Hat 1 to Hat 2, Sandy's probability of winning drops from 0.6 to 0.53; if she shifts to Hat 3, her probability of winning approaches 0.5. Here, it appears that increasing risk reduces the probability of winning.

To sum up, the above example suggests that an increase in risk works to one's advantage if the proportion of winners in the contest is small (below 0.5). Conversely, if the proportion of winners is high (above 0.5), an increase in risk reduces the probability of winning.

This analysis assumes, however, that only one of the contestants has the opportunity to manipulate risk. Insofar as that is true, opportunistic increase or decrease in risk is an important competitive advantage and can be the determining factor for whoever wins in a contest.

Consider, for example, an organization that, intentionally or unintentionally, sponsors a contest among many equally able employees to place the first few of them in positions with a high payoff. Typically, the proportion of winners is small, while the rewards for winning are disproportionately high relative to losing. Any employee who has special access to opportunities for greater risk in performance could enjoy substantive competitive advantages. For example, the protégé of a chief executive in a corporation might have greater discretion over actions than do other contestants.

Of course, shifting the mean of the performance distribution to an upper level by higher ability or greater effort would also have a positive impact on the probability of winning. However, in a contest with many equally able contestants who put in maximum possible effort to obtain the substantial maximum reward, as is often the case, opportunity for manipulating risk in performance is likely to be the determining factor in winning. Also, the competitive advantage gained by opportunistic risk taking *vis-à-vis* the advantage gained by increasing the mean of the performance distribution is likely to be much greater as the proportion of winners gets smaller.

What if all contestants had equal access to the choice of risk in performance and made such a choice strategically? In that case, in the example above, any one contestant would be better off choosing the highest-risk strategy (Hat 3) in the first version (where only the top draw wins) and the lowest-risk strategy (Hat 1) in the second version (where the top three draws out of five win), irrespective of other contestants' strategies. Consequently, all contestants should choose the highest-risk strategy in the first version and the lowest-risk strategy in the second version (which in formal game-theory terms would be called unique Nash equilibrium points).

Consider, for instance, an investment company that promises high payoffs to top-ranking fund managers who also would stand to gain from exceptional offers by competing investment companies. In such cases, many fund managers might engage in very high risks in order to increase their chances for the substantial leading prize, even sacrificing to some extent the expected value of their returns.

This might, in turn, severely escalate the risk faced by the company as a whole. There is now substantial empirical evidence that there is often much mid-year manipulation of risk by mutual fund managers for short-term gains. Underperforming funds, for example, tend to increase risk taking in order to boost short-term returns.

On the other hand, greater aggregate risk on the part of its employees could be beneficial to an organization that is itself engaged in a contest, for example an R&D race, with other organizations. The Singapore government, for example, conscious of the high payoffs associated with winning the regional race in internet-related activities, has been explicitly preaching the virtues of risk taking to its citizens.

In summary, as with quotas, contests could be used strategically by organizations to align risk behavior with their long-term goals. There might be a need at times to dampen severe risk taking by putting bounds on the range of discretion given to employees for their activities (such as curbing foolish risk taking by money managers). At other times, substantial rewards might be necessary to induce people to break the inertia in a stagnant organization.

Summary

As winner-takes-all values increasingly pervade our lives, analysts ponder on how to harness these for both individual and corporate good, writes **Anil Gaba**. Companies need to weigh incentives and motivation against associated risks. They may use contests and quotas to align employees' risk behavior with overall corporate goals. This sometimes means limiting severe risk taking and at other times offering substantial rewards for risk taking to overcome inertia.

Suggested further reading

Frank, R.H. and Cook, P.J. (1995) *The Winner-Take-All Society*, New York: The Free Press.

Gaba, A. and Kalra, A. (1999) "Risk behavior in response to quotas and contests," *Marketing Science*, 18, 417–34.

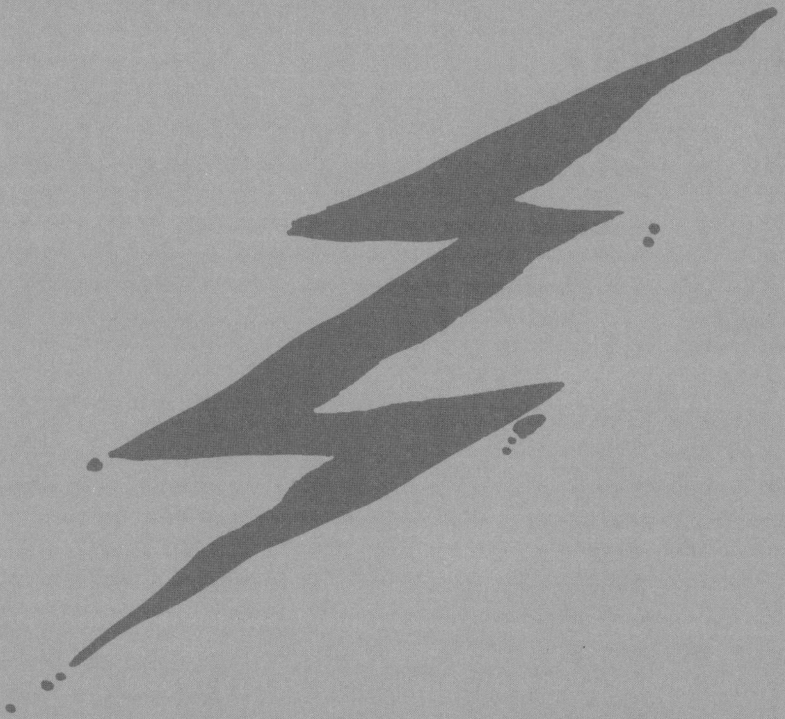

RISK STRATEGY

3

Contributors

Lisa Meulbroek is an associate professor of finance at Harvard Business School. Her research interests include corporate risk management, executive compensation, market efficiency, and corporate finance.

Benjamin Gomes-Casseres is a professor at Brandeis University's Graduate School of International Economics and Finance. He is author of *The Alliance Revolution* and a consultant to leading high-technology companies.

Jeffrey J. Reuer is an assistant professor of strategy and management at INSEAD in Fontainebleau, France. His current research focusses on international joint ventures, alliance dynamics, and corporate flexibility.

Michael J. Leiblein is an assistant professor of strategy and management in the Fisher College of Business at the Ohio State University. His current research focusses on the diffusion of new technologies and the effective co-ordination of resources between alliance or joint venture partners.

Tony Cram is a client director at Ashridge in the UK and a visiting professor at Universitätsseminar der Wirtschaft, Germany. He also teaches regularly at the University of Michigan. He specializes in the leisure industry and financial services, with a particular interest in the retail sector.

Rory F. Knight is dean emeritus and fellow in finance at Templeton College, University of Oxford. Dr Knight is a director of a number of internet companies.

Deborah J. Pretty is a research fellow at Templeton College, University of Oxford. Dr Pretty specializes in corporate risk management strategy, risk finance, governance, and value.

Contents

Total strategies for company-wide risk control 67

Lisa Meulbroek, Harvard Business School

Integrated risk management is the current topic of choice. Forward-thinking companies are rationalizing their risks for financial and strategic ends.

Alliances and risk: securing a place in the victory parade 74

Benjamin Gomes-Casseres, Graduate School of International Economics and Finance, Brandeis University

Alliances are a fruitful source of risk mitigation. Companies that team up can spread risks and capture new opportunities.

Real options: let the buyer beware 79

Jeffrey J. Reuer, INSEAD

Michael J. Leiblein, Fisher College of Business, Ohio State University

Real options are growing in popularity. They have their uses, yet managers should approach with caution.

Recession strategies: right moves for weathering the storms 86

Tony Cram, Ashridge

When the recession hits, many wish they were better prepared. This article offers some defensive guidelines.

The real benefits of corporate diversification 92

Rory F. Knight, Templeton College, University of Oxford

Deborah J. Pretty, Templeton College, University of Oxford

Corporate diversification was a concept of the 1980s. These authors argue that operational diversification adds little value – unlike geographical diversification.

Introduction

Risk and strategy are inextricably linked. Any strategic choice has its potential reward and, if it fails, potential costs. Large corporations face a variety of risk-related decisions, impinging on many different departments. In recent times many have tried to integrate these decisions in order to make the most efficient overall use of resources. The first article in this section describes the common techniques of integrated risk management and shows how risk management can be used to create real value in the organization. Elsewhere, authors consider the risks of alliance-making and corporate diversification, and propose strategies for coping with economic recession.

Total strategies for company-wide risk control

by Lisa Meulbroek

Managers have always attempted to measure and control the risks within their companies. However, the enormous growth and development in both financial and electronic technologies have created a richer palette of risk management techniques. "Enterprise," or "integrated," risk management is a prime instance, offering an important new opportunity for increasing shareholder value. Integrated risk management is the identification and assessment of the collective risks that affect a company's value, and the implementation of a company-wide strategy to manage them.

The insight offered by integrated risk management is that a company's risk profile is malleable; managers can choose to retain some risks while shedding others. Indeed, there is no safe harbor: failure to devise an active risk management strategy is a *de facto* decision to retain whatever risks arise in the course of business, without considering what the optimal mix might be.

Risk management has the potential to increase value in several ways: it makes financial distress less likely; it can lower the risk faced by managers who have most of their wealth invested in their company's stock; and it can reduce a company's tax burden. A progressive tax structure gives companies an incentive to smooth earnings in order to minimize taxes, and risk management enables such smoothing. It also increases a company's debt capacity, thereby capturing the incremental tax shield associated with that debt. Finally, by maintaining a particular risk level, risk management helps investors evaluate the company's performance.

Although long a theoretical prospect, integrated risk management has only recently become a practical possibility with the development of liquid markets for a broad set of financial instruments. Equal in importance to this evolution in capital markets is the cumulative experience and success in applying modern finance theory to the practice of risk management. In the past, risk management was rarely undertaken in a systematic and integrated fashion across the company. Today, managers can analyze and control various risks as part of a unified, or integrated, risk management policy.

Methods of integration

Companies have three ways of implementing risk management objectives: modifying the company's operations, adjusting its capital structure, and employing targetted financial instruments. These mechanisms interact to form the company's risk management strategy. Managers must weigh the advantages and disadvantages of any particular strategy to identify the best mix. An international airline, for instance, might choose to manage its exposure to volatile fuel prices operationally. When prices are high, it might instruct its pilots to fly more slowly (which in certain cases saves fuel), or it could decide to invest in more fuel-efficient aircraft. Of course, both of these operational measures come at a cost. If its planes fly too slowly, customers may defect for a speedier airline. Likewise, replacing its fleet of planes with more fuel-efficient models may prove more costly than the damage incurred by volatile fuel prices.

Clearly, the appropriate operational risk management techniques will differ by company. One operational method that Microsoft applies to manage risk is to use a greater proportion of temporary employees in the organization than one might normally expect. By reducing operating leverage (here, the fixed costs of a more permanent workforce), Microsoft has more flexibility to respond to unexpected shocks in demand, technology, or regulation, thereby improving its chances of survival, and mitigating the potential for even more severe collateral effects. In this manner, Microsoft's policy also reduces the risk borne by its permanent workforce, providing them with more job security than they would otherwise have in a volatile industry.

Consider the Walt Disney Company's operational risk management of weather risk. Bad weather dramatically reduces the number of theme-park visitors, exposing the giant entertainment enterprise to considerable weather-related risk. This risk extends to customers as well. A vacation destination with unpredictable weather conditions compels potential visitors to bear some weather risk. Disney's 1965 decision to build DisneyWorld in a warm and sunny location (Orlando, Florida) therefore reduced its own exposure and that of its customers to inclement weather. Yet the decision altered its risk exposure along other dimensions. At the time of Disney's purchase of 27,500 acres, Orlando was not particularly near any population centers and air travel was relatively expensive. One cost, therefore, of Disney's location decision was that most of its customers had to travel long distances to visit, increasing the company's exposure to fuel prices, the cost of air travel, and fluctuations in the economy.

For Disney, an alternative operational model is to have multiple theme parks close enough to major population centers that customers can observe the day's weather forecast and then decide whether to visit the theme park. In this model, inclement weather reduces visitor numbers (a risk to the company), but also lessens the customer's weather risk exposure. Because this type of theme park is likely to draw mostly single-day visitors, rather than multiple-day visitors who treat the park as a vacation destination, bad weather on any particular day will not lead to a ruined vacation. In its Disneyland Paris venture, such a strategy works well: visitors from Paris and surrounding population centers can reach the park in an hour or two, allowing them to bear the risk of poor weather themselves and giving them the flexibility to postpone the visit, reducing the company's risk of lost visitors.

Some risks cannot be managed operationally, either because no good operational approach exists, or because an operational solution is simply too expensive to implement or conflicts with the company's strategic goals. Targetted financial instruments such as derivatives (futures, forwards, or options) or insurance contracts can be an alternative to operational methods of reducing risk. Such instruments are available for many commodities, currencies, stock indices, and interest rates, and are even expanding to handle such risks as weather. Risk management techniques either reduce the probability of a risk occurring, or decrease the risk's impact on the company, should it occur.

Targetted financial instruments affect the company's risk profile in this latter sense: if a risk does occur, they attenuate or eliminate its effect on company value. By using targetted financial instruments, such as futures or forward contracts on jet fuel, an airline can set the price it pays for jet fuel for the duration of the contract, thereby reducing its exposure to volatility in fuel prices. Similarly, it could use currency forwards to hedge its foreign exchange risk. For Disney, purchasing insurance against bad weather could substitute for locating in a warm and sunny climate (though such insurance was not available in 1965). Its primary task is thus to evaluate whether locating close to a chilly but populous area, combined with weather insurance, is more valuable to it than physically locating in a temperate climate.

The benefit of risk management via targetted financial instruments is that companies are able to focus on a specific risk and hedge it at a low cost. Ironically, this ability to target risk precisely is the source of its main shortcoming: risk management using targetted financial instruments is possible only if financial instruments exist for the risk that one wants to target. Microsoft may find that few of its major risks are correlated with existing financial instruments, and therefore must depend on other risk management approaches.

Moreover, financial instruments only guard against risks that managers can foresee, both in type and magnitude. A forward position in fuel contracts does not help the airline much if the pilots' union decides to strike. The panoply of available financial instruments, however, continues to expand. The power and industrial group Enron, for instance, makes markets in gas and electricity, selling options and forwards. It has also launched trading operations in paper and pulp, coal, plastics, weather, even internet bandwidth.

When managers cannot precisely forecast the source or magnitude of a specific risk, they can use the company's capital structure as an all-purpose buffer. By decreasing the amount of debt in the capital structure, and increasing its equity component, managers reduce the shareholder's total risk exposure. A lower debt level means that the company has fewer fixed expenses, which translates into greater flexibility to respond to volatility that affects company value, whatever the source.

Microsoft makes extensive use of equity as an all-purpose risk cushion, complementing its operational policies. It has no outstanding debt; indeed, it currently holds approximately $18bn in cash. This no-leverage (or negative leverage) policy gives Microsoft a flexibility that is particularly valuable when the costs associated with financial distress are high. The low debt policy may also reflect an attempt to reduce the risk borne by some of its senior executives, who together own a substantial fraction of the outstanding shares. Microsoft's operational policy of using temporary employees and its financial policy of low leverage, although quite different in their application, are functionally equivalent. To that extent, they may be considered substitutes for one another. Even if similar in function, each policy, of course, has its particular costs as well as benefits. Temporary workers, for example, may not be as motivated as permanent employees. Furthermore, without debt, Microsoft loses out on valuable tax benefits.

The primary advantage of managing risk by using a larger proportion of equity in the capital structure is that equity is an all-purpose risk cushion or protector. There may be some risks that a company can precisely measure; these are most effectively shed through targetted risk management. Equity provides all-purpose protection against those risks that cannot be identified in advance, or for which no specific targetted financial instrument exists. The larger the amount of risk that cannot be accurately measured or shed, the larger the company's equity cushion needs to be. The cost of using equity as a risk management tool is that, by reducing debt, a company reduces the interest tax shield that debt provides. In contrast, managers modifying a company's risk profile operationally or via targetted financial instruments do not sacrifice the debt tax shield. Indeed, to the extent that managers reduce risks operationally or with targetted financial instruments, they increase the company's capacity to issue debt.

Thus the three risk management tools can serve as either substitutes or complements for one another. Because these tools can have similar effects on company risk, their use connects seemingly unrelated managerial decisions. For instance, because capital structure is one component of a company's risk management strategy, effective capital structure decisions cannot be made in isolation from its other risk management decisions. Managers' decision about the optimal debt-to-equity ratio for the company is inextricably linked to their decision about whether to build a plant in a foreign country, which is in turn linked to the decision about whether to broaden the company's product line.

Aggregate risk coverage

"Integration" refers both to the combined application of the three tools for implementing a risk management strategy, and to the aggregation of all the risks faced by the company (*see* Figure 1). Risk management entails managing the company's total risk, because it is the company's total exposure that determines whether the company can avoid financial distress. By aggregating risks, some individual risks within the company will partially or completely offset each other. Thus, in implementing hedging and insuring transactions to manage the risk of the company, one need only address the net exposures instead of covering each risk separately. This netting can significantly reduce the costs and improve the efficiency of risk management.

Integration of risk management can add value to a company by permitting the

Figure 1: Integration of ways to manage risk

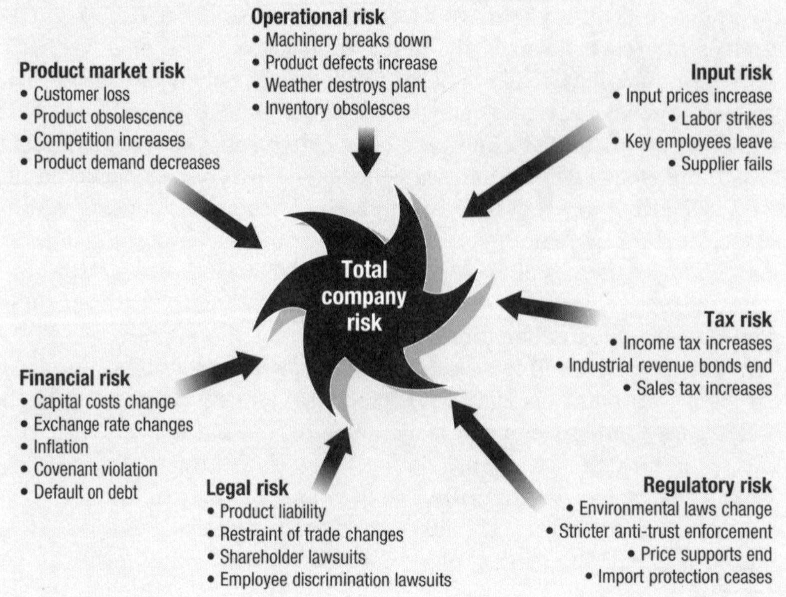

purchase of more efficient insurance contracts that provide a lower-cost way of managing its overall or "enterprise" risk. In 1997, the technology products group Honeywell purchased just such an insurance contract. This contract, the first of its kind, combined protection against traditionally insurable risks, such as property and casualty, and foreign exchange risk, a financial market risk more typically managed through derivative securities. The important innovation of the contract was that it covered Honeywell's aggregate losses, meaning that the policy had an aggregate deductible, rather than a separate deductible for each risk. By aggregating individual risks and then insuring the total, Honeywell was able to purchase a contract that cost 15 percent less than its previous contract, since the new policy cost less for underwriters American International Group (AIG), to produce.

Under the old system, with its collection of separate deductibles, Honeywell had bought more insurance coverage than it really wanted. To illustrate this principle, suppose that Honeywell faced three risks: losses from product liability, losses from fire, and losses from foreign exchange-rate exposures. Suppose further that the company is willing to "self-insure" against these risks up to a maximum total loss of $30m. The old system would have required a deductible of $10m on each of the three separate policies to achieve this goal, whereas the new system requires one aggregate deductible of $30m. Suppose further that the company experiences a product liability judgment of $25m and no losses from either fire or foreign exchange. Then, the separate-policy approach results in a $15m payment to Honeywell (the $25m loss net of the $10m deductible), even though the company was prepared to absorb the entire $25m loss, as this was within its pre-specified maximum loss of $30m.

In contrast, the aggregate policy with the combined $30m deductible does not pay Honeywell anything for the $25m loss, which did not exceed the deductible. Of course, after the fact, the company would be happy to have the greater coverage. However, beforehand, when it makes its risk management decisions, the company pays higher insurance premiums for that extra, unwanted coverage. If instead the company purchases a comprehensive policy covering all three types of risk, it pays less to receive the aggregate $30m deductible, receiving the coverage it actually wants.

The general principle exemplified by the Honeywell policy is that aggregate risk protection will almost always cost less than individual risk coverage, even when individual premiums are actuarially fair. Moreover, the aggregate coverage is better tailored to the company's risk management needs. Exposure of the company's value, after all, does not depend on the source of the risk *per se*; instead, it depends on the total risk. A company therefore wants insurance that provides compensation when the effect of the aggregated risks exceeds a pre-specified amount.

The inextricable relations of risk

In charting an effective risk management strategy, a manager must consider cross-business effects. By focussing narrowly on one specific risk, the manager may create or exacerbate other types of risk for the company. Such interactions between risks are not always obvious, especially when they occur among unrelated businesses within the company.

A subtle instance comes from the late 1980s. In 1988, investment bank Salomon Brothers attempted to move into the merchant-banking business on a large scale by leading an investment group in an unsuccessful effort to acquire control of the big tobacco and food group RJR Nabisco in a leveraged buyout. Although it did not succeed, the attempt signaled to bond-rating agencies and other stakeholders that Salomon was prepared to increase the total risk it faced. This change in its risk profile hurt its existing customer-based derivatives business, which had been a significant source of profits.

Salomon's prospective merchant-banking business would seem to have little connection to its existing customer-based derivatives business: the employees were different, the technology was different, the customers were different, even the buildings housing the businesses were different. Because Salomon owned both businesses, however, its shift into a riskier business affected the overall risk and creditworthiness of the company. The derivatives business was particularly sensitive to Salomon's credit risk; Salomon's strong and stable credit rating was essential to its customers. By its attempt to move into the merchant-banking business, Salomon showed its willingness to increase the company's overall risk exposure. That perception greatly impaired its ability to compete in the credit-sensitive customer-based derivatives business. Furthermore, the connection of Salomon's prospective merchant-banking business to the customer-based derivatives business did not materially benefit its merchant-banking business, because merchant banking is *not* a credit-sensitive business.

The Salomon example shows that when different businesses share the same corporate umbrella, the risk of each business is shared among all businesses. For Salomon, the combination of the businesses destroyed value, until financial engineering created an AAA-rated derivatives subsidiary that effectively decoupled the shared capital structure.

The Salomon example also underscores the fact that risk considerations permeate all of a company's major decisions. When a company changes its business strategy, it likely changes its risk profile, thereby either creating or destroying value. Risk management almost always requires tradeoffs to be made. These tradeoffs sometimes involve comparing the costs of reducing a particular risk with the benefits of that reduction; at other times, managers must trade off risks among businesses. Risk management decisions must be made on a company-wide level, because the consequences of managing any particular risk affect the value of the entire company.

Managers have always practiced some form of risk management, whether implicit or explicit. In a typical corporate structure, however, risks are dealt with separately. The treasury or finance department manages exchange-rate exposures and, perhaps, credit risk. Commodity traders, sometimes located within the purchasing area, focus on commodity price risk. Production and operations managers consider risks associated with the production process. The corporate insurance risk manager concentrates on property and casualty risks. Human resources may address employee risks. As a practical matter, then, managers of traditionally separate institutional units must co-ordinate their risk management activities if they are to implement an integrated risk management strategy.

The first step

With co-ordination as the first step, integrated risk management then calls for a "strategic," rather than a "tactical," approach. Tactical risk management, which is presently more common, has rather limited objectives. It usually involves the hedging of contracts or of other explicit future commitments of the company, such as interest-rate exposures on its debt issues. Consider a US dollar-based company that agrees to buy a machine from a German company for delivery in six months. Tactical hedging means that the company hedges any fluctuations in the US dollar/D-Mark exchange rates that affect the value of the contract before delivery occurs. Strategic currency hedging, in contrast, addresses the broader question of how exchange-rate fluctuations affect the value of the entire company. It takes into account how those fluctuations affect the company's competitive environment, including the pricing of its products, the quantity sold, the costs of its inputs, and the response of other companies in the same industry. As a consequence, a company can be completely hedged tactically, while still having substantial strategic exposure.

Since an integrated approach to risk management requires a thorough understanding of the company's operations, as well as its financial policies, risk management is clearly the responsibility of senior managers. It cannot be delegated to derivatives experts, nor can management of each individual risk be delegated to separate business units. Although management will no doubt seek counsel from managers of business units or projects, it must ultimately decide which risks are essential to the profitability of the company, taking into account cross-risk and cross-business effects, and develop a strategy for managing those risks.

The rapidly expanding universe of tools available for risk measurement and management offers managers significant opportunities for value creation, but this growth also creates new responsibilities. Managers must understand how to use these tools, and actively decide on their selective application. In the near future, risk management will play a significant role in corporate strategy.

Summary

Traditionally, companies have managed different kinds of risk individually: the corporate treasurer or finance director handles credit risk and foreign exchange risk, the human resources manager handles employment risk, and so on. Now, writes **Lisa Meulbroek**, integrated risk management offers managers the chance to draw together and rationalize the entire range of risks a company faces. Broadly, there are three ways of doing this: altering the company's operations, adjusting its capital structure, and employing financial instruments to reduce risk. Selective and co-ordinated use of these techniques permits senior managers not only to manage risks on a focussed and tactical basis, but to conceive and implement a longer-term, company-wide risk strategy.

Suggested further reading

Bodie, Z., Crane, D., Froot, K., Mason, S., Merton, R. *et al.* (1995) *The Global Financial System: A Functional Perspective*, Boston, MA: Harvard Business School Press (several chapters devoted solely to risk management).

Meulbroek, L. (2000) "Integrated risk management for the firm: a senior manager's guide," Harvard Business School Working Paper, Boston, MA: Harvard Business School.

Alliances and risk: securing a place in the victory parade

by Benjamin Gomes-Casseres

Thirty years ago, if you asked the chief financial officers (CFOs) of large companies why they used joint ventures, they would likely say: "To share risk." In fact, the modern joint venture format was all but invented by oil companies to do just that. Exploring for oil was a risky endeavor and a series of dry holes could be costly – better to share these costs with a partner, even if this also meant sharing the rewards of a successful strike.

Today, the CFO of a new-economy enterprise is likely to offer a more complex answer to the same question. Risk sharing will feature among the motivations for alliances, but it may not be as important as gaining access to complementary resources, influencing industry standards, or beating rivals in the rush to market. What they may not realize is that in these strategies, too, alliances are a way of managing risk.

Today's alliances not only help companies share the costs of risky projects, they also help them hedge risks, mitigate the costs of responding to unpredictable trends, and, most importantly, buy and shape options to exploit future opportunities.

However, both our old- and new-economy CFOs face an unpleasant paradox. To manage the business risks they face, they are choosing an organizational strategy that is itself notoriously risky – many joint ventures and other alliances end in nasty divorce or mutual disappointment. In a sense, alliance strategies enable companies to buy protection from business risk only by taking on additional "relationship" risks. The tragedy for many companies is that they have no comprehensive framework with which to evaluate this tradeoff. The risks of managing alliances are fairly well known, but the roles of alliances in managing business risk are not. Here we will focus on the latter and briefly summarize the former.

Uncertainty and alliances

The strategic risks that companies face stem from uncertainty in their technological, market, and competitive environments. This means that they cannot be confident of the payoff of a given strategic move, such as investment in a new plant or development of a new product. What can they do? One approach is to minimize the damage of a negative outcome. Another is to avoid committing to a definite strategy until the future is clearer. Yet a third policy is to try to influence the uncertainty itself. Sometimes a combination of policies can be used.

Alliances can help in all these approaches to strategic risk. To see why, we must begin by defining "alliance." An alliance is a unique organizational structure to enable co-operation between companies. It comes in many forms, from simple joint ventures to complex consortia and ever-changing co-development agreements. Regardless of the form, the alliance governs an ongoing, open-ended relationship between companies that themselves remain separately owned. One-off, arm's-length deals with clear terms and conditions are not alliances; neither are complete mergers or acquisitions. The beauty – as well as the challenge – of an alliance lies precisely in its flexibility and the partial commitments of its members.

As a rule, alliances enable companies to make incremental commitments to an unfolding strategy, a useful feature when environmental uncertainties preclude decisions that are more definite. In addition, the partial commitments involved in alliances leave the company with resources to invest in more than one such arrangement, thus spreading and diversifying the risk. At the same time, however, the open-ended nature of an alliance means that if not managed carefully, it can unravel and nullify all the potential benefits. If the partial commitments of members are not enough to compel them to act co-operatively, the alliance can be a recipe for strategic gridlock. The two sides of this coin are reviewed separately.

Managing strategic risks

Alliances help manage strategic risks by allowing companies to lower exposure to downside risks; hedge bets among multiple outcomes; reduce transition costs in a changing business; buy options on upside risks; and manage business risks directly.

Lower exposure to risk

Involving many partners in a risky venture reduces the exposure that each has to the possibility of failure. This technique is as old as capitalism; the English East India Company used it in the seventeenth century to finance risky voyages. In the twentieth century, oil exploration companies often teamed up. In today's high-tech economy, the explorers are not sailing to distant continents or drilling the earth – they are colonizing the sky or probing the depths of DNA and atomic structures.

A prime example is Iridium, the consortium of electronics, aerospace, and telecommunications companies that launched 66 satellites into space and initiated the first round-the-world telephone service in late 1998. The enterprise cost more than $5bn and Iridium filed for voluntary bankruptcy within a year.

Why? Many answers have been offered. Prime among them is that the project was overtaken by technological and market trends that were not foreseen when the initiative was launched. Being at the leading edge of technology and aiming to serve a market that did not yet exist brought huge risks for Iridium. Motorola, the US mobile telecommunications manufacturer, and its partners did well to lower their exposure to the possibility of failure. They are not alone. All the remaining satellite-communication projects under way are led by consortia of players seeking to share risk. Even Microsoft's Bill Gates has teamed up with the mobile phone pioneer Craig McCaw and Motorola to share in the next-generation Teledesic project.

This case shows why alliances can be valuable in lowering a company's risk exposure. Aside from the presence of uncertainty, the project itself is large and "lumpy" – a company cannot decide just to launch one satellite in an effort to lower its exposure. Similar conditions exist in bio-engineering research and in the push to create ever smaller structures on semiconductor chips, an area where alliances abound.

Hedge your bets

Another useful feature of alliances in bio-engineering and semiconductors is that they allow companies to hedge their bets among two or more competing technologies. This is also a chief reason that alliances in the dotcom world have proliferated so rapidly. In this strategy, not only is the company's exposure to failure in any one project reduced, but, more importantly, its chances of succeeding somewhere are increased.

Bill Gates uses this strategy too. Microsoft has been investing in a slew of companies offering competing solutions to address the coming convergence between the TV and the PC. No one knows exactly how this will occur. So, Microsoft has invested in AT&T to spur the rollout of high-speed internet access over telephone lines, in Nextel Communications to develop wireless internet access, and in Comcast to promote access over cable systems. It is likely that one or more of these options will pan out and that others will not. Either way, Microsoft is likely to have at least one winning bet. It may then use this to raise the ante on competitors.

Alliances are most useful in hedging your bets when there is uncertainty among competing future outcomes. This kind of uncertainty is common to the dotcom world in which there are likely to be one or only a few winners. Who will ultimately win the web browser war, Netscape or Microsoft? Who will win the online book battle, Amazon.com or barnesandnoble.com? In each case, it is likely to be one or the other company, or possibly both, but not anyone else. In these "winner-takes-all" markets, it pays suppliers, customers, and providers of complementary technologies to ally with several parties to secure a place in the triumphal parade.

Reduce your transition costs

In both hedging and risk-sharing strategies, the company takes a passive role after forming its alliances. As events unfold, the company is protected from excessive loss because of its portfolio of alliances. However, alliances are also used in the more active management of risk, as the next three sections reveal.

One common use of alliances is to change the capabilities and strategic position of a company. Xerox, the US printer and copier manufacturer, and Corning, a leading US glass and systems manufacturer, are among enterprises that are well known for having used joint ventures to enter new markets abroad and gain access to new technologies.

Other companies have used mergers and acquisitions for the same purpose; Daimler-Benz did so in acquiring Chrysler, becoming a German–US automotive group. When should a company, under pressure to change business capabilities or market position, use an alliance and when an acquisition? Differences in cost apart, these alternative strategies manage risk differently.

Two risks are inherent in any effort at transforming a company's business: the risk of setting off in the wrong direction; and the risk of stumbling badly, even when headed in the right direction. Using alliances rather than acquisitions can mean lower "transition costs" in both situations. An alliance lets a company test out the new direction and then retreat gracefully if it proves to be the wrong move. This is generally less costly than acquiring a company and then divesting it. An alliance also helps transfer knowledge and skills gradually while a partner maintains an interest in the business; an acquisition can well kill the spirit that promised to renew the acquiring company.

A case in point involves AT&T, the US telecoms carrier. For decades, computer and telecommunications companies had thought that someday their technologies would merge. However, in a scenario akin to the TV–PC convergence described above, no one knew when or precisely how this would happen. Even faced by this big uncertainty, AT&T charged ahead to acquire computer company NCR for $7.5bn in 1991. As it turned out, there was little synergy between the two and AT&T spun off its acquisition in 1996, after the latter racked up more than $3bn in losses. An initial alliance to test the idea might have saved money, time, and effort. Taking smaller steps can help managers gauge the terrain better and assist them in avoiding premature fatigue.

Buy options on the future

An alliance at an early stage of industry transformation can also be seen as a way of "buying" an option on future developments. The company first invests in an alliance and then has the option either to exit or to get more deeply involved after it sees how the business develops. The cost of entering a relationship is relatively small in this case, as is the cost of exit; but the value of the option to grow the relationship may be high. Let us take a brief detour into financial options.

An option, in the financial world, is the right to buy or sell a security within a given period at a pre-arranged price. It is not a definite commitment to do anything. If the option is not exercised within the period, it expires. The chief value of the option comes from the flexibility it offers to act in the future as new events unfold. Consequently, the higher the uncertainty in the environment about future events, the higher the value of this flexibility.

Corning Glass used alliances as options to explore and ultimately take leadership in optical fibers. When it started research on this technology in the 1970s, the idea of transmitting information in the form of light pulses through a glass fiber had not been tested outside the laboratory. Corning used a series of early alliances with telecommunications companies and research outfits to reduce technical uncertainties and develop a commercial solution. After it gathered new information, Corning launched a second wave of alliances, this time with early users and manufacturers. Its most important manufacturing ally was Siemens, which became a 50 percent partner in Siecor, the optical cable company that soon rose to a dominant position in the industry. By 1999, Corning's interest in optical fibers had grown such that it preferred to "exercise" its option fully to own and manage the business and it bought out Siemens's share.

Manage business risk directly

In all the strategies discussed so far, the company does not actually reduce the risk inherent in the project – it spreads this risk, hedges against it, or makes step-wise commitments tailored to changing market uncertainties. In our fifth strategy, alliances can actually reduce business risks directly by improving a project's chances of success. This strategy is often complementary to the others; a company may do what it can to make a project succeed, while also hedging its bets in case of failure.

The pharmaceutical industry has many examples of this type. Sometimes major pharmaceutical companies make multiple investments in bio-technology start-ups and in university laboratories, primarily to share risks and hedge their bets. At other times, however, they get deeply involved in shaping the agenda of a start-up or coaching it in marketing, the regulatory process, and other matters that can make or break a new drug. Often, this direct management of risk is reflected in complex sequences of decisions and milestone payments, designed to guide the start-up while also creating an option-like flexibility for the larger partner.

The deal between Abbott Laboratories, the US drug and medical products maker, and Japan's Takeda Chemical Industries is a good example. In 1977, they formed TAP Pharmaceuticals, a US-based joint venture that initially would have access to all of Takeda's R&D for use in the US market. This was a classic use of the options approach to alliances, as it was uncertain which compounds would turn out to be commercially viable in the US. Abbott did not just sit by and watch the uncertainties resolve themselves. Instead, it helped TAP develop a marketing strategy and sales force and manage the long and complex drug-approval process at the Federal Drug Administration. With Takeda's compound and Abbott's contributions to management, TAP Pharmaceuticals eventually developed Prevacid®, a block-buster drug that accounted for approximately $2bn in sales in 1999.

Here, too, alliances were useful in dealing with risks inherent in the project. Another important way in which today's alliances reduce business risk directly, particularly in hotly contested internet technologies, is by helping rivals agree on common standards. However, the risk protection offered by alliances is never free. Aside from the out-of-pocket costs of forming and managing alliances, the organizational strategy itself implies taking on additional risks.

Relationship risks in alliances

Management lore on alliances is full of anecdotes of messy relationships and of allies that turned into rivals. We need not emphasize that a poor structure or partner choice can doom an alliance from the start, nor that insufficient attention to post-deal alliance management can ruin a promising relationship (*see* Suggested further reading). Still, it may be useful to recap how companies can manage the relationship risk in their alliances:

- *Avoid "co-opetition."* The risk of conflict is high in alliances between rivals.
- *Define the scope carefully.* Even among companies that are not direct rivals, good fences make good neighbors, to borrow a phrase from the poet Robert Frost.
- *Do not ignore governance.* Careful structuring of the alliance in advance of the deal and continual adjustment thereafter are key to building a constructive relationship.
- *Build multiple bridges.* Enable relationships among partners to grow at many levels of their organizations.
- *Do not trust trust.* Personal chemistry is good and necessary, but it is no substitute for monitoring mechanisms, co-operation incentives, and organizational alignment.
- *Success begins at home.* Without a support system within your own organization, your external alliances are doomed to fail.
- *Do not stare at the downside, watch for the upside.* Failed alliances do not achieve what they set out to do, but successful alliances achieve much more than their original goals planned for.

Alliance strategy

These and other guidelines for alliance success have one thing in common: they treat the alliance as an evolving organization embedded in a dynamic strategy. An alliance, in this view, is much more than "the deal" that is typically announced with much fanfare in the business press.

A simple play on words summarizes this point: Companies should build "alliance strategies" not "strategic alliances." The difference is not semantic. Every manager has seen how excessive focus on the deal can lead to neglect *of the strategy behind the deal*. Why are we participating in an alliance? How will we manage it? How does this alliance fit our overall "constellation" of allies? How will we support it internally? These key questions go well beyond the closing of a deal. Effective use of alliances to manage risk requires such a dynamic perspective.

Summary

Large companies once embraced joint ventures to share the risk of large projects, but their motives today are more diverse. **Benjamin Gomes-Casseres** suggests that alliances can help companies hedge their bets between competing technology standards and can reduce the costs of major strategic change by bringing new skills and expertise to a participating company. An alliance might be regarded as an option on future developments – a company can either take it up or discard it according to changing conditions. And some alliances can enable business risks to be defused or managed directly. Despite these attractions, relationships between companies in an alliance are often risky in and of themselves. The author concludes with advice for ensuring that the company's allies do not become its enemies.

Suggested further reading

Das, T.K. and Teng, B.-S. (1999) "Managing risks in strategic alliances," *Academy of Management Executive*, (13) 4: 50–62.

Gomes-Casseres, B. (1996) *The Alliance Revolution: The New Shape of Business Rivalry*, Cambridge, MA: Harvard University Press.

Spekman, R.E., Isabella, L.A. and MacAvoy, T.C. (2000) *Alliance Competence: Maximizing the Value of Your Partnerships*, New York: Wiley.

Articles and links at www.alliancestrategy.com, especially "Do you really have an alliance strategy?" and "Strategy before structure."

Real options: let the buyer beware

by Jeffrey J. Reuer and Michael J. Leiblein

Executives keen to manage organizational risks are often well acquainted with financial options and other hedging instruments. Financial options, for instance, exist for foreign currencies, commodities, and corporate securities. But real options? What makes an option real, and how might companies use real options to manage risk?

What is real about real options?

In a narrow sense, the concept of real options applies the techniques developed in financial option theory to the analysis of non-financial, or real, assets. Like financial options, the fundamental characteristic of real options is that they confer the right,

Table 1: Comparing financial and real options

Financial options	Real options
• Financial options require no ongoing investment	• Real options often require substantial ongoing investments in managerial time and effort
• Financial options provide a proprietary claim on the asset at exercise	• Real options may provide only a non-proprietary or shared claim at exercise
• The exercise price for a financial option is fixed	• The exercise price for a real option may vary over time
• The underlying asset value is identical for all potential owners of a financial option	• The value of a real option is unique for each potential owner (e.g. due to learning, capabilities, synergy, etc.)
• Financial options are freely tradable or "liquid"	• Real options often require "sticky" investments that may be difficult to unwind

but not the obligation, to take some action in the future. The asymmetry between right and obligation makes real options attractive in creating value and managing risk.

The real option approach emphasizes that many investments create important, follow-on opportunities that a company may or may not subsequently exploit. Consequently, the real option approach highlights value that is contingent on earlier investments. For instance, while a given R&D investment may have a very low or even negative net present value, it may also provide platforms for future, favorable investments.

Real options bear some other similarities to financial options. For example, the value of both types of options increases with uncertainty. Further, by providing managers with discretion – rights but not obligations – financial and real options can help companies limit their downside risk while also gaining access to upside opportunities in the future.

However, unlike financial options, real options come into existence by the opportunities created by the company's strategic investments. Because their underlying assets do not trade in liquid markets, real options also present unique valuation challenges. Table 1 presents other comparisons between financial and real options.

In broader terms, the real options perspective has significant implications for the conception and implementation of strategy and risk management. Real options analysis encourages executives to confront fundamental sources of uncertainty proactively, rather than merely attempting to buffer against or avoid uncertainties. For example, real options analysis encourages managers to create value and reduce risk by making strategic investments that confer claims on potentially lucrative opportunities, actively monitoring various sources of uncertainty, and changing resource allocations appropriately in real time.

All of this sounds attractive enough on a general level, but why should companies invest in real options to manage risk if this is the role of financial instruments?

One rationale is that markets for financial options are incomplete. In other words, financial options simply might not exist to hedge certain kinds of uncertainties that matter to a company. For instance, from the perspective of sustaining competitive advantage, uncertainties relating to a technology or the moves of essential

Table 2: Illustrative real options

Option type	Description	Typical contexts
Growth	An early investment opens up future expansion opportunities	• Infrastructure investments • Investments in products with multiple generations • External corporate development
Abandonment	The presence of resale markets allows the firm to realize value from exiting markets with deteriorating conditions	• New product introductions • Capital-intensive industries
Switch	Product flexibility allows shifts in output mix; process flexibility permits shifts in inputs	• Consumer goods susceptible to volatile demand • Tapered vertical integration
Alter scale	Unexpectedly favorable or unfavorable market conditions lead the firm to expand or contract production	• Cyclical industries • Fashion goods
Defer	A lease or option to buy land allows the firm to wait to see if output prices justify investment	• Natural-resource extraction industries • Real estate development
Compound	Investments conferring multiple options of the types listed above	• Any of the above

Source: Adapted from Trigeorgis (1997)

competitors may be as important, if not more important, to a company than are price or currency uncertainties.

A second related consideration is the desired time horizon for risk protection. While financial options provide cover against uncertainties for relatively short periods, typically less than several months, many uncertainties to which a company is exposed are resolved only after more lengthy time intervals.

Clearly, there are various financial options such as calls and puts on commodities or currencies. In what specific forms do real options come? Just as there are many types of strategic investments, there is a multitude of real options as well (*see* Table 2). These different investments create different opportunities for future action, as discussed below.

A company can obtain a growth option by making a platform investment in a foreign location. While the company is not compelled to expand, should local demand turn out favorably the company can add manufacturing capacity or sell additional products through its distribution channels. The purchase price of this option can be seen as the initial sunk investment. By contrast, in many activities involving multiple stages, such as R&D or the rollout of marketing campaigns across products, early investment outlays create abandonment options.

Still other investments, such as leases, allow a company to hold open an option to defer investment. Once a company makes the investment, its option to defer expires. If managers intuitively account for the value of this option going to zero when making investment decisions, then this is one explanation of why companies often require new investments to generate returns significantly higher than their cost of capital.

Multinational networks

For the sake of concreteness, we would like to explore two specific types of real options that are important in the domain of international strategy and have often been viewed as central to flexibility enhancement and risk reduction – those created by multinational networks and international joint ventures.

Investments in geographically dispersed foreign subsidiaries confer the option to switch activities across borders in response to changes in currency markets, factor markets, or product markets. The ability to shift activities is likely to be particularly valuable when there are changes in local demand, labor expenses, other input costs, competitors' actions, or foreign exchange rates, all of which may vary across country boundaries in which the company has operations.

For example, suppose an industrial concern has production operations in Europe and Asia, and the devaluation of Asian currencies makes production in Europe and other locations costly on a relative basis. Since the company straddles countries having different currencies, it is able to shift production activities from countries with stronger currencies to countries with weaker currencies to achieve a lower cost structure (after accounting for transportation, switching and other costs).

How do rivals with operations in a single country fare? When a company's operations are concentrated in a single location, it is forced to bear the consequences of any uncertainties arising in that country. Purely domestic rivals simply have fewer degrees of freedom than their counterparts operating multinational networks.

Anecdotal evidence and research findings indicate that multinational companies do exercise such flexibility in their production decisions. In response to the 1997 Asian currency crisis, Asea Brown Boveri (ABB) and other companies shifted production from Europe and North America to their Asian facilities. Evidence also exists that companies with more significant foreign direct investment are able to mitigate their exposures to foreign exchange-rate movements.

The purchase and exercise of international options are not driven just by cost considerations, however. Demand-side factors are also pertinent. For instance, rising income levels or changing demand patterns in a developing country can cause local operations to expand over time. Competitive uncertainties also come into play. In fairly highly concentrated industries, multinational companies tend to imitate one another's international expansion initiatives to hold open competitive options in the future.

International joint ventures

International joint ventures represent a second form of international investment long held to enhance flexibility and reduce risk. While multinational networks provide a company with switching options, international joint ventures can confer growth options and reduce risk. There are several reasons for this:

- A company can reduce its inherent "liability of foreignness" – its lack of local knowledge, networks, familiarity with business customs, and so on – by taking on a local partner.

- Joint ventures enable a company to tap into the unique skills of a collaborator to shore up weaknesses in its own capability base.
- Parties reduce their income stream risk during the course of the joint venture by sharing equity.
- Finally, companies may reduce their risk of making resource commitments in uncertain industries by expanding sequentially. For instance, if a company has the right, but not the obligation, to buy out its partner, the company will go ahead and expand through acquisition if, at some point in the future, the value of the part of the joint venture it does not already own exceeds the buyout price. Since the company is not compelled to expand under unattractive circumstances, the option's terminal value has a floor of zero. Siemens has suggested that having a call option in its power engineering venture with Allis Chalmers was the most important part of its collaborative agreement.

The evidence examined

The previous section offers a brief sketch of the real options view and how companies might use international investments in geographically dispersed foreign subsidiaries and international joint ventures to reduce their downside risk while still grasping opportunities for the organization as a whole. But how does the "promise" that the theory holds out to companies actually stack up against the evidence, the "reality" that they generally experience?

We find that companies are not achieving the downside risk benefits that real option theory identifies. In a recent study, we analyzed over 300 US manufacturing companies to determine how their investments in foreign subsidiaries and international joint ventures affected their subsequent income stream risk, bankruptcy risk, and systematic risk. The results of this study revealed that the dispersion of foreign direct investment across different countries had no appreciable impact on any of these three measures of risk.

Even more surprisingly, and contrary to the predictions of real option theory, the study found that companies' investments in international joint ventures increased, rather than decreased, their subsequent income stream risk and bankruptcy risk, after accounting for other company and industry conditions. The same finding was evident for companies' investments in domestic joint ventures.

Managing risk through real options

Why are companies not realizing the benefits of multinational networks and international joint ventures as real option theory predicts? There are several potential reasons.

First, when a company invests in a real option such as a joint venture, it makes a limited initial investment in the hope of accessing future growth opportunities through expansion. However, unlike financial options, real options often require ongoing investments in the form of both physical and human capital.

To illustrate, consider an option to purchase BP Amoco stock. Once an investor purchases the option, it is put away for safekeeping. The investor monitors a clear market signal – the price of the stock – to determine if the gross value of exercising the call (that is, the current stock price) exceeds the strike price of the option.

In the case of a joint venture, several complexities arise. An investor likely needs to incur "carrying costs" arising from the ongoing management of the venture. This means that the company's downside risk is not necessarily limited to its initial

Table 3: Realizing benefits from real options: challenges and opportunities

Corporate readiness	Transaction design and execution
• Recognition of embedded options • Valuation and negotiation capabilities • Management and information systems • Global strategy • Organizational configuration	• Limiting carrying costs and co-ordination problems • Scanning multiple, complex environmental signals • Making a secure claim on upside opportunities

investment. In determining whether to expand, the value of the joint venture to the company is difficult to appraise, since the company needs to interpret multiple, complex cues from the environment relating to the venture's technology or product.

These complexities aside, it is also important to consider a second difference between financial and real options dealing with the security of the claim on the opportunities that the joint venture brings. For instance, suppose the demand for a venture's product surges, and a company seeks to buy out its partner. If a buyout price was not negotiated prior to the agreement, it is likely that the seller will appropriate some of the gains from expansion. For example, in 1985 what was then Ciba-Geigy paid $75m for a 50 percent stake in Ciba Corning Diagnostics, a medical diagnostics venture established with Corning Glass group of the US. In 1988, when the Swiss-based pharmaceutical company acquired the 50 percent of the venture it did not own, it was faced with paying a price of roughly $150m. Very few companies negotiate explicit option agreements into their international joint ventures.

We suspect that the gap between the promise of real option theory and the reality experienced by companies can also be explained by their differing readiness to use real options effectively. Many companies may not appreciate the options embedded in their investments. Others lack the capabilities to value real options and use the approach in their resource-allocation processes.

It is also likely that organizational history and complexity are obstacles standing in the way of realizing the value of real options in risk management. For instance, companies that expand internationally, based on a strategy of tailoring foreign subsidiaries to local needs on a market-by-market basis, will find it difficult to shift activities as suggested by real option theory. For other companies, information and other costs of co-ordinating a complex multinational may exceed the benefits of switching options.

Conclusion

Real option theory may provide useful prescriptions for companies to consider in increasingly complex and uncertain competitive contexts. Nevertheless, our study of real options in the international context suggests reasons for caution. For companies seeking to manage risk through investments in real options, we believe that they may increase their odds of success by attending to two basic challenges (*see* Table 3). First, companies need to be sensitive to the specifics of transaction design and execution. Examples include limiting carrying costs, defining relevant market cues to be monitored, and ensuring that the claim on the upside is secure. Second, they need to develop and support the capabilities necessary to implement real options. For instance, companies need to recognize when and how options are embedded in strategic investments, to acquire the skills to value and negotiate real options, and to develop appropriate management and information systems to limit co-ordination costs. By attending to these two fundamental challenges, companies may be in a better position to manage organizational risks through real options.

Summary

Real options – akin to financial options but for non-financial or real assets – are thought to be handy in limiting downside risk and capturing positive opportunities. Their effectiveness, however, is subject to a number of limitations. Many companies may not appreciate the options embedded in their investments. Others lack the capabilities to value real options and use them in allocating resources. International joint ventures supposedly enhance flexibility and reduce risk, while multinational networks provide the enterprise with switching options. **Jeffrey J. Reuer** and **Michael J. Leiblein** discuss the ways in which companies might usefully engage in ventures and networks to handle risk and opportunities. However, academic research suggests that the options specified do not reduce downside risk. Scattering foreign direct investment across different countries apparently has no appreciable impact on a range of important risk indicators. Surprisingly, joint ventures increase, rather than decrease, downside risk.

Suggested further reading

Kogut, B. and Kulatilaka, N. (1994) "Options thinking and platform investments: investing in opportunity," *California Management Review*, 36: 52–71.

Miller, K.D. and Reuer, J.J. (1998) "Firm strategy and economic exposure to foreign exchange rate movements," *Journal of International Business Studies*, 29: 493–514.

Rangan, S. (1998) "Do multinationals operate flexibly? Theory and evidence," *Journal of International Business Studies*, 29: 217–37.

Reuer, J.J. and Leiblein, M.J. (2000) "Downside risk implications of multinationality and international joint ventures," *Academy of Management Journal*, 43: 203–14.

Trigeorgis, L. (1997) *Real Options*, Cambridge, MA: MIT Press.

Recession strategies: right moves for weathering the storms

by Tony Cram

Recessions are dangerous beasts: they can creep up in an economy without warning, they may stalk a single sector, or damage wellbeing in a whole region. By the time the statistics confirm a second successive quarter without growth, managers will already be feeling the pain of defecting customers, inflexible suppliers, and demotivated employees. Managing the risk of recession involves more than studying manufacturing output figures to discern whether the downturn will strike next month or the month after that. There are four decisive steps that managers can take to fireproof their organizations against a harsh economic environment:

- reappraising today's market and its influence on new behaviors;
- challenging existing business assumptions in the short term;
- developing strategies for new circumstances in the medium term;
- accommodating the long term with plans for an upturn.

Today's market: new behaviors

Gauging market risks in today's climate means identifying changes and examining these changes closely for new insights. Companies can prepare for this by focussing on the micro-trends in their particular markets. They should review customer records to determine which segments, sub-segments, or individual accounts will first indicate an impending downturn in their market.

There are two points of entry to this analysis: historical and predictive. The historical method resurrects sales data for the months before the most recent recession, generally that of the early 1990s. A week-by-week assessment will indicate the trend-leading customers of the past.

For example, a UK manufacturer of crisps and other bagged snacks tracked early reductions in impulse purchases at the forecourt shops of fuel stations before the trend materialized in major retailers. Thus a sign in one channel may be an early warning of change elsewhere. By mapping the earliest indicators of the last recession, companies may identify the clients, sectors, and channels that they should scrutinize now for early warnings of trend changes.

The predictive approach monitors current customers to pinpoint those who lead emerging patterns. For example, Weyerhaeuser, the US forest products company, uses database software systems to rank its distributors on a range of factors, such as innovation. The same approach may be used to identify the most price-sensitive customers; monitoring their behavior will then show a wider trend.

In the business-to-business sector, the employment services company Manpower regularly surveys the employment market. In the US, its employment outlook survey checks the hiring intentions of 15,000 employers in 50 cities for the next quarter (at www.manpower.com). Certain countries outside the US are also covered. Such a process can indicate, by geographical area and industry category, emerging trends and sectors for concern.

In the business-to-consumer sector, similar, or more advanced, markets in other countries can often indicate important trends. For example, computer games manufacturers in Europe are endeavoring to understand the so-called "Pokémon effect" by studying the way the demand for Pokémon, the Japanese trading card game, diminished spending on computer games in the US in late summer 1999 and in the UK in spring 2000.

Consulting firms often use ratios of "enquiries to conversion" to flag sectors where unexpected changes frequently arise first, such as the IT industry. Manufacturers can be greatly assisted by going beyond immediate customers to understand the entire supply chain and stock levels at each level.

One might also study patterns in related industries in which experiences occur at an earlier stage. For example, curtain buying often follows investment in new carpets; thus a slowdown in the market for floor coverings gives caution to the vendors of curtains. The key question is: who are the bellwether clients and what changes affect them? These should then be subjected to scrutiny for insights and opportunities.

Managing the risk of customer defection involves determining their likely behavior. In a downturn, some customers will loyally maintain their purchases and make sacrifices elsewhere to do so. Other customers buy less or trade down the range; this may involve changing suppliers. Important questions are:

- Which customers are most loyal to the company?
- Which customers would economize within the product range or buy less frequently in case of recessionary pressure?
- Which customers would find a cheaper supplier?
- Which customers of upmarket competitors might buy from you instead?

Customer behavior may be affected by the degree of economic hardship. The managers of garden centers in Germany, for instance, believe that a minor economic downturn presents a big threat to their livelihood, since customers tend to economize in their gardens in order to continue to afford things perceived as more essential, such as holidays and new cars. Conversely, a more serious downturn represents good news for garden centers: unable to afford to travel or buy cars, customers redirect their expenditure to the garden where they will spend more time.

Alternatively, customer behavior may be influenced by external perceptions. Fears of conspicuous consumption may inhibit customers who are able to afford a product but are reluctant to draw attention to this in difficult economic times. In Sweden, for instance, this restraint can affect sales of Burberry coats and other luxury items, as well as lower-cost products such as women's magazines.

This analysis of customer behavior should create a compendium of opportunities and threats. Similarly, an analysis of competitors will contribute to the same list. Watching competitors is always critical, but at times of uncertainty it becomes vital. Which of your competitors are exposing themselves financially with new acquisitions, new ventures, and experimental activity? Do you recognize your competitors' vulnerabilities? How quickly could you respond? For example, customers typically become more cautious and risk averse when they feel less confident.

Recession alters the competitive context. Recession in other markets can compel companies to seek new markets: in the European package holiday market, for instance, Mediterranean resorts were badly hit by the sudden collapse of the Thai baht in September 1997, enabling long-haul destinations to match European prices and deliver a more unusual holiday experience.

Brands can move up or down market: BMW, the German carmaker, appears to present an increasing threat to mid-market motor manufacturers. Its sales of luxury 7-series and 5-series models declined by around 8 percent in 1999, while volumes of smaller 3-series cars were rising above 500,000 units. Plans are also under way for the 2002 launch of the BMW Mini.

What warning fences are you erecting to discourage new rivals? As a deliberate discouragement strategy, Procter & Gamble, the consumer products company, responds ferociously to new entrants and brand launches in its core sectors with aggressive levels of advertising, trade promotion and strong PR.

Challenging existing assumptions

The first challenge is to any current system of ranking customers. If a company faces an uncertain time, it should identify its essential accounts. There are five criteria: size, profitability, strategic importance, recession resilience, and loyalty. The first is clearly vital. If a company continues to supply Electricité de France, the state-owned French group that is the world's largest power company, for instance, this could send a clear signal of health to other utility companies in Europe. Likewise, being delisted would send dangerous messages to the market.

Another important criterion is recession resilience. Which sectors of your customer base will be most resilient to the impact of recession? Companies must use their knowledge of market conditions, expenditure preferences, and previous behaviors to forecast the likely impact of recession on their purchases. It is widely believed, for instance, that customers' affection for Hershey bars makes the US chocolate and foods group less vulnerable than its rivals to recession.

The final criterion for a key account is loyalty. Certain customers consistently demonstrate greater loyalty. They order all, or a higher proportion of, their requirements from one supplier. These customers may also provide other benefits: they may share information, have potential for cost reduction, conduct business dealings without hassle, be disposed to buy other lines or new products, or show willingness to recommend other potential buyers. For example, First Union Bank, the sixth largest bank holding company in the US, provides support facilities to all its customers, such as online tax returns and mortgage calculators, but offers greater assistance and services through phone-based representatives to the customers in a higher value or loyalty category. One UK consulting firm has recession contingencies that classify clients as loyalists, price demanders, or potential exits. For each group, strategies are defined.

Managers should ask certain questions when considering how to retain these customers. How might they help support and align their strategies with the loyal customers who are most likely to continue purchasing throughout an economic downturn and beyond? How might they drive down costs with simplified products, internet-based self-service, and minimal support for those who will respond to recession with price-based ultimatums? Finally, how might they manage the issues of fixed-cost, overhead recovery created by clients who cease buying from their companies?

A further challenge to companies facing recession relates to new customers. Normally, a company sees a new customer as a positive prospect. In a recession, this may not be so. Credit from a new supplier eager to win custom may be an easy solution for a failing company with scarce working capital. Delivering satisfying products and services in order to retain loyal customers must be a higher priority than winning new customers. According to Robert S. Kaplan and David P. Norton, founders of "The Balanced Scorecard," satisfied customers pay more quickly than dissatisfied ones. The secondary priority should be the selective acquisition of new customers, subject to a record of good payment performance and an analysis of the additional costs that may arise from setting up the commercial relationship.

New circumstances

Before any downturn materializes, there are five areas for strategy development, discussed below.

Products and services

Economic pressures tend to focus attention on value. Customers become more sensitive to waste. Are the imaginative facilities, secondary packaging, and dispensers now superfluous? In the same way that US fast-food group McDonald's convinces diners of the cleanliness of its restaurants by wiping the tables in front of their eyes, so companies must learn to make improvements in efficiency transparently obvious to their customers.

Companies should also consider simplifying the product range in certain ways: this can reduce the cost of complexity and drive down purchasing requirements, inventory, line changes, and reprocessing. Such simplification should take place before any downturn, so that benefits of cost savings, speed, and accuracy are available when pressure mounts.

Conversely, customers can be offered greater value through other kinds of additional services, even though they may not be central to the core product or service. DHL, an international courier company, allows customers to track their consignments on its website simply by entering an airway bill number. Mars, the fast-moving consumer goods company, has a website service for its Celebrations chocolate brand (at www.celebrations365.com). When customers log in the birth date of a particular friend, they receive an email reminder in time to buy a present. The major costs of such services are felt at development and launch – setting them up in pre-recessionary times might be seen as a low-cost insurance policy against customer defection.

Communications

In tougher times, it is important for companies to maintain (relative to competitors) or increase levels of advertising and customer communication. The UK market-research organization Taylor Nelson Sofres studied the 1991–92 recession in the UK, comparing expenditure on branding and market share for 127 brands in 46 product categories. It concluded that the highest-performing brands were those that also substantially raised their advertising expenditure; brands that cut marketing expenditure lost share. Buyers and consumers become more averse to risk as they lose confidence, so there is a powerful role for advertising as a means of reassurance.

For example, Oriflame, a Swedish direct-selling company that sells natural cosmetics in 52 countries, faced economic challenges in several of its markets and responded by increasing the publishing frequency of its catalog. It now produces more than 30m catalogs annually in 37 languages. Sales responded positively.

Public relations can also reassure the market and help to maintain confidence. The recommended approach is one of measured optimism, whereby genuine trading difficulties are recognized and balanced with elements of good news relative to the past, and the market's advantages are brought out in contrast to the problems of other markets. Corporate communications should feature facts, evidence, and information that customers can digest and – importantly – repeat to other potential customers. In recessionary times, potential customers are more cautious than normal. The reassurance of a personal recommendation has greater power than is normally the case. Building up word-of-mouth recommendations is an important part of recession risk management.

Distribution

When considering distribution and recession proofing, managers face two options. Robust and trusting relationships with suppliers through partnerships and long-term agreements are clearly advantageous during a downturn. Such relationships bring benefits in knowledge sharing, trend calibration, the testing of new technology, and the simplification of costly interactions. For example, by supporting wholesalers through difficult times, Unilever's subsidiaries have built up loyalty in a number of national markets.

In contrast, the internet offers opportunities for companies to streamline their distribution channels. For instance, American Airlines, Delta Air Lines, United Airlines, Continental Airlines, British Airways, and Air France have announced a joint venture that will run a business-to-business website for the airline industry. The airlines aim to save on procurement budgets, transaction costs, and inventory levels, and to cut the total number of suppliers.

Pricing

Pricing is a critical aspect of recession risk management because commercial difficulties quickly translate into price pressures. First, companies must identify and understand the nature of switching costs in their industries. What precisely are the costs borne by a customer who switches to a new supplier? Examples of financial costs are system setup, equipment costs, installations, new inventory, training in service and support, time delays through unfamiliarity, and increases in error rates. Caterpillar, a US manufacturer of earth-moving equipment, makes customers well aware of all these costs and argues that they more than justify any premium it charges over competitors.

There are also psychological costs such as fear, uncertainty, and doubt. These can be fueled by capturing and circulating real case histories of buyers who switched suppliers unwisely. These legends demonstrate company futures placed in jeopardy in return for small percentage savings. The advertising campaign by British Telecom on the theme of "welcome back" is an object lesson in building psychological barriers to customer switching. Why should current customers want to defect? After all, "thousands of customers are returning every month."

Employees

The fifth dimension concerns employees. Their abilities, level of understanding, morale, and motivation create organizational competencies. Under pressure, managers' ability to reward good performance may be constrained, and competitors may see salvation in recruiting the industry's best employees. In South Korea, this occurred when talented engineers and designers left the major industrial conglomerates such as LG Group, Samsung, and Hyundai to join smaller enterprises and internet start-ups.

A number of steps need to be taken to safeguard crucial parts of the workforce. These may be divided into tangible and intangible steps. In South Korea, one example of the former is the share option scheme offered to workers at Hyundai; and key researchers at Samsung benefit from a profit-sharing program. Intangible aspects include recognition and communication. Managers must replace a one-way communication flow of instructions to employees with a dialog dominated by messages from employees. They should regularly respond to employees' concerns by acting decisively and, most importantly, visibly, to inspire a feeling that "things are always improving around here."

At the onset of a recession, companies should calibrate the non-financial benefits of working for them – certainty, career enhancement, development experiences, comradeship, challenges, and recognition. They should find ways of reminding employees of these personal advantages. Barriers to competitor blandishments must be erected before the rival approaches. "Get your retaliation in first," as Mohammed Ali, the prizefighter, once said.

Turning downturn into upturn

Finally, if recession or downturn strikes an economy, sector, or region, companies should begin planning for its end at once. A task force must be established with the objective of drafting a strategy for the upturn. Such a strategy might include the identification of indicators of better times. It would certainly embrace tactics to recapture business lost to lower-priced competitors and would use every relationship-marketing technique to retain the customers it has gained.

Change is an opportunity – every time the economy changes pace, opportunities arise for new products and strategies. If growth continues unabated, all these recommendations will have strengthened the company's understanding of, and responsiveness towards, its customers. Managing the risk of recession builds a better business all round.

Summary

Recessions, like storms, often hit without warning, and judicious forecasting can help businesses that stand in their path. But how does a company identify the danger signs ahead of the pack? **Tony Cram** recommends it reviews micro-trends in its industry and closely scrutinizes its bellwether customers. Important customers should be ranked by size, profitability, strategic importance, and loyalty. Managers should also reassess their product ranges, increase communication with customers, guard against employee defection, and prepare defensive strategies for competitors' price cuts. Managing recession risk builds a better business all round, particularly if change is seen as an opportunity for new strategies.

The real benefits of corporate diversification

by Rory F. Knight and Deborah J. Pretty

Diversified companies choose to spread their production capacity across different sectors and countries. This allows them to minimize reliance on the fortunes of any one market. However, as more and more conglomerates choose to unbundle their businesses and focus on core operations, the value of diversification as an intangible asset is being questioned.

In 1996, following the lead of US giants AT&T and ITT, the diversified UK company, Hanson, announced that it would demerge its £11bn business. Hanson's former diversification strategy had been to minimize exposure to market cycles by operating across many industries. The company, led by Lord Hanson and Lord White, the conglomerate's two founders, had thus pursued an aggressive and acquisitive policy for 30 years.

In 1995, however, Hanson stock had underperformed the FTSE 100 by almost 50 percent and the company was under severe shareholder pressure to deliver more value. Since the demerger, Hanson stock has performed well, showing consistently better than expected earnings results.

At the time of writing, Tomkins, the UK buns-to-guns conglomerate, is being urged by investors to follow in Hanson's footsteps and demerge its unwieldy conglomerate. Since its purchase of Ranks Hovis McDougall, its food arm, Tomkins has underperformed the market by 70 percent. Even Granada's Gerry Robinson, who has for years rejected with aplomb the "conglomerate" label, is considering a demerger of his company into two separate businesses; hotels and catering, and media. What lies behind these changes in strategy?

The 1980s saw many conglomerate empires built. The 1990s saw several of these taken apart, piece by piece. Both strategies were sold in the name of value creation. This article will argue that the second strategy was implemented largely to correct the errors of the first.

What do theories say?

Discussing corporate diversification over the past 50 years, academics have claimed that it:

- lowers the variance in investors' portfolios;
- improves corporate ability to raise debt;
- reduces employment risk;
- heightens operating efficiency.

Portfolio theory

New York-based economist Harry Markowitz wrote a paper in 1952 that was to change the way people thought about diversification. He said that shareholders could reduce the variance of their investment returns by holding a diversified portfolio. Since stock returns are not perfectly correlated, the variability in returns of one stock can help to offset that of another stock. In this way, the overall variance in a portfolio of uncorrelated stocks is reduced.

Markowitz's Portfolio Theory shows that diversification by investors potentially eliminates the risk associated with the unique attributes that are specific to any given company: unique, specific, or unsystematic risk. Unsystematic risk can be removed entirely by investment in the market portfolio, which is a weighted investment in all stocks. Even small investors can obtain a diversified portfolio with low transaction costs by investing in a unit trust that is a reasonable surrogate for the market portfolio. However, the risk associated with exogenous economic factors that affect the market as a whole – market risk – cannot be removed (other than by international diversification) by a diversifying investment strategy since, by definition, all stocks in the market are affected in a similar direction.

Portfolio theory implies that, while diversification by investors is rational economic behavior, corporate diversification is redundant, since investors can diversify their own portfolios more cheaply and efficiently on the stock market. More specifically, a company does not achieve a lower cost of capital by corporate diversification or by other corporate hedging techniques.

Capital structure

A diversified company operates across several different earnings streams, which, because they are not perfectly correlated, offer some stability to the consolidated results produced at the company level. Since a diversified company generates a lower variance of returns than its specialized equivalent, the diversified company represents a lower risk to those who lend capital to the company. Lenders of capital, therefore, have an economic interest in corporate diversification. By reducing cash-flow volatility, diversification reduces the probability of loan default; credit risk is minimized.

Employment risk

Risk-averse managers would like stable salaries and security of employment, both of which are related to company performance. Whereas shareholders can diversify their investment income, managers seldom can diversify their income from employment. Managers, therefore, have an incentive to diversify the companies they control in order to reduce their employment risk. The managerial incentive to diversify is strong when mobility in the labor market is weak.

Where diversification by managers does not affect the company's expected returns, shareholder value may still be maximized. If, however, the cost of reducing employment risk is to achieve a lower expected stock return, then shareholders have an incentive to change managers' diversification policy. Given that the ability of shareholders to monitor management is less than perfect, it is likely that some opportunities for value destruction will remain.

Operating efficiency

Where a company's assets – tangible or intangible – are used to produce more than one type of good or service, or in more than one location, economies of scope may be generated. Tangible assets might include those generating goods for which demand is seasonal or variable or even is facing secular decline, or a capital asset with excess production capacity. Intangible assets could include managerial expertise, technical knowledge, existing marketing distribution systems, or the accumulation of goodwill.

Additionally, as René Stulz of Ohio State University suggested in 1990, access to greater free cash flows by diversified companies may result in making value-decreasing investments or investing in markets with little opportunity to earn reasonable returns. Potential adverse effects of cross-subsidization exist in diversified companies where failing divisions are sustained within the conglomerate.

The net effect of these diversification theories in relation to company performance remains unclear.

Diversification or spread?

This section presents some UK-based evidence in an attempt to shed some light on the theories outlined above. We analyzed corporate diversification – by business segment or geographical region – in relation to shareholder value for a portfolio of the largest 500 non-financial companies in the UK. The research shows that many of the benefits cited for business diversification either do not exist or go unrealized. In contrast, companies do appear to benefit, on average, from a perceived market value in geographical diversification.

The company's annual abnormal stock returns and its price–earnings ratio capture shareholder value. Annual abnormal returns reflect the extent to which a company has outperformed, or underperformed, market expectations over the year. These returns are risk adjusted and market-wide influences are stripped out. Figure 1 illustrates the average abnormal returns for companies, across different levels of business diversification. The abnormal returns are shown against the number of segments reported (NSEGREP) and by the number of four-digit Standard Industrial Classification (SIC) codes assigned to the company's operations (NSIC4).

Shareholder value is here shown as dramatically lower for diversified companies than for those with a single business focus. Indeed, diversified companies underperform significantly, even against the average return for the full portfolio.

These metrics, while useful because of their simplicity, do not recognize the distribution of the company's operations across industries or regions, and so suppress information relating to the importance to the company of each operation. Consequently, the authors also calculated the metrics of business diversification weighted by revenue generated from (or assets dedicated to) different business segments or regions. Analysis reveals a pattern that is almost identical to that shown in Figure 1. When the results are controlled for company size (since

Figure 1: Shareholder value by number of business segments

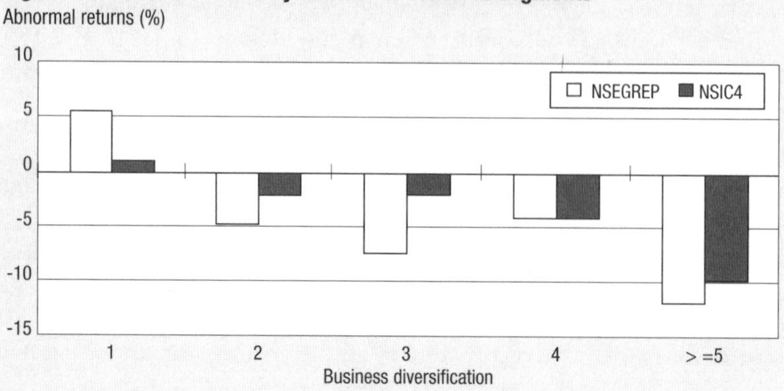

Figure 2: Shareholder value by geographic spread

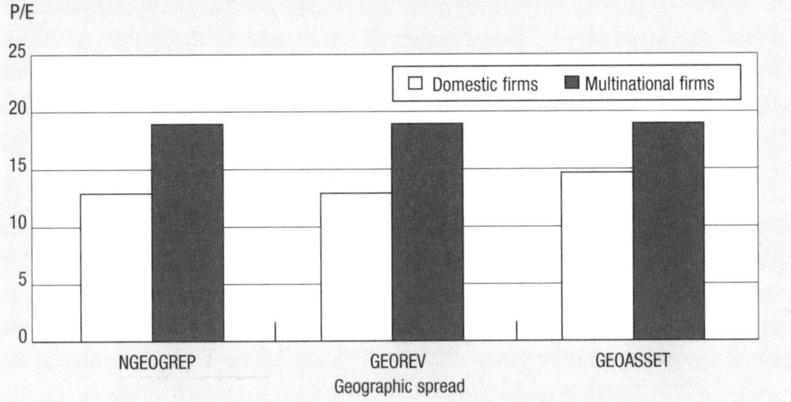

diversified companies tend to be large), the outcome is the same.

The results do not appear to carry through to measures of geographical diversification. A company appears to experience a significantly greater price–earnings ratio, for example, under a strategy of geographical diversification than does a purely domestic company. The results are shown in Figure 2, where NGEOGREP denotes the number of geographical regions reported, and GEOREV and GEOASSET provide the metrics that are weighted by revenue generated from, and by assets based in, each geographical region. For the purposes of this article, there are five possible geographical regions in which a UK company could operate: the United Kingdom, Continental Europe and Ireland, the Americas, Asia/Pacific and Australasia, and the rest of the world.

The evidence above reveals a market valuation "discount" for companies diversified by business segment and a market valuation "premium" for those stocks with a geographical spread of operations. The top performers, therefore, appear to be the specialist, global companies. The outcome of the banking battle in the UK for NatWest between the Royal Bank of Scotland and Bank of Scotland appears to support this logic. Ultimately, the major shareholders preferred the vision of greater cross-border reach to that of a stronger domestic presence.

A "conglomerate discount"

These results support Portfolio Theory and hold substantial implications for corporate restructuring efforts. Investors have easy access to stocks of different industries, so can diversify their portfolios across business segments more cheaply and easily than managers can. Managers face higher transaction costs. In this context, investment in a conglomerate is like investing in a unit trust, where shareholders are paying managers for central corporate functions, administration and co-ordination. It is unlikely that this mechanism represents an efficient use of owners' capital.

In contrast, many countries have yet to establish stock markets of sufficient critical mass and liquidity. As regards the geographical spread of operations, therefore, it makes sense that investors should rely partially on managers to diversify away company-specific risk. Managers can generate rewards for shareholders that the latter cannot achieve themselves.

Conglomerates present investors with a practical, analytical problem. Equity analysts tend to specialize in certain industries; a company diversified across many industries confuses any analysis of the company's true worth. Moreover, analysts will tend to evaluate each industry according to different criteria. For example, restaurants may be analyzed in terms of cash flow; packaged goods, by earnings. Increased focus makes it easier for analysts to understand the dynamics of a business, improves reporting and business visibility, and reduces uncertainty.

Where the conglomerate structure appears to have created value for shareholders, it is often where a particularly talented or charismatic personality has been present, and where employees and investors alike have placed confidence in that personality to bring, and hold, the disparate parts of the business into a cohesive whole. Take as an example the US conglomerate General Electric and the managerial talent and charisma that Jack Welch, its chief executive, has brought to bear on the enterprise. The evidence suggests, however, that cases where such "empire building" has delivered value to the shareholder appear to be the exception rather than the rule.

Of course, in any decision to diversify or focus, much will depend on the actual terms of the deal: the bid premium paid, the cost of the demerger, the terms of the share swap. What is clear from the evidence in this article, however, is that investors favor focus over conglomeration, and global spread over domesticity.

Summary

In the 1980s, the captains of industry built conglomerate empires in the name of diversification and value creation; in the 1990s, these empires were dismembered in the name of focus and, naturally, value creation. In this article, **Rory F. Knight** and **Deborah J. Pretty** argue that the second strategy came about in order to rectify the mistakes of the first. Corporate diversification was generally believed to add value by reducing investors' risk and the risk of managers employed in a single sector or region, as well as creating financing opportunities and economies of scope. Research shows that many of these benefits appear exaggerated: either they do not exist, or they go unrealized. Instead, geographical diversification does appear to offer market value. Shareholders seem to prefer a cross-border reach to a focussed domestic presence. Increased focus makes it easier for analysts to understand the dynamics of a business and improves reporting and business visibility.

Suggested further reading

Markowitz, H.M. (1952) "Portfolio selection," *Journal of Finance*, 7.

Stulz, R.M. (1990) "Managerial discretion and optimal financing policies," *Journal of Financial Economics*, 26.

Research sponsored by Marsh Limited. Copies of the full research report are available from enquiries@templeton-oxford.ac.uk

4

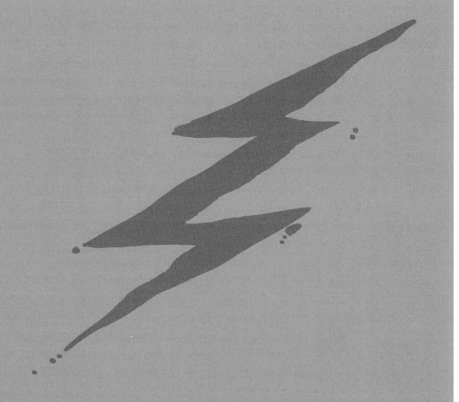

FINANCIAL RISK

Contributors

Gregory W. Brown is an assistant professor of finance at Kenan-Flagler Business School, the University of North Carolina at Chapel Hill. His research interests include corporate hedging, derivative securities, and risk management.

Philippe Jorion is a professor of finance at the Graduate School of Management at the University of California at Irvine. His books include *Big Bets Gone Bad: Derivatives and Bankruptcy in Orange County* (1995) and *Value at Risk: The New Benchmark for Managing Financial Risk* (2000). He is editor-in-chief of the *Journal of Risk*.

Paul Glasserman is a professor at the Columbia University Graduate School of Business. His research focusses on measuring the risk in financial portfolios and valuing and hedging derivative securities.

Suresh M. Sundaresan is Chase Manhattan Bank Professor of Finance and Economics at Columbia Business School, New York. His research interests include corporate debt, auctions, and derivatives.

Neil A. Doherty is a professor of insurance and risk management at the Wharton School of the University of Pennsylvania. His research interests include insurance pricing, optimal insurance, financial intermediaries, and risk management. He is the author of *Integrated Risk Management*, published by McGraw-Hill.

Contents

Seeking security in a volatile world 101
Gregory W. Brown, Kenan-Flagler Business School, University of North Carolina
This examination of how corporate financial risk management has developed to meet exposure on several new fronts argues that derivatives can be powerful tools.

The quest for precision through Value at Risk 109
Paul Glasserman, Columbia University Graduate School of Business
Most large financial institutions use Value at Risk to monitor potential losses. But banks and companies are beginning to realize that the concept makes assumptions that do not fully reflect reality.

Insurance and finance: new vehicles for driving value 114
Neil A. Doherty, Wharton School, University of Pennsylvania
Companies conventionally managed risk by hedging and insurance. Now, new insurance and financing instruments may present fresh opportunities.

Value, risk and control: a dynamic process in need of integration 119
Philippe Jorion, Graduate School of Management, University of California at Irvine
Value at Risk has revolutionized financial risk management, but may encourage some to exploit "risk holes" in the system.

Lenders and borrowers demand a creditable system 125
Suresh M. Sundaresan, Columbia Business School
Default is triggered in several different ways. Wise lenders should consider a range of models when calculating credit risk.

Introduction

Risk management was once synonymous with the management of a company's insurance interests. Yet since the 1970s, the emergence of new financial markets in derivatives has greatly expanded the number and size of opportunities available to corporate risk managers. As the first article in this section demonstrates, managers can now hedge against swings in currency rates, interest rates, and commodity prices. Subsequent articles deal with key financial models of risk management such as Value at Risk (VaR), issues in credit risk, and new finance and insurance instruments for corporate benefit.

Seeking security in a volatile world

by Gregory W. Brown

In the last 30 years, non-financial corporations of all shapes and sizes have awakened to the financial risks present in the new global economy. At the same time, the financial services industry has invented remarkable new products for managing these risks. How should companies make sense of all the new risks and risk management products available to them?

As product markets have become more global, so have the risks facing corporations. Before 1970, foreign exchange rates, interest rates, and commodity prices were only occasionally a concern for corporate managers. For example, the fixed exchange rates of the Bretton Woods era meant that a US company importing goods from Japan could know with great certainty the amount of US dollars it expected to pay for the coming year's sales.

Similarly, longer-term interest rates in most developed nations were relatively stable throughout much of the post-war period. As a consequence, financial officers had few worries over the costs of long-term borrowing. Even inflation and commodity price volatilities were low enough not to have an impact on the financial strategies of most large businesses.

In the 1970s, all of this changed: currencies floated, oil prices soared, and interest rates spiked. Financial officers had to start answering some very difficult questions regarding the effects of these new risks on business operations and, ultimately, corporate profits.

Volatility became a watchword associated with foreign exchange markets. The breakdown of the Bretton Woods system meant that exchange-rate volatility, measured by the monthly percentage changes in the yen/dollar exchange rate, went from near zero in the 1960s to double digits at times in the 1970s (*see* Figure 1).

Importers now faced uncertain costs and exporters became unsure of their revenues. Even localized businesses worried about new competition from foreign companies that had gleaned a comparative advantage from the volatile prices of currency and capital.

A similar shift occurred in the bond and commodity markets. US dollar long-term interest rates, which had been in a range of 2 to 5 percent since the Depression, rose to 10 percent by the end of 1979 and to more than 14 percent in the autumn of 1981 (*see* Figure 2). This period of economic and financial uncertainty also spilled over into commodity prices. Hard commodities were regarded as a hedge against rising inflation and volatile share prices.

The response of the financial community to the new era of uncertainty was nothing less than astounding. In the course of a decade (from the mid-1970s to the mid-1980s), an entirely new financial market emerged. The market's goal was to trade not assets, but risk itself. Although composed of many unique trading entities, this enterprise has collectively become known as the derivatives market.

Figure 1: Japanese yen per US dollar volatility*

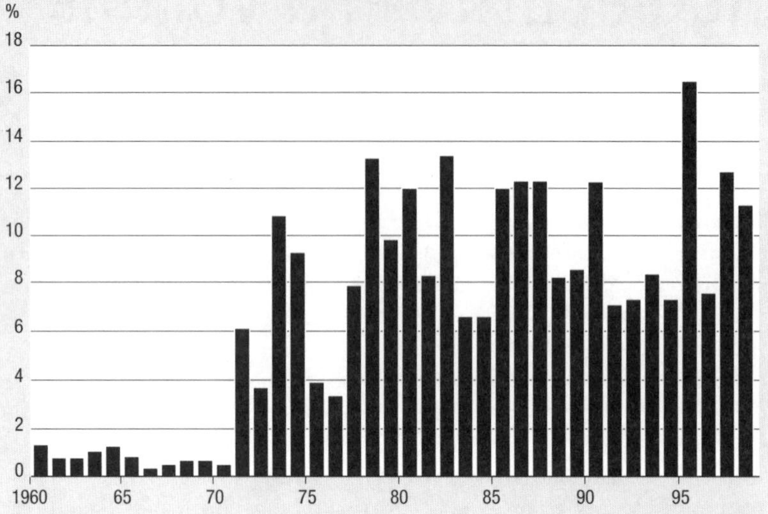

*Annual-based on monthly percent change

The rise of derivatives

Simply put, a derivative is any financial contract whose value is derived from the value of another "underlying" asset. A classic example is a commodity futures contract on wheat. In this contract one party agrees to buy a specific amount of wheat from the contract's counterparty on a specific future date for a specific price. The underlying asset is wheat and the futures contract is the derivative. Another common example is a stock warrant that gives the owner the option to purchase new shares in a seasoned equity offering. The warrant is a derivative, in this case an option, and the underlying asset is the stock.

In these contexts derivatives are nothing new. Forward and futures existed long

Figure 2: Yield on US Treasury bond with 10 years to maturity (monthly)

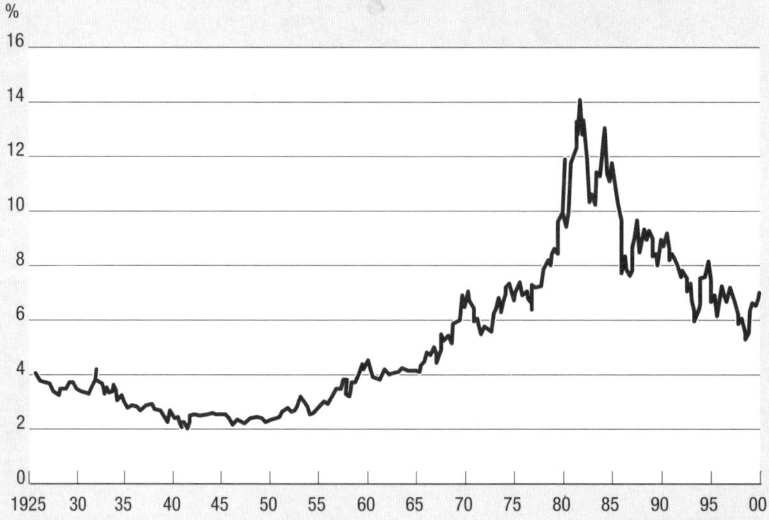

Yearly figures based on January

before the 1970s. There is evidence that ancient farmers used forward contracts (similar to futures) to sell their produce ahead of harvest. Organized futures exchanges were established in the US as far back as the 1800s. However, the derivatives market as we know it today began only in the 1970s and was the result of two unforeseen events.

The first was the already-mentioned financial uncertainty suddenly unleashed on the corporate world. The unexpected volatility in foreign exchange and capital markets meant that corporations now had a serious need for financial tools such as forward and option contracts on financial assets (instead of, or in some cases in addition to, hard commodities).

The second event was the invention of option pricing theory by three US academics: Fischer Black (then at Massachusetts Institute of Technology), Robert Merton (of Harvard Business School), and Myron Scholes (of Stanford University). The theoretical framework provided by these researchers allowed participants in the derivatives market to price financial derivatives and, more importantly, to create new products that would precisely fit the risk management needs of corporations. The contribution of this research to the success of the derivatives market was so significant that Merton and Scholes won the 1997 Nobel Prize for economics for their pioneering work.

The idea behind using derivatives to manage financial risk is quite simple in theory. Derivatives allow one party to transfer unwanted risk to another party that does not mind (or even desires) the risk. For example, consider a US-based manufacturer with sales in Germany that knows it will receive €10m in six months. The company is exposed to changes in the exchange rate between the US dollar and the euro; if the US dollar strengthens against the euro, the company will end up with fewer US dollars in six months.

To hedge this risk, the company can enter into a foreign currency forward contract that locks in the effective exchange rate it will use to transfer the euro to US dollars. In essence, it agrees to trade the $10m worth of euros for a fixed amount of US dollars and it is no longer subject to exchange-rate fluctuations. Typically, the derivatives dealer, often a bank, that sold the company the forward contract has another client (perhaps a German company with sales in the US) that is happy to take the opposite trade and both companies are left with lower exchange-rate risk.

Similar deals can be arranged with options. The US manufacturer could also purchase a put option on the dollar/euro exchange rate that guarantees a minimum exchange rate, but lets the company use a better exchange rate if the market rate in six months is more favorable. In this way, currency options are like an insurance contract that protects against a weakening euro.

Imagine now that the company wants to repatriate its foreign revenues every quarter for the next two years. In this case, the company might use a currency swap that provides a fixed exchange rate for all eight transactions. Swaps provide an efficient way of doing many (usually longer-term) hedges in a single transaction, and have become extremely popular in both currency and interest rate markets as risk management tools.

Finally, suppose the company's sales are spread throughout the year and not just realized on fixed dates. This implies that the company is exposed to the average exchange rate over the year. Now the company might use an Asian (or average-price) put option that provides protection based on the average exchange rate over the option's tenure.

The point is becoming clear: in practice, there may be complicated financial risks requiring complex derivative contracts as a hedge. For example, Microsoft uses "double average-rate basket" options to manage its foreign exchange exposure. (These options pay off as a function of the average exchange rate this quarter versus the average rate four quarters in the future, where the average rate is based on a group or "basket" of currencies.) These and other customized derivative contracts have emerged as a primary weapon in the risk management war.

Derivative contracts are even more popular in the fixed-income (interest rate) market than in the foreign exchange market. Here again, almost unimaginably complicated derivative contracts are regularly executed. One of the more common contracts combines an interest rate swap and an option (termed a "swaption") to create a hybrid derivative. Risk managers frequently use these and other tools to guarantee minimum funding rates, to lock in an interest rate until a bond can be issued, and to change fixed-rate debt into floating-rate debt (perhaps to match cash flows from floating-rate assets). Each of these undertakings has the potential to reduce the amount of interest rate risk a corporation faces.

Commodity derivatives, while somewhat less popular, have also come a long way since their humble beginnings. Perhaps the greatest change is the growth in the types of assets traded. Before the 1970s, almost all commodity derivatives were agricultural. Today, derivatives based on oil and gas, electricity, precious metals, even the weather, can easily be traded in many different markets.

However, derivatives are even more flexible than this. It is not uncommon to see derivatives based on multiple assets from different markets. For example, a swap contract might be written based on the difference between a fixed rate in one currency and a floating rate in another. It is hard to imagine a financial derivative contract that someone, somewhere, will not be willing to sell.

Weapons of destruction?

Despite their obvious power for managing risk, derivatives have acquired an aura of danger and mystery. It seems that every year new stories emerge of corporations, financial institutions, or investment companies "blowing up" because their derivative trades have gone bad. This has led some pundits to conclude that the risks involved in using derivatives are actually greater than those faced by not using derivatives. What is not usually reported about these incidents is that they inevitably involve either speculation (intentionally taking risks in hopes of profits) or shoddy oversight. Few episodes, if any, have been the result of derivatives *per se*.

In 1994, for example, the US consumer goods concern Procter & Gamble (P&G) lost nearly $200m on a complex interest rate swap. The swap itself was apparently designed to lower funding costs for P&G if interest rates behaved in a certain manner. Consequently, the swap amounted to a sophisticated bet on changes in future interest rates. For P&G, the loss was the result of both speculation and slack controls; the company should not have been betting on interest rates and, indeed, some would hold that its decision is a classic example of how not to use derivatives for risk management.

Derivatives are like most modern inventions: if used correctly, they are powerful and valuable tools. In the wrong hands, they are dangerous. The stories *not* told about derivatives represent the vast majority of cases where derivatives effectively reduce risk. In fact, almost all large, non-financial companies now use financial derivatives in some fashion and the trend is ever upwards.

Figure 3: Currency swaps*

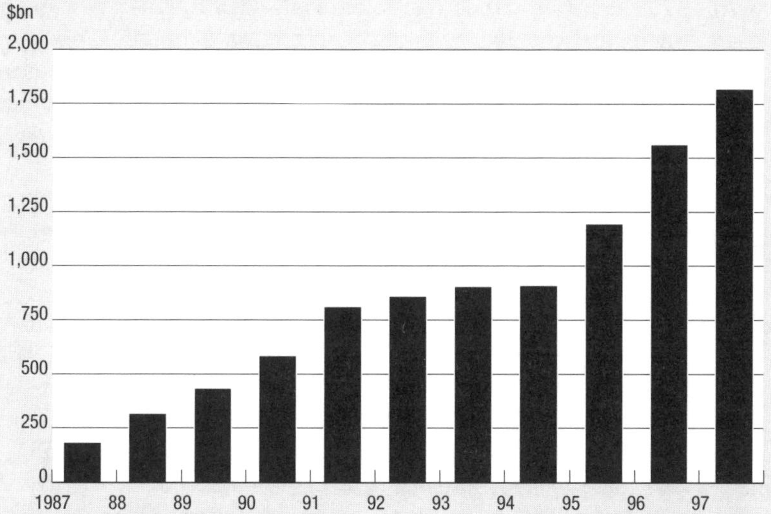

Source: International Swaps & Derivatives Association

*Notional value, outstanding contracts

Figures 3 and 4 show the massive and rapidly expanding use of interest rate and currency swaps. In 1997 (the last year for which there is comprehensive data), the notional value, or value of underlying assets, for interest rate swap contracts exceeded $20,000bn (roughly the size of all capital markets combined). For currency contracts, the notional value was almost $2,000bn. These values include contracts held by financial as well as non-financial institutions. However, studies indicate that usage by non-financial corporations is a significant portion of this total and is growing briskly.

Figure 4: Interest rate swaps*

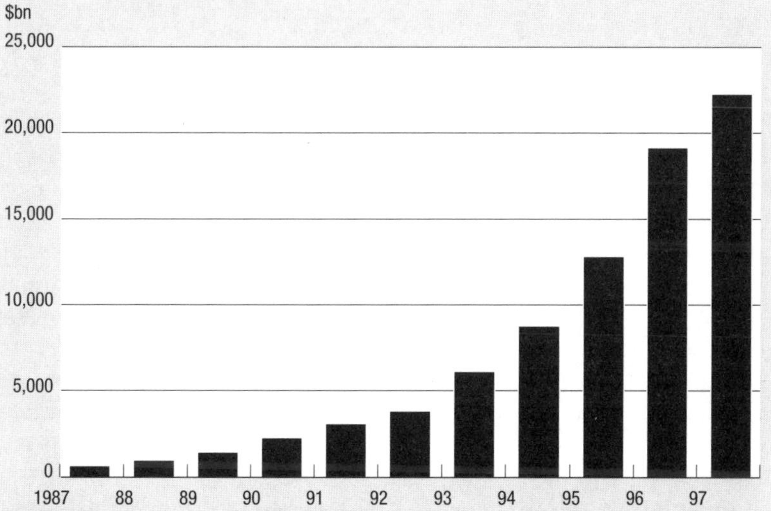

Source: International Swaps & Derivatives Association

*Notional value, outstanding contracts

A variety of research reports have also indicated that the intention (and behavior) of a typical corporate financial officer is to reduce risk with derivatives, not to speculate. Therefore, the logical conclusion is that, since most companies are using derivatives to reduce risk and only a few poorly managed businesses end up hurting themselves, risk management with derivatives is, as a whole, probably a beneficial undertaking.

But why manage risk?

All of the previous discussion has made a fundamental assumption: that financial risk is bad. It may seem obvious that financial risk is an undesirable exposure for a non-financial company. However, economists have a very specific way of thinking about financial risk and consider that it is not necessarily such an important concern for non-financial corporations.

There are two general types of risk, economic and financial. Economic risk is the uncertainty regarding the production of real goods and services in the economy. Financial risk is the uncertainty regarding the price of financial contracts that act as claims on these goods and services (such as stocks, bonds, and even currency itself). Derivative contracts and other types of financial risk management tools allow corporations to transfer financial risk between different parties, but not to eliminate it.

Take the example above of the forward contract that is ultimately a contract between a US company and a German company. No matter what happens to the dollar/euro exchange rate, one company will profit and the other will lose (by exactly the same amount). In fact, all derivatives have this property – in academic parlance, they are zero-sum games. This means that the total amount of financial risk in the economy is not directly affected by trading in derivative contracts.

How is it, then, that risk management benefits corporations? Most economists believe that financial risk and economic risk are intertwined. This means that changes in financial risk exposure for individual companies can have an impact on the real production of goods and services by business. The bottom line, however, is that managers must understand what underlying "real economic" risks they are using financial instruments to hedge against.

Returning to the example, assume that the US dollar strengthens substantially against the euro, so much so that had the US company not hedged, it would have not been able to make its interest payments and would have defaulted on its debt. A default is costly for the US company because it must renegotiate its debt. Management is distracted from running the business and important domestic expansion plans are delayed. These are all real economic costs to the US company, but by hedging currency risk it can avoid the costs of defaulting.

But what about the German company, which effectively had the other end of the deal? Had it not locked in an exchange rate with the forward contract, it would have been much better off with the stronger dollar. There will not be significant economic offsetting costs, because the German company would never have entered into the forward contract up-front (or even pursued the US sales) if it guaranteed the company a significant economic loss. So it was not the financial risk management itself but instead what the risk management avoided that provided the true economic benefit.

This is how economists view financial risk management, whether it is with derivative contracts or other types of financial contracts (such as issuing foreign debt or having foreign manufacturing facilities). Financial risk management allows companies to avoid real economic costs. An ideal financial risk management program understands exactly what potential costs the company faces, and designs the hedging strategy around these costs so as to minimize the expected chance of incurring them.

Academic researchers have expended considerable effort over the last two decades in identifying the types of economic costs that can be mitigated with financial risk management. Perhaps the greatest and most obvious of these are the financial distress costs alluded to already. Financial distress costs include the direct costs of renegotiating debt, restructuring a company, paying legal fees, and so on. While these can be significant, it is more likely that the indirect costs of financial distress are larger. These include less favorable terms from suppliers, loss of reputation and customers in the product market, loss of valued employees to competitors, and similar problems.

During the 1980s, some companies intentionally increased their chances of financial distress by adding significant debt (as a way of keeping management focussed on generating cash flow). In the 1990s, most companies improved their ability to cover interest expenses while at the same time expanding their financial risk management programs to lower the chance of financial distress. While there is no way to know for certain until the economy takes a downturn, the expanded financial risk management programs of the last 10 years may have noticeably reduced the expected costs associated with all types of financial distress.

There are other reasons for companies caring about managing exchange rate, interest rate, and commodity price risk. One has to do with the imperfect nature of capital markets. If companies need capital to undertake investments, there are two potential sources of funds. The company can either use internally generated funds (retained earnings) or raise money externally by floating new securities. Accessing external markets is costly, since there are issuance costs associated with new bonds or shares. If, instead, companies can increase their chances of funding projects by managing financial risks wisely, this will decrease the overall cost of making new investments.

Another reason involves the impact of financial risk on reported earnings. Financial risk can substantially increase the volatility of earnings, even when cash flows from operations are relatively stable. Investors have a hard time sorting out the two effects with only the limited amount of reported data. In addition, managers often hesitate to reveal potentially proprietary data that would help investors with the task. Accordingly, if financial risk management can remove some noise from earnings reports, this will allow investors more confidence in their valuation of the company. More often than not, this will lead to an increase in the estimated value.

This last explanation suggests a second fundamental source of value for financial risk management. If investors perceive a company as less risky, they will require a lower rate of return on their investment. This lower required return, or discount rate, implies a higher value for the corporation's shares. In a more general sense, if the costs of not hedging are correlated with overall economic activity (what financial economists call systematic risk), then reducing these costs lowers the overall risk in the economy. This is good news for everyone, not just the owners of companies, since it means that business cycles will be less extreme and individuals can worry less about their financial safety.

In short, the ability of corporations to transfer exchange rate, interest rate, and commodity price risk makes companies more valuable and the economy more secure, even in an environment where prices are more volatile than in the past. As the economy becomes more global, and financial risks more relevant for more companies, we should see a continuation of the trend toward active risk management. So even in a world of financial uncertainty, the rewards are palpable and the risks are manageable.

Summary

For most of the twentieth century, exchange rates were fixed and long-term interest rates were stable. With the breakdown of established financial norms in the 1970s, however, volatility sharply increased and, with it, corporate risk. In this article, **Gregory W. Brown** describes how corporate risk managers use derivatives to handle fluctuations in exchange rates, interest rates, and commodity prices. While a few well-publicised disasters have damaged public confidence in derivatives, the author argues that these products are merely tools – and that when properly used they are extremely powerful. Sound financial risk management allows companies to minimize the economic risks they face. When companies transfer exchange rate, interest rate, and commodity price risk, corporate value improves, as does overall economic wellbeing.

Suggested further reading

Bodnar, G.M., Hayt, G.S. and Marston, R.C. (1998) "Wharton survey of financial risk management by US non-financial firms," *Financial Management*, 27(4): 70–91.

Brown, G. and Chew, D. (eds) (1999) *Corporate Risk: Strategies and Management*, London: Risk Books.

Froot, K., Scharfstein, D. and Stein, J. (1993) "Risk management: coordinating corporate investment and financing policies," *Journal of Finance*, 48(5): 1629–58.

Géczy, C., Minton, B.A. and Schrand, C. (1997) "Why firms use currency derivatives," *Journal of Finance*, 52(4): 1323–54.

Graham, J.R. and Smith, C.W., Jr. (1999) "Tax incentives to hedge," *Journal of Finance*, 54(6): 2241–62.

Smithson, C.W. (1998) *Managing Financial Risk*, 3rd edn, McGraw-Hill.

Stulz, R. (1996) "Rethinking risk management," *Journal of Applied Corporate Finance*, 9(3): 8–24.

Tufano, P. (1996) "Who manages risk? An empirical examination of risk management practices in the gold mining industry," *Journal of Finance*, 51(4): 1097–137.

The quest for precision through Value at Risk

by Paul Glasserman

Discussions of financial risk can bring to mind the story of the six blind men describing an elephant. One man feels the trunk and concludes the elephant is like a snake. Another touches a leg and likens the beast to a tree. Each of the blind men manages to state something strictly correct, yet none of their descriptions fully captures all aspects of the creature.

Financial risk is at least as difficult to summarize as an elephant. The difficulty is not one of complete ignorance: like the blind men in the story, we can grope our way at least to some partially correct conclusions. Yet we are rarely able to give a complete picture of one of the most fundamental drivers of economic behavior.

At the risk of unfair oversimplification, the evolution of financial risk management over the past five years might be summarized as a quest to describe risk succinctly through a single number, Value at Risk or VaR. The quest has been championed by regulatory bodies, aided by a string of well-publicised financial disasters, fed by a growing software and consulting industry, and widely embraced by the financial companies and corporations exposed to the risk everyone is trying to measure. To what extent has the quest been successful? What lessons have been learned along the way?

We need to start by defining Value at Risk or VaR, which, briefly, is a percentile of a profit-and-loss distribution over a specified horizon. To give some life to that definition, let us consider an example. Suppose we have responsibility for measuring the risk in a portfolio of financial assets; the portfolio could consist of currencies, bonds, equities, derivatives, or a combination of these. We fix a time horizon over which to consider the risk – two weeks, for example. We might ask what the most is we could possibly lose on this portfolio over this period. The answer would be the worst-case loss. By definition, we can be 100 percent certain that losses from the portfolio will not exceed that amount. However, the worst-case loss gives too pessimistic a picture of risk, because the worst possible outcome is unlikely to occur. Instead, we might therefore ask for an amount (in dollars or pounds, say) such that we can be 95 percent certain that losses will not exceed that amount. The answer to that question is the Value at Risk. More precisely, it is the VaR for a two-week horizon and a 95 percent confidence level.

In reporting a VaR number, we understand that it is not a maximum loss. Indeed, if we regularly measure VaR at a 95 percent confidence level, then actual losses should exceed our estimate 5 percent of the time. If that is uncomfortable, we can use a 99 percent VaR and thus only underestimate 1 percent of the time. The point is that by not insisting on a 100 percent confidence level, we are providing a more realistic picture of losses a portfolio might suffer.

To appreciate the strengths and weaknesses of VaR, we should contrast it with other measures of risk. A simple but crude measure of the risk in a financial position is the outright exposure. A \$10m position in government bonds has an exposure of \$10m. So does a \$10m position in internet stocks. While it is theoretically possible to lose $10m in either case, large losses are certainly more likely in the second one. VaR tries to capture this.

Compare a $10m position in three-month government bonds with a $10m position in 30-year government bonds. The two are exposed to the same source of risk (US interest rates), but fixed-income managers have long understood that the longer maturity carries greater risk, because the value of long-term bonds is more sensitive to changes in interest rates. Sensitivity to interest-rate changes is thus an important risk measure in fixed-income markets. Sensitivities are also commonly used to measure and hedge the risks in options.

A difficulty in using sensitivities to measure risk is that they cannot be compared across markets and products. Duration measures, for example, are useful in comparing the risks in bonds issued by a single government, but they are much less useful in making international comparisons or comparing risks in bonds with other asset classes. In contrast, a VaR number is always calculated as an amount. A VaR of $55m is intended to measure the same level of risk, regardless of whether it applies to a portfolio of bonds, currencies, stocks, or options.

Students of modern portfolio theory are familiar with the statistical concept of standard deviation as a measure of risk. Standard deviation is used to measure the size of statistical fluctuations of many phenomena and the application to changes in portfolio value is natural. Like VaR, the standard deviation blends information about the probabilities of losses together with the size of losses. The most important difference between these two risk measures is that standard deviation implicitly assumes that profits and losses are mirror images of each other: a $1m loss has the same likelihood as a $1m gain, and the same for any other dollar amount. While this may be approximately true for simple instruments – say, a cash position in a major foreign currency – it is far from true when applied to options. Buying an option creates unlimited upside potential with no chance of losing more than the cost of the option. Conversely, writing options can produce unlimited downside risk with no possibility of profit beyond the premium earned on the sale of the option. By focussing only on the chance of large losses, VaR can capture this sort of asymmetry whereas standard deviation cannot.

A brief history

Two events have had a particularly strong impact on the widespread adoption of VaR in the financial sector and a third has encouraged its growth in the US corporate sector.

The first took place in Basle, Switzerland, in 1995. Meeting at the Bank for International Settlements, a committee of representatives from the central banks of 10 major western economies proposed new rules (amending a 1988 Basle accord) requiring financial institutions to hold capital against their exposure to market risk. The proposal, formally adopted in 1996, created an incentive for banks to develop sophisticated internal risk systems to calculate their VaR. Banks doing so could expect to see a reduction in the risk capital they would be required to hold to sustain trading activities, compared with banks that followed a standardized approach imposed by regulators to determine capital requirements. Thus, from the outset, regulatory relief has been an important factor in the growth of VaR.

The second important event took place on the World Wide Web. Starting in 1994, the US bank J.P. Morgan made its RiskMetrics system available to all over the internet at no cost. RiskMetrics (since then spun off in a joint venture with Reuters, the financial information group) provided financial data and a methodology to calculate a portfolio's Value at Risk. Other financial institutions and corporations were free to use the RiskMetrics VaR Calculator or download the RiskMetrics data to their own risk management systems. Third-party vendors quickly emerged providing risk management software tapping into RiskMetrics, making the methodology an instant benchmark.

The third event has probably had less total impact to date, but is one of the leading factors driving the use of VaR among US corporations. In 1997, the US Securities and Exchange Commission, concerned about undisclosed risks lurking in off-balance-sheet instruments, issued disclosure rules for the use of derivative securities by corporations. The rules allow corporations to choose one of three possible ways of disclosing risks from derivatives use: a tabulation of fair market value, a sensitivity measure, or VaR. Consequently, one can now read about VaR calculations in the annual reports of Microsoft, consumer products manufacturer Philip Morris, and many other major corporations.

Market realities

The approach to VaR popularized by J.P. Morgan is a good example of how it can be more effective to move aggressively with an imperfect solution than to wait until all the wrinkles have been smoothed out before taking action. The RiskMetrics methodology is based on a series of assumptions that simplify the calculation of VaR but do not always hold in practice. The developers of the methodology understood this; by now, most of its users probably do too. However, this simple methodology has usefully framed the discussion over how VaR should be calculated, and has helped focus efforts both in industry and academia on essential obstacles to estimating VaR accurately. Many of the important difficulties in determining VaR are best understood by contrasting market realities with these simplifying assumptions.

Markets are not normal

One of the central assumptions of the RiskMetrics approach and of many other VaR models is that market returns can be described by the statistical notion of a normal distribution. This is the familiar bell-shaped curve used to describe phenomena ranging from the heights of British prisoners to scores on school exams. A graphical record of returns on actively traded market instruments does at first glance bear resemblance to a normal curve: most returns fall in the middle near the average; very large moves up or down occur less frequently.

However, on closer inspection, market data deviates from the mathematical ideal of a normal distribution in a remarkably consistent way. Across virtually all major markets and asset classes, returns exhibit what statisticians (and increasingly risk managers) call "excess kurtosis." In simple terms, this means that too many observations occur near the center of the distribution – the curve is too peaked. But these values near the average are inevitably accompanied by an excess of very extreme values.

Imagine taking a bell-shaped lump of clay and squeezing the middle. Some of the clay gets pushed up, creating a higher peak, but some of it gets pushed down and out to the sides. This part corresponds to extreme market moves. Compared with the ideal of a normal distribution, the risk manager sees a world in which market prices move either too little or too much. This effect is particularly pronounced in measuring returns over short time horizons (for example, a day or a week). It is so pervasive that it comes close to qualifying as a law of nature in the financial world.

Portfolios are non-linear

Many VaR calculations assume that portfolio value moves in strict proportion to changes in market prices. This is often true. If you buy 100 shares of a stock at $23, then if the stock price increases by $1 your holdings increase in value by $100. If the stock price increases by $2 you make $200. The relation between the value of the portfolio and the market price of the stock can be described by a straight line. However, this type of linear relation often breaks down for portfolios that include derivatives. For example, the value of a call option on the stock might increase by $0.48 when the stock moves from $23 to $24 and then by $0.52 when the stock moves from $24 to $25. The relation between the stock price and the value of the option can no longer be described by a straight line. For portfolios consisting primarily of cash instruments, this may have little impact. However, for portfolios that include substantial positions in options, failing to capture this effect can render a VaR estimate meaningless.

The author's research, in collaboration with Philip Heidelberger of International Business Machines and Perwez Shahabuddin of Columbia University, has focussed on methods for estimating VaR that accurately capture the non-linear impact of options as well as the excess kurtosis characteristic of market data. This leads to more reliable VaR estimates, but it also puts greater data and computing demands on risk management systems.

Volatility is not constant

This may hardly seem surprising. Even a casual observer of financial news will note that markets appear more volatile at some times than at others. In risk management, volatility is used to describe a precise measure of market fluctuations (closely related to the standard deviation discussed above). While we know that volatility is not constant, accurately describing how volatility changes remains a challenge. Market data shows signs of "burstiness" or intermittency in volatility, with periods of high volatility engendering further volatility. A risk manager, therefore, cannot rely on a historical average level of volatility, but must forecast volatility based on current market conditions.

Volatility is also the key determinant of option value, so the difficulties in measuring volatility become particularly pronounced in calculating VaR for portfolios with options. The celebrated Black–Scholes formula, first published by economists Fischer Black and Myron Scholes in 1973, remains the cornerstone of option valuation. Nevertheless, it has been widely observed that market prices of options – especially on major equity indices such as the S&P 500 in the US – systematically deviate from this formula precisely because the formula assumes a constant level of volatility. Options that pay off in the event of a sharp decline in the S&P 500 are overpriced (according to a strict application of the Black–Scholes formula) relative to options that pay off in less extreme scenarios. Of course, when model and market disagree, the market is right and the model is wrong. Risk managers have become highly sensitive to this limitation of option theory; they have to be in order to see the risk in what would otherwise look like a profitable strategy of selling crash insurance on the S&P 500.

Markets move together, but nobody knows how

Many of the greatest financial risks arise from co-movements among market risk factors. In the summer of 1997, several Asian currencies experienced sharp drops in quick succession. The effect of the Russian default was felt in Latin American bond markets. An increase in the price of oil can adversely affect major stock markets. The most basic way to try to quantify the propensity of market rates to move together (or apart) is through the statistical concept of correlation. Accurate measurement of market correlations is indeed central to quantitative risk management; virtually all methods for calculating VaR rely at least implicitly on estimated correlations. However, it is now widely recognized that statistical correlation remains at best an imperfect description of the way markets move together when they make big moves. No measure of correlation could have captured the spread of the Asian currency crisis from the Thai bhat to the Korean won, for example. Sound risk management must therefore supplement VaR estimates with stress-testing scenarios outside the domain of statistical models.

It may be easier to meet the needs of regulators than the needs of the company

Risk management at many financial institutions (and to a lesser extent at non-financial corporations) entails two parallel sets of activities: providing the VaR reports required by regulators, and providing broader input on risk to the management of the company. These are never quite the same. Satisfying regulators, though perhaps onerous, is more straightforward, in part because their requirements apply to the company as a whole. Internally, a company needs to know not just how much risk capital is required for the entire company, but how this capital should be allocated among its units. This in turn raises questions concerning internal measurement of risk-adjusted performance. Does VaR provide an appropriate risk measure for determining risk-adjusted performance? Are profits earned on risky positions evidence of financial acumen or simply of risk taking? These types of questions remain an open challenge for the future of risk management.

Companies throughout the world have made enormous investments in the systems and staff needed to monitor and report VaR. Many have achieved the objective of complying with legal requirements or even obtaining regulatory relief through these investments. Has calculating VaR produced sounder risk management? Few companies would attest that this single number has by itself produced better business practices. However, the effort to measure VaR has undoubtedly brought a heightened awareness of fundamental issues in market risk management and of the data, systems, and expertise needed to monitor risk. The lessons learned along the way and the lessons still to be learned may well be more valuable than any VaR report. The blind men may never agree on a single description of the elephant, but they can surely learn much by trying.

Summary

Despite advances in finance and risk management, a satisfactory method for measuring the total financial risk faced by a business or bank at any time remains elusive, says **Paul Glasserman**. Value at Risk (VaR) is one attempt, and it has certainly helped people grapple with basic issues in market risk management. Regulatory concern over the use of derivatives has helped popularize this, as have the opportunities for risk capital savings by banks that develop sophisticated VaR measurement systems. After explaining the fundamental principles behind VaR and the landmarks in its history, the author goes on to outline some of the difficulties in its measurement. Questionable assumptions include a normal market, the linearity of portfolio values, and constancy of volatility. VaR's usefulness, he concludes, lies more in the processes and systems it encourages than in the substance of the single number it provides.

Suggested further reading

Alexander, C. (ed.) (1998) *Risk Management and Analysis*, Chichester: Wiley.

Duffie, D. and Pan, J. (1997) "An overview of Value at Risk," *Journal of Derivatives*, Spring, 7–49.

Glasserman, P., Heidelberger, P., and Shahabuddin, P. (2000) "Portfolio Value at Risk with heavy-tailed risk factors," PaineWebber Research Series, The Columbia University Graduate Business.

Jorion, P. (1997) *Value at Risk*, New York: McGraw-Hill.

Longerstaey, J. and Spencer, M. (1996) *RiskMetrics Technical Document*, www.riskmetrics.com/research/techdocs

Insurance and finance: new vehicles for driving value

by Neil A. Doherty

Risk management is about insurance and hedging. If a company is exposed to volatile cash flows and there is a set of costs associated with volatility, then an obvious way to control those costs is to reduce volatility, that is, to hedge the risk. The financial risk management literature has developed to reflect the two prongs of this proposition. On the one hand, researchers have asked why risk is costly to the company; simultaneously, they have sought to analyze and price existing hedging instruments and to derive new or derivative instruments to hedge new and exotic sources of risk.

However, hedging is not the only way a company can offset the cost of risk. If one understands the structural features of the company that cause risk to be a problem, then value can be created by adapting the structure of the company so that it is more robust to risk. For example, one reason risk is costly is that volatility increases the chance that any given company will become bankrupt. This, in turn, triggers a set of bankruptcy costs. A company is bankrupt when it is unable to meet its debt obligations. So the problem can be addressed by reducing the volatility (which reduces the probability of falling below a fixed debt obligation), or by keeping the risk and switching from debt to equity financing. Hedging and capital structure choices address the same corporate problem. As we address other reasons for risk being costly, we will see that the cost can be reduced by either reducing the risk or making the operation more resilient to a given level of risk.

A simple valuation model of the company

The starting point for identifying how risk management can create value is a simple valuation model of the company. The value of equity, V(E), is the value of the company, V(F), minus the value of debt, V(D).

$$V(E) = V(F) - V(D).$$

With limited liability, the value of debt is not its face value; rather, the face will be discounted to reflect the possibility of default. Default is often valued as a put option, known as the default put. The owners have the "option" to walk away from the debt and hand over the business to the creditors. Clearly, owners will only exercise this option when the value of the company falls below the amount owed to creditors. Thus, the value of debt is discounted from its face value, D, by the default put, P.

$$V(D) = D - P.$$

Putting together these two equations shows that this default put option increases the value of equity but reduces the value of the debt. Therefore, the default put is really a wealth transfer from creditors to shareholders made possible by limited liability.

$$V(E) = V(F) - D + P.$$

The default put can cause some mischief – this is where risk enters the picture. The key is seeing how risk affects the value of the put. If the company were performing well and had no risk, then bankruptcy would not be a threat. The default put would have no value, and debt would be valued at face. As risk is introduced and increases, the default put increases in value, which hurts creditors but benefits owners. If the company takes on risky activities, the shareholders keep any upside gain; but if things go awry, they can walk away from the downside. Owners now have an unhealthy interest in risk. The default put drives a wedge between the creditors and owners which, as we will see, leads to dysfunctional decisions.

Risk management is largely about correcting these decisions. In addition to the explanations given here, there are other reasons that risk can deplete corporate value. Risk can increase expected tax liabilities and it can reduce the effectiveness of managerial compensation systems designed to enhance performance.

Bankruptcy costs

Risk increases the probability of bankruptcy and increases the value of the default put. As we saw above, this will transfer wealth from creditors to shareholders. If this transfer could be anticipated, debt could be priced to reflect the risk and no one would be worse off. The value of the company would be the same and everyone would pay for what they get. The problem is that there is a set of deadweight costs associated with bankruptcy. Most transparent are legal costs. Subtler is the effect of removing the company from the normal discipline of the capital market and placing it under court supervision. This transfer can interfere with the process of value creation. These bankruptcy costs are borne *ex post* by the creditors, but will be anticipated in the price of debt. An appropriate risk management strategy is to reduce risk through insurance or hedging. However, the problem could have been tackled by reducing the company's leverage. A switch to more equity funding would also reduce the bankruptcy costs.

Dysfunctional investment decisions

Investment choices vary in their net present value (NPV) and in their risk profile. In the end, all stakeholders will benefit if the company selects projects that create the most overall value, that is, those with the highest NPV. However, the owners, who ultimately control decisions, can be tempted by the default put. High-risk projects will seem abnormally attractive to owners, since the increased upside potential is theirs but they walk from the increased downside. Instead of maximizing value, owners may be tempted to transfer value. Of course, creditors will anticipate this expropriatory behavior, growth and value will suffer, and the company will find debt financing more expensive.

There are typically three ways out of this predicament. First, if the company is healthy it might refrain from such high-risk decisions in order to enhance its reputation in credit markets. However, reputation is cheap when things are going wrong, as the US savings and loan crisis in the early 1990s vividly illustrates. (Here, US government bodies such as the Resolution Trust Corporation bought bad loans as a temporary step ahead of liquidating the institutions or reselling them to the market.)

The second approach is to commit to removing the risk from high-risk projects by hedging. This removes the distortions facing the owners. However, the third generic strategy comes from recognizing that the greater the leverage, the more acute the distortion. Project selection will improve and more value will be created if the company switches to a capital structure with less debt. Again, we see that risk management and leverage management are addressing the same root problem.

This incentive issue is an example of a principal–agent problem known as asset substitution. A related problem is known as underinvestment. Suppose some risky event occurs which is so severe that the company cannot pay its debt. However, the company still has opportunities to recover and even grow. In this situation, it may be advantageous for the shareholders to walk away rather than investing in positive NPV recovery projects. The problem is that the main benefit of the investment is to prop up debt that otherwise would have been in default. Therefore, the shareholders may not even be able to recover the cost of investment, let alone the NPV. This problem can be avoided in several ways. Since there is clearly a potential mutual gain from investment and recovery, the post-loss situation is ripe for a renegotiation of the debt. A pre-emptive strategy is to hedge against those events that might place the company in such a plight. However, there is a third approach. The root problem is with the level of debt. Had the company initially chosen more equity financing, it might have avoided these post-loss distortions.

Financing post-loss investments

The next hypothesis about why risk is costly relies on the differential costs of internal and external sources of funding. Various transaction costs are associated with external funding, notably the principal–agent costs considered above. Since internal funds are less costly, these are usually the preferred funding for new investments. Businesses typically manage their cash to provide orderly funding of new investments. However, a sudden loss can absorb cash and leave the company unable to finance new investment except with more costly external funds. Because of the increased costs, some new projects will fail to meet the capital budgeting criterion and their value will be lost. This has been used as an explanation for hedging behavior, so-called "cash-flow hedging." Hedges such as insurance protect the company's cash from these sudden shocks and ensure that its ongoing investment program is properly funded. However, other risk management strategies are available. Had the company operated with less leverage, it would have increased its net income and been able to absorb income shocks more readily. The company could have alleviated the problem by its choice of capital structure.

Emerging hybrids

The various explanations of the costs of risk given here suggest that managing leverage provides similar benefits to hedging or insuring risk. Lower leverage reduces the value of the troublesome default put options and alleviates their distorting effects. However, there is the rub. Debt is fine when things are going well. The problem arises when something goes wrong (the big liability suit or foreign exchange loss). It would seem a shame to sacrifice the benefits of some debt financing (such as preferred tax status) simply because debt becomes embarrassing when things go awry. Some of the instruments that are now appearing permit finer tuning.

Bankruptcy costs arise because the company cannot honor debt after a loss of value. Asset substitution and underinvestment problems arise because debt has distorting effects after a loss of company value. The post-loss financing problem is a story about the need for capital after a large shock to the company's earnings. These descriptions suggest a contingent approach to the company's capital structure. A market for such contingent financing instruments is developing. Many of these new instruments are being used by insurance companies to manage the risk stemming from their insurance portfolios, but are being experimented with by non-insurance companies.

Forgivable debt

The idea that principal or interest on debt be forgiven if some defined event occurs is not new. Early insurance contracts, known as bottomry, took the form of a loan to a merchant, which was forgiven if the ship were lost. Structured debt has been issued in which the principal or interest was related to oil prices and other commodity prices. Other examples include catastrophe bonds (where principal or interest is forgiven if some natural catastrophe occurs) and credit-linked notes (where a bond issuer such as a bank can have the debt reduced by adverse credit performance on its loan portfolio). These instruments provide a hedge for an issuer whose value is tied to the forgiveness trigger. For example, airlines can hedge against oil-price risk with a bond whose principal is tied to oil prices. Insurers and reinsurers can hedge their catastrophe risk with catastrophe bonds (widely known as "cat bonds").

The use of cat bonds by reinsurers to hedge natural-hazard risk is in some ways a little strained. The debt issue does not provide working capital to the insurer; it merely provides collateral that eliminates credit risk for the hedge contract. A more natural use of debt forgiveness is for non-insurance companies to include in their capital-structure debt whose principal or interest is linked to peripheral risks, such as liability claims, property losses, or foreign exchange rate changes.

The virtue of these instruments is that the company can keep debt on its books, but naturally reduces its leverage if some feared event happens. The problem of bankruptcy costs is addressed, and the distortions in investment decisions described above can be ameliorated. Why would investors hold these bonds? A simple answer is that they have a higher yield. However, there are other benefits to bondholders. Bankruptcy costs are avoided if things do go wrong. Second, the bonds would otherwise be subject to default risk. Forgiveness is a way of formalizing the type of renegotiation that might occur anyway. Most importantly, by forgiving debt when things go wrong rather than walking away, shareholders keep some downside risk. This will encourage them to make safer investment decisions.

Reverse convertible debt

A more revolutionary instrument that can achieve similar benefits is a new form of debt conversion, reverse convertible debt (RCD). An example of this was issued by the Netherlands diversified financial group ING. With RCD, the debt is converted to equity at the option of the company. The conversion option is exercised when the company value falls. Like forgivable debt, the business automatically reduces leverage when things go wrong. The benefits of RCD are also very similar to those of forgivable debt. A simple RCD issue would be triggered by a fall in the stock price. Like other insurance-linked securities, a further trigger could be added to protect against specific events (such as insurable losses).

Risk management is largely about financing: how to pay for post-loss investments so the company can recover and prosper after some risky event. Here we encounter contingent financing. The commonplace version is a line of credit. However, our logic suggests that post-loss leverage is the problem, not the solution. A more natural candidate is contingent equity. An interesting newcomer on this scene is the catastrophe equity put designed by insurance brokers Aon. To avoid having to raise new equity after a loss when the share price is depressed, the company issues a put option to sell its own shares to a counterparty at an agreed price (possibly including a second trigger, such as property or liability loss). This enables the company to recapitalize on favorable terms so that it can take full advantage of post-loss investment opportunities.

From indemnity to value creation

Over recent decades, there has been a decline in corporate insurance buying, particularly by larger companies. Some recent evidence suggests that companies with lower leverage are less likely to insure and hedge than more levered, high-growth companies. This trend should come as no surprise, since managing risk and managing leverage essentially involve the same activities – aligning the incentives of corporate stakeholders and ensuring security of funding for value-enhancing investments, particularly after a loss.

Recognition of the relationship can be a threat or an opportunity for the insurance industry. The traditional indemnity products offered by insurers are expensive and involve significant transaction costs. Furthermore, indemnifying a loss does not necessarily match the financing needs of the company. For example, no funding is needed if replacement of the destroyed asset would be a negative NPV investment. An equity injection equal to the cost of a liability settlement seems arbitrary if the suit has changed the expected NPV on new investment opportunities. A more appropriate question is this: If such an event happens, what capital is needed? As this question is asked, one will see greater use of instruments such as structured debt and contingent capital. If insurers recognize that the risk management paradigm is changing from indemnity to value creation, they can stem the flow and be lively players in the evolving corporate risk management marketplace.

Summary

Managing risk boils down to questions of insurance and hedging, writes **Neil A. Doherty**. Hedging aims to control risks attached to volatile cash flows. One reason risk is costly is that volatility increases the possibility that a company will go bankrupt. This article looks at default puts in the context of the way risk management creates value and suggests that the choice of internal or external funding has a direct impact on risk costs. Managing leverage can offer benefits similar to those of hedging or insuring risk, while some of the newer instruments in the portfolio allow for more finely tuned approaches to financing debt. With risk management so closely tied to "financing," it is natural that a market for contingent financing is also emerging. The apparent trend in larger companies to reduce the volume of insurance purchased could be countered if insurers accepted that the shift was away from indemnity to value creation. Among other topics discussed are cat bonds – which in times of calamity essentially reduce the leverage of debt on the books – and reverse convertible debt, a way of converting equity so as to generate benefits similar to forgivable debt.

Value, risk and control: a dynamic process in need of integration

by Philippe Jorion

It is only seven years since the financial industry emerged from the pre-history of financial risk management. This started when the Group of Thirty (G-30), a private, non-profit, international body composed of senior representatives of the private and public sectors and academia, established best practice for dealing with derivatives risk following the derivatives disasters of the early 1990s. Among other recommendations, the G-30 suggested there was a need to quantify financial market risk with a uniform measure of risk called Value at Risk.

VaR is a remarkably simple concept. It summarizes the downside risk of a portfolio into one single number, taking into account leverage and diversification effects. For instance, in its latest annual report the US bank J.P. Morgan states that its aggregate VaR is about $22m. Thus the bank, one of the pioneers in risk management, may say that for 95 percent of the time it does not expect to lose more than $22m on a given day. Originally, the main appeal of VaR was to describe risk in dollars – or whatever base currency is used – making it far more transparent and easier to grasp than previous measures. As importantly, the process of computing VaR brings a better understanding of the risks facing an institution. It is the first step toward better control and management of financial risk. VaR also represents the amount of economic capital necessary to support a business, which is an essential component of "economic value added" measures. This explains why VaR has become the "standard benchmark" for measuring financial risk.

Since then, the industry has truly experienced a revolution in risk management. The VaR concept has expanded from market risk to credit risk and is now being applied to other forms such as operational risk. The use of VaR, once confined to commercial banks, is spreading to other financial institutions, to institutional investors, and to corporate treasury departments. Academic and practitioner research in risk management is likewise developing at high speed.

These events can be viewed as extensions of the main idea behind VaR, which is to quantify risk at company-wide level. At the same time, they stem from the recognition that, once some risks are quantified and used to compute a capital charge, financial risks tend to slip toward areas where they are not measured. The central thesis of this article is that, ideally, risk management systems should provide comprehensive views of company-wide risk.

The galaxy of risks

Figure 1 classifies the risks facing institutions into business and non-business risks, the latter being further classified into event risks and financial risks. Admittedly, these are somewhat arbitrary classifications, as there is some overlap across categories.

Business risks generally are those that the corporation willingly assumes to create a competitive advantage and add value for shareholders. This risk pertains to the product market in which a company operates and includes product technology, design, and sales. Business risk is symmetrical, since it can create both gains and losses. Fundamentally, corporations are "paid" to take business risk.

Financial risks are associated with the effect of financial variables. These risks are also symmetrical, as they can create both gains and losses. Institutions are "paid" to manage financial risks.

Market risk arises from movements in the level or volatility of market prices. Credit risk arises because counterparties may be unwilling or unable to fulfill contractual obligations. Losses due to credit risk, however, can occur before the actual default when reflected in market prices. Corporate bond prices, for instance, anticipate credit losses, thereby interweaving credit risk with market risk. Liquidity risk takes two forms, asset liquidity risk and funding liquidity risk. Asset liquidity risk arises when a transaction cannot be conducted at prevailing market prices due to the size of the position relative to normal trading lots. Funding liquidity risk, also

Figure 1: Company-wide risks

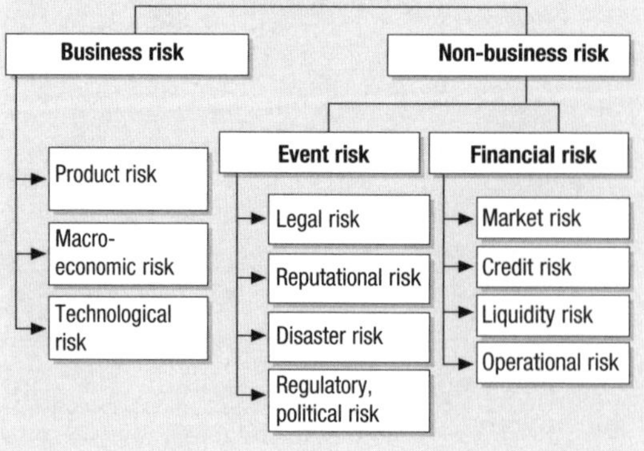

known as cash-flow risk, refers to the inability to meet payment obligations. As for operational risk, there is still no widely accepted definition. Sometimes it is narrowly defined as risk arising from operations, including human and technical errors. Others define it more broadly as the risk of direct and indirect loss resulting from failed or inadequate process, systems, and people, or from external events.

Event risks can generally be ascribed to other, negative events, outside the control of the institution. Event risks only create losses, some of which can be covered by traditional insurance. Institutions "pay" to mitigate event risks.

Using VaR to control risk

By now, VaR systems have become ubiquitous. All respectable banks have implemented some type of VaR system to measure and control risk. Such systems can also be used to design risk-based capital charges. These are ideally suited to dealing with a bonus-based compensation system for traders – those such as an option that has high upside, but limited downside. The problem is that such reward systems can be a recipe for disaster. Indeed, they create an incentive for "going for broke," as happened with Nick Leeson, the 28-year-old trader who in 1995 single-handedly brought down Barings, Britain's oldest investment bank. Alternatively, some traders inflate their profits, as happened with Kyriacos Papouis, a former interest-rate options trader who cost NatWest Markets, the investment banking arm of National Westminster Bank, some $130m by mispricing derivatives.

VaR systems can address the fundamental tension between creating incentives for traders to perform and making sure they take on risks that are reasonable from the institution's viewpoint. The solution lies in measures such as RAROC (risk-adjusted return on capital), which penalize profits for risk. Trading positions with greater risk need a greater amount of economic capital to absorb unexpected losses. VaR is such a measure of economic capital. The purpose of RAROC is to adjust trading profits by the remuneration of this risk capital. There is no better mechanism for making traders pay attention to their risk. This is not to say that trader profits have to be decreased. For normal risks, we could still have the same average compensation. Instead, relative to current practices, profits are adjusted down for greater than average risks and up for lower than average risks.

Such a system was implemented a while ago by Bankers Trust in the US. By now, it is becoming more common for risk managers to have some input into traders' compensation. The same rationale justifies risk-based capital charges set by bank regulators. Commercial banks should hold an amount of capital that is consistent with their risk-taking profile, as with traders. Otherwise, these banks may have an incentive to take on too much risk, at the expense of government insurance deposit funds or the stability of the financial system. This explains why the Basle committee of the Bank for International Settlements established minimum levels of capital in 1988.

Gaming the system

A potential problem with this approach is that the agent subject to risk-based charges may have an incentive to "game the system." This is what I would call the "VaR dialectic" issue. If a supervisor imposes a VaR-based charge to penalize traders for the risks they are incurring, traders may try to decrease VaR artificially. In other words, they could move into markets or securities that appear to have low risk for the wrong reasons. For instance, currency traders could take positions in currencies with fixed exchange rates, which have low historical volatility but perhaps high devaluation risk. They could alternatively attempt to exploit "risk holes" in the system. It is then the responsibility of the risk manager to understand the limitations of the VaR system. This is why risk management is as much an art form as a science. It is a dynamic process that does not stop at one number.

Similar reactions have occurred as a result of the Basle capital adequacy requirements for credit risk. The risk assessment was so crude that the banking industry has since found ways around the capital charges, in particular through securitization of loans or using new financial instruments such as credit derivatives. In response, bank regulators have proposed an improved capital requirement scheme.

This possibility of "gaming" explains why control systems are generally less efficient than was initially believed. This is not an indictment of VaR systems, but rather a reminder that benefits from technological innovations are often diminished by unforeseen side effects.

The interaction of risks

There is another side effect of risk measurement systems. The danger is that, once financial risks are quantified in some areas, they could slip toward areas where they are not measured, creating a false sense of security.

This risk is much more subtle and dangerous than is usually recognized. The prime example is that of Long-Term Capital Management (LTCM), the US hedge fund that failed spectacularly in 1998, endangering the global financial system. In its marketing materials, LTCM advertised itself as having a level of market risk similar to that of US equities, that is, about 15 percent per annum. The fund was essentially maximizing its expected return subject to a constraint on VaR. LTCM was specializing in "convergence trades," which attempt to benefit from small discrepancies in prices. Together with a constrained optimization, this explains why the $5bn in equity capital was leveraged into $125bn in assets and some $1.25tr in total face value for its derivatives positions (also known as notional, or contracted principal amounts). The problem is that the optimization ignored another component of financial risk – liquidity. LTCM was so enormous that it was unable to adjust its positions quickly as its trades turned sour. By focussing on market risk, it took on an exposure to liquidity risk to which it was blindsided.

Another example is Bankers Trust. It used its RAROC methodology to reward sales staff by a compensation formula that accounted for profits as well as a measure of market risk. This, however, missed another important component of risk, which involves damage to client relationships. In 1994, the bank became embroiled in a high-profile lawsuit with the US consumer products company Procter & Gamble that created adverse publicity. This is an example of reputational risk, which can be viewed as the damage, in addition to immediate monetary losses, caused to the ongoing business of an institution due to a damaged reputation. The bank's profit-driven culture and sole focus on market risk created an exposure to reputational risk.

The syndicated eurodollar loan is a further illustration. At the beginning of the 1980s, US banks were eager to lend to developing countries, but did not want exposure to market risk, that is, currency and interest-rate risk. Hence, eurodollar loans were denominated in dollars (no currency risk) and were payable on a floating rate basis (no interest risk). However, after US interest rates skyrocketed in the early 1980s and the dollar appreciated, countries such as Mexico and Brazil went into default, unable to make the floating dollar payments on their loans. In short, market risk had been transformed into credit risk.

Integrated risk management

The point is that attempts at controlling one type of risk may end up creating another. The only protection against this is enterprise-wide risk management (ERM), or "integrated" risk management. ERM aims at measuring, controlling, and managing the overall risk of the institution across all risk categories and business lines using a consistent methodology. This is slowly being made possible by a convergence in methods used to quantify financial risk from the finance and insurance industry. Computing and telecommunications developments are also making such integration technologically feasible.

Consider an institution that has measured the economic capital required to support its market/liquidity risk, credit risk, and operational risk. Figure 2 presents a typical breakdown of financial risks for a commercial bank. For instance, the bank may require \$2.5bn to cover operational risk, \$6bn to cover credit risk and \$1.5bn to cover market/liquidity risk, taken separately. These capital charges are basically VaR measures of downside risk. Next, the overall charge must be totted up from the various components.

If the risks are independent, we could compute the total capital charge as \$6.7bn only. The overall charge will be less than the total of individual charges due to diversification effects. In this situation the bank can carry less economic capital, as it would be highly unlikely for it to suffer the worst loss at the same time across the three categories. (In technical terms, the standard deviation of the sum is not the sum of standard deviations, but instead the square root of the variance that, with independent events, is the sum of the individual variances.)

The problem is not only of measuring various risks, but also their interaction. If the worst losses could occur at the same time across the three categories (or have perfect correlations), the total economic charge needs to be the sum of individual charges, or a full \$10bn, which is quite a lot higher. Thus the interaction of risks plays a crucial role in the total charge for financial risks.

At an even more fundamental level, this example further demonstrates the need for a consistent measurement technique across all risk categories. If market risk is measured using VaR tools that provide a fair reflection of economic risks, but other risks are not, there will be a danger of risks shifting away from fairly measured market risk into other risk classes. As one consultant reflected: "Is it an accident banks are now looking for growth in areas where they do not directly allocate capital and where risk is difficult to manage, rather than in basic trading and lending where businesses now have to pay their own way?"

This trend toward broader recognition of risk is embodied in the latest proposal of the Basle Committee for setting risk-based capital charges for commercial banks. So far, the capital charges guard against credit risk and, to some extent, market risk. It is widely recognized, however, that operational risk can be a significant source of losses in the banking industry. In exchange for lowering capital charges on credit risk, the Basle Committee has proposed to establish new charges for operational risk. The goal is to have regulatory capital charges that are in line with economic capital, creating the least amount of distortions in markets.

Figure 2: Setting up a company-wide charge for financial risks

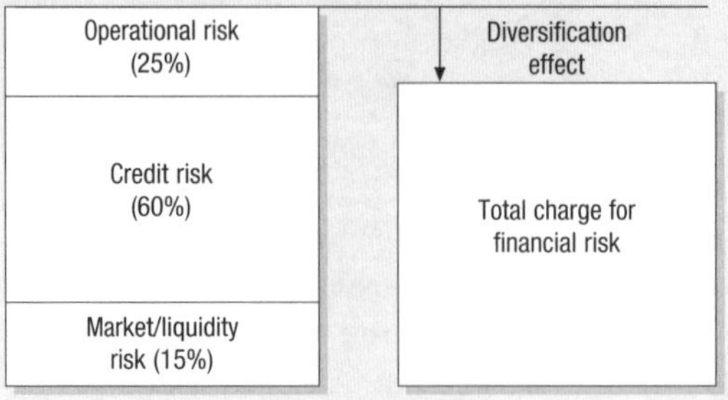

The final frontier

The industry is fast learning that it should take a comprehensive approach to risk management. A piecemeal approach can miss significant risks or, worse, push risks into less visible places and create a misleading sense of safety. What is required is the application of consistent risk measurement techniques across various sources of risk. Organizational structures also need to be rearranged so as to give company-wide risk authority to a single individual, or committee. The "silo" mentality of separately storing responsibilities for market, credit, and operational risks will no longer do.

The upside of this vast effort is an improved understanding of risks facing institutions. At a minimum, this will lower hedging costs, by pruning unnecessary transactions and taking advantage of diversification. At a more strategic level, the trend toward company-wide risk management will lead to better allocation of capital, taking into account not only rewards but also risks across business lines.

Summary

Value at Risk (VaR), a simple indicator that has revolutionized risk management in the past few years, is not a panacea, notes **Philippe Jorion**. VaR was initially designed to avoid bank disasters. Today, it is a ubiquitous measure of risk in the financial markets, but should not lull managers into a false sense of security. Indeed, controlling one kind of risk may give rise to other, more subtle and dangerous types. Risk management remains as much an art form as a science, a dynamic process that does not stop with just one number. This article offers an overview of issues involved, including business and non-business risk, event and financial risk. Ideally, risk management systems should be comprehensive, involving an enterprise-wide approach that in turn ensures that capital is more efficiently deployed.

Suggested further reading

Basle Committee on Banking Supervision (1999) *A New Capital Adequacy Framework*, Basle, www.bis.org/publ/bcbs50.pdf

Jorion, P. (1999) "Risk management lessons from long-term capital management," University of California at Irvine, www.gsm.uci.edu/~jorion/ltcm.pdf

Jorion, P. (2000) *Value at Risk: The New Benchmark for Managing Financial Risk*, McGraw-Hill.

Lenders and borrowers demand a creditable system

by Suresh M. Sundaresan

When one party lends money to another, the risk that the borrower may not be willing or able to repay the loan at regular intervals – or indeed at all – is called credit risk. On a small scale, this might happen when a shopkeeper borrows money from the local bank and finds that cash-flow problems make it impossible to pay the interest on the loan. On a larger scale, portfolio managers might invest in credit-risky contracts such as sovereign and corporate bonds. Commercial banks, the International Monetary Fund, and the World Bank face the largest-scale credit risk in their loans to large corporations, governments, and institutions.

There are several ways in which borrowers can be said to default on a loan: missed or delayed disbursement of contractual obligations (such as interest payments, sinking fund payments, or principal payments); going bankrupt or falling into receivership; experiencing distressed exchanges (when debt holders exchange their old bonds for new bonds, which may have less value); and becoming liquidated (when the company's assets are sold off). Each one of these events is an example of a credit event.

Such events can be costly to borrowers and lenders, as the renegotiations that follow often soak up the time of senior managers. Legal bankruptcy procedures can whittle away valuable resources of the stock holders and bond holders; renegotiating loans can be expensive, as can debt service reductions and potential liquidations. A credit event may also lead to a lower recovery rate on the loan or bond obligations. In such situations, the lender may get less than the figure specified in the contract.

In 1998, all these things occurred when the Russian government decided to impose a 90-day moratorium on debt payments. Foreign lenders to Russia took hefty losses: the *Washington Post* estimated that the losses to banks and securities companies exceeded $6bn. It was thought that around 720 banks would face liquidation.

So, investors are keenly interested in determining the probability of default on a loan as well as the potential recovery rates in the event that default occurs. Together, the probability of default and the recovery rates determine the value of a credit-risky security.

How can we estimate the future recovery rate on a loan? There are many institutional factors, including the following:

- the relative bargaining positions of lenders and borrowers;
- the underlying bankruptcy code and its enforceability – this is especially important in the distinction between a sovereign loan and a corporate debt;
- the access to collateral in the event of default – this is related to the presence or absence of a bankruptcy code, which formalizes access to collateral;
- the seniority of the loan or bond and whether it is secured or not;
- the availability of secured collateral and its value under financial distress;
- multiple creditors and the existence or absence of bank debt.

The presence of any different creditors can severely hamper co-ordination in a reorganization plan. The presence of a bank loan helps bond holders in the sense that the bank closely monitors the borrower. On the other hand, since bank loans are typically senior and secured, bond holders' access to collateral may be curtailed.

Debt can be a loan extended by a bank or a syndicate of banks. It can also be in the form of bonds issued by the borrowers that are held by many investors across the globe. Credit markets in recent times have witnessed an explosive growth in bond markets. This growth has often come at the expense of loan markets in some areas, such as corporate debt markets and sovereign debt markets. In November 1999, the Bank of England reported that the UK corporate borrowers used debt securities for 35 percent of their borrowing needs in the 1998–99 period, whereas their reliance on bonds was under 20 percent in 1990.

The sovereign bond market today is nearly as big as the sovereign loan market, whereas the sovereign bond markets were quite small in 1980. Extensive securitization of loan portfolios and bonds over the last decade has resulted in a widespread distribution of credit risk to many bond holders. Many debt securities and investors in capital markets are now subject to credit risk.

What causes default?

Macro-economic factors such as recession or a collapse in exchange rates may cause borrowers to default on loans. During the depression years of the 1930s, there was a significant increase in the number of defaults in the US. More recently, the Asian financial crisis of 1997 started with a precipitous drop in exchange rates. Domestic borrowers from countries such as Indonesia, Malaysia, and Thailand who had borrowed in dollars were hardest hit. Bankruptcies were also accentuated by structural deficiencies in the bank sector.

Default may also be due to company-specific or industry-specific factors. For example, in the east Asian crisis, many companies that went bankrupt had very high ratio of debt to equity. In part, this was due to the lack of development of equity markets and the scarcity of equity capital.

Finally, even though the borrower is in a position to make the debt service payments, it may choose to default to extract additional concessions from the lender. Such strategic default may arise as a result of imperfect information, the high cost of default to lenders, and structural deficiencies in the process of financial distress resolution.

Information about the financial health of borrowers comes from two important sources: rating agencies and the market. Moody's, Standard & Poor's, and Fitch IBCA, for example, regularly produce information about the credit standing of borrowers that significantly influences the cost of their credit. The prices of stocks and bonds issued by the borrower also contain valuable information about credit risk of the borrower. An increase in credit risk translates into lower equity and bond prices, other things being equal.

The bankruptcy code

The cornerstone of debt contracting is the bankruptcy code. The rubric of the code defines the rights and responsibilities of creditors and borrowers in the event of default, anchors the process of co-ordination, renegotiation, and restructuring for a financially troubled borrower, and formalizes the lender's access to the borrower's collateral.

The bankruptcy code balances two conflicting forces: on the one hand, the integrity of a debt contract must be upheld so that *ex ante* lenders have an incentive to lend money in exchange for debt contracts. This implies a strict enforcement of the absolute priority rule, which respects the seniority of debt holders over equity holders in their rights to residual cash flows.

On the other hand, the code must prevent the enforced liquidation of companies that suffer from nothing more than a lack of liquidity. Often, to prevent such liquidations, it may be necessary to inject additional capital into the distressed company, which may only be forthcoming at a higher priority than existing debt claims.

The bankruptcy code differs from country to country. The perceived efficiency, enforceability, and fairness of a particular country's code have a major influence on the development of credit markets. Investors' perception of the code as "borrower friendly" or "lender friendly" has important implications for the spreads. The bankruptcy code in the US is regarded as borrower friendly due to the fact that the debtor remains in control. On the other hand, the code in the UK, which operates on the principle of receivership, is perceived as lender friendly. Lenders might charge a higher rate in a country where the code is perceived to be borrower friendly.

In most countries, the code has three important provisions. First, when a company seeks protection under the bankruptcy code, all payments to creditors are suspended. This ensures that there is no "rush to the exit" by creditors who may have an incentive to cut a deal with the borrower at the expense of other creditors. This moratorium on debt payments is specified *ex ante* – as opposed to the *ex post* (and unilateral) moratorium on debt payments enforced by Russia in 1998. The period of automatic stay varies from country to country.

Second, the judiciary authorities play an active role in supervising the process of reorganizing a bankrupt company's affairs. Major decisions cannot be taken without the approval of the court. If the court is not satisfied with the reorganization plan proposed by the existing management, it may appoint a new management team.

Finally, under the US Bankruptcy Code the borrower remains in control on bankruptcy filing, though at the request of the creditors the bankruptcy court can change the company's management. The rationale for this provision is that the borrower is in a better position than the creditors to turn around the company and should therefore get the first shot. The receivership doctrine works in reverse, giving creditors the first opportunity at reorganization.

Models of credit risk

Lenders and borrowers use models of credit risk to help address various issues. Asset managers and other lenders are interested in knowing the spreads that they should demand for investing in credit-risky securities such as loans and bonds. Bankers are interested in evaluating the overall credit risk of their loan portfolios. Borrowers would like to know the effect of placing some contractual features and bond covenants on the pricing of their debt issues. Likewise, investors may wish to know the value of converting bonds to equity.

Structural approach

The structural approach to credit risk focusses purely on the borrower's balance sheet and on calculations of the value of the borrower's assets and liabilities. At any point, the model tells the user how close the asset value of the borrower is to the default trigger, and delivers estimates of default probabilities based on information contained in the balance sheet. Market factors can also be included in the model. Default in this model is never a surprise.

The structural approach suggests the following relationship: the value of credit-risky debt equals the value of risk-free debt less the value of the put option to default. In other words, investors will pay less for a corporate bond than they would be willing to pay for an otherwise identical government bond that is free of default. This intuition leads to the following important conclusions:

- The spread between the government bond price and the corporate bond price increases with the volatility of the underlying assets of the company. As the assets become riskier, the option to default becomes more valuable, and cautious investors will demand a higher discount to buy such corporate debt.
- The spread increases with leverage. If the company has more debt, it is more likely to default, and investors will demand a higher spread.
- The spread typically increases with time to maturity of the loan. This is due to the fact that with a longer maturity loan, the borrower's option to default is more valuable.

Structural approach with strategic default

This approach focusses on the bankruptcy code, liquidation costs, and the bargaining power of lenders and borrowers. It is based on the idea that lenders and borrowers prefer to renegotiate debt contracts rather than liquidate the company, which is costly to both. Since the lenders know beforehand that recontracting will occur later, they typically charge a premium in the pricing of loans. The presence or absence of a bankruptcy code, its perceived "friendliness" to lenders or borrowers, and the existence of a credible threat (such as trade sanctions or seizure of exports) serve to set the bargaining boundaries and hence the spreads.

Reduced form models

Reduced form models do not specify who the lenders and borrowers are, but concentrate specifically on the probability of default and the recovery rates. The lynchpin in this class of models is the absence of arbitrage. In other words, these models operate under the assumption that investors behave rationally and do not "leave any money on the table." The focus of these models is the time to default. By their very nature, default is a surprise event in the reduced form models. These models are particularly valuable in the pricing of credit derivatives.

Managing credit risk

The management of credit risk has to be addressed at two levels: at the institutional, legal, and judicial structure of the economy; and at the level of contractual and organizational provisions. The financial architecture of the country encompasses a well-established bankruptcy code, securities and corporate law, its judicial system, and an enforcement mechanism for compliance of legal contracts. Debt markets will only develop if this architecture is sound.

On the second level, contractual and organizational provisions might include marking positions to market frequently so that the losses and gains are realized periodically; requiring collateral when counterparties owe more than a threshold level; contingent provisions whereby if the counterparty's credit rating is downgraded, all positions are marked to market; and requiring that the portfolio of credit risks is diversified across industries and the globe. Most contracts also specify that cash flows should be netted so that the overall credit exposure is managed more efficiently. In this context, netting means that if A owes B $2m and B owes A $1.5m, then rather than each of them making these payments, A will make a payment of $0.5m to B.

Organizational provisions might include several safeguards: credit committees consisting of senior managers should exercise control over which institutions can act as counterparties to a financial transaction, such as an interest rate swap; there might be an internal credit-scoring system, which is already common practice in many financial institutions; and the measurement of credit exposure using simulated scenarios and stress testing – already a popular technique.

While these provisions are often adequate, they may not be sufficient when there is a major "flight to quality" precipitated by a macro-economic shock to a large region. The Asian crisis of 1997 and its aftermath clearly form such an example. Prudent interventions by central banks and agencies such as the IMF and the World Bank might help mitigate some of the problems, but reforming the financial architecture will provide the best means of developing healthy credit markets.

Summary

When the Russian government defaulted on its debts in 1998, western banks, governments, and businesses with credit in Russia were left $6bn short. In this article, **Suresh Sundaresan** explains the main issues of credit risk and the financial and legal structures that enable credit to be sought and given. He examines different kinds of default, the nature of information on credit risk, and differences in bankruptcy codes in the US and UK. Finally, he describes three models of credit risk.

OPERATIONAL RISK

5

Contributors

Leslie Willcocks is a Fellow in the Oxford Institute of Information Management at Templeton College, University of Oxford. He is joint editor of the *Journal of Information Technology*.

Chris Sauer is a Fellow in the Oxford Institute of Information Management at Templeton College, University of Oxford. He is joint editor of the *Journal of Information Technology*.

Gary D. Eppen is deputy dean and Ralph and Dorothy Keller Distinguished Service Professor of Operations Management at the University of Chicago Graduate School of Business. His research activities include analytic models and empirical data for improving productivity in manufacturing and service organizations. He is particularly interested in international operations and supply chain management.

Christoph H. Loch is an associate professor of operations management at INSEAD. His research interests include product development, management of R&D, technology management, and status competition in organizations.

Arnd Huchzermeier is professor of production management at the Otto-Beisheim Graduate School of Management of WHU in Vallendar near Koblenz, Germany. His research interests include real options/risk management in R&D and start-up ventures, supply chain optimization, promotion planning, product bundling, and pricing strategies.

Clive Smallman is a senior research associate and James Tye, British Safety Council Fellow in Safety, Health and Environmental Management at the University of Cambridge, Judge Institute of Management Studies.

Andrew Robinson is a lecturer in financial economics at the University of Bradford Management Centre.

Gareth John is an independent consultant in strategy, planning, and research, with a background in marketing advertising and communications.

Philip Bell is a business risks manager at the insurance company Royal & SunAlliance.

Contents

High risks and hidden costs in IT outsourcing 135
Leslie Willcocks, Templeton College, University of Oxford
Chris Sauer, Templeton College, University of Oxford
A corporate decision to buy IT solutions from third parties carries a tradeoff between risk and advantage.

Charting a course through the perils of production 141
Gary D. Eppen, University of Chicago Graduate School of Business
Risks associated with the design-to-delivery cycle include production and delivery systems, currency fluctuations, and political issues.

Hiding behind risk in fear of innovation 147
Christoph H. Loch, INSEAD
Arnd Huchzermeier, Otto-Beisheim Graduate School of Management, WHU
This article suggests there are flaws in some of the tools that financial controllers use to measure project returns and argues for more flexibility.

Unhealthy attitudes that endanger good performance 152
Clive Smallman, Judge Institute of Management Studies, University of Cambridge
Andrew Robinson, University of Bradford Management Centre
Gareth John
Workplace injuries cost US businesses enormous amounts each year. Even so, health and safety remains a poor relation in the lexicon of management topics.

Product failure and the growing culture of claims 156
Philip Bell, Royal & SunAlliance
No company is completely immune from the possibility of product flaws. Where injury occurs, compensation bills can run into billions.

Introduction

Operational risk covers a multitude of issues in the day-to-day running of a company's operations, including health and safety, fraud, product failure, manufacturing breakdown, or quality problems. In the past 20 years, IT has joined this list as a significant source of company risk. The danger it poses has increased along with the fashion for outsourcing – when a company puts valued operations in the hands of another company, it must also institute systematic checks to ensure that the outsourced function is reliable and secure.

High risks and hidden costs in IT outsourcing

by Leslie Willcocks and Chris Sauer

Information technology (IT) outsourcing is the handing over to a third party of the management and operation of IT assets and activities. This is not the only way of using the market for external IT services. For example, buying in resources to be managed by the client company – sometimes called "insourcing" – is also widely practiced. The sourcing of IT projects is a tradeoff between managing downside risk and maximizing the opportunity to achieve competitive advantage. Both practices have their attendant risks. To be successful, ultimately each requires active, if different, in-house management involvement.

Why focus on the specific risks of IT outsourcing? First, because survey and case research into global practices shows a rising trend of expenditure. E-business makes great demands on companies and managers will often conclude that the only way to meet short deadlines for new technology projects is to contract for specialist services. On the authors' figures, global IT outsourcing revenues were $100bn in 1998. These will rise to $120bn in 2002 and $150bn in 2004. By that year, on average 30–35 percent of a corporation's IT budget will be outsourced. Having a third of their IT under external control makes it essential for managers to have a clear understanding of the attendant risks and how to mitigate them.

Second, research consistently demonstrates that despite the growing maturity of vendors and their clients, the practice of IT outsourcing continues to be a high-risk, hidden-cost process. Consider the UK division of the major US retailer Sears. In early 1996, it outsourced most of its IT on a 10-year, "no tender" basis to a single supplier – a deal worth £344m. This was brokered largely as a financial rescue package for the troubled group. Within 17 months, and with the resignation of the chief executive, the board could no longer see sufficient business advantage in the arrangement. The cost to Sears of implementing, then terminating, the deal exceeded £55m.

Most experiences are not as stark. One reason is that in the leading UK and US markets some 73 percent of organizations take a selective outsourcing route. Typically, they outsource only between 15 and 30 percent of the IT budget and use different suppliers to fulfill specific needs. In 2000, some 21 percent of organizations were largely expected to do IT in-house with no significant outsourcing contracts.

In the authors' case research, selective and in-house sourcing had success rates of 77 percent and 76 percent respectively, but only 38 percent of total outsourcing deals (80 percent or more of IT outsourced) were successful, 35 percent failed and 27 percent had "mixed" results. Nevertheless, a recent research study found a quarter of organizations encountering serious and difficult problems in IT outsourcing. Moreover, hidden costs, followed by the credibility of vendor's claims, continue to be the top single risks materializing as significant negative outcomes in outsourcing deals.

Clearly, it becomes important to develop a risk-profiling framework for setting up and running IT outsourcing. Based on more than 250 case histories that the authors

Figure 1: IT outsourcing: risk analysis framework

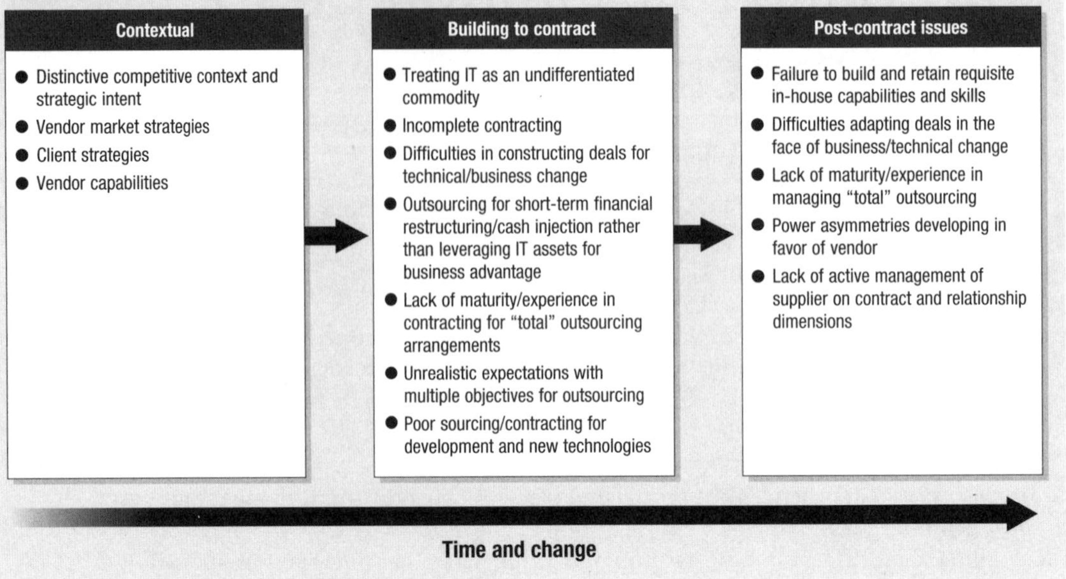

studied between 1991 and 2000, Figure 1 highlights the most salient risks experienced in IT outsourcing. We will now illustrate these risks, and discuss practical ways of managing them.

Contextual
Distinctive competitive context and strategic intent
Vendor market strategies
Client strategies
Vendor capabilities
Building to contract
Treating IT as an undifferentiated commodity
Incomplete contracting
Difficulties in constructing deals for technical/business change
Outsourcing for short-term financial restructuring/cash injection rather than leveraging IT assets for business advantage
Lack of maturity/experience in contracting for "total" outsourcing arrangements
Unrealistic expectations with multiple objectives for outsourcing
Poor sourcing/contracting for development and new technologies
Post-contract issues
Failure to build and retain requisite in-house capabilities and skills
Difficulties adapting deals in the face of business/technical change
Lack of maturity/experience in managing "total" outsourcing
Power asymmetries developing in favor of vendor
Lack of active management of supplier on contract and relationship dimensions
Time and change

IT advantage or disadvantage?

In 1994, Sir John Browne, chief executive of oil major BP (now BP Amoco), stated: "Failure to outsource our commodity IT will permanently impair the future competitiveness of our business." In a highly competitive sector, the risk he identified was that of a loss of focus on core competencies if the company did not outsource. In the group, BP Exploration's total outsourcing contracts with three suppliers proved highly successful in this regard. A "best-of-breed" approach was adopted to supplier selection. Contracts were kept to five years (considered a reasonable period given the speed of business and technological change), in-house measurement systems were established, and the remaining group of skilled IT managers proved successful at monitoring and working with multiple suppliers.

However, the contextual risks shown in Figure 1 can be difficult to surmount. Some studies suggest that strategic disadvantage can be one outcome from outsourcing. In a study of 54 businesses over five years, reported in 1998, Peter Weill and Marianne Broadbent of Melbourne Business School found that those outsourcing at a faster rate had indeed achieved lower costs, but had also experienced greater strategic losses compared with organizations that did less outsourcing. Losses included:

- significantly increasing information systems staff turnover;
- longer time to market for new products;
- lower perceived product and service quality than their competitors;
- slower rate of increase in revenue per employee;
- lower return on assets.

The present authors' research supports the notion that managers who pursue growth and faster time to market risk making the business strategically and operationally inflexible if they outsource principally for cost-reduction purposes. For example, in 1994 Xerox signed a 10-year global single-supplier deal. Where cost reductions did take place, they may have restricted Xerox's ability to cope with a major change in marketing structure. In late 1999, Xerox lost control of its billing and sales commissions systems, with big consequences for profitability. In other words, there must be a match between business strategy and what outsourcing is set up to achieve. Consider also Capital One, the US credit card group with 12,000 employees, 1,000 of them in IT. According to its president, Nigel Morris: "If you have a business that churns out products, then outsourcing makes sense. But . . . IT is our central nervous system . . . if I outsourced tomorrow I might save a dollar or two on each account, but I would lose flexibility, and value and service levels."

Further risks reside in not understanding a supplier's competitive and client strategies and its essential capabilities. For example, while outsourcing remains a growth market, vendors will be tempted to devote their attention and energies to winning new contracts rather than servicing existing ones.

On the first issue, a supplier may well be keen to enter a new marketplace, as for example Perot Systems, the US services company, was in the early 1990s in the UK. Alternatively, a supplier may seek to boost growth by offering favorable deals, its view being that as other, more profitable, contracts come along it can shift its key human resources to these, at the same time finding ways of building revenue from the original contracts.

Suppliers that make losses or have slim margins may indulge in opportunistic behavior (unless the client is of central significance). Such behavior may include efforts to reinterpret contracts and create new modes of revenue generation.

Checking that a deal is based on reasonable profit for the supplier can be a risk-mitigating exercise here. Government agencies particularly need to heed this point. Where there are requirements to select the cheapest supplier, they may secure fewer tenders in the first place. Subsequently, they experience difficult relationships with their vendors because the contract does not allow for reasonable profit.

Some large suppliers also have long-term strategies to dominate vertical markets, for example military logistics. In these cases, a supplier may well offer very favorable terms and service over the early years of a deal, but its overall objective would be to make switching costs prohibitive and to build up a monopoly of experience and a track record in that market that would dissuade competitors. There is a risk that a vendor that secures a client on a long-term basis becomes gradually more and more powerful and can begin to dictate price and service regimes. Clearly, it is in their long-term interest for client companies to retain sourcing flexibility by encouraging competition, thereby retaining the power to influence the vendor's behavior.

Companies must also be wary of a supplier's claims of capabilities and resources. Even the largest suppliers experience skills shortages, or "stickiness," in making the skills they do have available to specific clients. When in the mid-1990s EDS claimed in its bid to South Australia government that it had 100,000 people available worldwide, the challenge for the client was to determine how many were realistically not already committed, and able to travel to and work in Australia. Unless they stipulate otherwise, clients may well have their old staff hired back to them, gaining no real influx of new skills.

Often suppliers have to subcontract. In the big deals we studied, frequently more than 30 percent of the work involved a multi-supplier contract in disguise. This was particularly true in technical consulting, desktop hardware and installation, network specialists, and software specialists. There are a number of risks here. Suppliers do not always manage other suppliers better than the client could. They may charge more and add less value than if the client undertook the work.

Responsibilities and intellectual property rights can be less than transparent. It becomes all too easy for responsibilities to fall through the cracks of these increasingly complex relationships as one supplier plays the client off against others.

Some companies have addressed these risks by taking an equity share in the supplier to which they have outsourced IT. The best-known example is GM-EDS, with EDS operating as a subsidiary of the motor car giant. Elsewhere, the Commonwealth Bank of Australia took equity in EDS Australia, and Australian developer Lend Lease took equity in IBM Global Services (Australia). This may prove an excellent business investment, but it remains to be seen how far it helps mitigate outsourcing risk. Where the equity holding is managed by an asset management unit rather than the chief information officer, that unit will support whatever strategy the supplier has for maximizing its returns, ahead of pressing for better service for its own organization.

Pitfalls and pick-me-ups

In the authors' research, failed or failing IT outsourcing deals invariably exhibited all the practices shown in Figure 1 during the course of the contract. Problems and disappointments occurred if any one of these risky paths was selected. In 1992, the UK regional power supplier East Midlands Electricity (EME) totally outsourced to a single supplier on a 12-year deal worth £150m. Within three years, its board accepted that significant parts of its IT, previously viewed as an "undifferentiated commodity," were in fact critical to the evolution of the company's business strategy. The company began to rebuild its in-house resources, but was restricted by its outsourcing contract, the terms of which Perot Systems showed no signs of breaking. Eventually, the contract was terminated five years early in 1999, as EME's acquisition by Powergen, the UK's third largest electricity generator, triggered a let-out clause.

Some of the most disappointing deals were signed in the early 1990s either as financial rescue packages or to achieve cost savings – these deals were for total outsourcing over a long period to a single supplier. Companies usually contract for 10 years or more in order to establish a strategic relationship with the supplier. However, contracting for IT services for such a length of time is very difficult. As John Cross, IT director at BP Amoco, pointed out in 1999: "In the course of five years we experienced two generations of technology." Incomplete contracting is frequently the result.

Another feature of long contracts is that power asymmetries develop in favor of the vendor. In many of these deals, the supplier sought to recoup its investments in the second five years and found many opportunities to make excess charges for services not covered in the original contract. The explicitness of the contract and service measures emerged as critical, not least because in practice employees move on, and contracts can be continually reinterpreted to favor one side or the other. None of this is helped when the client fails to build requisite in-house capabilities to keep control of its IT destiny.

Success in total IT outsourcing has taken a variety of routes. On the evidence, it requires mature management and long experience of IT outsourcing, as shown in the BP Exploration case mentioned above. It also needs complete and creative contracting. We have seen successful uses of flexible pricing: for example shares in vendor savings, "open book" accounting, third-party benchmarking, and obtaining reduced fees after comparing these with a supplier's other customers.

We have also seen companies begin with small, short-term contracts that they later convert to large, long-term deals, and the use of competitive bidding for further work beyond the first contract in order to provide a continuing incentive for the supplier. Effective contracts also allow managers to revisit price/performance criteria, which they can benchmark against a fast-changing IT labor and services marketplace.

Large "total" outsourcing contracts are often successful mainly in stable, well-understood areas of IT activity such as infrastructure/mainframe operations. Less typically, Philips Electronics, the Netherlands-based consumer electronics company, and Origin, its computer services subsidiary, entered a strategic alliance where Philips spun off its entire IT function in a shared risk/reward and joint venture with an existing supplier. Others hope to spread their risks by signing multiple suppliers to five- to seven-year contracts. Others still were single supplier deals that took on board the above prescriptions, had detailed contracts, and were also high profile, with the suppliers wary of adverse publicity in specific countries or markets. British Aerospace's alliance with CSC or the UK's Inland Revenue Service's deal with EDS fall into this category.

Post-contract management

Failures in dealing with the issues of context and building to contract flow through into what actually happens at the post-contract stage, the point of implementation. But even if a deal is well set up, IT outsourcing can still founder. Risks arise from not staying flexible in the face of unexpected but inevitable business and technical change, not managing the relationship well, not making the most of the business relationship, and not maintaining a power balance between the parties.

Short-term contracts, multiple suppliers, the possibility of competition, and the possibility of future work have all been used to incentivize suppliers. For example, one IT director, asked why he went for short-term contracts, commented: "It's amazing the service you get when the contract is coming up for renewal." Managers need to use various stratagems to gain and hold the full attention of the supplier. John Yard, IT director in the 1993–2003 UK Inland Revenue–EDS deal, has made the point explicitly: "I see myself as in direct competition for the supplier's attention with all its other customers."

In running any IT sourcing arrangement, the greatest risk that companies face resides in trying to retain employees with appropriate skills and capabilities. David Feeny and Leslie Willcocks have identified nine such skills. These include business-related skills such as relationship building and business systems thinking; technology-related skills such as IT architecture and problem solving; skills for managing external suppliers such as contract facilitation, informed buying, contract monitoring, and vendor development; and the governance and co-ordination capabilities that come from effective leadership. Companies that build these in-house stand a far greater chance of keeping IT outsourcing arrangements on track.

In practice, too many companies see IT outsourcing as an opportunity to offload headcount – a real risk if done indiscriminately. Another less serious mistake is to appoint the wrong people to these roles, something the authors found even among relatively mature users of the IT services market. Conventional information systems models suggest a structure with fewer staff – but all with distinctive, high-performance capabilities. Frequently, these are skills not provided by existing, retained staff. IT outsourcing requires intensive management, in fact, but of a different kind from more traditional IT functions. It has also become clear that appointing one person, usually the "contract manager," to fulfill several of these roles lowers resulting performance. This may, however, be a pragmatic tradeoff in smaller client organizations.

From risk to business advantage

Generally, selective sourcing to multiple suppliers – on relatively short-term, detailed, and regularly revisited contracts – has been the more effective approach to mitigating the risks of external IT outsourcing.

On IT development projects, in situations where the technology is new and unstable, where there is little relevant IT experience of the technology, and business requirements are unclear or changing, "insourcing" presents a far safer approach. This is not to say that total outsourcing is not feasible; rather, it means that risk analysis, and mitigation techniques, become even more required practices.

In the 1990–2000 period, the authors' research has shown that organizations that selectively outsource achieve most of their limited, realistic expectations. We have also seen a small number of organizations achieve strategic business goals by outsourcing IT on a large scale, for example facilitating and supporting major organizational change at British Gas in the 1990s; achieving direct profit revenue generation through joint venturing with a supplier partner at Philips Electronics; redirecting the business and IT into core competencies as at BP Exploration; and strengthening resources and flexibility in technology and service to underpin the business's strategic direction, as at the US chemicals, pharmaceuticals, and agricultural products group DuPont. All underwent and managed the potential risks detailed in Figure 1.

As the focus of IT outsourcing shifts to supplier-supported e-business projects, the use of application service providers, business service providers, managed network services, new forms of outsourced e-fulfilment, and customer relationship management, some critical issues in risk management arise. Radical forms of large-scale outsourcing are now emerging; it should be remembered that the new principles underlying large-scale outsourcing at the networking industry kingpin Cisco Systems are not that far from those underlying the original "virtual organization" – the Italian clothing group Benetton – in the late 1980s. Ignoring all we have learned about the risks in IT outsourcing and how to manage them would be a very risky business indeed.

Summary

As e-business fuels IT expenditure, companies should take a hard look at the related risks, say **Leslie Willcocks** and **Chris Sauer**. A corporate decision to buy IT solutions from third parties carries a tradeoff between risk and advantage. There are numerous examples of companies being burnt by high-risk, hidden-cost solutions. The authors recommend a prudent approach to such issues as IT sourcing contracts, supplier claims, the risk behind disguised multi-supplier contracts, supplier capabilities and resources, single-supplier and long-term deals. Success in total IT outsourcing requires managerial maturity and experience. Too many companies regard IT outsourcing as a chance to reduce costs and headcount – but they face real risks if they trim their capabilities and skills too vigorously. Finally, the authors note that, for some large suppliers, the long-term aim is to dominate vertical markets. Their favorable initial terms may disguise a goal of making switching costs prohibitive.

Suggested further reading

Feeny, D. and Willcocks, L. (1998) "Core IS capabilities for exploiting IT," *Sloan Management Review*, June.

Kern, T. and Willcocks, L. (2001) *The Relationship Advantage*, Oxford: Oxford University Press.

Lacity, M. and Willcocks, L. (2000) *Global IT Outsourcing: Search For Business Advantage*, Chichester: Wiley.

Lacity, M. and Willcocks, L. (2000) "Inside IT outsourcing: a state-of-the-art report," Templeton College, University of Oxford, April.

Sauer, C. (1999) "Deciding the future for IS failures: not the decision you might think," in Galliers, R.D. and Currie, W. (eds), *Re-Thinking Management Information Systems*, Oxford: Oxford University Press, Oxford.

Sauer, C., Yetton, P. and Associates (1997) *Steps to the Future: Fresh Thinking on the Management of IT-based Organizational Transformation*, San Francisco: Jossey Bass.

Weill, P. and Broadbent, M. (1998) *Leveraging the New Infrastructure*, Boston, MA: Harvard Business School Press.

Charting a course through the perils of production

by Gary D. Eppen

The topic of *operations* deals with the design, creation, and delivery of goods and services. It includes traditional activities such as the creation and distribution of physical goods (production and logistics), as well as "back-office" processes in the service industry, for example producing mortgages, managing patients, scheduling consultants, staffing, and designing call centers.

Managing risk effectively is critical to success in operations, but the word "risk" itself is not as commonly used in operations as it is in the field of finance. The management of risk takes place under a variety of labels in a wide number of locations throughout organizations.

Risk at two levels

Risk in operations occurs at the micro-level within the production and delivery systems of the organization. It is also important at the macro-level in the form of operating exposure due to currency fluctuations in international operations and political risk. A number of approaches have been developed to help managers deal with the various forms of risk.

In order to discuss mastering risk at the micro-level in operations, it is useful to talk about processes. A process is any series of activities that produces physical goods or information. Two examples from the many available include production systems that make crankshafts and the series of steps that convert customer demand into production orders in a factory.

Mastering risk at the micro-level in operations means managing the variability produced by these processes. There are two fundamental approaches to this management challenge. First, one can change the process so that the amount of variability in the output of the system is reduced. This is often called process improvement. Alternatively, or perhaps in addition, one seeks ways to mitigate the impact of the variability on the organization.

Process improvement

The idea of controlling the variability in a process dates back to Walter A. Shewhart, who invented the control chart in 1924. His concept had real staying power, and even today you will find control charts in manufacturing plants all over the world.

For example, John Deere, the world's biggest maker of farm tractors, uses a so-called X-bar chart to control the assembly process on the cabs that protect operators from hazards of weather, noise, and tractor rollovers. Periodically, a completed cab is pulled from the product stream and examined using a checklist of key product quality attributes. Findings are reviewed and scored for impact on customer satisfaction and comfort. The score is then calculated and plotted on a control chart.

If this score falls within specified limits (shown in Figure 1 as Upper Control Limit and Lower Control Limit), which are determined on the basis of the natural variation in the process, production continues. Otherwise, the production process must be stopped, inspected, and if necessary adjusted. Responsibility is assigned for corrective action in process improvements and projects are monitored until changes demonstrate effective improvement. This procedure is followed not only in Deere's US assembly plants, but also in Europe, Asia, and South America.

Figure 1: Assembly audit control chart

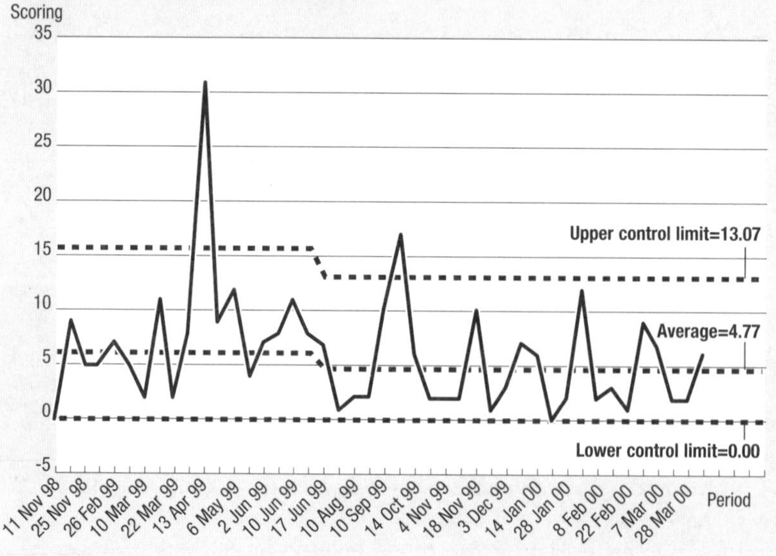

Total quality management

Somewhere along the line the purpose of the control chart changed. Originally, it signaled a change in the output of the system. If the control chart indicated that the variability in the output of the process increased, management was to inspect the process to see if an adjustment was needed. About 1950, under the leadership of Dr W. Edwards Deming, the academic behind much of Japanese management philosophy, and Joseph M. Juran, another pioneer of total quality management, charts became part of a total quality management (TQM) program. Charts were used to measure variability and the goal was to continue to reduce the variability in processes until zero defects became an obtainable goal. (Indeed, today, Deere uses the chart described above in exactly that way.) Japanese manufacturing companies led the world in adopting and perfecting process improvement (risk reduction), and the impact on the demand for Japanese products is well known.

TQM started to make an important impact on manufacturing in the US in the second half of the 1970s. For example, the US electronics group Motorola, then under the leadership of former chief executive Robert Galvin, made process improvement a central part of its corporate strategy. The Motorola approach was dubbed the six-sigma system and became the guideline for all Motorola processes, not just manufacturing. The basic idea was to improve processes so that the probability of a defect was essentially zero.

The goal of a TQM company is to take variability (risk) out of the entire process of producing a good or service. Thus the principles were extended to include parts and materials purchased from suppliers. With TQM, the practice of inspecting parts before they were assembled into the final product disappeared. For example, Molex, the world's number two maker of connectors, produces the connector for the central control module (computer) in all General Motors' vehicles. This is a highly sophisticated connector, yet it moves directly from Molex to the GM assembly line without passing through an acceptance sampling procedure.

Batching causes variability

The concept of reducing variability (risk) in a process extends beyond manufacturing processes. The order arrival process provides a good example. Jay Forrester, a professor at the Massachusetts Institute of Technology and father of Industrial Dynamics, observed that the process of passing orders from customer to retailer to wholesaler and finally to manufacturer could dramatically increase the variability in the original demand. That is, the variability that the manufacturer observed in orders arriving at the plant could well be an order of magnitude greater than the variability in the original demand. More recent publications refer to this as the bullwhip effect.

In essence, batching orders causes the increase in variability that one observes in a supply chain of this sort. Consider, for example, a retailer with a demand that varies from 70 to 130 and averages 100 items per week. The retailer orders every fortnight from a wholesaler, which in turn orders every month from the manufacturer. Under reasonable assumptions, it seems that the manufacturer would see a demand stream that consists of three weeks of no demand and then an order for somewhere between 340 and 460 units. Thus the manufacturer can either produce at a regular rate of around 100 units a week and carry inventory to meet the order, or invest in enough capacity to produce the 400 or so units in one go to fulfill the order.

Eliminating batching and the self-induced variability enables manufacturers to smooth output and reduce inventory levels in the supply chain. Today, manufacturers such as Procter & Gamble, the US consumer products company, receive information on actual customer demand directly from their biggest customers such as Wal-Mart, the US retail giant. Price scanners and electronic data transmission make this a simple but important process.

In manufacturing, batching (producing items in long production runs) is induced by long and costly setups. In logistics, batching (delivering several weeks of demand at one time) is caused by infrequent deliveries (long lead times). These forms of batching also produce increased variability. The attack on setup times and lead times is well documented. In the automobile industry, Japanese carmaker Toyota led the charge in reducing setup times on presses from more than 10 hours to under a minute. Just-in-time delivery systems, common in the auto industry, mean frequent deliveries. These initiatives are well known, but they are not commonly identified as approaches to reducing risk.

Reducing risk with flexibility

In many situations, process improvement as applied to manufacturing systems can reduce the variability to such an extent that the risk of a defective product is essentially eliminated. However, the demand for a number of products and services includes a level of what we might label irreducible variability, that is, variability inherently generated by customers. Operations managers face the challenge of dealing with that uncertainty in a cost-effective manner.

Delay strategies are a powerful tool in the battle against demand uncertainty. The fundamental idea behind delay strategies is simple. Think of the process of producing and delivering a product or service as being defined by a series of steps. The strategy is to delay giving the product or service a specific definition until as late in these series of steps as possible. For this discussion, there are two basic parts to the definition of a product: a specific feature that distinguishes otherwise identical items, and a specific destination for an item that is distributed among several locations. Here are two examples.

Electronics manufacturer Hewlett-Packard sells printers in western Europe. In general, a different power source and set of instructions are required for each country. In the original design, the power source was an integral part of the printer. Printers were assembled in Vancouver, Washington, packaged along with appropriate instruction materials, and shipped to European warehouses.

The process was redesigned based on the principle of delay. The printer itself now serves all countries. The power source is built into the power cord. Printers can be assembled in the US and shipped in bulk to warehouses in Europe. When an order arrives, the printer and its appropriate power cord and instructions are packaged and despatched to the customer. This change substantially reduced the level of inventory needed to satisfy uncertain demand – very important for a product that measures obsolescence in months.

The underlying force behind delay strategies is the same as that for diversified financial stock portfolios. When random variables, such as the demand from two different European countries, are added together, some of the randomness tends to "cancel out," reducing the risk.

The world's biggest maker of earthmoving equipment, Caterpillar, uses this delay strategy in designing its international parts supply system. The direct costs of having a piece of heavy earthmoving equipment out of service are large and the possible impact on the cost of a multimillion-dollar project is huge. Thus Caterpillar makes prompt delivery of repair parts central to its marketing strategy. Its supply system depends on a series of searches in the following sequence: first check the nearest local distributor, then the nearest regional warehouse, then the other regional warehouses, and finally contact the manufacturing unit. Note that inventory at the regional warehouse is not defined by location until it is called for and sent to a local distributor. The effectiveness of this supply chain is again based on the risk-reducing property of adding random demands.

Macro-risks

Companies that compete internationally may face a risk commonly called operating exposure. This is provoked by exchange-rate fluctuations. A company that incurs production costs in one currency and collects sales revenue in another suffers an operating exposure. The strategy for minimizing this risk is to find alternative ways to manage cash flows so that the risk only applies to the profit stream rather than entire revenue or cost stream. There are many examples.

Japanese carmaker Honda began supplying demand for its vehicles by importing finished products from Japan. Today, Honda's Anna engine plant near Maryville, Ohio, meets demand for Honda automobiles in North America and supplies engines for vehicles exported to Europe. An increasing proportion of the materials in these vehicles comes from US-based suppliers. In particular, in 2000, Honda is scheduled to produce more than one million engines at its Anna plant, while a new plant near Birmingham, Alabama, will start producing engines and cars in 2002. When it reaches full capacity in 2003, this plant will add another 120,000 units to Honda's capacity. Under this arrangement, both the revenues and the costs of supplying North American demand are denominated in US dollars.

Lufthansa, the German airline, collects revenues in US dollars from US customers flying to Europe. It reduces its operating exposure by increasing the proportion of servicing that it carries out on its fleet of planes when these are in the US. Thus its US dollar expenditures more closely match dollar-denominated revenues.

Political risk occurs because company assets or the future revenue stream from a project can be altered by government action. The impact can come from actions as extreme as war or a dramatic change in the government, or from something as common as the ongoing regulatory process. One extreme example of political risk was the decision by the Iranian government to seize the assets of western countries during the 1979 Islamic Revolution. In retaliation, the US froze Iranian assets under its jurisdiction, and today some $20m is still tied up.

It does not take a revolution or a war for government to have a significant impact on business. Everyday government regulations can have positive or negative effects on individual businesses. UOP, a leading US technology provider to the oil industry, has seen both sides of the coin with MTBE. This petrol additive reduces levels of air pollution from the exhausts of internal combustion engines. UOP holds patents on the MTBE production process. Thus when the government passed stricter air quality requirements, MTBE seemed to be an answer and demand for production processes and UOP's services accelerated.

However, as a news agency report in March 2000 shows, the future for the product is grim. The report said the Clinton administration was to phase out MTBE as a petrol additive because it posed a risk to public health or the environment. The report added that while MTBE reduced emissions of smog, it had been linked to groundwater pollution in California and elsewhere. The US environmental protection agency plans to "significantly reduce or eliminate" use of MTBE under legislation allowing the agency to ban chemicals "deemed to pose an unreasonable risk to the public or the environment."

Unfortunately, there are no standard techniques such as control charts that can be used to minimize political risk. However, progressive companies use tools such as decision analysis based on decision trees and scenario analysis to help them understand the risks associated with a given business opportunity. In addition, with so much cheap and fast computing capacity available, companies can use mathematical models to help the decision-making process and reduce the impact of variability. Airline seat-pricing models are a ready example of this. The ability to determine how many seats of various types to have available at different times enables airlines to make more efficient use of capacity and reduces cash-flow variability.

Nevertheless, it is hard to imagine a model that could forecast that MTBE would move from being an anti-pollutant to a pollutant. However, a good probabilistic model would certainly indicate that a product such as MTBE might fail for a variety of reasons and would therefore incorporate the high cost of such a failure. This approach provides substantial motivation for companies to invest in R&D aimed at developing new products and processes that will provide new opportunities in case of such a failure.

A deterministic view of the world, a view that does not explicitly consider risk, misses that point. Consider how the UOP example ends. Thanks to its investment in R&D, its new INALK process will make use of much of the equipment that produces MTBE. That means the demise of the additive will be much less painful to those who built MTBE plants and, coincidentally, offers new opportunities and cash flows for UOP.

In short, variability and risk are an integral part of the business of producing and delivering goods and services. There are a variety of approaches that help manage those risks and several analytic techniques that make it easier to understand them. Good managers make use of both.

Summary

Operations is a subject that covers the full design-to-delivery cycle for producing goods and services. **Gary D. Eppen** suggests that variability and risk are significant issues in manufacturing and delivery. Control charts – first seen in the 1920s and still found in plants around the world – were an early attempt to track change and, later, to reduce the variability in output caused by processes used to make goods and services. Operations risk occurs at the micro-level – production and delivery systems – and at the macro-level – currency fluctuations and political risk. This article discusses how different techniques – among which are the computer-based tools of scenario analysis, decision trees, and probability models – address these two levels of risk.

Suggested further reading

Forrester, J. (1961) *Industrial Dynamics*, Productivity Press.

Hammond, J. et. al. (1998) *Smart Choices: A Practical Guide to Making Better Decisions*, Boston, MA: Harvard Business School Press.

Schonberger, R.J. (1982) *Japanese Manufacturing Techniques*, New York: The Free Press.

Hiding behind risk in fear of innovation

by Christoph H. Loch and Arnd Huchzermeier

All over the world, financial controllers evaluate research and development projects according to the following logic: the project plan implies certain costs over time, and its target implies later revenues and profits. Neither costs nor revenues can be planned exactly, only within certain ranges, so managers have to forecast some kind of "expected value." The manager discounts back to the present to represent the time value of money (100 today is better than 100 a year from now). Typically, the "riskier" the project is – or the wider the possible range of profits and costs – the higher the risk-averse manager sets the discount "hurdle rate," or the minimum return on investment required from the project in order to win funding. This is the so-called "discounted cash flow analysis," which produces the project's financial evaluation and is taken as a measure of the project's attractiveness.

Over the past 20 years, finance and management researchers have discovered that this method is conceptually flawed because it fails to give managers the flexibility to change their course of action during the project. However, the method has a more insidious aspect: it embodies the control mentality that permeates so many organizations. Once a project plan, a budget, and a schedule are established, employees are rewarded for achieving these rather than for doing the best they can. As one manager told the authors: "In our environment, meeting targets is appreciated more than exceeding targets."

In such an environment, any deviation from the expected environment, or from the plan, is seen as a downside. "Risk" has become synonymous with "downside." Only companies that are able to evaluate upsides in risky projects, as well as downsides, can hope to achieve those upsides. If you only evaluate (and thus reward) the fulfilment of specific targets, at best that is all you will get.

Opportunities, not failures

Yet uncertainty also creates opportunities. Project teams can experiment with technical solutions, they can adjust product features, they can target additional uses by customers, or they can adjust the product's positioning. The flexibility of managers to make such adjustments in mid-course is often referred to as "real options."

Consider Figure 1: the bar represents the possible range of project outcomes, from best to worst. The planned target is somewhere in the middle, but things can go from better to worse. Unfortunately, the "best" outcome usually requires greater expenditure. However, in an organization that adheres to the control mentality, the team will not be allowed the extra budget, since this deviates from the plan. So, the upside is excluded, while the downside remains. The result is predictable: on average, the results of the project will be worse than planned.

Now, imagine that we track the project over time and if things go badly, we can decide to end it. This is called an "abandonment option." It can exclude the low end of project outcomes (the second bar in the figure) and therefore increase the project's

Figure 1: The value of decision flexibility in a project

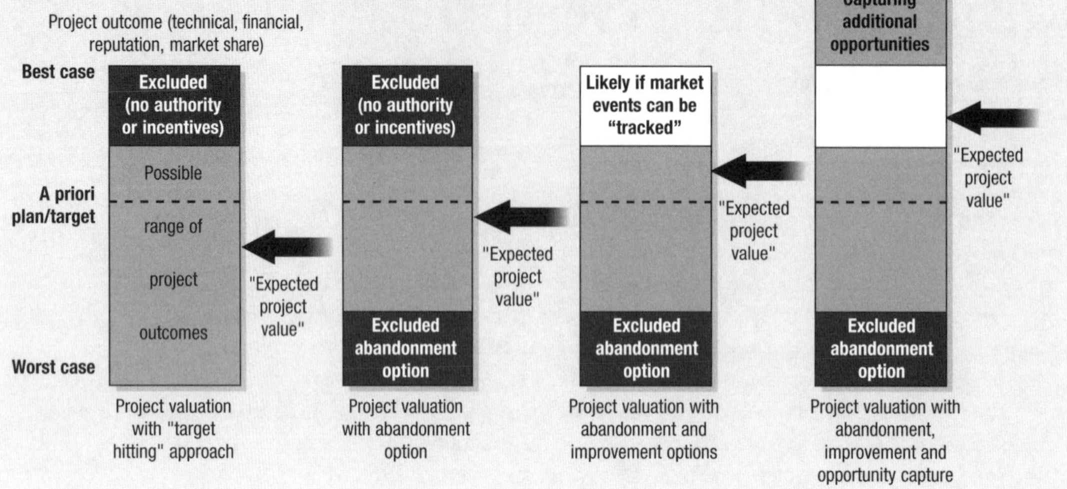

expected value. What if we can also track opportunities, and change the project's approach and activities to take advantage of them if they occur? This is called an "improvement option," shown in the third bar in the figure. It will again increase the expected project value. Finally, maybe we can even identify opportunities that were not foreseen at all at the outset (and thus not included in the "possible range"). If we can somehow identify them when they occur, and capture them, we can increase the project value even more.

Our research shows that these options can be extremely valuable. Only if the existence of flexibility during the project can be included in its valuation can R&D managers be rewarded for "chasing" opportunities for improvement and growth rather than for creating costly insurance against project failures. The latter is a source of the often-lamented lack of "entrepreneurial spirit": in a control mentality, R&D managers are not rewarded for pursuing opportunities.

Abandonment options

Formal "go/no go" decisions are widely used in projects. Work is conducted in phases, such as project requirements, feasibility, specifications, detailed development, testing, and launch or implementation. Each phase is followed by a "gate" at which senior managers can review the current chance of meeting the targets and decide, in light of this review, whether to continue. Once it becomes very unlikely that a certain "required" performance or return will be delivered, a formal decision is made to stop the project. Such a decision is quite common in the pharmaceutical industry, where development projects are terminated as soon as the negative side effects of the drugs under development are discovered.

Abandoning projects aggressively can have a powerful positive effect on an organization: stopping "losers" early frees up scarce and valuable R&D resources for new projects with a potentially higher value. This allows the organization to start more R&D projects than it has capacity to handle – as only the ones with the highest value are pushed all the way.

This does, however, require some organizational discipline. There is no room for pet projects or for adherence to past ideas because someone is not willing to admit to a mistake. There are numerous well-known cases where an organization could not muster the will to stop doomed projects. Nevertheless, once an organization has the discipline, project values go up and more projects can be started, as "bets" on the future.

Improvement options

Managers can take advantage of new events over the course of a project in three ways, which we call "improvement options": the option to improve some aspect of technical performance, the option to change the target market and the option to change the attributes of the final product. Note that this requires a delay of the "specification freeze" – the point after which the product design is no longer allowed to change. Whenever the specification is changed in a project, costs rise, because work based on the original specification has to be redone. Fear of reworking leads to a generally accepted rule of thumb: "Freeze specifications early." Once a team understands the nature of an improvement option, it can make a decision on whether to change, weighing costs against benefits. In practice, improvement options are difficult to use toward the end of a project, because that is when costs typically escalate (in consumer goods, for example, 80 percent of all development costs occur during launch).

Take CargoLifter, a German company that is developing an airship to transport very large and heavy goods, such as power generation turbines. For the first airship (due to make its maiden flight in 2001), the freeze of design specifications has been maximally postponed to take advantage of new technologies as they become available (steering mechanisms, rudders, light-weight engines and so on). In addition, the decision whether to serve the cargo market or the passenger travel market, or both, will be constantly reviewed until a short time before launch.

Consider a different example: in the early 1990s, British Telecommunications developed a telephone handset with a number display, allowing the recipient of a call to see the caller's number. After extensive market testing, however, BT realized that what customers really wanted was to know who had called them last. It changed the technical features of the project from hardware (a telephone handset) to software and service (a number the customer could ring to find out who had last called them).

The revenue model also changed completely. After launch, it turned out that BT did not even have to charge customers for calling the information number (this was the planned direct revenue comparable to selling the number-display handset). Rather, it made money from the additional call volume generated from customers immediately calling back the person responsible for the missed call. (There were also downside risks, of course: some opposed the project because people feared they could no longer make "anonymous" inquiries to companies. BT therefore allows callers to conceal their identity.) Thus, the project changed both technically and in terms of market positioning. The resulting value generated by massive additional telephone traffic was much higher than planned project value from a niche high-end handset.

What is the impact on project evaluation? Project changes as described above cannot be foreseen perfectly, but scenarios with probabilities can often be estimated. Scenarios acknowledge explicitly that the default plan may have to be changed over the course of the project. Such estimates, if available, offer two benefits:

- the organization can treat projects with a higher upside as more attractive;
- it can give the team rewards for achieving the upsides rather than just the default plan.

Opportunity capture

Opportunity capture results from a possible, but not "plannable," opportunity for a project in the future. In pharmaceutical research, active mechanisms (molecules) often have potential, but uncertain, disease applications (called "indications" in the industry) that differ from the "primary" indication for which the molecules are developed. For example, the sexual stimulant Viagra was originally developed to treat a heart condition.

It is sometimes possible to estimate the potential value from such unexpected opportunities, although the opportunities themselves cannot be planned. This sounds paradoxical, but let us consider the example of a pharmaceutical company that had to decide which of several central nervous system drug research projects it should pursue.

A serotonin-based molecule looked more attractive in the standard analysis than a calcium-based molecule. However, a researcher dug up company statistics of past projects, showing that the chance of additional indications discovered later, during clinical development, was surprisingly high. Moreover, it was much higher for the calcium molecule class than for serotonin-based molecules (60 percent against 40 percent) because of the lower "specificity" of the chemical mechanism of action for calcium. No particular additional indication could be predicted or planned, but based on the past statistics, the researchers could estimate the overall chance of one occurring at all. Moreover, the statistics showed that additional indications tended to be as profitable, on average, as the primary indications. When this was included in the financial analysis, the calcium project looked much more attractive.

The regional European airline Crossair is another example. In 1996, Crossair invested in a project to introduce a "differential global positioning system" (DGPS) in its aircraft. DGPS improves the accuracy of a standard (non-military) GPS by constantly comparing the measured co-ordinates of a nearby reference station with its true co-ordinates, and using the error to correct the measured position of the aircraft. This system could allow landing under difficult conditions at airports that did not have automatic guidance equipment and Crossair benefitted by being the first to market. In spite of successful tests and on-schedule technical completion, however, implementation of the system ultimately failed for reasons beyond the company's control.

Thus, the project seemed like a failure for Crossair. However, in 1998 it became clear that the supplier of Crossair's planes would stop making small commercial aircraft. Crossair had to find a different partner. After long discussions, it joined up with another manufacturer as a lead customer with a significant influence on the aircraft's design. Crossair's expertise with DGPS was a significant factor in achieving this, making the original DGPS investment highly valuable.

The lesson is clear: the evaluation of a project by simple financial criteria greatly underestimates its value if unforeseen opportunities are significant. The apparent paradox is that individual opportunities cannot, by definition, be included in the project evaluation, but it is often possible to estimate the overall likelihood of an opportunity, and of the range of its value. Of course, every senior R&D manager's reaction after reading this will be to say: "If I allow this value to be included in project plans, I open the floodgates to dream stories that people will tell to justify their pet projects." Thus speaks the budget and control mentality. Yet venture capitalists and entrepreneurs do this all the time: they coldly evaluate the possibility of future opportunities. The key is to make the claim transparent, to question and justify it, and to include it if the possibility is there.

Once all information about the risks is calculated, and the resulting upsides and downsides are considered, it turns out that a higher discounting hurdle for the R&D project is not necessary. It is subjective, in any case. Financial analysts orient themselves on benchmark projects with the "same" risks to set the hurdle rate, but projects with the same risks are a fiction, which makes this method as arbitrary as any other. A hurdle rate is nothing but a proxy for risks that are not at all understood. It is cleaner to discount at the company's cost of capital (or at the "opportunity cost" of the returns of other projects that are displaced by the project in question).

Make no mistake: it is expensive to put the systems and processes in place that can identify the options, monitor them during the project, and make the decision to pursue them when they arrive. However, it enhances a project's value if a company can do so. This boost to value is open to large companies as well as start-up companies, if they reassess the ways in which they consider and implement projects.

Summary

Christoph H. Loch and **Arnd Huchzermeier** suggest there are flaws in some of the tools that financial controllers use to gauge hoped-for returns from a project. Furthermore, their methods encourage a control mentality that too often regards risk as synonymous with downside, and can hamper potentially lucrative initiatives. Success in a risky project implies rewarding those who chase opportunity rather than betting against failure. R&D managers should act as entrepreneurs and be rewarded for exercising managerial flexibility, even if this conflicts with an organization's natural desire for disciplined project implementation. Lateral thinkers will also consider "opportunity capture" – of which Viagra is an example – so as not to overlook a project's unplanned potential.

Suggested further reading

Huchzermeier, A. and Loch, C. (2000) "Project management under risk: using the real options approach to evaluate flexibility in R&D," *Management Science*.

Loch, C. (1999) "Cross-Air," case study, INSEAD.

Loch, C. and Bode-Greuel, K. (2000) "Expansion options: evaluating strategic opportunities from research projects," working paper, INSEAD.

Unhealthy attitudes that endanger good performance

by Clive Smallman, Andrew Robinson and Gareth John

Much of risk management is rightly concerned with assessing and mitigating the effects of financial volatility, bad debt, and liquidity problems. Companies talk of strategic risk specific to the markets or industries within which they work, and legal risk – the province of corporate lawyers – is also well developed. Each of these areas of risk management is important, but they tend to obscure a category of risk that has the power to break companies.

Operational risks accrue in the functioning of business processes and in the behaviors of people in charge of those processes. Disasters abound in this context: Challenger, Piper Alpha, Chernobyl, Bhopal, *Exxon Valdez*, and the *Herald of Free Enterprise* all mark failures in safety or transport processes and in senior management. In finance, Barings, BCCI, Credit Lyonnais, Sumitomo, and the Korean banking collapse also represent process failures initiated wittingly and unwittingly by people. In addition, business is not alone in being prone to crisis: healthcare has also suffered from more than its share of operational failures.

Hence it is no surprise that new regulatory initiatives have rekindled interest in such risks. In the UK, for example, the change to the Combined Code on Corporate Governance now demands that companies listed on the London Stock Exchange report on significant risks to their businesses and the mitigating measures they have undertaken. Also, the British government has plans to introduce an offense of "corporate killing," a matter that may come to preoccupy public transport operators.

One area of operational risk, workplace health and safety, has been with us for quite some time, and until recently has remained relatively undervalued. Why? In answering that question, we may learn lessons that enhance our understanding of the entire field of operational risk.

The nature of the problem

Aside from environment and taxation, health and safety has more legislation devoted to it than any other business issue, yet it is not generally mentioned in the same breath as risk management. In fact, adherence to good health and safety practices is crucial not only to the efficient functioning of processes but also to corporate reputation and performance. After short cuts were reported in safety and quality procedures at British Nuclear Fuel's reprocessing plant at Sellafield, the damage to shareholders' confidence in the company eventually led half the board members to resign. Indeed, the UK's Health and Safety Executive intends to exploit the power of public humiliation by "naming and shaming" companies that disregard health and safety law.

That said, by common consent the price of life remains relatively cheap. In a recent case, Special Steel of Attercliffe, Sheffield was ordered to pay £40,000 in fines and costs after an employee was crushed to death under a bundle of steel bars. In another case, a 16-year-old lost his left arm following an incident at WFS (Iron and Steel) metal scrapyard near Barnsley, South Yorkshire. The price? £14,000 plus

£1,138 costs. OCS Cleaning South was fined £19,000 plus £3,331 costs after one of its employees fell six floors to his death during a window-cleaning operation. These may seem to be isolated incidents, but injury and illness at work occur in all sectors of industry and commerce.

In the US, the Bureau of Labor Statistics reported that in 1998 the number of fatal work injuries totalled 6,026. Approximately six million injuries were reported in private industry workplaces during 1998. If the number of people afflicted by work-related injury and illness seems a little abstract, then the economic effect of such matters may bring the issue into sharp focus.

According to the National Safety Council of America, work-related injuries in 1998 cost that country $125.1bn. That is a little over 1 percent of forecast gross domestic product (GDP), or nearly three times the combined 1998 profits of the top five Fortune 500 companies. In the UK, the Health and Safety Executive has placed the total cost to British employers of physical injury and illness in the workplace at between £9bn and £12.6bn and to society at between £14.5bn and £18.1bn, or 2.1 to 2.6 percent of GDP. Official statistics aside, in 1998 the TUC won a total of £308m in compensation for victims of workplace injury and illness, an increase of 9 percent over 1997. The picture in the developing world is worse and almost certainly understated. In summary, health and safety in the workplace matters, not simply because of ethics, but also because of economic common sense. What do aspiring and practicing managers think?

The education gap

Managers in the making have little exposure to health and safety issues, since the subject is not generally taught at business schools, nor does it appear in executive development programs. Furthermore, a straw poll of MBA students finds health and safety management regarded with barely concealed contempt – it seems it adds no value to the career aspirations of new generations of managers. In universities across America, Europe, and Australia, health and safety teaching is usually found in engineering, chemistry, or industrial technology departments. At one level this is understandable, since health and safety is not generally regarded as "glamorous"; in other words, it is rarely linked to managerial performance appraisal, except perhaps for specialists. At another level, given health and safety's inextricable link with environmental issues, it seems incongruous that it does not receive the same amount of attention as its "green" sibling, but then perhaps we come back to the issue of profile. The belated greening of industry is very definitely high on the corporate agenda, even if it appears to be passé or, worse still, cosmetic; health and safety simply does not carry the same cachet.

Health and safety is not presently on the management education agenda. Instead, it seems consigned to be a purely technical issue, despite economic evidence to the contrary, the best efforts of professional bodies to show otherwise, and a legal requirement that directors sign off on health and safety.

Managerial attitudes to health and safety

In spite of entrenched opinion against developing the management curriculum to include health and safety, research suggests that the topic may be moving up the managerial list of priorities. In a study commissioned by the British Safety Council, the market research agency MORI assessed the attitude to health and safety of 102 directors in major UK companies across a range of sectors. The findings suggest that health and safety is an important determinant of performance. While the evidence seems to indicate that it has a strong relationship with the bottom line in the form of insurance premiums, sales, or profit, it also suggests a strong link to more intangible issues, such as brand value, employee morale, and customer satisfaction.

In another study (again funded by the British Safety Council), a small panel of directors was interviewed at length. The research team found that health and safety is an important board-level issue, since it presents a serious potential threat to reputation and profits. Good health and safety performance is increasingly seen as part of corporate culture and a source of pride among managers. The arguments for health and safety are moving on from a simple preoccupation with legal compliance. Among the most sophisticated companies, health and safety is not viewed as a separate function but as part of broader initiatives that target productivity, competitiveness, and profitability.

Health and safety performance can have an impact on corporate reputation, but in a negative rather than a positive sense – a good workplace record goes unnoticed, while a poor record can place a company at a disadvantage by impairing its status in the eyes of one or more of its stakeholders. At the most senior level, companies have little idea of costs and expenditure on matters relating to health and safety. Nor do they assess their return on such investment, finding this concept unpalatable.

Best practice

As we noted earlier, part of the problem with health and safety is that it is still identified in rather narrow technical terms, despite the importance attached to it by senior managers. Often it is deemed to be the province of specialists, and more often still it is paradoxically seen as counterproductive, as yet another cost to be borne by the productive side of the business. However, good health and safety management requires systems auditing, behavioral auditing, and consultation. Such processes not only reveal minor health and safety issues, but also can demonstrate serious flaws in business processes. They are a vital part of the maintenance of an organization and its production systems.

At the highest level, the successful management of health and safety requires clear objectives, policy, and operational standards. However, these can only be fully effective where they are integrated across the value chain, from inbound logistics, through production and operations, marketing and sales, outbound logistics, to after-sales support. In other words, health and safety should have equal standing with both commercial and operational issues.

Academics Sue Cox and Robin Tait (*see* Suggested further reading) described the fundamental elements of success in health and safety. They include:

- well-defined objectives and policy;
- demonstrably strong management commitment, competence, and leadership;
- provision of adequate resources;
- agreed and justified standards and procedures;
- consultation with the workforce;
- effective performance monitoring and feedback;
- effective incident-investigation procedures;
- systematic and comprehensive selection, induction, and training processes and programs;

- promotion of principles of good job design, including positive attitudes and intrinsic motivation, responsibility and meaning;
- effective communication;
- well-practiced and effective procedures;
- the support of professionals.

The reader might note the absence of the words "health and safety" from the above list. This is purposeful since, by our earlier argument, the skills of good management should be the skills of good health and safety management. In particular, the skills of leadership and especially communication are at the absolute forefront of maintaining an excellent health and safety performance.

The key lies in balancing the development and health of people with productivity and profits, as Robert Rosen and Lisa Berger point out (*see* Suggested further reading). They describe the distinctive anatomy of a healthy company as one where ideals, goals, respect, values, and mission are shared, balanced against the need to deliver. Health and safety at work ("healthy people as appreciating assets") is singled out for particular attention. The depth and breadth of the assembled evidence are impressive. So too are the contributing organizations, including Intel, Levi-Strauss, Johnson and Johnson, and General Electric, lending significant credibility to support the central message that shareholder value can be balanced with employee (and managerial) wellbeing.

In a sense, this is an argument for broadening the base of Robert Kaplan and David Norton's concept of "the balanced scorecard," in order to include more detailed measures of the effectiveness and efficiency of internal business processes. These sit alongside measures of financial performance, customer satisfaction, and innovation and learning, with the aim of reflecting the true complexity of corporate performance, rather than the picture that relies solely on financial indicators. The reader might observe that this seems a long way from health and safety, but at the fundamental level, health and safety is about risks associated with the production or service processes of companies, and the people who operate these processes. In this sense, it reflects behaviors associated with significant operational risks.

Reflecting operational risk

As discussed earlier, the requirements of the Combined Code on Corporate Governance mean that organizations need to consider and report on their handling of significant risks. Some of this can be done with orthodox tools; much of it cannot, since the behaviors and attitudes of people are not easily assessed, especially by mathematical constructs, however sophisticated. It is time for the lessons on managing health and safety (such as auditing organizational culture in order to assess attitudes to health and safety risks) to be hauled out of their "silo" and be applied to other areas of operational risk.

Health and safety matters in organizations, and not solely because it is the "right thing." It is a genuine economic force and reflects behaviors that, left unchecked, can damage the financial standing of the company, either directly or through damage to corporate standing. We have seen that directors take this issue seriously and that certain metrics may help to mitigate the major factors. Such tools will continue to appear, but it is up to managers to use them. Furthermore, it is for management educators to put these issues on the curriculum; the trick is in demonstrating to people that there is value in health and safety, and not just for their own sake. It holds important lessons for dealing with other types of operational risks.

Being in business is risky – that is the nature of business – but why take risks that are not necessary? It makes no sense for a company that has invested in the development of its employees' knowledge, experience, and skills to take any kind of risk with their health and lives.

Summary

Workplace injuries cost US businesses $125bn in 1998, or more than 1 percent of GDP. Even so, health and safety is treated as the poor relation of core management topics, say **Clive Smallman**, **Andrew Robinson** and **Gareth John**. It has none of the glamor of strategy or marketing, and cannot readily serve the career interests of aspiring managers. New research, however, shows that executives are increasingly aware of the performance-related benefits of a good health and safety policy. They admit that safety concerns are paramount and, indeed, are willing to spend more than adequately on attaining high standards. The best companies achieve a virtuous balance between employee wellbeing and shareholder value.

Suggested further reading

Cox, S. and Tait, R. (1998) *Safety Reliability and Risk Management*, 2nd edn, London: Butterworth Heinemann.

Kaplan, R. and Norton, D.A. (1992) "The balanced scorecard," *Harvard Business Review*, January–February.

Robinson, A. and Smallman, C. (2000) "The healthy workplace," University of Cambridge Research Papers in Management, WP05.

Rosen, R. and Berger, L. (1991) *The Healthy Company*, New York: Tarcher Putnam. *See* www.healthycompanies.com for more information about the Healthy Company concept.

Product failure and the growing culture of claims

by Philip Bell

All companies are likely to produce or supply defective products at some stage. In many circumstances, the product will not cause any harm, but will merely fail to fulfill its intended function, and is usually replaced following a customer complaint. Product liability arises where the defective product causes injury to persons or damages property. All sellers of goods, whether they be manufacturers, importers, wholesalers, or retailers, may incur a liability to pay compensation for the harm caused.

Liability may arise in tort, by contract, or, in Europe, under the EU's 1985 Directive on Product Liability. Liability in tort arises from negligence and is based on the idea that a supplier of goods owes a duty to the consumer to take reasonable care. In the UK, this principle was established in 1932 (in *Donoghue v Stevenson*), when a woman became ill after drinking some of the contents of an opaque bottle that was found to include a decomposed snail. Liability in contract arises from agreements between the parties to the contract, but also includes the implied terms that apply to all agreements to sell goods – namely, that they are fit for their intended purpose and of sufficient quality to be sold.

The 1985 EU Product Liability Directive was enacted in the UK as the first part of the Consumer Protection Act 1987, and was designed to make it easier for people to bring claims against suppliers of defective products. The act meant that it was no longer necessary for a claimant to prove that someone in the chain of supply had been negligent. However, the claimant must still show that there has been injury or damage, that there is a defect in the product, and that this defect caused the injury or the damage. The directive has been introduced into the law of all member states and has also been adopted by other countries such as the Czech Republic.

How can managers defend their companies against the risk of these claims? There are several defenses, the most notable being the development risks defense. This prevents producers from being liable for defects or dangers of which they could not possibly have known as they were beyond scientific and technological knowledge at the time the product was supplied. This defense was optional in the EU Directive and applies in most European countries apart from Luxembourg, Finland, and Norway. Spain does not permit it for food and medicinal products, and France does not allow it for products derived from the human body. Elsewhere in the world, territories such as Australia and Japan allow the defense but it is unlikely to succeed in the US, where the liability laws are determined at state level. A federal bill to introduce the defense into the US was rejected in 1998.

Product liability claims against suppliers have been increasing steadily in recent years. This is not because products are becoming more dangerous. In fact, scientific and technological advances have made it easier to pinpoint defects and identify a causal link from the product to the injury or harm. In addition, safety standards have generally improved. The principal reason that claim numbers have increased is that social attitudes toward claims have changed. The public is today much more conscious of its right to bring claims against companies.

This consciousness has been fueled by solicitors' advertisements, the development of legal expenses insurance, and media coverage focussing on the entitlement of individuals to compensation. Compensation levels for personal injury continue to rise, and a recent decision by the Court of Appeal will increase the amounts awarded for pain and suffering. In the UK, moreover, the widespread introduction of conditional fee arrangements (usually referred to as "no win/no fee") in 2000 gave everyone the same access to justice. Legal aid funding for personal injury claims is no longer available.

These changes in society mirror those in the US in the mid-1980s, where companies faced a crisis over product liability. Claim numbers were spiraling out of control, as was the cost of claims, the level of which is decided by a jury. Attorneys' fees for winning an action were usually calculated as a percentage of the compensation awarded (and could be as high as 40 percent). Since jury members were aware of this, they increased the award accordingly. A strict liability basis was interpreted literally and many court decisions were based on a "deep pocket" principle – the party who was in the best position to pay the compensation was found liable. A system of "joint and several liability" also means that a supplier who may be only partially to blame can be held 100 percent liable; class actions mean that a number of producers of the same product can be liable according to their market share if the fault cannot be established against any specific producer.

The availability of insurance to many businesses became scarce and some insurers failed. While the crisis was averted by rising premiums and by the fact that many businesses chose to self-insure much of the risk, the liability system remains in place and needs to be understood by any business intending to sell products in the US.

Procedures and products

Customer satisfaction is essential to business success. It is important, therefore, for the supplier (whether a manufacturer, importer, wholesaler, or retailer) to adopt appropriate measures to avoid supplying defective products. The main responsibility for this lies with the manufacturer, but importers and wholesalers should also ensure that the products they handle and supply meet the relevant standards of safety. In addition, if goods are stored, packed, or broken down for distribution, importers and wholesalers should make sure that defects are not introduced during this phase of the product supply cycle. Retailers should make certain that, in case of a claim, they could identify their suppliers to enable the claim to be passed back down the chain of supply.

A product might be defective through an inadequate design, the use of defective raw materials, failure to provide a safety device, inadequate labeling, or poorly written instructions on use. Instructions are a common cause of problems with imported goods, but liability for any injuries suffered by the consumer is likely to rest with the importer, especially if the source of the product is outside the EU.

Methods for minimizing manufacturing defects are well known, but managers can take a few simple precautions in reviewing product safety. Committees for safety and design review with representatives from a cross-section of managerial functions should meet regularly to ensure that procedures for handling customer complaints are robust. It may only be possible to defend a claim where good documentation is available, showing clearly the history of development and proof of safety in, for example, field tests. Proper quality assurance procedures should be adopted, such as the globally recognized ISO 9000 "Quality Systems," which establish minimum requirements for product manufacture and the provision of services.

Product recall

If it becomes necessary to withdraw a product because it is discovered to be potentially dangerous, recall procedures can ensure that the faulty products are traceable. These procedures should be in place well before potential disaster strikes – it is no good trying to establish a recall plan while in the middle of a crisis. The plan should be put together as part of the management control process, but it will need to be sufficiently flexible to respond to the specific crisis.

Once the problem has been identified, managers will need to ascertain the number of batches affected, enabling them to decide whether a full recall is required or if the problem can be addressed in the field (the fault might easily be rectified at the point of wholesale or retail). Additional staff and storage space may be needed to complete the recall and modifications required to correct the problem. In some instances, products may need to be destroyed and safe disposal arranged. Where the manufacturer deals with a network of wholesalers, retailers, agents, and local subsidiaries, it may decide to impose its own conditions on the network to ensure that identical systems and records exist to improve the effectiveness of the recall.

A crucial part of any recall plan will be communications with customers and local or national press. While no manufacturer wishes to instigate a recall, good public relations is vital once the recall has been announced. The motor industry provides a good example of best practice: when car manufacturers need to recall defective vehicles, they tend to have well-rehearsed recall procedures and clear communications to customers that cause the minimum of inconvenience.

Liability insurance

Most businesses purchase product liability insurance, although there is no compulsion on them to do so. Insurance is not a substitute for risk management and insurers will expect the policy holder to have sound procedures to reduce the risk.

The insurer will take control of claims where injury to persons or damage to property is alleged, investigate the circumstances, and settle the claim in the most efficient manner. Where liability on the supplier is clear, the aim will be to settle as quickly as possible and on the most favorable terms. Where liability is disputed, the insurer funds the cost of any litigation. If compensation is ultimately awarded, it will be funded by the insurer.

Policies contain a limit of indemnity that represents the maximum amount the insurer will pay in any period of insurance (usually 12 months). If a business wishes to purchase protection above the level the insurer may wish to offer, extra insurance can usually be obtained by means of "excess product liability insurance." This means that the insurer will respond to claims in the event of exhaustion of the indemnity limit under the main policy. In many instances, the legal costs of defending claims are payable by the insurer in addition to the policy limit.

In deciding on the appropriate level to purchase, it is important to remember that a defective batch may lead to many claims. Serious injury claims can take a number of years to settle and will be paid in accordance with the law prevailing at the time, not when the injury happened. Compensation for serious personal injury claims can amount to several millions of pounds, particularly where permanent healthcare is required and there is a significant loss of future earnings. Products such as pharmaceuticals rarely produce claims, but if they do, the number and cost can be substantial. Products containing asbestos have also cost the insurance industry many millions of pounds in compensation.

Insurance will not cover all of the financial consequences to the business. There can be serious brand repercussions arising from the supply of defective products, valued customers and contracts may be lost, and there could be a serious interruption to production, particularly if the offending product needs to be redesigned or new safety features added. Valuable management time may be diverted to investigate the circumstances or to oversee a recall. It is quite possible for the uninsured losses to exceed the claims for compensation, which could be devastating for some businesses – particularly those that concentrate on a single product line or that are surrounded by competitors keen to exploit the situation.

European developments

The EU issued a communication explaining its position on an element of policy called the precautionary principle. The principle originated in Germany in the 1970s as an element of domestic policy, and was first recognized at international level in the World Charter for Nature, adopted by the UN General Assembly in 1982. Subsequently, it was incorporated into various international conventions on environmental protection.

The basic objective of the principle is to assist in the management of risk. Among its aims, the communication seeks to build a common understanding of how to assess, appraise, manage, and communicate risks that science is not yet able to evaluate fully. It also seeks to establish guidelines for applying the principle. The communication is intended to inspire debate on how it might be applied within the EU and internationally.

The principle potentially poses a fundamental challenge to the conventional legal and political conventions on safety concerns and to the extent to which we have come to rely on science to provide us with answers. No one yet knows how the principle will be applied in practice or the scope of compliance. So what is the nature of this potential change? In a consultation paper issued by the EU in 1999, it was suggested that courts would be justified in inferring or assuming a causal link between the injury or damage and the defect, and would place the responsibility wholly on the producer to disprove the link. Claims are unlikely to succeed at present, but if new legislation reverses the burden of proof, it could encourage many more claims, including many spurious and dubious ones, particularly in areas where scientific knowledge is not particularly well advanced. A liability to pay compensation due to the inability of a producer to show what scientists have not yet discovered could have serious consequences for business, insurers, and product innovation.

At the moment, insurers do not believe there is any need for such action, as the question of proof is not a major issue when dealing with product liability claims. Since so many claims are settled without recourse to the courts, it is thought, there is little reason to rush headlong into change.

Controversially, the consultation paper also discusses the possible abolition of the development risks defense. Innovation and development always include a certain residual risk, which – being unforeseen and unknown by industry – is difficult for insurers to underwrite. Indeed, abolition of the development risks defense would seem to contradict the EU communication on the precautionary principle, which suggests that where the producer had gone through due process to ensure that a product was safe according to the current state of scientific and technical knowledge, it would be inequitable to attribute liability or blame to the producer if the product subsequently proved to be harmful – particularly if the producer was complying with a government permit or standard.

Europe's influence in the area of product liability will undoubtedly increase in the next decade. In future, it will be critical for business to embrace the concept of product safety within its culture if it has not yet done so, to protect its commercial interests as well as those of its insurer. Society determines safety standards and appropriate levels of compensation, and the combined impact will continue to challenge businesses to raise their standards.

Summary

No company is completely immune from the possibility of product flaws, writes **Philip Bell**. Usually no harm is done and faulty products can easily be replaced. In cases where injury occurs, however, companies can face compensation bills running into billions of pounds. Further, Europeans are following North Americans in becoming more aware of their rights in product liability cases and are less willing to tolerate corporate mistakes. Manufacturers (and importers and wholesalers) should establish robust design and safety systems, and thoroughly test their procedures for product recall in case of a major liability problem.

6

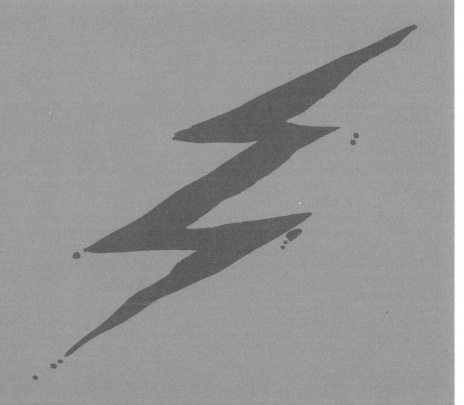

REGULATION AND POLITICAL RISK

Contributors

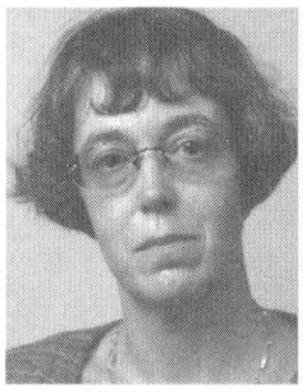

Bridget Hutter is Peacock Professor of Risk Management at the London School of Economics and Director of the Centre for the Analysis of Risk and Regulation. Her current research interests focus on corporate responses to regulation. More generally, she is interested in the regulation of economic life, most especially the control of risk in business organizations.

Marvin Zonis is a professor at the University of Chicago Graduate School of Business, where he teaches international political economy, leadership, and business strategy in the era of e-commerce. He also heads Marvin Zonis & Associates, political risk consultants.

Michael Power is P.D. Leake Professor of Accounting at the London School of Economics and Director of the Centre for the Analysis of Risk and Regulation. His research interests include auditing, internal control, and corporate governance.

Sam Wilkin is director of research and development at Marvin Zonis & Associates. He specializes in political risk analysis, management, and strategy for direct investors.

Julian Randall is a partner in the commercial litigation and professional liability team of the international law practice Barlow Lyde and Gilbert.

Martin Stone is risk analysis director for Control Risks Group. He is a specialist on Algerian affairs and Islamic extremism, and author of *The Agony of Algeria* (Columbia University Press, 1997).

Bridget Treacy is a partner in the corporate and finance team of the international law practice Barlow Lyde and Gilbert. She is also a member of the firm's IT law and e-commerce groups.

Philip M. Nichols is an associate professor of legal studies at the Wharton School of the University of Pennsylvania.

Contents

Risk management and business regulation 165
Bridget Hutter, London School of Economics
Michael Power, London School of Economics
Edicts on running businesses are unfashionable. This article describes the complex relationship between regulators and risk managers.

Digital buccaneers caught in a legal web 169
Julian Randall, Barlow Lyde and Gilbert
Bridget Treacy, Barlow Lyde and Gilbert
This article focusses on the legal dangers for aspiring e-businesses. It warns of national differences in e-commerce law and contractual, jurisdictional, and other risks.

Driving defensively through a minefield of political risk 176
Marvin Zonis, University of Chicago Graduate School of Business
Sam Wilkin, Marvin Zonis & Associates
Multinationals often monitor politics in countries where they operate. This article recommends a comprehensive framework for analyzing political risk.

Scourges that strike at the heart of global business 181
Martin Stone, Control Risks Group
For many companies, kidnap, terrorism, war, and crime are the biggest security threats they face. This author offers advice for managers operating in danger zones.

Dealing with an eruption of corruption 187
Philip M. Nichols, Wharton School, University of Pennsylvania
Bribery is an insidious problem that can blight companies and the wider economy, but some useful responses can be advocated.

Introduction

While financial markets have been subject to deregulation in recent times, governments in industrialized countries continue to legislate widely on corporate matters. The outcome of such legislation is partly determined by the relationship between companies and regulators, as the first article in this section reveals. In a global economy, political and security risks must figure highly in multinational companies' assessments. Here authors examine the issues of kidnap, political instability, terrorism, and bribery.

Risk management and business regulation

by Bridget Hutter and Michael Power

The regulation of business and corporate risk management are inextricably related. Regulation is one way in which risks are managed in modern societies, and corporate risk management is a form of self-regulation, although senior management would not articulate it in such terms. In practice, the distinction between regulation and risk management is becoming blurred as risk management blueprints influence the design of regulatory systems. This is particularly evident in the latest thinking of the UK Financial Services Authority, the country's chief financial regulator, which is required to maintain market confidence and protect consumers. The FSA's new operating framework builds on its earlier, risk-based approaches to regulation, and recognizes that the nature and intensity of its relationship with a regulated firm will depend on the risk assessment of that firm. Accordingly, the FSA's approach to regulation is converging with the risk management practice of the very entities that it regulates.

Demands on governments to regulate risks are increasing. The by-products of new developments in such areas as food technology, public transport systems, e-commerce, and lifetime financial planning may be unintended dangers to health, safety, and physical and financial security. Add to this concerns with the global impact of financial instability and environmental pollution, and it is clear that risk permeates regulatory agendas. Governments have typically intervened to regulate these risks, many of which are created by organizations rather than by nature, but they are hampered by two important factors. First, state regulation tends to be national, or at best regional, in scope, whereas risks are increasingly transnational in character. Second, the capacity of states to design and implement effective regulation of risks is constrained by the need to work with regulated entities.

Regulatory practice can take many forms. State regulation through the use of the law – popularly known as command-and-control regulation – is perhaps the best-known method. It is also the least loved by business and, according to regulation theorists, not always successful. But this is just one form of regulation and there are many others. For example, existing commercial incentives may be exploited, or the state may co-opt the self-governing powers of the company. Systems of "enforced self-regulation" combine state and corporate regulation; they seek to penetrate the everyday life of the company and to harness its management tools in such a way as to align regulatory objectives and corporate strategy.

This style of regulation is now visible in many areas, such as environment, health and safety, and corporate governance. It includes the code introduced in the UK following the governance lessons learned from the collapse of Robert Maxwell's business empire in 1991. Most advanced industrialized countries rely on a regime of standards requiring companies to develop their own risk management systems and internal rules. An important area where regulatory systems and risk management meet is the corporate internal control system.

Internal control

For many years, internal control was largely a private affair for organizations, at best only loosely connected to formal regulatory systems and a matter of interest to a few humble corporate specialists, mainly auditors and quality control experts. However, this situation has changed dramatically. Systems of enforced self-regulation increasingly focus on the technical features of internal control systems, such as those for financial and environmental regulation.

In the 1990s, internal control also moved to the center of discussions about corporate governance. In 1991, an influential conceptual framework for thinking about internal control (the "COSO" framework) was developed in North America by the professional services firm Coopers & Lybrand under the auspices of the Treadway Commission. COSO (the Committee of Sponsoring Organizations) and other similar documents broadened the concept of control, making possible the alignment of corporate governance and risk management. In the UK, this convergence of thinking about governance, risk management, and regulation is epitomized by the Turnbull report.

The Turnbull report and its underlying thinking support a growing market for corporate advice in the public and private sectors, both in the UK and overseas. Its significance lies both in the specific recommendations it contains and in the regulatory style that it signifies: the concept of control is broadened, tightly linked to risk analysis, and enjoined as an imperative of "good" management. Disparate demands for risk management to become a senior executive preoccupation coalesce in Turnbull and in its support for a top-down, integrated corporate risk management policy.

The management of compliance

Although risk and regulation are increasingly intertwined, they are not perfectly aligned, so compliance remains an important issue for organizations. Yet it is not always clear what constitutes compliance. For example, regulatory laws are often vague, involving broad statutory standards and delegating a good deal of discretion to regulatory officials. Regulation is typically designed to be adaptable and flexible to changing technology, knowledge, and the circumstances of individual companies and sites, so it necessarily leaves scope for interpretation. Thus, compliance is fundamentally a creative process involving negotiation and interaction between regulatory agencies and those they regulate.

Determining what is meant by compliance involves assessing the risks associated with any given activity and their acceptability. One of the central difficulties of regulating industrial and commercial activity is finding a balance between the purpose of regulation – for instance controlling risks to health and safety at work or reducing risks to the environment – and its cost. In practice, regulators refer to the absolute and relative monetary costs of regulatory demands and the general economic climate, both nationally and regionally, and between sectors and companies.

Regulation, not risk elimination, runs through the legal system, including the courts. For example, judgment was recently handed down in the UK case of the oil tanker *Sea Empress*. In February 1996, an inexperienced port authority pilot ran the tanker aground at the entrance to Milford Haven estuary, spilling 72,000 tonnes of crude oil and causing widespread environmental damage to the Pembrokeshire southern coastline of Wales. The Milford Haven Port Authority was fined £4m costs, the judge noting that the level of the fine was based on the authority's ability to pay and the gravity of the pollution. But the judge added that he sympathized with arguments that the local area could suffer "a double economic blow" with the incident and the level of the fine. In March 2000, the Court of Appeal reduced the fine to £750,000 on similar grounds.

Another important issue about the meaning of compliance is that our understanding of risk changes, as does public and managerial tolerance of risk. As the case of BSE shows, expert opinion may be divided over the sources and causes of risk and theories about both can change over time. Moreover, political factors may intervene in determining acceptable levels of risk. The initial link between BSE and the brain disease CJD was made on the basis of 10 Britons dying from a new strain of CJD. This led to a Europe-wide ban on imports of British beef and a vigorous campaign by the British government to challenge the legality of the ban and the scientific evidence on which it was based. Compliance is also determined by regulators' knowledge of organizations, that is, their specific knowledge about a site, its machinery, processes, equipment, and personnel.

Based on experience and training, the regulator will make assessments of the organization's compliance "culture" – its commitment to regulatory objectives, its record of compliance, the quality of its management, and its capacity to comply. These considerations influence the regulator's motives to intervene in a company's affairs and are often formalized as guidance for regulatory officials. For example, the UK Environment Agency's criteria for prosecution include the extent to which non-compliance could have been foreseen, the intent of the offender, the history of offending, and the offender's attitude. The application of these criteria will, of course, depend on the willingness and ability of an organization to self-regulate.

So, what does this mean for "compliance risk management"? If compliance is emergent – the outcome of negotiation and interaction – businesses may be genuinely unsure what compliance is. Furthermore, companies and the managers within them may differ greatly in their understanding of regulation. Research shows that while small businesses are often confused about regulation, large companies use regulators as a source of information. Small companies tend to be less able to self-regulate and more ready to accept regulatory requirements, whereas large companies are more inclined to challenge regulation. Attempts to co-opt corporate risk management systems or to guide and advise them are not well understood by businesses, which tend to perceive regulators in a policing role.

Studies of corporate responses to occupational health and safety regulation suggest that there may be wide variations in the attitudes and expectations of safety departments in large companies. The reason is that guidance about compliance with occupational health and safety regulation is differentially interpreted across a large organization. A case study of the UK's former nationalized rail company British Railways found that departments implemented the general health and safety commitment in their own way. Consequently, there was no standard response across the organization. Poor communication emerged as a main obstacle to successful compliance risk management. Fragmentation of the company meant that important risk information was kept at a departmental level. More generally, when risk information is kept isolated in separate divisions or departments of an organization, understanding and decision making at the senior level become impossible.

The implications

These examples suggest that compliance is a complex phenomenon at the interface between risk and regulation. Regulation is both a form of risk management and a source of compliance risk. As regulation seeks to operate increasingly with the grain of organizational life, risk management in its broadest sense represents the continuation of regulatory programs within businesses. Accordingly, the inside of the organization is increasingly recognized as a "regulatory space" in which the various facets of compliance are determined.

The process of convergence between regulatory ambitions and organizational priorities is not smooth or guaranteed. Corporate responses to regulation are poorly understood, and little is known about the extent and normality of compliance. The regulatory process involves multiple agents: inspectors are co-opted into organizational processes at the same time as aspects of risk management are outsourced. Compliance officers and corporate risk managers wrestle with their dual roles as regulator and as internal adviser. Auditors and consultants also play an increasingly influential role in determining the understanding and management of compliance.

In short, the corporation is becoming an arena for intense competition as internal and external auditors, legal specialists, health and safety officers, inspectors, and others seek a pre-eminent foothold in the market for internal advice, and in the market for defining regulatory compliance. Accordingly, the policy agenda for the future is to use these resources to improve the alignment of corporate risk management practices and regulatory regimes. Yet, since the active market for interpretation of compliance is global, the capabilities and horizons of national regulators are likely to remain challenged in the future.

Summary

The interaction of government and business in regulating risks is complex and subtle, write **Bridget Hutter** and **Michael Power**. The state can impose rules directly by "command-and-control" legislation or can encourage internal control systems, such as that described by the UK's Turnbull report. When judging whether a company has complied with the rules for risk management, regulators have wide discretion to take into account its particular circumstances and its "culture" of compliance. Moreover, regulators and corporate risk managers must play a dual role – as both the enforcers of compliance and internal advisers to the process of risk management.

Suggested further reading

The Committee of Sponsoring Organizations (1992) *Internal Control – Integrated Framework.*

Hutter, B.M. (1997) *Compliance: Regulation and Environment*, Oxford: Clarendon Press.

Institute of Chartered Accountants in England and Wales (1999) *Internal Control: Guidance for the Directors of Listed Companies Incorporated in the United Kingdom*, London: ICAEW.

Power, M. (2000) "The new risk management," *European Business Forum*, 1(1): 60–61.

Digital buccaneers caught in a legal web

by Julian Randall and Bridget Treacy

It is tempting to think of the internet as a wild and lawless frontier where a buccaneering spirit is the most important quality a business can have. In reality, the internet allows us to do what we have always done more quickly and cheaply, and sometimes in different ways. Stepping into cyberspace is no reason to abandon the worthy disciplines of planning and risk avoidance that lie behind most successful businesses.

E-commerce has yet to spawn its own laws or legal precedents on any great scale. In fact, one of the main sources of e-commerce risk is that there are too many laws governing activity on the internet. A danger for any internet business is that it inadvertently infringes the established laws of the countries in which it trades, and fails to take account of new patterns of trading that might bring it up against well-established, but unfamiliar, legal issues.

These difficulties are well exemplified by internet trade across the EU. The drive to harmonize the economies of EU states has focussed on creating a level playing field for the manufacture and sale of goods and services across international boundaries. Until now, it has not been possible to export retail services without significant investment in outlets in the foreign market or a well-developed mail-order system. In setting up such a structure, retailers must also investigate local laws, taxes, and requirements.

Websites, by contrast, are accessible from countries of which the owner of the website may never have heard and with whose laws they may be unfamiliar. This can cause difficulties for the unwary, even when dealing with such a leading internet economy as the US. For example, the UK airline Virgin Atlantic ran into difficulties when advertising (via its UK-based website) a transatlantic fare in terms that are entirely conventional in the UK (such as "Fly from London to New York for £*x* return, plus taxes and booking fee – please contact your local travel agents for details"). In the US, however, it is not enough simply to refer to the fact that additional charges are payable. A company must set out the exact cost of the taxes and booking fees. While Virgin Atlantic incurred only a relatively trivial fine, the adverse publicity was potentially damaging. Likewise, the consumer protection laws of Germany put significant restrictions on the discounts and other benefits that a retailer can offer to consumers.

New legislation should attempt to address this essential feature of e-commerce – that it cuts across different taxation, regulatory, and consumer protection regimes in different jurisdictions. At present, it is not clear to what extent legislative proposals will succeed. Attempts within the EU to harmonize retail markets are in their infancy – it is politically difficult for elected governments to change their consumer protection laws to accommodate the needs of international business or the agendas of other countries. EU members are unlikely to share the same goals over e-commerce legislation. Even if they are able to agree, they may not wish to do so at the risk of losing control over the way in which business is conducted and, in particular, the way in which it is taxed.

Policing the problems of data protection

The internet may have greatly facilitated global commerce and communication, but differences in national attitudes to data protection are causing legal problems for companies that wish to operate across national borders. In the EU, there is broad agreement that individuals have certain rights over information concerning them and that companies should be prevented from collecting, using, sharing or selling those data without their permission. The EU directive on data protection, passed in October 1998, laid down four basic principles:

- Individuals should be able to obtain and make corrections to information that is held about them by companies or institutions.
- Companies must gain their customers' consent before storing or using information about them.
- Companies must only use data for the original purpose that was expressed at the time of collection, unless the customer agrees otherwise.
- Companies must not obtain more data on individuals than they need to carry out their stated purpose.

Crucially, the directive also provides that data should not be sent to countries that do not follow the same rules. That includes the US, which has no federal laws governing the "right to privacy" in commercial transactions and no independent ombudsman on data issues. US attitudes surrounding the use of personal data are generally more relaxed than those of the EU – companies have routinely used transaction records and mailing lists without gaining the permission of the relevant consumers. There are also few restrictions governing the secondary use of data in the US. Credit-card companies, for instance, are not obliged to ask cardholders if they can use their data for other purposes, nor even to tell them if they have already done so.

These national differences on data privacy have profound consequences for industries that operate in Europe and the US. When, for example, a European airline wishes to arrange a connecting flight for a passenger via a US airline, compliance with the directive entails that it gains the passenger's permission before using the relevant data to complete the transaction. In theory, any company with subsidiaries in Europe and the US could face prosecution for exchanging data on individuals without authorisation.

For two years, no agreement could be reached that satisfied both sides. In March 2000, however, EU and US negotiators agreed to recommend a system of self-regulation – the so-called "safe harbour" principle – under which US companies will sign up to certain standards of privacy on a voluntary basis. These companies would then be deemed to comply with EU privacy rules and would be able to conduct business in Europe. Any violation of the rules would trigger sanctions against the offending company. At the time of writing, the scheme awaits approval by the US authorities, EU member states and the European Parliament.

There are a number of current initiatives within the EU, including:

- the Electronic Signatures Directive, which promotes a framework for the legal recognition of electronic signatures;
- the E-Commerce Directive, which seeks to encourage e-business by dealing with a number of issues, notably that of which country's laws will govern the online provision of goods and services;
- the Distance Selling Directive, which seeks to provide additional protection (including a seven-day cooling-off period) to consumers who purchase goods and services without coming face to face with the supplier;
- the Distance Marketing of Financial Services Directive, which seeks to regulate the long-distance sales of financial services;
- the Data Protection Directive, which seeks to strengthen protection for those whose details or data might be held online (*see* box).

In the UK, the Electronic Commerce Bill seeks to promote e-business by establishing a system of independent approval for providers of cryptography services, and permitting electronic signatures as evidence to prove the authenticity of a document.

Whether any of these initiatives will meet the need for legal harmonization across different jurisdictions of the EU remains to be seen. In any event, until there is worldwide harmonization of laws applicable to those trading on the internet, any business making use of the internet should be aware of the risks.

The risks of going online

In the age of e-commerce, the speed with which competitors emerge and technology brings change to accepted modes of business can put pressure on managers to move quickly to adopt an e-business strategy. It is imperative that organizations take appropriate steps to manage the associated legal risks. Many of the issues with which internet businesses grapple can be avoided or minimized by an early assessment of the risks.

During the early stages of planning and implementing an e-business strategy, some legal advice will be required, particularly in relation to software development and/or web development contracts, contracts with IT consultants, and systems integration contracts. The key issues are to define the services to be provided, to set milestones for the completion of those services, and to agree acceptance-testing criteria and procedures. Failure to do so can result in some costly remedial work and delays.

More generally, companies should consider four kinds of legal risks before embarking on an e-commerce strategy: contractual risks, jurisdictional risks, intellectual property rights, and internal or content-related risks.

Contractual risks

There is no legal obstacle to entering into a contract over the internet unless the contract is one of the narrow category of agreements that has to be concluded by a deed or in writing. Again, however, this is an area where companies can be caught out by the requirements of local law. A forthcoming e-commerce bill in the US will provide for digital signatures to be given the force of law (in the US). The EU's E-Commerce Directive at present requires that all electronic contracts be given the same force as written contracts. These provisions, if enacted, will help avoid misunderstandings in those jurisdictions, but may also create an expectation in Europe and the US that electronic contracts are always enforceable, when in fact they will not be valid in some parts of the world.

A major contractual risk – often overlooked – is the need to agree the terms on which parties do business over the internet. If a company sets up a website to carry out transactions, the website must be designed in such a way that customers cannot place an order unless they have first agreed to be bound by the terms and conditions on which the business is trading. These terms and conditions must be accessible to customers before any order is placed, and ideally should require customers to signal their acceptance (for example, by clicking on an icon).

Crucially, the terms of trading should incorporate a clause excluding or limiting the amount of damages that can be obtained for breach of contract (which is often the most important term of the contract). Most developed legal systems require that any clause seeking to exclude or limit damages should be brought clearly to the attention of the potential customer. In determining whether an exclusion clause is reasonable for the purposes of, say, the Unfair Contract Terms Act in the UK, a court will examine how clearly it is incorporated. If it is tucked away in a difficult-to-access part of the website, for instance, the clause may be ineffective.

It is also essential for any company offering goods and services over the internet to control the contractual process by inviting customers to make the contractual "offer," which the company is then free to accept or reject. The alternative is for the company to make the contractual offer through the website, which is, in effect, an offer to the whole world, which the customer can then accept or reject.

In 1999, for example, the UK retailer Argos inadvertently offered television sets for sale on its website at a price of £3 rather than £300. Unsurprisingly, the site was besieged with orders, which Argos subsequently refused on the basis that the website was analogous to a shop window display (in legal terms, "an invitation to treat"), and that the contractual "offer" was not made by Argos's display of goods but by the customer's placement of an order. That left Argos in the position of retaining the discretion to accept or reject any orders placed through the website. In that case, the submission of an order did not bind Argos to a contract – if the website had been structured otherwise (as many are), it would have done.

Paying careful attention to contractual controls is also important if there is a jurisdiction in which a business does not wish to trade. By controlling the contractual process, a business can reject offers received from customers with, say, a delivery address in a particular jurisdiction.

Jurisdictional risk

One of the legal challenges associated with any international business is to ensure that the company's preferred legal system applies to particular transactions. Certain jurisdictions, notably the US, have already demonstrated a willingness to exercise jurisdiction over internet-related disputes, often where the link to that country is, at best, tenuous. This is a significant risk factor, given the vagaries of jury awards and the possibility of punitive damages in the US.

Generally, transactions entered into via the internet will be governed by the same rules of private international law as any other cross-border transaction. By the same conventions, therefore, it is advisable for companies to stipulate in the contract which countries' law will apply and the jurisdiction in which any dispute should be dealt with (although the companies' choice of jurisdiction may not always prevail).

From a risk management perspective, it is preferable for parties to specify jurisdiction and governing law in their contracts. Considerations to take into account when selecting the jurisdiction include:

- How will the choice of law be applied within the chosen jurisdiction?
- Can the outcome of a dispute in the chosen jurisdiction be predicted with any certainty?
- How long will it take to reach a resolution of a dispute in the chosen jurisdiction?
- What are the costs of proceeding in the chosen jurisdiction?
- Will a judgment in the chosen jurisdiction be enforceable against the potential defendant?
- Where are the defendant's assets?

Intellectual property rights

While it may seem obvious, organizations often overlook the fact that intellectual property rights are territorial in nature; securing a trademark within one country does not mean that one is entitled to use that trademark in all other jurisdictions. Setting up a website without registering a trademark in key jurisdictions puts a business at risk of infringing another's right to use the same trademark. It is therefore important to secure intellectual property rights in key jurisdictions and, having done so, to defend those rights.

An unresolved issue in this sphere is whether new methods of business will be universal, as one might expect, or whether the effect of traditional law will put a brake on such developments. Article 27 of the World Trade Organization's agreement on Trade Related Aspects of Intellectual Property Rights suggests that patents should be available for any inventive process, even if that process is simply a novel way of delivering a service over the internet. We may therefore see a growth in monopolies by patent of methods of conducting business over the net (and, indeed, other IT database systems).

Internal or content-related risk

Email encourages informality and speed in communication. In these circumstances, defamatory material is more likely to be disseminated and there is a greater risk of breach of confidence and breach of copyright.

From the perspective of an employer, giving employees access to email gives rise to a risk to the employer of being prosecuted for defamatory emails sent by employees. The risk is similar in nature to that of an employee writing a defamatory letter on a company letterhead, yet it is much higher by virtue of email's speed and relative informality. The UK insurance group Norwich Union and the utility company British Gas have been involved in claims that they are vicariously liable for the defamatory emails of their employees. From a risk management perspective, companies are well advised to ensure that an email protocol is adopted and enforced.

Companies should also be wary of occasional instances of staff downloading offensive or sexually explicit material that is displayed as a screensaver. Employers should be aware that permitting the display of such material in the workplace might result in a claim from other employees for sexual harassment.

Innocent assistance

Businesses such as internet service providers or chatroom hosts often permit the posting or publication by others of material on their website. This places these businesses under significant additional risk, and it is not yet clear to what extent these passive disseminators of information have an obligation to monitor content posted on their website.

This risk is illustrated by the recent English case, *Godfrey v Demon Internet*. Defamation in England involves the making of a defamatory statement, referring to the victim, which is "published" to a third party. In the case of *Godfrey v Demon Internet*, Dr. Laurence Godfrey discovered that "squalid, obscene and defamatory" material about him had been posted on a virtual noticeboard provided by internet service provider Demon Internet. Dr. Godfrey contacted Demon Internet's managers and asked them to remove the offending material; they refused and Dr. Godfrey sued for libel. The court held that, while Demon Internet was not the author or the "publisher," it had disseminated the information and, once it was notified of the libel, it could not be said to have taken reasonable care that it was not contributing to the publication of the libel. On this basis, the defence of "innocent dissemination" was not available to Demon Internet.

On the face of it, it is only fair that Dr. Godfrey should have some redress if he faces "squalid" defamation, and that an internet service provider should not be able simply to ignore his plight. However, any requirement that an internet service provider must vet what appears on its site threatens the free flow of information that is a fundamental characteristic of the internet. Any complaint about any message on a service provider's site will, it is to be assumed, be enough to notify it officially, and it will then be required to make a decision as to whether the material is defamatory. Reaching such a judgment would involve management time and, often, legal costs – the practical solution must be simply to delete any information about which a complaint is made, thus potentially stifling the free transfer of information on the net.

In the US, the First Amendment right to free expression has created a different attitude in this area. Section 509 of the Telecommunications Decency Act 1997 provides that a service provider is not to be considered as a "publisher" of material provided by a third party, and also protects the service provider in relation to any actions taken by it in good faith to restrict access to material that the provider might consider "obscene, lewd, lascivious, filthy, excessively violent, harassing, or otherwise objectionable."

The practical effect of this enactment was seen in the 1997 case of *Zeran v AOL*. The US service provider AOL was sued in respect of a bulletin-board message posted by an unconnected third party. The court ruled that the effect of the act was to create "federal immunity to any cause of action that would make [the service provider] liable for information originating with a third party user of the service." The court stated that all claims seeking to construe the role of internet service provider as being analogous to that of a publisher would likewise be barred.

The practical effect of this might well be that a US-based internet service provider growing up under the protection of the Telecommunications Decency Act might not appreciate that its exposure to defamation actions around the world is very much greater than at home. It could also be forgiven for failing to realize that one publication might lead to numerous actions around the world. Dr. Godfrey has launched a number of similar claims, which have reportedly already brought him an estimated A$10,000 in an out-of-court settlement from an Australian PC user group and other victories against New Zealand Telecom and Toronto Star's On-line Organization.

Further, providers of auction sites and exchanges that facilitate the sale of goods or services may, in the absence of very rigorous self-policing, find that they are in fact facilitating the sale of illegal material. In the US, Yahoo! is reportedly facing legal proceedings from Japanese computer games companies Sega and Nintendo alleging that counterfeit games are being sold through its online auction site. More recently, the International League Against Racism and Anti-Semitism has issued proceedings in Paris against Yahoo!, claiming that it is hosting auctions of Nazi-related paraphernalia. In France the sale or display of items that incite racism, including Nazi paraphernalia, is illegal.

Conclusion

The internet may have the potential to turn the world into a single marketplace in which transactions are completed between businesses or sales are made to consumers that are very difficult to pin down to a particular jurisdiction (or for interested jurisdictions to tax or to regulate). This is exciting to some and, no doubt, worrying to others, but it seems unlikely that individual states will be able to stand against the tide. A comprehensive global approach to regulation, policing, and, if necessary, taxing of e-commerce is clearly highly desirable. Until such structures are in place, however, any business stepping into cyberspace must be aware that the fact that its managers have never heard of an arcane piece of local law in a far-flung country is likely to cut very little ice with the local lawyers.

The risks of infringing those laws and the other risks described in this article can be minimized (if not, perhaps, eliminated) by careful planning at an early stage, in particular as to the contractual terms of trading and jurisdiction.

Summary

The internet holds out great opportunities for both start-ups and established businesses, but creates a range of legal pitfalls, say **Julian Randall** and **Bridget Treacy**. If a company offers goods or services internationally over a website, it may find itself infringing the laws of any number of countries in which it trades. Contractual difficulties may also arise from transactions conducted over the internet, particularly when the terms of the contract are not clearly stated and readily accessible to users. Cross-border transactions that fail to specify the laws under which the transaction takes place can create jurisdictional problems, and trademarks or intellectual property registered in one country may have no force in others. Finally, the authors sound a warning to companies that freely transfer their customers' data across borders – different states can have radically different laws governing data privacy.

Driving defensively through a minefield of political risk

by Marvin Zonis and Sam Wilkin

Political risks come in many forms. Consider these recent cases:

- An international energy company invested in Indonesia in the early 1990s, during that country's long-running economic boom. By involving a crony of then President Suharto in the project, the company was able to negotiate highly favorable contract terms with the state-owned electricity utility. Its projected rates of return were excellent. Then, in 1997, the Asian economic crisis hit. In the wake of widespread political instability and economic meltdown, the state-owned electricity utility was effectively bankrupt, running a deficit of $2.6bn. Not only was the foreign energy company forced into a lengthy contract renegotiation process, but also contract terms (and therefore rates of return) were likely to be far less favorable than initially projected and government lawyers were marshaling a corruption case.
- A Canada-based energy company decided to undertake a major expansion of a power project to produce new energy supplies for Canada and for export to the state of New York in the US. However, the project soon ran foul of both Indian tribes and environmentalist non-governmental organizations (NGOs). Both these groups waged a sophisticated media campaign against the project. The company attempted to respond with a public relations campaign of its own, but was unsuccessful. Eventually, the New York Power Authority pulled out, depriving the project of 30 percent of its expected revenues and leaving the Canadian company with substantial sunk costs on its books.
- In the early 1990s, several US energy companies entered India. The country suffered no major economic crisis or political instability, but by 2000, a majority of the power-generation projects in the country had been abandoned. One US company was forced to obtain 150 bureaucratic clearances for its project and the state government renegotiated its power-purchase agreement four times. In addition, politicians took the company to court on charges of corruption. The company spent some $27m in legal and administrative fees before ultimately pulling out, after seven years of delays.

These three cases all occurred in the energy industry, but there the similarities end. One company suffered because of the sudden onset of a political crisis; another, because of the political actions of NGOs; and the third, because cumulative bureaucratic obstacles made the profitable conduct of business impossible.

The complexities are further compounded. Why did these projects go wrong? Did the companies fail to assess risks accurately? Did they pursue overly aggressive negotiating strategies? Did they lack the knowledge necessary to operate in difficult environments? Did they fail to cultivate support in the communities where their investments were located?

Nearly all companies that venture abroad face political risk in one form or another. Even businesses that operate only in Europe and North America may experience the hazards of NGO action or regulatory change.

Yet companies differ widely in the risks they face and their need for political risk management capabilities. Companies need to prioritize the political risks to which they are exposed and develop appropriate, effective risk management strategies to deal with the most serious threats. A definition of political risk, a framework for identifying and prioritizing political risks, and pointers for companies undertaking the task of political risk management are set out here.

Defining political risk

Political risk is uncertainty that stems, in whole or in part, from the exercise of power by governmental and non-governmental actors. Political instability and politicized government policy pose the best-known political risks. Political violence, expropriation and creeping expropriation, contract frustration, and currency inconvertibility are among typical hazards.

These risks can affect a company's value in many ways. Risks such as expropriation and sabotage can have an impact on its assets. Risks such as kidnapping and local hiring requirements can affect personnel. Risks such as social unrest and export requirements can affect operations. Risks such as tax hikes and hyperinflation can affect commercial activity, while risks such as currency crises and capital controls can affect transfers.

This diversity of risks and their effects mean that, operationally, "political risk" carries very different connotations for different companies (and all too often for different people within the same company). For instance, a multinational bank holding the sovereign debt of a developing country will be mainly concerned with that country's macro-economic policy decisions, since such decisions will directly affect the value of the debt. However, if the bank has no physical presence in the country, it will be far less concerned with risks such as political violence or expropriation.

By contrast, an oil company with a drilling operation in the same country will be deeply concerned with security issues and with its own relationship with the host government. However, if the oil company sells the oil outside the country, the country's macro-economic policies will have relatively little impact on the oil company's operations.

The term "political risk" covers a variety of threats, with a variety of impacts. How can a company decide which threats matter most, and where (and how) these threats need to be addressed? The first step is to define a "common language" on political risk that focusses on the areas that concern the company. This common language facilitates dialog between different regional and functional groups within the company. The second step is to use a broadly focussed framework for identifying political risks and to apply it systematically to the company's operations. An example of such a framework is given below.

A political risk framework

Companies that take an *ad hoc* approach to dealing with risks often expend too much effort on dealing with easily identified political risks, while leaving other, sometimes more critical risks untouched. Even more commonly, these companies will focus their political risk management efforts on areas where improvements are hard to achieve, giving short shrift to areas where improved political risk management could deliver quick results.

Another common problem is that companies will take a reactive approach to political risk. In this case, they usually end up with a political risk management strategy that emphasizes damage control. Such strategies are unnecessarily expensive. In political risk management, an ounce of prevention is certainly worth a pound of cure. Political risks are generally far easier to handle before they evolve into full-blown crises. Companies that rely on damage-control strategies must employ top management personnel – often backed by big-name lawyers and ex-diplomats – to handle high-profile, high-pressure negotiations. Once made, political decisions are hard to reverse, because reputations are publicly on the line. Far better to identify risks in advance, and influence host government and NGO actions before reputational concerns about "losing face" arise.

The key to developing a proactive, broadly focussed political risk management strategy is to adopt a comprehensive and systematic view of factors driving political risks. This will allow the company to identify the locus of problems, assess where improvements are easiest to achieve, and lay out a plan of action.

The factors that drive political risk can be broken down into three basic areas: external drivers such as political instability and poor public policy, interaction drivers based on the relationships between the company and external actors, and internal drivers such as the quality of the company's political risk management processes.

External drivers

External drivers of political risk can be subdivided into several categories. The classic drivers are incidents of political instability (such as riots and coups) and poor public policy (such as hyperinflation and currency crises). These types of political risk attract the headlines (as in Indonesia, Russia, and Brazil) and often dominate the attention of political risk managers.

However, an external driver of political risk that is frequently overlooked is a weak institutional framework. For direct investors, drivers in this area (such as corrupt regulatory agencies and ineffective legal systems) can be more critical than headline-generating political and economic developments. Weak political institutions pose the threat of a "death of a thousand cuts," such as that suffered by the power plant in India described earlier. Weak political institutions include such hazards as failing legal systems, biased regulatory systems, and the inability of the government to provide expected services (such as infrastructure and security).

In most cases, the company cannot influence these drivers of risk (it cannot make the host country more stable, or alter its basic macro-economic policy decisions). Hence, the company needs to focus on assessing these risks accurately, and managing their impacts (for instance, by buying political risk insurance).

Interaction drivers

Interaction drivers can be split into categories based on the relationship involved. Companies typically have many relationships that influence political risk levels. The most common include relationships with home-country and host-country governments, with local governments in the host country, and with regulators. If these relationships turn sour, political risk levels will increase.

Other important relationships include those with local communities and the labor force. Community demands can lead to government intervention – as happened in the case of the Canadian energy company discussed earlier. In addition, one of the most common reasons for unwanted host government intervention is labor issues. Several academic studies have found that companies with large labor forces and companies with well-organized labor forces experience higher levels of political risk. Labor unions can be extremely effective in seeking government action. Labor regulations are typically complex and subject to intense political pressure.

Another relationship whose importance has increased in recent years is that between companies and NGOs. Because of the internet, information about a company's far-flung investment activities can be disseminated rapidly and easily, and multiple NGOs can effectively co-ordinate their actions (as they demonstrated so powerfully at the World Trade Organization's Seattle ministerial meeting in December 1999). When NGOs are involved, a company's Value at Risk in an investment project exceeds the value of the project itself, since NGOs can affect a company's global reputation as well as consumer behavior. For instance, Talisman, a Canadian oil company with substantial investments in the Sudan, found that accusations of its complicity in human rights violations did severe damage to its international reputation. Because of pressure from human rights activists, pension funds of US state governments sold off holdings in the company's shares.

A final relationship that drives the impact of political risks is the company's relationship with shareholders. Again, the internet is an essential component. The World Wide Web has made monitoring a company's foreign activities much simpler. Increasing the challenge, shareholders have seen companies hobbled in recent years by high-visibility crises in Mexico, Indonesia, Thailand, Russia, and Brazil. When shareholders obtain information about foreign political events from the media, they are likely to respond to negative events by hammering the company's share price (as seen in the example of the company investing in the Sudan). It is therefore critical for the company to present its political risk management strategy to shareholders in a compelling fashion, before political risk crises hit, and to follow this with status updates when problems do occur.

Interaction-based drivers of risk differ from external drivers in that the quality of the company's relationship with external actors strongly affects risk levels. Hence, the company can influence both the probability and the impacts of these political risks.

Internal drivers

Internal drivers can fall into a variety of categories, which may vary from company to company. One basic category is organization. Problems in this area can have profound effects on the company's ability to deal successfully with political risks. For instance, there is often difficulty aligning management incentives with the political risk management goals of the company as a whole. A common story is that project developers are compensated based on the value of the projects they originate. Hence, developers have an incentive to downplay political risks that might lead to the rejection of a project. Equally common is a situation in which country managers have the primary objective of increasing the value of assets under their control. They therefore have a tendency to downplay any increases in risk levels that might induce the company to lower its exposures.

Another category of internal drivers is information related. Many companies created internal political risk analysis functions in the early 1980s, in response to incidents of severe political instability (especially the 1979 Iranian revolution) and widespread expropriations of foreign direct investment. However, information-related problems proved difficult to overcome for many of these companies. One typical problem was that internally produced risk assessments were too lengthy or abstract to be useful. Another problem was that risk assessments – although they were generated within the company – were not credible to the company. Even when the assessments were right, managers did not believe them and failed to act on their recommendations. Consequently, most companies had dismantled or cut back their political risk analysis function by the end of the decade. In 1982, the Association of Political Risk Analysts reached a peak membership of 400. In 1994, it was disbanded.

There are several other groupings of internal drivers of political risk that vary from company to company. For instance, policy-related risks include problems with managers failing to obey risk management policies (such as policies that forbid campaign donations), or problems with the absence or incompleteness of these policies. Risk relating to the use of specific risk management techniques arise when companies select the wrong type of risk mitigation strategy (as when they purchase political risk insurance coverage that does not completely cover their exposures). "Human capital" risks include problems that arise when staff are not qualified to deal with political problems (such as when project managers attempt to avoid dealing with the host government, "stick to business," and fail to cultivate a positive relationship).

A company with superb capability in political risk management can defuse risks before they escalate. A company with little capability can turn a low-risk investment into a high-risk one (as when it provokes regulators to intervene). The probabilities and impacts of internal drivers of risk are completely determined by the quality of the company's political risk management capabilities.

Systematic approach

A company can use a framework such as that described above to identify the vital drivers of the political risks it faces. This can be the responsibility of the company's political risk or government relations department, or of a management committee convened by a top executive. Having identified political risks, managers should turn their attention to building political risk management capabilities. These capabilities include risk management policies, business processes, organization, human capital, methodologies, reports, systems, and data. The company must determine the capabilities that, if improved, will most effectively address the risk drivers identified in the previous step. It can then set out a plan of action to improve its capabilities.

Taking a systematic approach to political risk management does not necessarily need to be very elaborate. Indeed, businesses that take a systematic approach may find they are currently expending effort unnecessarily. A detailed political risk quantification scheme for cash-flow analysis may be useful, but perhaps not as useful as a government relations scheme that could save a project a company might otherwise be forced to abandon. Ultimately, this will depend on the existing competencies of the company and the drivers of the political risks to which it is exposed. How far the company proceeds in developing its political risk management capabilities, and in what areas, should depend on a comprehensive assessment using a systematic political risk framework.

Summary

Failure to manage political risks effectively can expose an enterprise to costly damage, warn **Marvin Zonis** and **Sam Wilkin**. The term "political risk" covers a variety of threats, with impacts that vary according to a company's specific exposures. The challenge for companies is to decide which threats matter most, and where (and how) these need to be addressed. The authors advise companies to adopt a comprehensive and systematic view of factors that drive political risks. This will allow managers to identify the locus of problems, assess where improvements can be achieved, and set out a plan of action. A company that successfully matches its risk management capabilities to the political risks it faces can defuse risks before they escalate. On the other hand, a company with underdeveloped capabilities can inadvertently turn a low-risk investment into a high-risk one.

Scourges that strike at the heart of global business

by Martin Stone

The range of events and developments that managers label as "security risks" is on the increase. They can be broadly categorized as security of personnel, physical assets, and financial assets, though there are real differences in the impact these have on a business. Generally, the more spectacular and visible "human" risks tend to generate more attention and demand more management time. Employees, the media, and the public understandably tend to be more interested in an event that affects real people rather than money, buildings, or assets.

Security events also have the potential to affect a great deal more than reputation, income, or production. There is an intricate connection between security events and risks that can be classified as political, financial, operational, reputational, and so on. The way in which a company protects its assets from guerrillas and terrorists could inadvertently implicate it in a wider debate about human rights, particularly if, as is often necessary, such protection involves the use of armed guards and army units. This may not jeopardize financial performance immediately, but it could potentially undermine shareholders' confidence and even the company's ability to attract the brightest and most qualified staff.

Businesses with global aspirations expand into new countries and expose themselves to a greater number of risks. An analysis of the business risks that globalization generates to some extent involves a discussion of the backlash against the issue that, as one leading commentator has remarked, "is a broad phenomenon that is fed by many different emotions and anxieties that have been triggered by [globalization] and the challenges of adapting to it." Often, this means that forces involved in globalization attract security problems, for example where the growing gap between rich and poor fuels crime, extremism, and terrorism. International business is usually seen as the main agent of globalization – and thus growing poverty – and is often singled out for attack. However, this article will focus on three key areas of security risk for international business: kidnap, terrorism, and crime.

Managing kidnap risk

Kidnapping – the taking of hostages for financial or political ends – is a significant risk to companies in many countries, though one that is prone to exaggeration. While, in purely statistical terms, the likelihood of being a kidnap victim is far lower than that of being a road traffic accident victim, the risk of abduction tends to distort perceptions of a country's security risk profile out of all proportion to reality. Some companies ignore, for example, the evidence before their eyes – that many businesses operate successfully and profitably in Colombia, in spite of its reputation for kidnap. Even so, during 1999 the number of reported kidnaps reached its highest-ever level, and continuing economic pressures in Russia and the Far East are likely to exacerbate the situation in those areas in the near future.

There are two main types of kidnaps: those carried out by criminal gangs to raise money – "cash criminals" – and those perpetrated by extremists and activists motivated by political, religious, or other causes. Cash criminals are responsible for the vast majority of kidnaps, though there is much overlap with political terrorists staging kidnaps to raise money for their causes. There is a wide range of objectives of political kidnaps: to extort money or political concessions over policy or resources; to obtain publicity; to intimidate witnesses; or to undermine a country's attractiveness to foreign investors.

The incidence of kidnap is notoriously difficult to quantify, however. Reliable information is hard to ascertain, as kidnaps – particularly of local staff – often go unreported (*see* Figure 1). The annual number of kidnaps worldwide probably does not exceed 20,000 and, on average, one in 10 people kidnapped is subsequently killed. Compare this with the approximately 22,000 murders that occur in the US

Figure 1: Top ten kidnap ranking: 1992–99

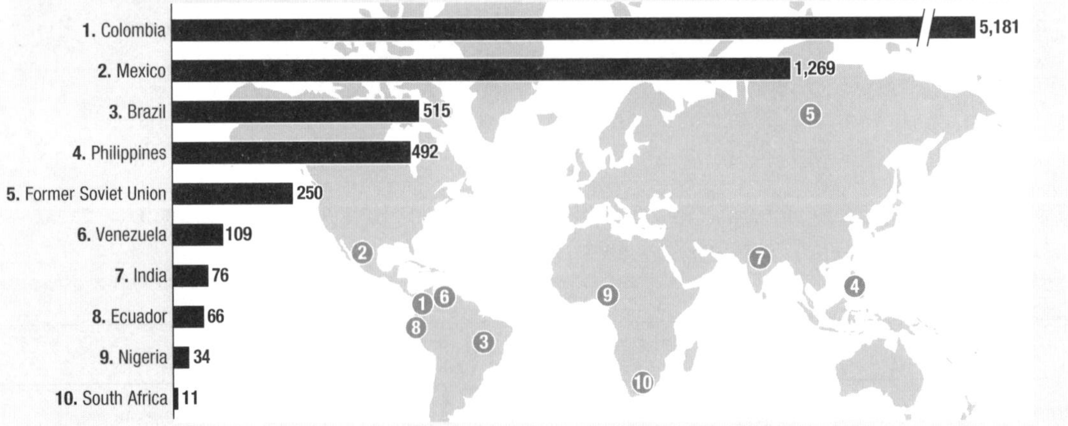

Source: Hiscox Group, April 2000 (www.hiscox.com). Note: figures refer to recorded kidnaps for which there is reliable information. (Former Soviet Union refers to Russia and other CIS member states.)

every year. Moreover, kidnap incidents, partly because of their rarity, tend to grab the headlines, inflating the incidence and impact of the problem.

Some kidnap for ransom is merely another form of extortion. In Russia, for instance, criminal gangs have preyed on foreign companies with unusual skill and experience, offering themselves as joint venture partners assisting investors with navigating the labyrinth of Russian bureaucracy. If thwarted, the gang may turn from subtle extortion to heavy-handed abduction, with a tendency to gratuitous violence in retribution. In Chechnya, kidnaps tend to be long-drawn-out affairs, where the financial demands are high and non-negotiable, and the conditions in which the victims are held both harsh and debilitating.

Kidnaps may occur during chance encounters, but more often than not kidnappers ascertain the routines of the employees and plan an abduction accordingly. There are thus several straightforward strategies that companies can follow to minimize the possibility of employees and managers being kidnapped for ransom:

- Conduct a thorough assessment of the risk of being kidnapped.
- Implement any necessary security measures, such as changes to personal or corporate profile and to lifestyle. Simple lifestyle changes may include avoiding a predictable routine and a high media profile, or arranging for the installation of an alarm system.
- Ensure that protection extends – where necessary – to spouses and children.
- Consider undergoing a kidnap survival course. Such courses outline the stages of a kidnap and the structure of negotiations.
- Consider kidnap insurance. Insurance is, for obvious security reasons, very sensitive, and should be discussed only with the company's risk manager, or with the corporate or family insurance broker. Disclosure that an individual holds kidnap insurance usually invalidates the policy.

If an employee or a family member is kidnapped, the company or family may also contact reputable consulting companies that specialize in crisis management. The authorities should always be informed (at the highest possible level), but in some countries it is not desirable to involve the police in any way. Police officers may even be part of the kidnap or may be prepared to leak sensitive information regarding the state of negotiations. An experienced crisis management company can assist in preparing a strategy for negotiation and may offer advice during negotiations that helps minimize the length of captivity.

A kidnap is the most traumatic situation that an individual or family is ever likely to face. Fortunately, most kidnap situations are resolved with the release of the victim. Professional counseling after release is essential if the kidnap is not to do any lasting psychological harm.

Steering clear of terrorism

It is in the nature of terrorism to "kill one, scare a thousand." Once again, statistically speaking, one is much more likely to be frightened by terrorists than targetted by them. That said, some terrorists do single out companies on grounds of their nationality, or purely because they are business concerns. In Turkey, Greece, Colombia, and Peru, for example, ultra-leftist groups have over the years staged occasional – and usually small-scale – bombings of US and other western businesses, but the number of countries affected is becoming smaller, and the threat of terrorist attack is very rarely cited as a significant factor in a withdrawal decision.

Figure 2: Terrorist attacks against business

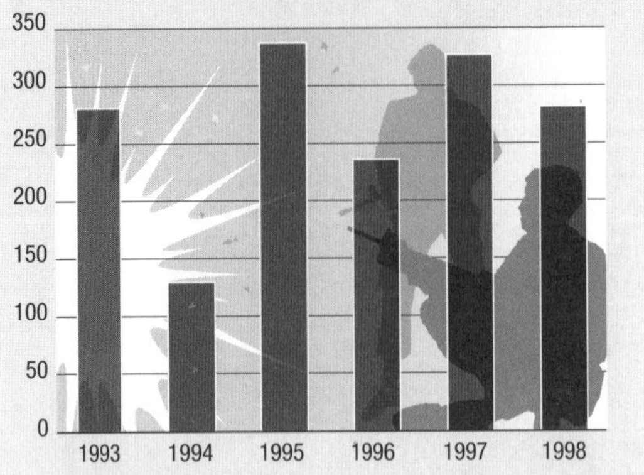

Source: US State Department

A misleading picture? Raw data shows between 150 and 330 direct terrorist attacks against business each year. However, bombings of oil pipelines in Colombia – which are viewed as US targets – account disproportionately for this total. For instance, in 1998 there were 77 such attacks (27 percent of the total). The majority were small-scale attacks with minor consequences.

Civilians or officials are always more likely to be caught up in bombings or attacks than company employees, even though company property is often targetted. Indeed, specific businesses were not the primary target in any of the 12 most notorious terrorist acts of the 1990s, whether reckoned in terms of the political implications or the numbers of fatalities (*see* Figure 2).

However, while terrorism is declining in frequency, the individual incidents that do take place – such as the dual bombings of the US embassies in Nairobi and Dar-es-Salaam in August 1998 – are actually killing more people: the so-called "high impact, low-risk" scenario. For instance, figures from the US State Department show that, in the 1970s, fatalities occurred in 17 percent of incidents, whereas in 1995, at least one person was killed in 29 percent of terrorist incidents.

This is to a large extent caused by the fact that attacks by religious extremists are more likely to be lethal than those carried out by secular terrorists. Religious extremists were involved in 25 percent of incidents in 1995, but they were responsible for 58 percent of all fatalities.

Terrorism has the potential to do much greater harm to business when terrorists strike at the economy in the belief that it represents any government's weakest and most sensitive point. This was the case when the IRA planted bombs in the City of London, the capital's financial heart, London's Docklands area, and central Manchester between 1996 and 1998, causing many millions of pounds worth of damage, and much more in costs from disruption and business interruption. Indeed, the tactics of disruption are often seen in a "mature" terrorist campaign, where essential utilities as well as transport infrastructure are targetted. Again, the cost resulting from disruption and delay has a far greater impact in financial terms than more "traditional" attacks in public places.

The practicality of managing terrorism risk depends very much on the specific situation. In Algeria, where seven workers in a foreign oil-related business were murdered by terrorists in 1995, all foreign extractive companies continue to employ security co-ordinators, who liaise with the local security and law enforcement authorities to carefully plan employees' movements and protect worksites and residences. Travel in and out of the oil and gas desert towns is carefully controlled, with most foreigners flying directly on charter aircraft to Hassi Messaoud, Algeria's oil "capital." The situation is roughly the same in other places under realistic terrorist threat, such as Colombia and Angola.

Terrorism risk management is clearly a less straightforward proposition in industrialized countries, where the targetting tends to be much more diffuse and the risks less definable. In the absence of reliable intelligence that can help to form an accurate picture of terrorists' potential business targets, companies are obliged to monitor a potential attacker's methodologies and tactics. They can formulate their own conclusions about the realistic level of threat to their assets and ensure that appropriate security protocols are in place.

Loss due to crime

Business is more likely to suffer a loss due to criminal reasons than any other security risk, and the risk of being targetted will feature much more often in decisions not to invest, or to withdraw, than will kidnap or terrorism.

Certain countries have a reputation as particularly crime ridden, usually with justification. For instance, crime has more than doubled in Russia since 1991, and the real situation is likely to be much worse; since many people believe that the police are ineffective, they fail to report crimes. Levels of violent crime have risen rapidly: there were more than 30,000 murders in 1999, a rate per head almost three times greater than that of the US. Although most violence occurs in domestic and alcohol-related disputes, and in rivalry between Russian businesses and crime gangs, there is a strong incidental risk to business visitors.

South Africa, particularly the Johannesburg area, is another country that has become notorious for crime. One of the reasons is chronic underfunding of the police service and the departure of thousands of officers to take up posts in the private security sector. No improvement is forecast for at least the next five years and the government's new anti-crime strategies are unlikely to be effective in the interim. Business has effectively fled from downtown Johannesburg to US-style, suburban satellites such as Sandton; but crime has followed it there, too.

For all foreign territories, an appreciation of the realistic level of threat to a business is critical. Local employees will usually underestimate the extent of any problem, while outsiders tend to exaggerate it. Although there are no internationally accepted standards of reporting on crime figures due to wide differences between national police forces, fortunately it is relatively straightforward to analyze crime trends around the world. For instance, theft is the most common crime reported, followed by burglary, though theft rates are higher for industrial countries than for non-industrial countries. Similarly, most cities have similar patterns for homicide and for robbery rates, though several Latin American, Northern European cities, New York and other US cities tend to suffer from above-average murder rates.

In most cases, a detailed city map of high-risk areas can be prepared for distribution to expatriates and local employees; residences and worksites should be surveyed and appropriate security measures installed. In the highest-risk situations, special arrangements are often put in place for staff, ranging from 24-hour close protection to advice on varying routines and steering clear of certain districts.

On the most practical level, business must also address crime where it affects travelers, again, by awareness and education. For instance, travelers through Bogota and Lagos airports can reduce their exposure to snatch thieves by simple procedures such as strapping their laptops to their body, being aware of common scams, and ensuring that they are met at the airport by someone they know. In some Latin American cities, laptop thefts are increasingly common: copying sensitive or crucial data on to floppy disks, stored separately, should be the minimum procedure every business traveler adopts. Travelers face the highest risk when they arrive disoriented in an unfamiliar city, and advice on the best, safest, and most reliable route to their hotel is invaluable.

The co-ordination of travel risk advice tends to be a combined effort of the security director's office (or the human resources department) and the travel planning office. Many companies find a system where externally sourced information and analysis – supported by in-company knowledge – is automatically supplied to travelers, or their administrators, when they purchase a ticket or make a hotel reservation. This ensures consistency of approach and avoids overreliance on travel anecdotes or "war stories" that tend to circulate within companies. What happened six – or even three – months ago may well be entirely irrelevant in a fast-moving situation.

Summary

Security events – risk to personnel, physical assets, and financial assets – are a growth industry, writes **Martin Stone**. Still worse, they have the potential to affect far more than a company's income or production. Indeed, these risk events often carry political, financial, operational, or reputational implications. The public perception of how a company counters risk – which may involve using army units and armed guards – can have an impact on shareholder confidence and staff morale. This article notes that kidnap and terrorism are real hazards in the global marketplace, but that individual perceptions of the dangers often exaggerate the reality. Terrorism, while declining in frequency, has now become more deadly. However, business is more likely to suffer losses from a criminal act than from any other type of security risk. Crime, not kidnap or terrorism, is thus more important in decisions about investment or withdrawal.

Suggested further reading

Clutterbuck, R. (1987) *Kidnap, Hijack and Extortion*, Basingstoke: Macmillan.

Herring, R. (1983) *Managing International Risk*, Cambridge: Cambridge University Press.

Howell, L. (ed.) (1998) *The Handbook of Country and Political Risk Analysis*, East Syracuse, NY: PRS.

Monti-Belkaoui, J. and Riahi-Belkaoui, A. (1998) *The Nature, Estimation, and Management of Political Risk*, Westport, CT: Quorum Books.

Moran, T. (1998) *Managing International Political Risk*, Oxford: Blackwell.

Stone, M. (1997) "Managing political risk in the international arena," in Fundamentals of the Natural Gas Industry, *Petroleum Economist*.

Stone, M. (ed.) (1999) *Outlook 2000: Global Risk Forecast*, London: Control Risks Group.

Dealing with an eruption of corruption

by Philip M. Nichols

Corruption and bribery have moved to the forefront in discussions about the business environment. James Wolfensohn, president of the World Bank, regularly identifies bribery as among the greatest threats to global economic development. US vice president Al Gore convened an international symposium on global corruption in 1999. Numerous political and business leaders – from Benjamin Netanyahu, former Israeli prime minister, to Lockheed Martin, the world's largest defense contractor – are dealing with or have recently dealt with corruption charges.

A company that encounters a bribe request or contemplates offering a bribe faces four risks: criminal prosecution, dysfunctional relationships, damage to reputation, and the destruction of markets. There are several strategies for dealing with bribe requests, including payment of the bribe, individual corporate codes, and industry-wide standards.

Criminal prosecution

Criminal prosecution for the payment of bribes abroad constitutes a serious risk. Two years ago, only US residents faced criminal liability in their home country for paying bribes while abroad. Today, at least 20 countries have such laws and 14 more will soon enact them. Countries that now prohibit the payment of bribes to foreign officials include Austria, Belgium, Canada, Germany, Japan, Korea, and the UK. These countries are required by an Organization for Economic Co-operation and Development (OECD) convention to criminalize transnational bribery (Convention on Combating Bribery of Foreign Public Officials in International Business Transactions).

The Organization of American States' Inter-American Convention against Corruption, which was signed by most countries in the Americas in 1996, also requires members to criminalize transnational bribery, although implementation has been somewhat slower than for the OECD measure.

The effect of these two treaties is that both the northern and the western hemispheres will soon have a comprehensive system of laws prohibiting the payment of bribes to foreign government officials.

At the same time, the world has experienced what Moisés Naím, editor of the US journal *Foreign Policy*, in a 1995 article refers to as a "corruption eruption." Bribe demands occur at a staggering rate. Most of the comparative evidence is anecdotal: people involved in international business for many decades often say that the number of countries in which one could expect a large bribe demand has risen from a handful to most. This increase, it must be noted, is due in part to an increase in the offer of bribes by companies doing business abroad.

Transparency International, a non-governmental organization based in Berlin, Germany, has made considerable effort to educate governments and businesses about corruption and has accumulated some of the most comprehensive data existing on corruption. The TI Corruption Perception Index provides frightening evidence of how pervasive bribe requests are. This index correlates a number of surveys, polls, and other country ratings on the amount of bribe requests perceived by business people who regularly conduct business in those countries.

A score of 10 indicates a perception that bribe requests are never made, while a zero score indicates a perception that bribe requests are always made. In the 1999 index, for example, Denmark scores 10, the UK scores 8.6, and the US scores 7.5.

Two-thirds expect bribes

What is daunting is that of the 99 countries included in the 1999 index, 66 score 5.0 or lower. In other words, in two-thirds of the countries in this index, business considers it at least as likely as not that a bribe request will be made in any given transaction. These include some of the world's most populous countries, such as China, which scored 3.4, India, 2.9, Indonesia, 1.7, and Pakistan, 2.2. A manager therefore faces a world in which both the penalties for paying and the demand to pay bribes are very large.

The risk of criminal enforcement is very real. Those who supported the passage of anti-corruption legislation envisioned two primary means of finding lawbreakers. One is government investigation, both of their own and of their competitors' nationals. The end of the cold war has reduced the need for intelligence agencies to gather strategic intelligence, so now they collect commercial intelligence. The US is already reported to have used bribery information supplied by intelligence agencies on contracts in Latin America and the Middle East. Other countries will undoubtedly also use similar information.

The other means of finding lawbreakers is competitors. Competitors have every reason to inform authorities when a company violates laws against bribery of foreign officials. Indeed, one of the premises of such laws is that they resolve the "assurance problem" among competitors. In a system in which decisions are made based on bribes paid rather than on quality and price, economic actors are rewarded for diverting resources from quality to bribes. The *kaçak* – "contraband" – buildings that collapsed during the 1999 earthquakes in Turkey are vivid examples. They collapsed because they were not built to Turkish codes. In turn, this was because it was cheaper to erect a substandard building and bribe a building inspector than it was to meet the cost of satisfying the building code.

Rather than providing goods that kill their users, most businesses probably want to sell high-quality goods or services. However, the cost of supplying high quality and bribes is so much greater than that of low quality and bribes that high-quality providers risk being driven out of business by those preferring the low road.

Laws that outlaw the payment of bribes provide assurance to those who want to provide quality that others will not cheat. Competitors should report credible suspicions of bribe giving, and will probably do so.

The penalties for violating these laws can be severe. In the US, penalties include incarceration, fines, and disqualification from doing business with the US government. Pending legislation in France will impose a 15-year prison sentence on certain types of bribery. In South Korea, a five-year prison sentence and a 10m won fine may be imposed, while half the profits of the underlying transaction can be confiscated. Even in Norway, which has the least punitive of the new laws, bribery of foreign government officials is punishable by a year in jail.

Criminal penalties and fines are serious risks. It must be noted, however, that there are risks other than criminal ones from paying bribes. A bribe creates a dysfunctional relationship between the bribe payer and the bribe taker. Although bribe-taking officials and the business people with whom they work may be a feature of a culture where bribe payments are a regular part of doing business, the larger society in general will almost certainly not accept bribery.

Thus bribery everywhere is conducted behind closed doors and kept secret. Both bribe giver and bribe taker consume time, energy, and resources to keep secret that aspect of their relationship. For obvious reasons, the quality of corrupt relationships has received little study, but those who have endured them often describe them as unhealthy, unstable, and unenforceable.

Bribes hurt reputations

The payment of bribes also creates a threefold risk for business reputation. First, a company risks its reputation among the broader masses of a country where it pays bribes. Even if bureaucrats and businesses consider large bribes to be normal business practice in any one country, its general population almost certainly does not. For example, those who conducted business with the family of former Indonesian President Suharto suffered much reputational damage after the regime in that country changed.

Second, the paying of a bribe means that your reputation to bureaucrats becomes one of being a bribe payer. One European businessman told this author that after his company made its first few payments, bribery became part of the normal course of business for it because bureaucrats worldwide expected similar treatment.

Third, using bribes abroad puts the business's domestic reputation at risk. Disapproval of businesses paying bribes has not yet reached the levels of opprobrium reserved for enterprises that degrade the environment or abuse human rights. Yet as public anger against bribe paying grows, it is possible that the associated reputational risk will worsen.

A fourth risk attached to bribery is degradation of markets. The economist Paolo Mauro, in his article "Corruption and Growth," finds a direct link between high levels of corruption and low levels of foreign direct investment. Harvard's Shang-Jin Wei, in a 1997 working paper, also finds a significant negative relationship between corruption and economic growth. Less rigorously – but perhaps more frighteningly – the collapse of the Nigerian middle class and resistance by many in central and eastern Europe to market reforms have been attributed to corruption. The list of countries that have been politically or economically destabilized by corruption is long and growing. Businesses with long-term interests in a particular country are poorly served by a strategy that contemplates bribery.

Strategies exist for dealing with bribe requests. The least effective – but one that is used by some companies – is to pay the bribes. US companies, which unlike their counterparts elsewhere, have operated for more than 20 years under laws that prohibit bribe payments to foreign officials, often try it through local agents. Authorizing payment of a bribe is just as illegal and otherwise harmful as a direct bribe payment; it does not shield a US company from liability under US law, and probably will not shield businesses in other countries from such liability under their own laws. US businesses also can try to describe the bribe as a "facilitating payment." Under US law, bribes to foreign officials are legal if they are made in order to get a bureaucrat to do something the bureaucrat should have done anyway. The legality of such "grease payments," however, may be unique to US law and certainly should not be counted on by those subject to other legal regimes.

Most managers should rebut bribe requests. Viable companies can say "no." In the mid-1970s, for example, the US electronics group Motorola not only refused a bribe request from a Latin American official but also said it would not conduct business in that country until the regime changed. Refusal of bribe requests requires a corporate culture that supports the refusal of such requests. One of the most effective means of doing this is with a simple corporate code for managers and employees, affiliates and potential business partners. At a minimum, the code should refer to the laws that bind the company and prohibit bribery of foreign officials. The code should also describe the decision-making line for bribe requests and assure managers that the company will back them when they refuse to pay a bribe.

Building this into the corporate culture is possible and can bring competitive advantage. The leading oil company Texaco, for example, earned such a fearsome reputation for not acceding to bribe requests that even at remote African border crossings, Texaco's Jeeps are sometimes waved through without any requests for a bribe.

Corporate codes, however, do not solve the assurance problem: they do not prove to a company that its competitors are not bribing. Thomas Dunfee and David Hess, of the University of Pennsylvania, have developed industry-wide standards that they call the "C2 Principles" for dealing with bribe requests. These principles cover company policy for outlawing the payment of bribes, public reports on bribe requests, and outside auditing of any possible improper payments.

Bribery is a real and growing threat to business. The payment of bribes incurs the risk of criminal prosecution, dysfunctional relationships, damage to reputation, and degradation of markets. Companies can mitigate such risk by building a corporate culture that refuses bribe requests and by establishing company codes to ensure that employees, agents, and affiliates follow suit.

Summary

Corruption and bribery are hot business topics. **Philip M. Nichols** notes that some believe it may even pose a critical threat to global economic development. Bribery demands are a real and rising peril for business where criminal prosecution for paying a bribe is a serious risk. This article warns that paying a bribe opens the door to criminal prosecution, dysfunctional relationships, damaged reputations, and degradation of markets – where those preferring the low road drive out high-quality providers. It speculates that once the public outcry against bribe paying becomes as prevalent as it is on environmental issues, the bribery risk for corporate reputations will rise significantly. A good defense is to encourage an anti-bribery corporate culture and provide employees, agents, and affiliates with a clear code of conduct.

Suggested further reading

Hess, D. and Dunfee, T. (2001) "Fighting corruption: a principled approach: the C2 Principles," Zicklin Center Working Paper Series, *Cornell International Law Journal*, 33.

Mauro, P. (1995) "Corruption and Growth," *Quarterly Journal of Economics*, 110: 681.

Naím, M. (1995) "The Corruption Eruption," *Brown Journal of World Affairs*, 11: 245.

Wei, S.J. (1997) "Why is corruption so much more taxing than tax?: Arbitrariness kills," National Bureau of Economic Research Working Paper no. 6255.

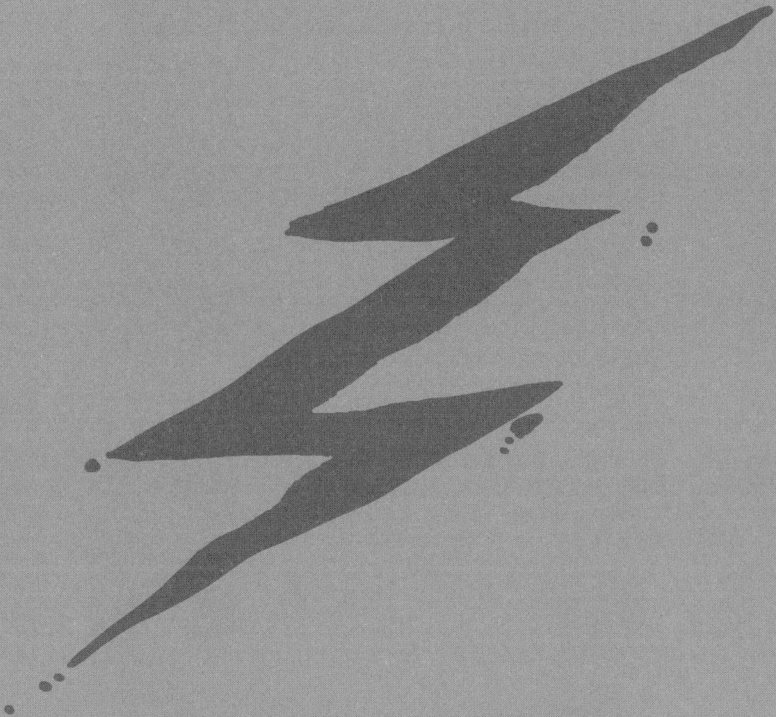

INSURANCE AND SYSTEMIC RISK

7

Contributors

Gerry Dickinson is a professor of international insurance at the City University Business School, London. His research interests include strategic and financial management in insurance enterprises, risk management, and regulation. He is a deputy secretary-general of the Geneva Association, an international association for the study of insurance economics.

Allan M. Malz is a partner in the RiskMetrics Group LLC and is responsible for the DataMetrics risk data service. Formerly with the Federal Reserve Bank of New York, he conducts research on extracting market forecasts and risk perceptions from derivatives prices and on option risks.

Frederic S. Mishkin is the Alfred Lerner Professor of Banking and Financial Institutions at the Graduate School of Business, Columbia University. He is a former director of research and executive vice president at the Federal Reserve Bank of New York and author of *The Economics of Money, Banking and Financial Markets.*

Tim Shepheard-Walwyn is Director, Group Risk and a member of the Executive Committee at Barclays Bank. Formerly he was a managing director in the group risk department at UBS.

Christopher C. Finger is a partner in the RiskMetrics Group LLC and is primarily responsible for research on the CreditMetrics model, including its application to asset-backed securitizations. He also contributes to research into market risk, simulation methods, and the application of risk models in emerging markets.

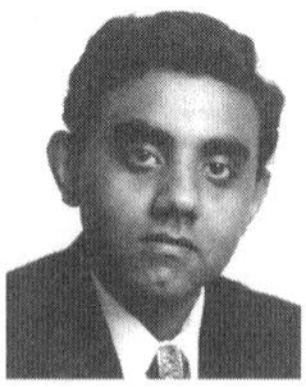

Akash Deep is an assistant professor at Harvard University. His research focusses on derivative securities, corporate and portfolio risk management, privatization, and asset management at foundations and financial institutions.

Contents

Insurance finds a blend of innovation and tradition 195
Gerry Dickinson, City University Business School
Convention is blending with tradition in the insurance business and novel types of policies have evolved to meet expanding corporate risk management needs.

Securing a safety net against economic free fall 202
Frederic S. Mishkin, Graduate School of Business, Columbia University
The overall financial system is profoundly shaken when a bank goes bust. This article describes some of the ways in which regulators can reduce systemic risk.

Welcome to this week's one-in-a-million event 207
Christopher C. Finger, RiskMetrics Group LLC
Allan M. Malz, RiskMetrics Group LLC
If you thought the 1987 US equities crash was a highly unexpected affair, spare a thought for those who model risk. These authors review the strengths and weaknesses of models used in risk assessment.

Capital ideas that face dissension in the banks 213
Tim Shepheard-Walwyn, Barclays Bank
The Basle Committee set minimum capital requirements back in 1988. Today, these methods beg reassessment.

A firm foundation for project finance 218
Akash Deep, Harvard University
Project finance is flavor of the month in countries committing to flagship development. How can the related risks be reduced?

Introduction

The increasingly complex needs of corporate risk managers have encouraged convergence between the domains of insurance and financial markets. As the opening article in this section points out, new forms of insurance such as ART (alternative risk transfer) are in many ways akin to derivatives instruments; ultimately, though, they demonstrate the limits of insurance. Elsewhere in this section, authors describe the nature of financial shocks and the systems designed to prevent them; the reliability of financial risk models; the mismatch of banking regulations and risk management techniques; and risk reduction in project finance.

Insurance finds a blend of innovation and tradition

by Gerry Dickinson

The concepts and processes of risk management first arose in the 1950s because of companies' need to systematize their insurance buying. Insurance markets have existed for many years and corporations have been able to choose whether to transfer risks on to these markets or to retain them within the corporation (to self-insure). Further, because the causes of insurable risks, or their potential severity of loss, often entailed human error or malfeasance, such losses were to some degree controllable. Thus managers began to consider systems for loss prevention and, later, for the economic control of losses should they occur. There were incentives to do this, since insurance prices tended to reflect the claims experience of the corporation.

Over time, insurance markets have widened their product range. Insurance brokers have strongly influenced this development by virtue of their role as intermediaries between corporate insurance buyers and insurance suppliers.

Earlier types of insurance were mainly concerned with protecting physical assets, such as buildings, plant and equipment, goods in transit, and vehicles of transportation. In the past few decades, insurance contracts have broadened in purpose, from protecting assets to protecting corporate income against certain causes of loss. One example of this product development has been the growth of business interruption (consequential loss) insurance. This enables corporations to insure against the loss of corporate income – and the associated expenses of continuing a disrupted operation – caused by physical damage, accidents, or other insurable contingencies. Similarly, the development of credit insurance, whether relating to domestic or export sales, afforded a means of protecting, or stabilizing, the corporate income stream.

The growth of a more litigious society – reinforced by safety and environmental impairment legislation – has brought an increase in scale and scope of liability insurance and enabled corporate income (and net worth) to be protected from legal suits for negligence from customers, employees, or a variety of third parties. In respect of liability of employers to their employees, legislation has been introduced in many countries that requires the compulsory purchase of insurance cover. There are clear limits to the extent that insurance can protect or stabilize income streams and this raises the issue of what types of risk are insurable. This will be discussed later.

One further class of insurance that companies now purchase is group insurance that offers employee benefits. This includes group pension schemes, group disability and accident schemes, and group health insurance schemes. These types of insurance are not directly concerned with protecting corporate assets or income.

Captive growth

Increasingly since the 1960s, larger corporations have created and used their own, in-house insurance operations, called captive insurance companies, primarily as a means of co-ordinating insurance buying across the global enterprise. It is estimated that in 1999 there were more than 4,200 "captives" worldwide. Most of these are wholly owned subsidiaries, but some are organized on a group ownership basis.

The growth of captives has been stimulated by occasional limitations in the supply of insurance in certain markets, or when the supply price of insurance has risen sharply. Centralized insurance buying allows corporations to exploit both their buying power and the greater flexibility of the international reinsurance market.

Tax considerations have always played some role in the location of captives offshore. A favorable tax regime allows companies to build up contingency reserves to fund self-insured losses more effectively. The less onerous regulatory and capital requirements of many offshore locations have also been a factor. With tax authorities in North America, Europe, and other jurisdictions seeking to moderate the use of offshore tax havens, companies have begun forming onshore captive insurance companies. Many European captives are based in Dublin and Luxembourg; in the US, they can be found in Vermont. However, offshore locations remain the main domicile for captives, and Bermuda is the largest of these.

Limitations of insurance markets

Although insurance markets have widened their product range over time, there are limits to the types of corporate risks that can be insured. Some are due to regulatory factors, and some to the nature of insurance itself.

National insurance legislation in individual countries specifies the types of insurance or risk transfer products an insurance company can offer. With greater liberalization of national legislations, insurers have been able to widen the range of products they offer, but limitations still remain. For example, a derivative contract would not count as an insurance product under most national insurance regulations and hence could not be supplied directly by an insurance company. Similarly, the commercial or business risks of an enterprise are not usually considered insurable.

Even within the scope of insurance regulations, there are also market limitations. First, the risk transfer relationship must clearly define the legal trigger of a potential loss at a point in time and ensure that the contract itself is enforceable. Second, insurance can only be supplied in a sustainable way if it can be adequately priced: an insurer must have sufficient information to estimate the underlying loss distributions.

One particular aspect of a pricing problem is adverse selection, where the buyer has more information about the probability or severity of loss than the insurance company itself. This is more likely in commercial than personal insurance, since the corporate buyer is usually well informed. If the degree of adverse selection is high, supply will be curtailed over time.

Third, insurance supply can be inhibited if the insurance buyer has less incentive to take reasonable care or to invest in loss-prevention measures. This problem – known as moral hazard – exists to some degree in all insurance contracts, but is reduced in practice through such contractual arrangements as the use of deductibles and profit share incentives.

In terms of the global insurance market, there is a limit to the industry's capacity to absorb extremely large losses, mainly from natural catastrophes, earthquakes, hurricanes, and so on. Even though the insurance industry has an effective international mechanism for risk sharing through reinsurance, the capacity of the global insurance market is, in the last analysis, restricted by the size of its capital base. The capital base of the world's non-life insurance and reinsurance was about \$400bn in 1999, which, though large, is still significantly smaller than the size of global capital markets.

The cost of capital

The insurance industry's supply of insurance is also constrained by the fact that regulation requires an insurance company to hold a certain level of capital to protect against insolvency. Apart from the additional value of services that insurance companies supply, such as risk assessment, loss prevention, engineering, and claims management services, when a company purchases insurance it is in effect renting capital from the insurance company to cover the possibility that losses will be higher than expected.

Insurance is thus a form of contingent capital. If a corporation did not buy insurance at all, it would have to hold a higher level of working capital to absorb large fluctuations in its cash flows or hold extra lines of credit with the banking system. For companies, the fact that insurance companies have more liquid capital and more diversified risk portfolios means that the cost of insurance is often lower than the cost of holding extra working capital. Similarly, when insurers themselves transfer risks to other insurers (that is, to reinsurers), they are in effect renting the capital of these reinsurers. However, there are diminishing returns to the efficiency of insurance as a form of contingent capital. Global reinsurance markets at the end of the risk transfer chain are required by regulation to hold capital just in case it is needed. Over time, this cost will be passed on to consumers in higher premiums.

Moreover, the effective cost of holding capital against large potential losses increases as probability of loss decreases. This point can be illustrated by a simple example. Assume the cost of capital of a large reinsurance company is 12 percent and the rate of return earned on the investment of the capital funds that it holds to cover large potential losses is 8 percent. Thus, its marginal cost of holding capital is 4 percent. If, however, the probability of paying a very large loss is 0.1 (in other words, the loss is likely to occur only one year in every ten), the effective cost of holding capital can approach 40 percent per year. More direct contingent claims on global capital markets through risk securitization are likely to be cheaper.

The emergence of ART

During the 1990s, corporations were offered new ways of financing their insurance risks, known collectively as alternative risk transfer (ART). Excluding insurance placements through captive insurance companies, there are three types of alternative risk transfer: finite risk insurances (and financial (re)insurances); insurance derivatives; and securitization of insurance risks directly on to capital markets.

Several factors influenced the development of ART: a lack of capacity for larger-scale risks from time to time, due to an imbalance between the supply and demand of insurance over the underwriting cycle; attempts by progressive insurers and brokers to introduce new types of product for the corporate sector; and investment banks wishing to enter the insurance market to exploit their product development expertise in derivatives and securitization.

Finite risk insurances and financial (re)insurances are extensions of conventional types of insurance. They differ from conventional insurance in that the contracts are longer, typically three to five years, and they often involve a packaging of different kinds of insurance, including some risks that are difficult to place.

In addition, finite risk insurance usually possesses a profit-sharing feature, such that if the claims costs of the corporation vary unexpectedly, there is some *ex post* adjustment in the premium cost. Because of its tailor-made character, finite risk insurance represented an attempt by insurance companies to develop longer term risk-sharing relationships with corporations. As the name implies, there are limits to the degree of risk transfer in finite risk programs, and thus they provide a mezzanine layer of risk financing between self-insurance and conventional types of insurance.

The second area of ART – insurance derivatives – evolved in the mid-1990s. For a long time, insurance had been seen as a potential area of product development for derivatives, in part because a conventional insurance contract can theoretically be seen as a put option sold by an insurance company.

However, the development of derivatives as a mechanism of risk financing for corporate insurance risks has been limited, for two main reasons. First, there are no suitable indices on which derivatives can be based. Second, derivatives require that the underlying economic variable being tracked is relatively homogeneous. This requirement is often not met for corporate insurance risks, since these represent a heterogeneous bundle of risks, many of which may be specific to an industry.

In 2000, the only active traded derivative market was the property catastrophe options market at the Chicago Board of Trade (CBOT), which was set up in 1992. The Catastrophe Risk Exchange (CATEX) in New York was set up in 1996 as a loss swap market for insurers, but has since evolved into something that is closer to an insurance exchange than a traded derivative market. These markets were developed primarily to assist US insurance companies in managing their claims experience in the event of large catastrophic losses. They have been of limited use to corporations, even to the captive insurance companies of US corporations.

Figure 1: Insurance risk securitization through a bond issue

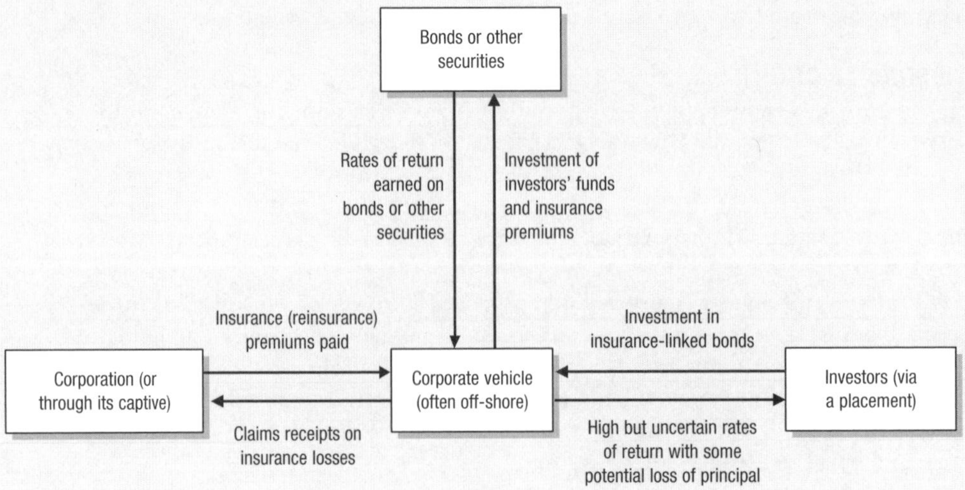

More recently, weather derivatives have been introduced, based on indices of rainfall, snowfall, and temperature. The statistics to estimate the underlying probability distributions on which these indices are based are derived from meteorological sources. It is clear that these derivatives, though useful, appeal only to certain types of businesses. Finally, ART also includes the securitization of insurance risks directly on to capital markets. Growth here is likely to continue in the longer term, especially for large potential losses facing corporations and for important projects. Two mechanisms for securitization have evolved, one based on bond instruments and the other on equity instruments. Specialist divisions of insurers and brokers have often collaborated with investment banks to develop tailor-made products for corporations to transfer their risks on to capital markets.

Bond securitization products seek to model the underlying loss experience on a portfolio of insurance risks within the corporation. In essence, they are low-grade bonds, offering investors an uncertain rate of return. These bonds are attractive for both their high expected rates of interest and their low systematic or "market" risk. The underlying insurance losses are largely random in nature, which can assist in efficient portfolio diversification. Figure 1 illustrates the typical mechanism of a risk securitization through a bond issue.

Equity-based securitization products are a form of contingent claim on equity markets. Technically speaking, they are a put option on the equity market since the

Figure 2: Risk transfer network for corporate risks

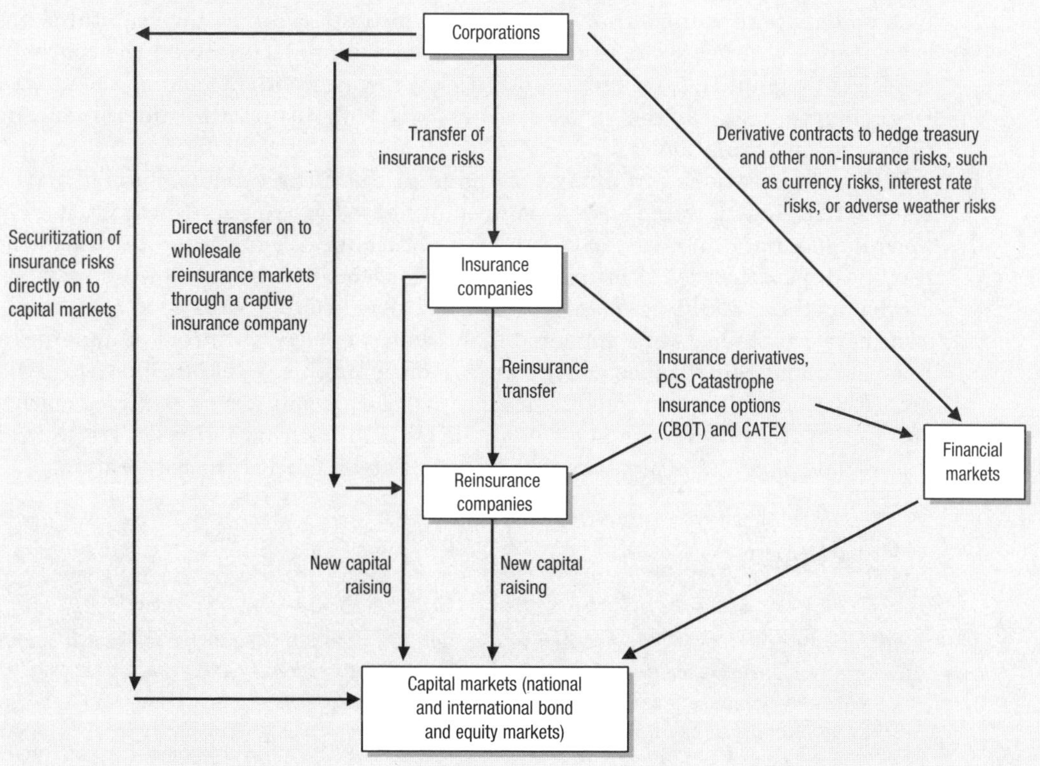

Conventional insurance and ART

Alternative risk transfer (ART) is a misleading expression. From a company's point of view, conventional insurance and ART are more complementary than competing. But there are economies of scale in issuing capital market products. However, large insurers and reinsurers are now beginning to use their balance sheet strength to mediate in securitization issues for corporations that do not have the size or credit ratings to tap the capital markets directly. One can consider the optimal financing of a corporation's insurable risks as lying on a distribution of potential losses by size (*see* Figure 3). At lower levels of loss (low severity and high frequency), companies are likely to self-insure and perhaps use some form of finite risk insurance cover. At a higher level of loss severity, a conventional insurance program will continue to play an important role (or a reinsurance program if risk transfer is through a captive insurance company). Risk securitization finds its market position at the top end of the loss severity spectrum (*see* Figure 3).

Figure 3: The spectrum of risk financing

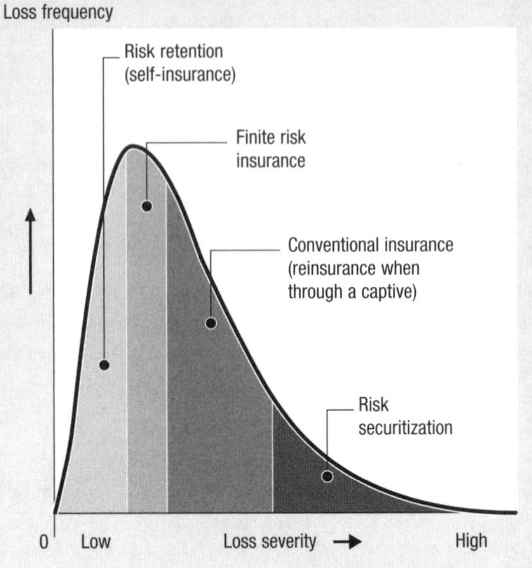

issuer is selling equity on to the market. A theoretical advantage of equity-based instruments is that they are a form of "just-in-time" capital, since capital is only raised when a large loss takes place. Equity-based products extend the concept of contingent capital that exists in conventional insurance and thus has the effect of removing the capital cost constraint imposed on insurance and reinsurance companies by regulation.

Risk securitizations are likely to expand in the future and companies may, to some extent, switch from bond-based to equity-based instruments – the greater risk appetite of equity markets makes them a natural bearer of corporate risks. Since the mid-1990s, the cost of insurance and reinsurance has been below its long-term economic cost, mainly because of market oversupply. Thus the cost of risk securitization products has appeared high when compared with that of underpriced insurance and reinsurance contracts. A more appropriate balance between risk securitization and conventional insurance will come about when insurance markets rise to their natural economic level, as the cycle in insurance prices corrects itself. Figure 2 on page 199 depicts the risk transfer network facing the corporation.

Conclusion

What are the challenges facing the management of insurance risks within companies?

- Since the purchase of conventional insurance and ART products are both types of contingent external capital, pressure will increase on managers to integrate these decisions, as well as hedging decisions for treasury risks, into the wider capital-raising and capital structure decisions of the corporation. This also applies to risk retention policies.

- The search for efficiency will encourage greater co-ordination between insurance risk managers and treasury risk managers, since the financing of insurance risks through insurance contracts and the hedging of financial risks through derivative contracts play essentially the same role within the enterprise.
- There is a growing recognition among senior managers, prompted in part by corporate governance concerns, that the company should adopt a comprehensive and robust risk management strategy. This, in turn, will lead to greater efforts to integrate insurance and treasury risk management processes into the overall risk management systems of the enterprise. In the final analysis, insurance risks and treasury risks emanate from the corporate strategies and activities of the enterprise.

Summary

The rise of corporate risk management as a systematic activity has stimulated the development of novel forms of insurance, writes **Gerry Dickinson**. Conventionally, companies used insurers to protect their physical assets; the market now offers insurance to cover such events as business interruption, product liability, and environmental impairment. In addition, large companies are increasingly insuring their own risks through in-house insurance companies, or "captives." Alternative risk transfer offers insurance companies further ways of serving sophisticated customers and of entering territory usually inhabited by investment banks. However, the scope and scale of insurance markets is limited by inflexible regulation and by certain defining characteristics of insurance itself.

Suggested further reading

Dickinson, G.M. (1998) "The economic role of the insurance sector in the risk transfer–capital market nexus," *Geneva Papers on Risk and Insurance*, No. 89, October.

Punter, A. (2000) "New solutions for the financing of risk," *Journal of Insurance Research & Practice*, Chartered Insurance Institute, No. 2, July.

Williams, C.A., Jr., Smith, M.L. and Young, P.C. (1997) *Risk Management and Insurance*, 8th edn, McGraw-Hill.

Securing a safety net against economic free fall

by Frederic S. Mishkin

For the financial system to remain healthy, managers of financial companies must actively manage the risks they face to keep their companies viable. Managing these risks is the focus of this book. However, there are potentially highly dangerous shocks beyond the control of individual managers that can strike the financial system as a whole. The collective term for these threats is systemic risk.

Who should manage such risks? Obviously, only government can do so. The question is: how should they manage them and what role does this imply for government involvement in the financial system?

Why does systemic risk occur?

To answer these questions, we must first understand why systemic risk occurs and why it can be such a problem. Systemic risk occurs when there is a sudden, usually unexpected, event that disrupts financial markets, making them unable to channel funds effectively to those with the most productive investment opportunities. If this happens, business and households, starved of funds, stop spending and a severe economic downturn, perhaps even a depression, results.

Banking panics are one manifestation of systemic risk and provide a good illustration of how such risk can occur. Consider a situation in which there is no government safety net for the banking system (such as deposit insurance) and a major bank failure occurs. Depositors at this bank suffer losses, and other depositors at other banks begin to wonder whether their bank might also be insolvent. Because banks pay back depositors on a "first come, first served" basis, depositors who arrive at the bank first will get all their money back, while those later in line will suffer large losses if the bank fails. Once a major bank failure occurs, depositors have a strong incentive to rush to other banks and withdraw deposits, provoking what is naturally enough called a bank run. The withdrawal of deposits can trigger the failure of other banks, which provokes further bank failures, and so on. This snowball effect, often referred to as contagion, can then lead to a full-scale bank panic, in which a substantial portion of the banking system goes out of business and the economy suffers a severe economic downturn.

Government safety net

The systemic risk created by panics can be limited by government provision of a safety net for the banking system. One common way to do this is to provide government-guaranteed deposit insurance. If depositors will not suffer losses when a bank fails, they have no incentive to start a run on the bank even when they are concerned about the bank's health: they still get 100 cents on the dollar no matter what happens. Deposit insurance can therefore short-circuit bank runs and prevent bank panics.

Another way of providing a government safety net is through what is called the "lender of last resort." Faced with a potential banking panic, the central bank can provide liquidity to financial institutions to keep them afloat. It should only do so when these institutions are solvent but illiquid, or when the government needs time to marshal the funds to close institutions down or take them over in an orderly manner. In recent years, the US Federal Reserve has engaged in its role as lender of last resort several times. For example, in 1984 it lent $5bn to the Continental Illinois National Bank to prop it up.

Central banks can also act as lender of last resort to prevent systemic risk, even when another part of the financial system – not the banking system – is threatened. The most important recent example of this was the Federal Reserve's intervention immediately after the stock market crash of October 19, 1987. Just before the market opened on October 20, Alan Greenspan, chairman of the Federal Reserve Board, announced the Federal Reserve System's "readiness to serve as a source of liquidity to support the economic and financial system." Liquidity was injected into the system and banks were encouraged to lend to stockbrokers which needed large amounts of funds ($1.5bn for Kidder Peabody and Goldman Sachs alone) to clear their customers' margin accounts. The market immediately recovered and the business cycle continued.

Another example occurred in autumn 1998, straight after the Russian financial crisis and the near-failure of the Long Term Capital Management hedge fund simultaneously roiled US capital markets. Then the Fed also took pre-emptive action to avoid systemic risk by lowering its federal funds rate by 75 basis points.

International financial organizations such as the International Monetary Fund (IMF) have also taken on the role of lender of last resort. Billions of dollars were provided to Mexico and Argentina during the 1994–95 Tequila crisis, to east Asia during its crisis of 1997–98, and to Brazil in 1999.

Although a government safety net is able to keep systemic risk from spinning out of control, it is a mixed blessing. A safety net creates the well-known problem of moral hazard common to all insurance arrangements. When a financial institution knows the government will come to its rescue, it has incentives to take on greater risk because the government will bail it out. Provision of a safety net can thus lead to precisely the outcome the safety net is intended to prevent: the safety net encourages risk taking in the financial system, which makes systemic risk and financial fragility more likely. Can moral hazard be prevented? If so, how?

Regulation and supervision

Moral hazard can be constrained – and systemic risk minimized – by regulation and supervision. Once governments provide a safety net, they must implement regulations to limit the amount of risk that financial institutions can take. They can do this in several ways.

First, governments restrict the assets that financial institutions can hold and the activities in which they can engage. In many countries, for example, banks are restricted from holding common stock, which is considered too risky, or are not allowed to engage in activities unrelated to core banking.

Second, financial institutions are encouraged to diversify their asset holdings in order to reduce the overall riskiness of their balance sheet, for example with restrictions on their lending too much to any one customer.

Third, financial institutions are required to hold a minimal level of capital, which is often tied to the riskiness of their activities – the famous Basle Accord on bank capital requirements is one such example. Requiring sufficient amounts of capital not only ensures that the financial institution has a cushion against losses on its assets, but also reduces its incentives to take on risk. When a financial institution is forced to hold a large amount of capital, it has more to lose if it fails and is thus more likely to pursue less risky activities. Fourth, financial institutions are required to follow standard accounting principles and disclose a wide range of information about the risks they are incurring and the quality of their portfolio of assets.

Such regulations, however, are not by themselves sufficient to limit systemic risk and ensure the health of financial institutions, because the institutions they attempt to regulate may try to avoid them. The government must also engage in prudential supervision, in which financial institutions are subjected to periodic examination, both on- and off-site, to monitor whether they have sufficient capital and are complying with other regulations that limit risk taking.

In recent years, government examinations of financial institutions have begun to focus more on assessing the soundness of institutional management processes for controlling risk. Examinations that focus only on the position of an institution's balance sheet at a particular point in time are no longer adequate in a world in which financial innovation has produced new markets and instruments that make it easy to make huge bets quickly.

In this new financial environment, an institution that is quite healthy at a particular point in time can be driven into insolvency extremely rapidly from trading losses – forcefully demonstrated by the failure of the UK-based Barings bank in 1995. Thus, examinations that take only a snapshot of an institution at a point in time may not show whether it will face excessive risk in the near future. Bank examiners in many countries, for example, now have to give a separate risk management rating for the institutions they supervise; this rating then plays an important role in determining whether the bank is given a clean bill of health.

To limit systemic risk, it is not good enough to have stringent regulations in place. It is also crucial that prudential supervisors perform their jobs rigorously and do not engage in what is known as "regulatory forbearance" – in other words, fail to enforce regulations.

The most damaging form of regulatory forbearance occurs when supervisors allow financial institutions with insufficient capital to remain in operation. For example, in the 1980s US government regulators allowed savings and loan associations to include in their capital calculations a high value for intangible capital, in effect lowering capital requirements substantially and enabling many undercapitalized institutions to stay in business.

Undercapitalized institutions have tremendous incentives to take huge bets, particularly if they are insolvent, because if the bets come in they will be out of the hole, but if the bets turn sour the institutions have lost little in any case – once you are broke, it can't get any worse. Indeed, this is exactly what happened to undercapitalized savings and loans, leading to massive loan losses that cost US taxpayers considerably more than $100bn.

Although we hope that government officials act in the interest of the public, this is often not the case, and this also applies to prudential supervisors. Supervisors are human beings: they often try to escape blame for poor performance by sweeping things under the rug. By engaging in regulatory forbearance and allowing undercapitalized institutions to stay in operation, they can avoid acknowledging problem institutions and hope that time and good luck will improve the situation of these institutions and bring them back to health. Even if the institution does not recover, the supervisor may be able to avoid having the failure occur on their watch by moving to another job, often in the private sector, before the failure becomes known. Supervisors, in the interest of protecting their careers, can also be unduly influenced by politicians, who can lean on them to take it easy on financial institutions that have made big political contributions.

Systemic risk on the increase

In the last 20 years, systemic risk has become a growing problem. Before the 1980s, bank failures and financial crises were rare events in western industrialized nations. Between 1945 and 1980 in the US, there were on average fewer than 10 commercial bank failures per year. By the late 1980s, the annual number of bank failures had risen to more than 200. By the early 1990s, the Scandinavian countries Norway, Sweden, and Finland found themselves in a banking crisis, with bailout costs ranging from 4 to 11 percent of gross domestic product (GDP). Finland, which had the worst crisis, consequently experienced a very severe economic contraction.

Estimates suggest that Japan's banking problems will cost taxpayers over 10 percent of GDP and that the banking crisis in Mexico in 1994–95 will impose a cost of 20 percent of GDP on Mexican taxpayers. These losses pale in comparison to those incurred by the east Asian countries that experienced severe financial crises in 1997 and 1998. World Bank estimates suggest that the cost of cleaning up the Indonesian financial sector will exceed 50 percent of GDP. Further, the depression and the resulting economic hardship in that country because of the financial collapse have been disastrous.

Why has systemic risk become more of a problem? In recent years, there has been a growing trend toward the liberalization of financial systems in many economies and the globalization of international capital markets. This has provided new opportunities for risk taking by financial institutions.

In addition, the expectation by market participants that governments would come to the rescue of their financial sectors and offer a safety net has increased, and these expectations have been validated by huge bailouts, often conducted with the assistance of international financial organizations such as the IMF. Financial institutions have more incentive for moral hazard, so substantial increases in systemic risk have occurred.

What can be done?

I have described the basic ingredients that are required to manage systemic risk and promote the safety and soundness of financial systems throughout the world. Prudential supervisors must be given the incentives and resources to do their jobs properly: that is, enforce adequate restrictions on risky activities and assets, impose capital requirements that are sufficient to provide an adequate cushion for negative shocks to balance sheets, and not engage in regulatory forbearance, which allows insolvent institutions to continue to operate.

Making sure that prudential supervision works properly to manage systemic risk is easier said than done, but positive steps have been taken in this direction. In the US, the Federal Deposit Insurance Corporation Improvement Act (FDICIA) of 1991 implemented "prompt corrective action" provisions, which require bank supervisors to intervene earlier and more vigorously when a bank gets into trouble. Prompt corrective action has been spreading to many other countries. Bank capital requirements have been beefed up through the work of the Basle Committee on

Bank Supervision, operating under the auspices of the Bank for International Settlements. International banking standards have been proposed for countries that would have been able to borrow from multilateral institutions such as the IMF.

There is hope of improving the management of systemic risk, a task that should be a high priority for all those in the world of finance. Failure to manage systemic risk not only harms financial institutions, but when systemic risk gets out of hand it makes it harder for people to get loans, whether for purchasing a house or for building plant and equipment with which to increase productivity.

Further, when systemic risk leads to a financial crisis in which the financial system seizes up, depressions can result, with high unemployment, severe economic hardship, and the threat of political instability.

The last 20 years have not been good ones in terms of managing systemic risk. Let us hope that governments, banks, and financial institutions have learned the lesson and the future will bring considerable improvement.

Summary

The failure of a large financial institution has profound financial and psychological impacts on the overall financial system. Not only can the institution's creditors lose their capital, but the public may fear for the solvency of other financial institutions and cause them to fail too. In this article, **Frederic S. Mishkin** sets out how government or regulatory authorities attempt to reduce systemic risk. A government safety net, either with government-guaranteed deposit insurance or through the mechanism of a "lender of last resort" restoring liquidity and confidence to the financial system, can prevent the spread of systemic risk and financial panic. However, because a safety net can encourage risk taking, it must be combined with proper supervision of institutions by regulators to ensure that robust risk management strategies are established and observed.

Welcome to this week's one-in-a-million event

by Christopher C. Finger and Allan M. Malz

The concept of "normal distribution" has had a remarkable hold on thinking in a range of disciplines. Risk management and finance are no exceptions. The normal distribution was first formulated in the eighteenth century as a way of summarizing and forecasting physical phenomena. It was discovered in the nineteenth century that a great number of biological measures, such as the distribution of height in a population, also obey a normal law.

In the early twentieth century, the grip of the normal distribution was extended to finance when French mathematician Louis Bachelier discovered that successive changes in asset prices are approximately normal. The very name "normal" came about because this distribution seems to govern so many measurable phenomena.

Today, standard risk assessment techniques are based firmly on the normal distribution. Value at Risk (VaR), one of the basic and most common measures of financial risk, estimates the worst loss that a portfolio might suffer with a given small likelihood. The standard methods to compute VaR use forecasting techniques that assume that asset returns follow a normal distribution.

The standard model is not bad, since in fact it performs remarkably well. Regulators have, since 1998, allowed banks to use these models to determine minimum capital requirements, and the US Securities and Exchange Commission recently authorized corporations to disclose their derivatives exposures through standard VaR estimates.

Unfortunately, the models are not perfect. The differences between the normal distribution and real-world return distributions are small numerically, but extremely important practically for banks and corporations exposed to market prices.

Limitations of the standard model

What does it mean to say the standard model is "wrong"? Failure is an elusive concept here, since statistical models are not designed to give exact results. A VaR estimate states a portfolio's potential loss with only, say, a 95 percent level of certainty; it follows that even when the model works perfectly, there will be 5 percent of cases where the realized loss is greater. So one "excession" (a result that falls outside a given range) of the VaR does not constitute a failure, nor does a period of 100 days in which the VaR estimate is exceeded six times invalidate the argument that the VaR bounds the portfolio loss with 95 percent probability.

That said, certain individual moves are so large as to undermine the model's assumptions. The 40 percent depreciation of the Mexican peso in the week of December 19, 1994 was one such case. Assuming the standard model for the peso, we would have concluded that only one move of that magnitude was to be expected during the life of the universe. Forced to choose between admitting to the model's fallibility and the idea that we have been privileged to witness such a rare event, even the most egotistical among us would admit the model's shortcomings. Statisticians refer to such a decision as rejecting the null hypothesis that the model is reliable.

Figure 1: Exchange rate

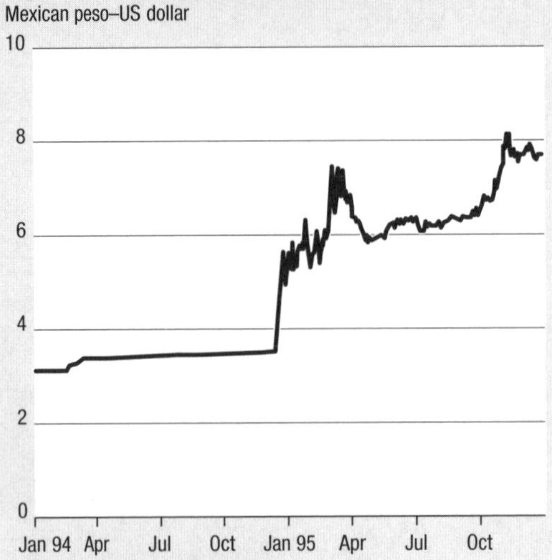

Source: DataMetrics (RiskMetrics Group)

Even during the relatively short lifespan of the authors of this piece, several of these one-in-a-million events have occurred: the US equity crash of October 1987; the breakdown of the European exchange rate mechanism in 1992; the plunge in copper prices in 1996; the devaluation of the peso in 1994, and of the Thai baht, Philippine peso, and Malaysian dollar in 1997. The puzzling frequency of these large moves, which experts call "fat tails," reminds one of the words of US sports commentators, who during the college football season routinely refer to "this week's game of the century."

Improving the models

The high number of model failures clearly indicates the need for improved models. Indeed, each new crisis generates a flurry of research activity, attempting to improve the mathematics of the models, or to enhance the information feeding them.

The mathematical improvements tend to focus on the way risk measures are derived from a set of historical data. To derive risk measures requires assumptions about the behavior of financial variables. One standard assumption is time-stationarity – that is, that the characteristics of a given asset (and in particular its volatility) do not change over time. Under this assumption, to estimate the volatility of a particular market factor, it is best to observe it over a long period, and consider each day of the period equally.

The frequency of large asset price moves and much other evidence indicate that the financial markets are not time-stationary, but exhibit volatility clustering. Volatility clustering implies that it is better to allow more recent behavior of the asset to have greater influence on volatility estimates. Consider the magnitude of returns on the dollar–yen exchange rate, seen in Figure 2. This rate was evidently more volatile late in 1998 than, say, in 1996. Were we to have estimated the volatility of the Japanese yen in mid-1998 using all of the available history, we would have understated its subsequent volatility. Allowing the recent behavior of the yen to drive our estimate yields a more accurate forecast.

Figure 2: Magnitude of dollar–yen returns 1994–1999

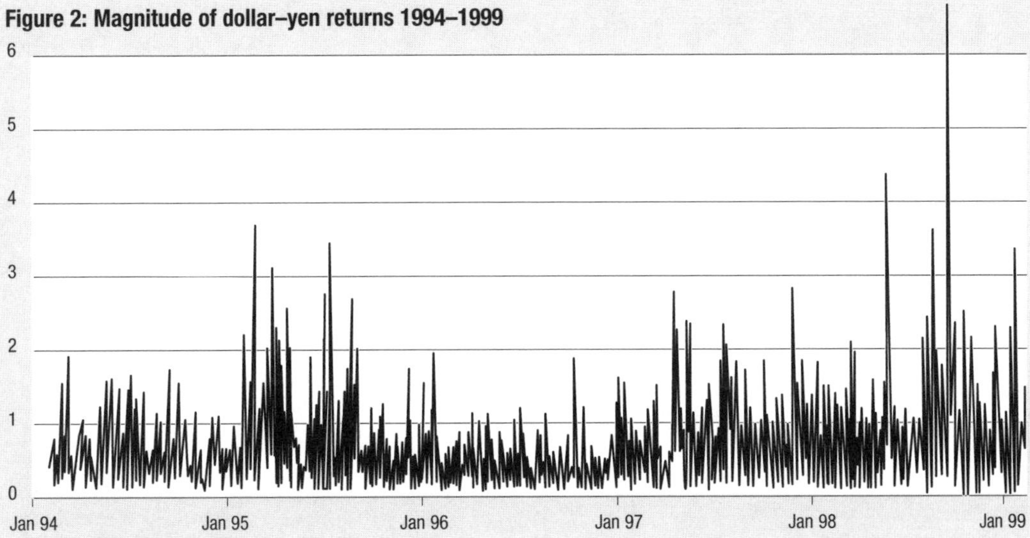

Source: DataMetrics (RiskMetrics Group)

Additionally, a branch of statistics called extreme value theory (EVT) is employed to describe the largest market moves. EVT recognizes that the problem with establishing statistical laws about rare events is that they are indeed rare. It attempts to exploit what little we know as fully as possible, and can be thought of as a law of large numbers for the extremes rather than the average of a distribution. The classic law of large numbers states that, for example, the proportion of heads in a large number of coin tosses is very close to one half, and even tells us the probability that the proportion of heads is, say, less than 49 percent. Similarly, EVT gives us probability laws for the rarest of market returns over a long period.

Despite the sophistication of these mathematical models, they can only extrapolate from the information they are given. The other route to improved models is to enhance the quality of this information. For instance, options are bets on market volatility, so their prices reflect market opinion on future volatility. Option-implied volatilities are therefore quite sensitive indicators of market expectations – or anxieties – about imminent large price moves. A good example is the behavior of the implied volatilities of options on the US dollar–Thai baht exchange rate in the weeks before the baht peg to the dollar was broken on July 2, 1997 (*see* Figure 3). The spot rate hardly budged as the exchange rate came under pressure; after all, it was still pegged. However, implied volatilities rose sharply, indicating that the markets were distinctly aware of the possibility of a baht devaluation.

Stress testing

Regrettably, there is a limit to forecasting enhancements, and there will always be market events that defy the models. This is where stress tests come in. As a recent report from the Bank for International Settlements notes, stress tests "enable managers to track a company's exposure to price changes during events that are considered plausible, without obliging them to develop a statistical model for such events." Specifically, a stress test is an examination of a portfolio under a specific set

Figure 3: US dollar–Thai baht exchange rate and implied volatility

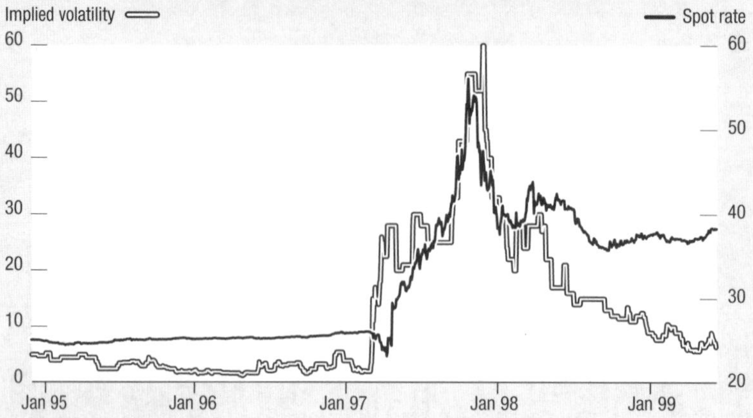

Source: DataMetrics (RiskMetrics Group)

of market moves (scenarios). What the standard model leaves out should drive what the stress test scenarios include. Stress tests are a crucial addition to VaR in forming a more complete "picture of risk" and in answering the corporate treasurer's or investor's real question: "What can go badly wrong?"

Scenarios can be historical, in which case we would apply the market moves observed in a past crisis. The result would be, for example, the earnings shortfall that would result were the Asian crisis of 1997 to be repeated. Historical scenarios are attractive because all relationships between markets are specified at once. On the other hand, no one believes that exactly the same combination of market moves will recur. It is therefore common to specify hypothetical scenarios: events that are plausible, but that have never occurred previously. Hypothesizing a scenario for one market is straightforward; the difficulty arises in specifying relationships between markets that would be likely in such a crisis scenario. To understand the difficulty, we have to see how market linkages shift during a crisis.

Market linkages in crises

Corporate treasurers and investors generally know the greatest exposures of their plans and portfolios to large changes in particular risk factors. The real surprises stem from the changed relationships among risk factors in stress periods, which can lead to far more serious losses than a large move in just one market rate. In currency crises, for example, devaluations typically induce interest rate shocks as the central bank scrambles to defend the currency. More surprising to market participants have been the implications of devaluations on credit quality: the weakened currency compromises the ability of domestic borrowers to meet foreign currency liabilities.

Currency crises often spread. The Tequila Effect, a phenomenon eerily repeated in the Asian turmoil of 1997, was a textbook example of contagion. Following the December 1994 decline in the Mexican peso, Mexican interest rates spiked and the equity market fell. Investors, rationally or not, pulled out of countries they felt resembled Mexico. As a result, equity markets fell in Brazil and Argentina, and later in Thailand and Indonesia. Even the US dollar depreciated sharply relative to the D-Mark and the yen. In the end, the standard models failed in these cases not only in forecasting the initial move but also in recognizing that other large moves would follow.

Figure 4: US 30-year swap spread, 1998

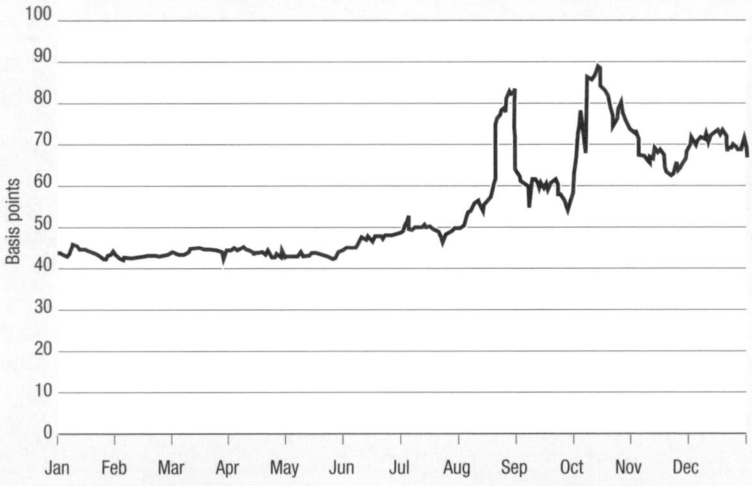

Source: DataMetrics (RiskMetrics Group)

The counterpart to contagion is another risk management buzzword, correlation breakdown. Here, previously reliable relationships between asset prices cease to hold. The events of the autumn of 1998 provide the classic example. Generally, the yields on US Treasury bonds (which are risk free) and those on bonds issued by a good-quality bank or corporation (which are risky) tend to rise and fall together. The yields on risky bonds will be higher, to compensate the investor for the risks that the issuer will fail to pay (credit risk) and that the bond will be difficult to sell (liquidity risk). The difference in yields, or spread, is generally quite stable, however, since the credit and liquidity risks do not change markedly from day to day.

Market participants rely on this stability in hedges, using US Treasury bonds to offset the risk of other fixed-income positions. However, in the fall of 1998, in reaction to the Russian default, investors flocked to US Treasury bonds. The sudden demand drove down Treasury yields much more than other interest rates, resulting in a widening of spreads (Figure 4) and heavy losses on positions that anticipated that the historical relationships would hold. The standard models, relying on data from a period where the relationship was stable, underestimated the likelihood of spreads moving to this extent.

The last example highlights a critical point: any model is only as good as the information that goes into it. If the information merely represents a historical period when relationships are as they are now, it should not be surprising that models do not predict the relationships to break down. As simple as this sounds, history is replete with surprised bankers and treasurers:

- Recently auctioned (on-the-run) Treasury bonds are highly liquid and typically trade at a premium to older (off-the-run) Treasury issues, although there are no essential differences between them. Perceptive traders exploit the discrepancy to profit when the prices of the bonds converge. However, in periods such as the fall of 1998, where linkages change, the prices can diverge further, resulting in significant losses.
- Companies may borrow in a foreign currency to achieve lower interest rates than

if they borrowed domestically. Usually, companies just end up lowering their interest costs, but occasionally, as in Europe in 1992 or Asia in 1997, the result is a serious foreign-exchange loss.

- Selling out-of-the-money "puts" on equity indices (that is, receiving payment up front for providing protection against losses) is a lucrative business as long as equity prices keep increasing and the protection is never needed.

For years at a time, these strategies can look like a free lunch – a steady return with no losses. Yet each of these strategies has incurred spectacular losses on occasions in the last decade. A risk manager who expects a model to recognize the risky nature of these strategies while using only the most recent information is as myopic as the traders or treasurers who claim that the profits are without risk.

In the past, the practice was to ignore the risks of sudden changes in price relationships, and define a hypothetical scenario by specifying the move for a small set of markets and assuming the remaining markets did not change. Market events, including the Asian crisis in 1997 and the aftermath of the Russian default in 1998, taught us that relationships change in crises, and that ignoring these relationships when stipulating a scenario renders the exercise meaningless. Managers now are more mindful of the potential of contagion and correlation breakdown, and a practice of predictive stress testing has emerged: stress moves for a select set of market factors are specified, and moves for the remaining markets are obtained through a model that incorporates market relationships.

Conclusion

This article addresses historical events in the financial markets and rationalizes the inability of risk models to forecast the most spectacular of these. The moral, however, is not to cast the models out, but to know them better. As our examples illustrate, the models are only as good as the assumptions and the information on which they rely. Prudence thus requires that any model be complemented with analysis of situations that the model will not forecast or address, using surprises from the past as a guide. When used properly, the resulting picture of risk can highlight weaknesses in portfolios and financial plans that standard models overlook.

Summary

Risk assessment technique models perform well but are not perfect – witness the 1987 US equities crash or the 1994 Mexican peso crisis which, if the models were to be believed, were once-in-a-millennium events. **Christopher C. Finger** and **Allan M. Malz** consider why risk models failed to anticipate the rash of spectacular recent financial events. However, they warn against throwing the baby out with the bath water. While a mathematical model may be at the cutting edge, it is only as good as its underlying assumptions and information inputs. Stress tests – which examine a portfolio under a specific set of market moves or scenarios – are critical supplements for obtaining a complete "picture of risk" and answering investor concerns about the downside. Taking past surprises as a guide, prudence suggests that any risk model should be measured against situations that the model itself cannot forecast or address.

Suggested further reading

Committee on the Global Financial System (2000) "Stress testing by large financial institutions: current practice and aggregation issues," Basle, March (available at www.bis.org/publ/cgfs14.htm).

Capital ideas that face dissension in the banks

by Tim Shepheard-Walwyn

Ever since a common international standard for regulatory capital was first established in 1988 by the Basle Committee, the international banking supervision body, the link between the risk that a bank assumes and the capital it is required to hold by its regulator has been pivotal in the overall banking approach to capital and risk management.

Over time, however, markets have developed and banks have improved their internal risk measurement and capital management systems. A gap has appeared between the regulatory capital requirements of the Basle Committee and the amount of "economic capital" that banks would choose to hold as a protection against the risk if they could use their own internal risk measures.

Calculating capital requirement

The background to the problem lies with the existing Basle Committee methodology for calculating the capital requirement for credit risk. The formula requires a bank to maintain a fixed amount of capital against each of its assets, without distinguishing between the riskiness of different classes of borrower. Thus, the same amount of capital must be set aside for a £100m loan to a triple-A-rated corporate borrower as for a £100m portfolio of loans to small start-up businesses. Yet statistical analysis shows that the risk of lending to the latter group of borrowers may be hundreds of times more hazardous than lending to the former.

Furthermore, the Basle approach is at odds with a central principle of modern risk management, which recognizes that the individual risks in a portfolio of assets can offset one another in a systematic way because different assets behave differently – otherwise referred to as co-variance effects. Consequently, the Basle formula requires a bank to hold the same amount of capital against a single loan of £100m to one borrower as it must for ten loans of £10m to different borrowers with the same credit rating. This is despite the fact that the likelihood of all ten borrowers defaulting simultaneously is many times less than the probability of any single borrower defaulting.

The absence of allowances for portfolio effects of this type – which can significantly reduce the amount of credit risk a bank faces – is now recognized as a serious weakness in the existing Basle methodology and a foremost cause of the gap between regulatory and economic capital. The problems created by the gap between economic capital and the Basle system are well known to both regulators and industry practitioners. Several attempts have been made to address this issue.

The most significant development was the Basle Committee's introduction in 1996 of the market risk amendment to take account of the risk that banks face from changes in the market prices of their portfolios of traded assets. This permitted banks to use their own Value at Risk models to calculate the regulatory capital requirement, with the express objective of aligning the regulatory capital requirement with banks' internal measurements for economic capital.

However, for most banks, market risk accounts for only a small proportion of their overall risk profile. Despite changes in financial markets, the credit risk charge remains the most significant factor in determining the regulatory capital requirement for the majority of banks, and this is where divergence between economic and regulatory capital is most pronounced. As a result, the Basle Committee announced in June 1999 that it would review the 1988 Basle Accord, with a view to aligning banks' regulatory capital requirements for credit risk and their economic credit risk.

Risk mitigation effects

To achieve this, the committee is considering basing capital requirements on banks' own internal rating systems, which assess the relative riskiness of their different classes of counterparties. It will also consider making allowance for risk mitigation effects from guarantees and other credit risk reduction techniques, such as collateral and credit derivative transactions. It has indicated it might later consider allowing banks to calculate their regulatory capital requirements for credit risk by using their internal credit models. These calculate the economic capital requirement for credit risk by taking into account the overall effect of individual transactions on the bank's total credit risk at a portfolio level.

The committee also recognizes another important issue. Banks increasingly distinguish between the "expected loss" and the "unexpected loss" in determining the economic capital required to protect against credit risk. At the time the original Basle Accord was agreed in 1988, banks did not generally appreciate the significance of this distinction. Credit losses were regarded as random events and capital was seen as a buffer against all losses.

However, with the application of modern statistical approaches to credit risk, banks now appreciate that there is an "expected loss" or average likelihood of a loss for any particular class of borrower. "Expected loss" is seen as a cost of extending credit and is charged to the borrower as part of the credit spread. This means that, provided the bank has estimated its expected loss accurately, it should be able to cover most of its credit losses using its income from credit spreads. The bank will only need to use its capital to cover those cases where its actual losses exceed its expected losses – its "unexpected losses." Therefore, any attempt to align regulatory and economic capital has to recognize that economic capital is only relevant to a measure of unexpected, not expected, loss.

However, this comparatively recent recognition has a potentially profound impact on the search for an effective alignment between regulatory capital requirements and the banks' own risk capital measures, and is reflected in current discussions on how the Basle Committee should set capital standards for "other risks." This is now central to the discussion about the future of regulatory capital. The committee recognizes that the overall effect of moving toward a more economically precise measure of credit risk – particularly one based on unexpected loss measures – will almost certainly mean a reduction in the total regulatory capital requirement for credit risk for any individual bank.

A move toward a more economically appropriate capital requirement for credit risk is likely to reduce the total amount of regulatory capital in the financial system unless compensating action is taken elsewhere. Thus, the Basle Committee has decided that any change to the regulatory regime for credit risk needs to be accompanied by an additional requirement for "other risks," which it takes to include such operational risks as rogue trading and systems failures, as well as the interest rate risk that banks carry in the banking book. Unsurprisingly, perhaps, consensus on "other risks" is proving difficult to achieve. The question of how a bank determines overall economic capital requirements for all its business risks has only recently attracted attention.

Given the high profile of debate over these issues, it may seem strange to argue that the problem now facing the industry and the regulators is the lack of a sound theoretical basis for determining the capital a bank requires to support its business. In the context of corporate finance theory, however, financial and non-financial firms have always taken different approaches to determining capital. We therefore need to understand the assumptions underlying the conventional analyses of bank capital structures. Recent changes in banking raise important questions about the suitability of such analyses.

In standard corporate finance theory, the cost of capital to a company reflects the overall riskiness of prospective earnings. Importantly, it is assumed that this cost is unaffected by any decision on the relative mix of equity and debt that the company holds. This means that, differential tax treatment of equity and debt apart, the decision about how much equity the company holds is one of how the risk in the future earnings stream is best shared between debt and equity holders. It follows that the economic or risk capital charge attributable to any particular business or investment is simply the weighted average cost of funding the business. This is an accurate reflection of the market's assessment of the overall corporate risk profile and of the hurdle rate the business faces in adding value for the shareholder.

In banking, however, the importance of deposits in funding business means that this approach to determining the optimal capital structure and allocating capital to a business does not work. Unlike a normal business, where the funding choice is between debt and equity, a bank has three sources of financing – equity, bond finance, and deposits. The most significant part is a bank's deposit base. On a day-to-day basis there is little, if any, link between the "riskiness" or prospective volatility of bank earnings and the cost of deposits. The weighted average cost of its funds does not reflect a bank's risk profile, and thus the decision between debt and equity financing is not cost neutral. It will always be more expensive for a bank to fund its business out of capital than from additional deposits.

Linking risk measures and capital

As a result of these differences, an alternative approach has emerged for determining the economic capital required by banks, which seeks to establish a direct link between risk measures and capital. It assumes that a direct analysis of the bank's risks can be made and that the economic capital the bank needs to protect it can be derived from these measures. This is achieved by analyzing the riskiness of the individual elements of the bank's balance sheet and current activities.

If, for example, a bank holds a particular portfolio of loans or trading positions, it seeks to estimate the unexpected loss associated with the credit and market risk in those portfolios and to derive the amount of potential loss associated with this risk. The logical extension of this approach is what the Basle Committee has adopted with respect to "other risks." It recommends that banks identify all other risks associated with their activities so as to calculate the unexpected loss associated with each additional class of risk, then add up each class of economic capital to reach a total requirement for economic capital. These associated risks include transaction processing, fraud, and reputational risk.

Recently, however, the limitations of this method have become increasingly clear. The central role of equity for a bank is no different from that at any other company owned by shareholders and with various forms of debt on its balance sheet. A chief reason for maintaining equity capital is to provide a bank with a buffer against future earnings volatility, and in particular against loss risk at any particular point in time. From this simple definition of the purpose of equity, we can draw two very important conclusions. First, we cannot make any meaningful statement about a bank's risk profile and consequently its economic capital requirement unless we also have information about expected earnings. Second, the volatility of the bank's expected future earnings is likely to be significant in determining its appropriate economic capital requirement.

Corporate finance theory

The recognition that the appropriateness of a bank's economic capital structure can only be assessed in the context of its potential future earnings stream is not surprising when considered in terms of corporate finance theory. The theory sees this as the primary risk for which companies require equity.

Moreover, there is plenty of solid evidence in banks' stock market performance to support the idea that market perceptions about the scale and volatility of prospective earnings are critical in determining banks' market valuations. Indeed, recent uncertainty about the possible impact of the internet on banks' earnings potential and the speedy bank response to this confirm that senior managers are fully aware of the importance of the market view.

That a large part of a bank's economic capital exists to protect against future earnings risk has profound implications both for how capital adequacy needs to be assessed within banks, and for allocating capital to various business activities to ensure that risk is properly captured and rewarded. This also helps to explain why the Basle Committee's proposals to introduce a capital requirement for "other risks" have hit difficulties. It is trying to estimate economic and regulatory capital using a theoretical framework that ignores prospective bank earnings.

It may, indeed, be true for many banks that the largest element in their economic capital requirement exists to cover risks other than credit and market risks. However, such risks cannot be measured by estimating the causes of earnings volatility – such as credit, market and operational risk – alone. It has to be considered against the level of earnings it affects. So, for example, a bank with a credit risk measure of $500m has a much lower requirement for capital to protect against a potential loss when its earnings are $1,000m a year than if they were $300m a year. The standard methodology for determining bank capital ignores this. However, it is growing in importance as banks increase the amount of earnings obtained from activities – such as investment advice, private banking, and fund management – unrelated to their balance sheets.

A further issue is yet to be resolved. Should the regulatory capital requirements set by the Basle Committee be the same as the economic capital requirements that banks determine for themselves, or should the regulatory requirement be different but still consistent with the way that banks calculate economic capital?

Concerns differ

To date – and in the course of this article – it has been assumed that the two measures should be the same. However, it is becoming clear that the concerns of the regulatory authorities differ from those of bank managers. Managers aim to set economic capital so as to optimize the risk-adjusted return to their shareholders over the medium term. The regulator seeks to ensure that the bank has sufficient capital to protect against a potential systemic shock over a relatively short time horizon.

These are not inconsistent objectives. It is clearly in the manager's interests to ensure that the bank can survive a systemic shock. However, the amount of capital it needs to do so and the amount of economic capital it needs to optimize shareholder returns over the medium term are not necessarily identical. In general, it is likely that the amount of economic capital a bank holds would be appreciably more than the amount of capital it would need to absorb a systemic shock. Most banks recognize that such a shock could occur and that they need sufficient capital to survive it and to remain in business thereafter.

Moreover, as previous articles in this book have noted, the way a company estimates the scale of its exposure to a systemic event (and hence estimates the capital it needs to protect against that event) is more likely to be based on scenario planning and stress-testing techniques. This contrasts with the volatility-based methods that banks typically use to estimate the amount of economic capital needed to meet shareholder expectations about earnings volatility.

It is thus clear that the discussion about an appropriate future regulatory capital framework – and particularly how "other risks" fit into the framework – is still rudimentary. But it is already possible to see what will be required for a system that will make corporate responsibility for shareholder returns consistent with the needs of regulators to protect against systemic risk. There are a number of important considerations:

- economic capital measures that provide an adequate level of assurance to bank shareholders that they will be suitably protected against prospective future earnings volatility over the medium term;
- regulatory capital requirements to protect against systemic risk over the relatively short term;
- regulatory capital requirements that incorporate all potential sources of loss that could affect bank earnings and based on stress tests;
- regulatory capital requirements that take into account the earnings capability of the company to protect itself against potential loss sources;
- regulatory capital requirements consistent with the bank's own estimates of potential exposure to such stress events. This amount would generally be expected to be less than the economic capital the bank decides it needs to protect against potential earnings volatility over the longer term.

Agreement here should provide a solid basis for developing a new approach to regulatory capital. However, the continuing absence of agreement is likely to perpetuate problems now being encountered in trying to establish a new, sustainable replacement for the 1988 Basle Accord.

Summary
The Basle Committee's 1988 minimum capital requirements for financial institutions are showing their age. From the banker's perspective, **Tim Shepheard-Walwyn** notes that in approaching capital and risk management issues, banks can tap increasingly sophisticated measuring techniques. This throws up some important differences in opinion for banks and regulators. Currently, both sides are wrangling over the question of how to tally regulatory capital requirements with banks' desires to optimize capital levels. Modern statistical approaches can now accurately determine expected and unexpected losses. Some argue that the gap between regulatory capital requirements and levels favored by banks could be narrowed. With both parties defending different corners, convergence may be a challenge.

Suggested further reading

Basle Committee on Banking Supervision (1999) *A New Capital Adequacy Framework.*

Hawawini, G. and Viallet, C. (1998) *Finance for Executives*, South Western College Publishing.

Matten, C. (2000) *Managing Bank Capital*, Wiley.

Shepheard-Walwyn, T. and Litterman, R. (1998) "Building a coherent risk measurement and capital optimization model for financial firms," *Federal Reserve Bank of New York Economic Policy Review.*

Shepheard-Walwyn, T. and Rohner, M. (2000) "Equity at risk – an alternative approach to setting regulatory capital standards for internationally active financial firms," International Financial Risk Institute Discussion Paper, at www.risk.ifci.ch

A firm foundation for project finance

by Akash Deep

In the past few years, both industrialized and developing countries have increasingly used project finance to fund transactions involving the construction, privatization, and concession of large infrastructure projects. These have included power-generation plants, toll roads, bridges, and development of oil and gas reserves. Notable examples are the Eurotunnel between France and the UK (worth $16bn), the Trans Alaska Pipeline System Project ($7.7bn), the Sincor Heavy Oil Project in Venezuela ($4.5bn), the Hibernia Oil Field Project off the coast of Newfoundland ($4.1bn), and the Melbourne City Link Project ($1.2bn). Private-sector investment in project finance deals rose to almost $100bn in 1998. It is expected to grow significantly in the next few years.

Project finance involves creating a separate legal and economic entity with the primary role of setting up an organizational structure and obtaining the necessary financial resources to develop and manage a project. The main, and crucial, distinction from conventional financial structures is that repayment to debt and equity providers depends solely on the capacity of the project to generate cash flows, with typically no recourse to the sponsor's balance sheets or assets.

Given the myriad risks embedded in all projects, reliance on the project itself as the sole source of revenue makes careful risk management imperative for project finance transactions. The first reason for this is that both the debtors and project owners face a lack of diversification. The returns that both participants expect depend strictly on one source of income, the project.

The second reason concerns the large size and long tenure of projects. According to a recent study, the average amount in project finance exceeds $500m, while the average maturity is close to 20 years. These characteristics, together with high leverage ratios, represent important sources of risk. In addition, many projects are financed by international sources, exposing them to risks associated with unstable exchange rates, different legal jurisdictions, and varied political regimes.

While the prime objective of risk management in project finance is to ensure that the project remains financially viable, there are other risks involved that cannot be tackled solely by the standard tools of financial risk management. Project finance also requires the use of innovative contractual structures that can facilitate a transfer of risks between the project, its sponsors and contractors, loan and debt providers, equity holders, the government, insurance agencies, and, in some cases, multilateral organizations. It is the establishment of these contractual agreements that makes risk management in project finance a complex and painstaking process that can often take many years and cost millions of dollars.

Although the final risk structure will vary from project to project according to the negotiating positions of the various parties, the fundamental principle of project finance remains the same: each risk should be allocated to the party that can best control or manage it. Sources of risk, as mentioned before, are varied and extend through all the phases of the project. These risks can be classified under the following broad areas: development and construction, operation and maintenance, financial risks, political and legal risks, environmental risks, and *force majeure.*

Development and construction

Development and construction risks range from studying the feasibility of the project and obtaining government permits to the raising of funds for construction. Other related risks involve technology, the likelihood of cost overruns and delays, and the successful transfer of the project from the contractor to the operator.

Given this large menu of risks, it is not surprising that traditionally expensive, short-term bank loans were the only option for construction financing. They would be refinanced to longer-term loans, debt and equity, after the completion of construction. After all, how could one seek financing for, say, 20 years, to be redeemed from the project's cash flows, when the revenue-generating asset was not even in place? By carefully parceling out these risks through strong completion guarantees from, and incentives to, the project contractor, even this can be achieved.

For example, in 1997, TermoEmcali, a combined-cycle gas-fired power-generating facility in Cali, Colombia, was the first power project in that country to finance its construction with $165m "out of the box," 17¾-year bonds (representing 79 percent of the total project loan) a good two years before the planned commencement of operation. This aggressive financing scheme was facilitated by entering a fixed-price turnkey construction contract with affiliates of Bechtel, the largest private US construction company.

Explicit turnkey contracts can be expensive, however. So instead, the Sutton

Bridge power station, a $450m project in Lincolnshire, UK, used a variety of strategies. These included schedule and performance-liquidated damages that involve monetary compensation for failure to meet deadlines and/or predetermined performance levels, totaling 50 percent of the project cost, along with completion bonuses, to create what was, in effect, a turnkey engineering, procurement, and construction contract with General Electric International, a wholly owned subsidiary of GE of the US, and subsidiary contractors.

Operation and maintenance

The assessment of risks over the second major phase in the life of the project – operation and maintenance – is fundamental, because these affect its long-term viability and determine the level of funds that both sponsors and lenders will receive throughout its life. Such risks primarily encompass the technological and economic aspects of the project: the failure to achieve adequate performance, the risk of technological obsolescence, the risk of inadequate demand, the possible entrance of new competitors, and the cost and availability of material and labor.

The risk of the project meeting specific performance criteria is best mitigated by making this a part of the construction agreement with the contractor. However, addressing maintenance risk is equally important to ensure undisrupted cash flows from the project asset. For example, the 30-year concession for construction and upgrading of the 418km N3 toll road in South Africa, the largest project finance transaction in that country, was exposed to the risk of overloaded trucks causing severe road damage that could increase maintenance costs significantly. (One overloaded truck can cause the same amount of damage as 18 legal vehicles.) The sponsors are mitigating this risk by installing moving and static weighbridges, and have agreed to provide technical and administrative assistance to enable the authorities to enforce the law regarding the overloading of vehicles on the highway.

Of course, the primary risk that a project faces is economic: will it generate sufficient revenue by certain dates to meet its financing obligations? If large parts of these risks are borne by the financiers, this can hamper the rating of the project and could even make it impossible to seek cheaper financing in capital markets, leaving more expensive bank loans as the only option. However, long-term procurement and supply contracts that stabilize both the volume and the price of the output can be used to mitigate these in many cases.

Financing instruments

Risks can also arise from the financial structure adopted for the project. Sponsors and lenders need to review the exposure of cash flows from the project to changes in exchange-rate volatility and convertibility, inflation, and interest rates. While these can have a strong impact on revenues from the project, they are generally outside the control of the participants and hence need to be addressed via financial instruments or contracts.

One of the catalysts in the rapid development of international project finance has been the adoption of US Rule 144A by the Securities and Exchange Commission (SEC), which allows institutional investors to engage in secondary trading of privately placed debt. This has greatly widened the risk appetite, efficiency, and liquidity of the debt market for project finance, and thus made it attractive for international issuers to raise dollar debt without having to meet strict, time-consuming SEC regulations.

However, most projects have revenues denominated in local currency, whose depreciation may significantly increase the cost of their dollar debt obligations, especially due to the long amortization period of project debt. The Mexican and Asian crises, which caused significant project finance defaults, have brought the risk of currency fluctuations into sharp focus.

In industrialized countries, which have developed financial markets and relatively stable macro-economic fundamentals, most financial risks can be hedged through standard derivative instruments such as swaps, futures, and options. In developing countries, however, regulations often do not permit normal hedging instruments such as forwards or futures. In such situations, non-delivery forward exchange-rate contracts (NDF) have proven to be excellent tools for managing currency risk.

An NDF differs from standard forward contracts in that physical exchange is not contemplated; instead, the notional value of the contract is evaluated based on a pre-determined formula and one party makes a net payment to the other. In some cases, long-term contracts that involve the host government have also been employed.

In the 1998 Caderyta project financing, which consisted of the upgrading and expansion of the Pemex refinery in Mexico, the contract included a $2bn interest-rate swap that hedged all of the floating interest-rate exposure of the project. On the other hand, in the 1999 Cross Israel $1.35bn, 30-year toll road concession, $850m was raised locally at floating interest rates, but no hedging was possible. Hence, the deal included a special mechanism whereby if, at the end of the 4½-year construction period, the average interest cost exceeded the expected level, the toll could be increased. Similarly, if the interest cost were less than expected, the toll would be reduced. Additionally, the toll would be adjusted on a yearly basis for inflation as well as currency fluctuations that might affect the $250m international debt denominated in dollars.

The law, politics, and environment

In assessing legal and political risks in project finance, it is fundamental to have a clear understanding of the historical and social environment of the country in which the project is being developed. These risks can include political instability, issues of sovereignty, corruption, and regulatory changes, such as the introduction of tariffs and quotas, deregulation, and expropriation.

Risk managers should seek to mitigate these risks through governmental agreements. In the $616m Liabin B coal-fired plant, the first Chinese infrastructure project to be financed entirely with foreign capital, the concession agreement provided sweeping government guarantees. This included clauses that entitled the project to compensatory payments in case of any significant changes in law, including tax and environmental regulations, that might prevent the company from fulfilling its obligations to lenders.

In the absence of such guarantees, projects can seek political risk insurance from such organizations as the World Bank's Multilateral Investment Guarantee Agency; the Overseas Private Investment Corporation (OPIC), an arm of the US government; export credit agencies and private insurers. Political risk insurance has become particularly important to lenders in the wake of the Asian financial crisis and sovereign defaults by Russia, Indonesia, and Pakistan. The Trident energy power project in Thailand, one of the few project finance deals to close in 1998, was financed entirely from debt that included political risk insurance or that provided by Thai government-owned agencies. Similarly, a $200m debt offering by the Telefonica del Peru telecommunications project in Peru was launched in 1999 backed to the full amount by OPIC.

Legal and political risks become more pronounced in cross-border and binational projects. For example, the Buenos Aires–Colonia bridge project, which consists of a 42km bridge uniting Argentina and Uruguay across the Rio de la Plata river, required a bilateral treaty, which, once ratified by both senates, will supersede the laws of both countries unless challenged constitutionally. The treaty sets up a bi-national commission to administer the project and defines all-important legislation that might affect its performance. This includes tax and labor laws, protection against expropriation and development rights for complementary projects.

Environmental risks can translate into higher costs both during the implementation phase and throughout the operation of the project. These include the costs of external audits that determine potential outside problems such as pollution, the implementation of mechanisms that reduce contamination, and clean-up costs. Project managers can address environmental risks through negotiations with the government of the host country, as in the case of the Chinese Liabin B project. Alternately, they can conform to more universal standards, such as the Colombian TermoEmcali project, which was built in compliance with World Bank environmental standards. It was also agreed that if any changes in environmental laws hindered the project's economics, these costs would simply be passed through to the government.

Force majeure

Finally, *force majeure* risks generated by events such as floods, fire, and wars must be taken into account. Although the sponsors or lenders of the project cannot directly manage these risks, they can hedge against many of them through insurance contracts. The sponsor of the Jamnagar project, a $2bn refinery and petrochemical complex on the India–Pakistan border, had conventional insurance, but this did not cover damage in case of war. Therefore, in July 1999, after a few months of intensified military action across the border, the sponsors sought war insurance coverage for the project.

Conclusion

As individuals and companies continue to master the different risks associated with project finance, we can expect new financing opportunities to emerge from the realms of capital markets. Currently, most international funding is denominated in US dollars, but as the euro acquires greater importance in world markets, it is likely that new finance projects across the world will demand euro debt, resulting in a widening of international funding sources.

Further, it is expected that the trend toward securitization of project finance loans will gain momentum. Although each project will have specific contractual agreements, effective risk management will seek to standardize projects so that they can be pooled and sold in capital markets. This will address the primary source of risk in project finance, the lack of diversification.

As opportunities for project finance continue to expand and financial markets develop instruments to fund these projects, precise risk management that provides the right blend of innovative financial and contractual hedging mechanisms will be fundamental for the success of any project.

Summary

Industrialized and developing countries increasingly use project finance to build, privatize, and operate flagship developments. Project finance relies solely on the ability of the project to make repayments to sponsors and lenders. As a result, writes **Akash Deep**, a risk manager's primary focus is ensuring the financial viability of the project in the face of its risk exposure. Project finance risks cover development and construction, operation and maintenance, financial risk, political and legal risk, environmental risk, and *force majeure*. The article argues that innovative and highly complex contractual structures can be used in successfully managing these risks. Further, it suggests that fresh financing opportunities will emerge as capital market participants begin to master project finance risks.

Suggested further reading

Ahmed, P.A. and Fang, X. (1999) "Project finance in developing countries," International Finance Corporation, *Lessons of Experience*, No. 7.

Benoit, P. (1996) "Project finance at the World Bank: an overview of policies and instruments," World Bank Technical Paper, No. 312.

Buljevich, E.C. and Park, Y.S. (1999) *Project Financing and the International Financial Markets*, Kluwer Academic.

Finnerty, J.D. (1996) *Project Financing: Asset-Based Financial Engineering*, J. Wiley.

Hoffman, S.L. (1998) *The Law and Business of International Project Finance: A Resource for Governments, Sponsors, Lenders, Lawyers, and Project Participants*, Kluwer Law International.

EMERGING ISSUES IN RISK

8

Contributors

Eric K. Clemons is a professor of information strategy, systems, and economics at the Wharton School of the University of Pennsylvania. His research and teaching interests are in the area of information technology and competitive strategy, with a focus on successful implementation of e-commerce initiatives.

Paul Willman is a professor of organizational behavior and industrial relations at London Business School and Director of the Centre for Organizational Research at London Business School. His research interests include industrial relations and risk management.

Bernd Schmitt is professor of business at Columbia Business School in New York and founder and executive director of the Center on Global Brand Leadership.

David Brotzen is a founder of Brotzen Mayne Limited, a corporate reputation consultancy. He was formerly European head of crisis management at Hill & Knowlton, an international public relations agency.

Nigel Nicholson is a professor of organizational behavior at London Business School. His research interests include leadership skills, personality and executive behavior, group processes, and decision making.

Contents

Gauging the power play in the new economy 229
Eric K. Clemons, Wharton School, University of Pennsylvania
Strategic risks posed by the internet are a time bomb in waiting. This article warns of how changes in business focus are set to cause upheavals.

Branding puts a high value on reputation management 236
Bernd Schmitt, Columbia Business School
Branding is now about lifestyle and brands are rocketing in value. Protecting brands and managing reputation are mission-critical skills.

Folly, fantasy, and roguery: a social psychology of finance risk disasters 241
Nigel Nicholson, London Business School
Paul Willman, London Business School
In the world of high finance, basic forces like ego, fear, and greed appear to override the traditional belief that markets always act rationally.

Wise words and firm resolve when times get tough 246
David Brotzen, Brotzen Mayne Ltd
Protecting corporate reputations in times of disaster requires well-planned strategies and rigorously trained executives. This article highlights the perils of neglect.

Introduction

Born of financial deregulation, nurtured by globalization and confirmed by the arrival of the internet, "change" has been a recurrent theme in business literature in the past two decades. The transformations wrought by these forces have created entirely new risks that companies are only beginning to address. Subtler changes, such as a widespread public intolerance of corporate interests and the increased importance of corporate reputation, demand a sophisticated awareness of social and legal issues.

Gauging the power play in the new economy

by Eric K. Clemons

E-commerce is primarily about "commerce," not about "e;" companies want to use bits to sell physical goods, not use physical goods to sell bits. Therefore, this article focusses on the strategic risks associated with launching e-commerce ventures, rather than the electronic or technical risks associated with e-commerce. For instance, we examine what happens when a website destroys industry profitability, rather than, say, the problems of a retail website that experiences frequent crashes.

This strategic perspective is not new: competitive strategy has for centuries been about the deployment of economic resources, to force a desired outcome, in the presence of uncertainty and hostile intent. However, e-commerce has changed so many of the risks, and altered the value of so many resources, that strategic plans and strategic risk assessments require a fresh look. For that reason, the practice of combat economics will play a central role in reviewing and preparing for the risks associated with e-commerce. This is based on the deployment of economic resources, in order to force an outcome, in the presence of strategic uncertainty and hostile intent.

There are myriad risks associated with e-commerce, many of which overlap with the risks of old-economy companies. Four of the most important are structural risk, channel risk, sourcing risk, and general risks of strategic uncertainty. We examine each of these in turn.

Structural risk

A common risk of e-commerce is that companies design their business strategies in such a way that industry structure makes them inherently unprofitable, or they exploit for profit the very inefficiencies that the e-commerce transformation will assuredly eliminate.

Examples might include online vendors of commodity products, such as bestselling books or compact discs, which are now sold at the cost the vendors are charged by the publishers. Customer loyalty strategies apart, the practice of buying *Harry Potter and the Prisoner of Azkaban* for $9.97 and selling it to a customer for $9.97 does not offer long-term profitability.

Most large consumer web-based retailers are still in their growth stage, and, like the online retailer Amazon.com, they are still paying to acquire customers and market share. It is too early to determine whether consumers will remain loyal to these sites, allowing these retailers time to harvest profits and cover the costs of their acquisition, or whether the web's empowerment of consumer choice will mean that customers constantly migrate to the lowest-cost online seller. If the web is as liberating and empowering as most accounts have led us to believe, all business models based on paying to acquire share are flawed.

In another example, many electronic exchanges rely on the presence of excess production materials, such as glass or steel products. We cannot yet determine whether their business model – profit from liquidating excess production and overstock – will succeed, or whether the web's ability to enable careful co-ordination between industrial customers and their producers will lead to channel optimization. Such co-ordination would eliminate production mistakes, and thus would eliminate the excess inventory on which these exchanges hoped to trade.

Channel risk

Companies have always used a distribution channel to move their products and services through a chain of intermediaries to the final consumer. Airlines use computerized reservations systems to enable travel agencies to sell seats to passengers. Cereal and detergent companies use wholesalers, who sell to retailers, who sell to consumers.

Inevitably, e-commerce will alter some of these channels: British Airways provides seats directly to passengers and Unilever may in future provide detergent directly to households. This throws up a number of questions. Which companies will remain in the channel and which will be ousted? What if changes in industry structure require that a company changes its channel strategy, reaching out directly to its customers? What if it does this too soon and is punished by its current channel partners? What if it fails to do this soon enough, and loses out to those partners or its competitors?

Branding and customer loyalty play an important part in answers to these questions. Consider the market for packaged consumer goods in supermarkets. Traditional stores such as Sainsbury or Tesco in the UK, Carrefour in France, or Wal-Mart in the US carry multiple brands of the same product to avoid losing sales to consumers who care about the brands they purchase. But what if a Sainsbury online store or an electronic Wal-Mart knew precisely what each consumer wanted, and could identify the consumers without any significant brand loyalty? Shoppers who wanted Viva paper towels would get Viva, and shoppers who wanted Bounty paper towels would get Bounty. Shoppers with no strong preference, however, would get whatever the online vendor wanted them to get, which would almost certainly be the product with the highest margins for the vendor.

Indeed, physical stores have to display products so that customers with strong preferences will be able to find what they want, otherwise there is some risk that they might leave the store. In the physical environment, manufacturers have to pay for preferential treatment, such as end-of-aisle displays and promotional programs, but to some extent they still get a free ride – at least some shelf space is provided for the display of their products to avoid losing brand-loyal customers. Thus they are carried on the shelves for view even by customers without a preference for their brand. On the internet, however, the vendor can reconfigure the "store" for each customer, knowingly showing brand-loyal online consumers their preferences, and showing the vast majority whatever is most profitable for the store. This, of course, leads to a bidding war, as manufacturers are forced to cut the prices that they charge the store operator, or offer discounts and overrides, to bid for virtual shelf space in the store. Companies with weak brands may be doomed if they allow the channel to become dynamically reconfigurable in this way.

What if, instead, the manufacturer attempts to launch an internet sales channel itself? Perhaps the question should be, what would the online vendor do to the first paper-towel manufacturer, or the first detergent manufacturer, that attempted a bypass strategy? It is safe to assume that the retailer would respond, and would respond rapidly, by decreasing shelf space, increasing prices, or taking other actions to reduce sales of the offending manufacturer's goods.

Further, the internet retail market is not yet sufficiently developed for manufacturers to disregard their old distribution partners. Electronic home shopping in the US, for instance, has captured less than 1 percent of total grocery sales in the decade or so of its operation. How rapid has the stores' response been to manufacturers' threatened bypass strategies? Not surprisingly, intermediaries have launched their punishment strategies almost immediately after the bypass or direct distribution strategy is announced, well before any consumer adoption has occurred. The experience in the US has been that adoption of alternative distribution systems is slow, punishment by traditional channel intermediaries is immediate, and the results are often catastrophic for the manufacturer.

These two analyses together suggest that many manufacturers and suppliers are doomed if they fail to anticipate the impacts of electronic distribution on their weak brands, and do not respond in a way that prevents online vendors and retailers gaining the advantage. They are also doomed if they attempt a bypass strategy and then are severely punished by the online vendor.

Lest this appear a purely theoretical concern, experience in the US highlights these risks explicitly. Five years ago a travel agent might have received a 10 percent commission on all tickets, which at today's prices would translate to more than $200 for a full-fare round trip to San Francisco, or, in the agent's ideal world, more than $1,000 for booking Concorde. Airlines have effectively squeezed the agencies, and though they still perform ticketing services, most airlines have capped commissions at the smaller of 8 percent or $35; the pain caused by this loss of income has been significant. In contrast, powerful US retailers such as Home Depot have been able to threaten immediate and effective punishment of any supplier that attempts to reach consumers directly, while retaining the ability to direct sales to whichever brand Home Depot chooses to promote. The advent of a Home Depot website will greatly increase its power in this respect.

Detailed simulation models can assist in making accurate predictions and formulating strategic responses. Managers should consider a series of factors, including brand loyalty, channel preferences, the need for a broad market basket to attract consumers, percentage in play (that is, the proportion of consumers who are not constrained by existing contracts), and cost structures. These models are useful also for determining what might need to be changed in order to assure long-term survival. Certain actions can be quite effective for manufacturers:

- The single best play for manufacturers is to strengthen their brands. This limits the retailer's ability to shift market share or extort lower costs in the future. It also limits the retailer's ability to punish manufacturers if they do launch a bypass strategy.
- Where bypass strategies appear necessary but the conditions needed for their success are lacking, other actions can reduce punishment. The most obvious of these is to launch a website with other brands, ideally with direct competitors; Sainsbury can punish Surf or Tide, but it probably cannot punish both together.
- Simulation models suggest that encouraging more rapid channel adoption through pricing or other actions can be a compelling strategy if the right factors are selected and the speed of adoption is sufficient to limit the period of loss making. For example, online ordering can be accelerated by targetting customers,

offering incentives only to the most profitable. Launching an online sales site with a sufficient number of partners or with a sufficient range of offerings is another way to speed adoption – in most industries, customers want a bundle of products and demand a certain range of choices.

Sourcing risk

Two forms of sourcing risk concern us here: the risk of strategic dependence (resulting from a small number of alternative suppliers and the resulting loss of bargaining power) and the risk of loss of critical expertise (theft of an intellectual asset and the loss of competitive advantage). In other words, what if an organization becomes dependent on one or more critical suppliers? How will this affect the price it charges and the profits that it is able to retain? Further, what if it transfers critical information resources to a strategic supplier, which then decides to compete directly with it? How does it protect itself?

Imagine a bank in eastern Europe that purchased a non-standard IT and e-commerce platform running software that was available only from the original hardware manufacturer. This manufacturer would come to exert huge influence over the bank, since the bank would be obliged to pay virtually whatever it requested for enhancements and changes not explicitly noted in the original contract.

What, then, does this suggest about strategic dependence of alliances for rapid web entry? Many would now argue that strategic alliances in the new economy are all too often plagued with post-contractual bargaining over small numbers: one party, usually the purchaser of web-entry services, finds itself totally dependent on the other, with no immediately available alternative supplier of essential services. Not surprisingly, the dependent party falls victim to opportunistic repricing, or strategic holdups, and is forced to pay significantly higher prices in order to progress. The problem might disappear if binding, verifiable, long-term contracts were written and enforced; in the rapidly changing and highly uncertain e-commerce environment, however, neither party is usually willing to enter into such binding, long-term agreements.

Now consider a company with a novel way of doing business, perhaps a new strategy for auctioning unused tickets to consumers. This might attract both consumers and airlines: consumers get to fly and the airline will sell more tickets without forcing traditional customers to purchase their seats at auction.

Suppose the developer of the auction idea forms an alliance with a website host with large market share. The benefits are clear: the auctioneer gains additional market share and the website owner wins additional traffic. But what if the website owner decides to steal the idea and operate it alone, without sharing revenues with or providing any payments to the auctioneer?

Again, lest this appear a purely hypothetical situation, precisely this litigation is under way between the patent holder of an online auction model for air travel and its initial web partner. The patent holder believed its patent would offer adequate protection; its partner decided to risk attempting to break the patent in court.

Managers must assess these risks in a disciplined fashion: particularly those of partnerships or alliances, of sourcing, and of the intentionally limited or temporary transfer of intellectual assets. This discipline contains four basic components:

- *Close assessment of a supplier's pre-contractual claims.* Failing to uncover the hidden details of a potential supplier may lead to the selection of a company that can neither deliver a quality service for entry into electronic markets, nor deliver it on time or on budget.

- *Monitoring of contractual private information.* Managers must gauge the efforts made by their partners and suppliers and the quality of service delivered. Is your internet partner delivering according to the criteria you set, such as clicks and eyeballs, or sales and profits? If not, why not? Is it because the market is more competitive than anticipated, because the vendor is late, or is failing to invest properly in advertising?
- *Small numbers bargaining.* After a contract begins, parties often have to bargain over what to do next. At these bargaining sessions, the dominant party usually explains what the terms will be and the weak party is forced to concur. This applies when there are few sellers (as in the case of Microsoft and Intel) or few buyers (with Home Depot and Wal-Mart). Thus, even if relations with a supplier appear harmonious, it is good risk management practice for companies to seek alternatives. If this is impossible, what factors might limit, say, the vendor's ability to raise its prices in the future?
- *Poaching and theft of intellectual assets.* Managers must identify exactly what needs to be disclosed or shared to make a partnership successful. Can they limit the partner's subsequent use of that knowledge or restrict its direct competition with them? Can they limit its possibilities of forming alliances with important competitors, or its ability to sell them valuable proprietary information and expertise?

Risks of strategic uncertainty

What if managers misread market trends and prepare for the wrong future? This has always been a potential problem when setting any long-term strategy. However, today's technological change is causing uncertainties in consumer behavior and rapid changes in the competitive environment. Decisions must be made and actions taken long before these strategic uncertainties have been resolved.

Managers must identify the critical strategic uncertainties in their industry, those I call "strategic drivers." These are the things one cannot know when planning, but which really matter the most. Imagine, for instance, that the Oracle at Delphi informed Wal-Mart's headquarters in Arkansas that after the year 2003 no consumer would ever buy shelf-stable products – detergent, paper products, canned beans, coffee, or tea – in a store again, but would only shop for these goods online. Advance knowledge of this strategic driver would immediately overturn the company's plans for geographical expansion and the construction of new stores.

Managers can identify strategic drivers by developing and examining alternative futures for their industry and company using a powerful risk management technique called scenario analysis. Each scenario must be planned in detail with the company's industry-specific expertise, and managers should specify the deployment of their critical economic resources in order to obtain the desired economic outcomes.

During recent work at Wharton, companies have developed scenarios determined largely by strategic drivers concerning uncertainty in consumer behavior. It is generally agreed that technical measures of e-commerce will be trending up, and trending up quickly – these measures include network speeds, total numbers of consumers online, and numbers of websites. However, important uncertainties remain in consumer behavior.

Will customers form lasting relationships with web vendors, or will all transactions be based on best currently available price? Stockbrokers who believed they had strong relationships with their customers were rudely awakened by the surprise popularity of internet share trading. Where does the demise of the long-term relationship leave Amazon.com, with its strategy of taking spectacular losses in order to buy market share? That is, how will it ever be able to charge enough to recover its acquisition costs? It may have invested heavily in training customers to shop online for books and other commodities, but the balance sheet hole created by subsidizing consumers' purchases may never be completely refilled. This need not be considered too far-fetched; while Citibank invested heavily in encouraging customers to leave their local high street banks and shop for the best credit-card deal, the first real winner was Capital One, which piggy-backed on Citibank's transformation of consumer behavior.

Will customers buy market baskets and bundles, or will they buy individual products and package their own bundles? (A market basket is, of course, a collection of items purchased together in a supermarket or other retailer. A bundle is more complex, and represents a collection of items that must function together. If I want a portable digital-imaging platform, I need a digital camera, a laptop, and a portable printer, all of which must work together.)

If customers shop for baskets and bundles, high street banks can lose money on free checking accounts and make it up on profitable credit cards. However, if customers are willing to take their checking accounts from Barclays while switching their credit cards to Capital One, this could pose a problem for Barclays. Similarly, Amazon.com may be able to justify selling bestselling novels at cost if this attracts customers who fill their online shopping carts with more profitable offerings. However, if online shoppers opportunistically pick off each store's loss leaders, this retailing strategy will require fundamental re-examination.

When performing scenario analysis, it is customary to pick values for these drivers, assume that these values will occur, and examine the futures that each set of values creates. Such an examination might reveal what strategies we would pursue and what resources we might require. To return to our earlier retail example, assume that customers buy individual products, one at a time, with no loyalty either to the product or its website. I may buy Surf (detergent) and Bounty (kitchen towels) from two websites today, but Tide (detergent) and Viva (kitchen towels) from two different websites tomorrow.

It is not too difficult to see how manufacturers would need to respond. They would:

- cut costs to offer consumers the best deals, probably using web-based logistics and supply chain management;
- control channels, again to offer consumers the best deals, almost certainly requiring a web presence;
- invest in product differentiation to blunt direct market competition;
- invest in websites, including community information sites, to exploit differentiation – that is, differentiation is of no use unless the consumer is aware of it;
- anticipate that most intermediary functions would be reduced in this scenario – hence they would anticipate that intermediaries would seek to force a transition to a scenario that they find more attractive and more profitable.

How do managers develop specific strategies for dealing with each scenario? By examining the economics of these future worlds. What resources will we need? How

Liquidity risk in electronic markets

Liquidity – the presence of buyers and sellers – is the single greatest determinant of the relative attractiveness of a trading site. The presence of buyers and sellers means that one can readily transform an asset into cash, or cash into the asset, fast enough to do so without being forced to hold an unwanted position, and easily enough to do so without affecting market price. Liquidity creates what is called a "participation externality": a market's attractiveness is self-reinforcing. The presence of sellers attracts buyers, which attracts more sellers. In other words, once a market has gained liquidity, it is sufficiently attractive that it is difficult to displace it. If you are lucky enough to own liquidity, this effect is called the central market defense; it is called the liquidity trap if you control a new alternative electronic market but you cannot convince anyone to trade on it. The New York Stock Exchange enjoys its position as the central market (if you like it), or its investors are stuck trading there as a result of the liquidity trap (if you do not like it).

The first e-commerce wave dealt with B2C, or business-to-consumer e-commerce; Amazon is perhaps the best-known company of this wave. The next wave of e-commerce was B2B, or business-to-business, with such companies as CommerceOne and Ariba capturing investors' attention. The new wave is B2X, or industrial exchanges. For example, Rooster.com integrates egg producers and their trading partners up and down the value chain. MetalSite trades ferrous metals, eMetra trades non-ferrous metals, and sites have been proposed for everything from excess glass production to sashimi-grade yellowfin tuna.

For such exchanges to flourish, each will require liquidity. Liquidity is the greatest advantage a market can enjoy. Conversely, once a market has been launched, if it fails to capture liquidity it becomes marked in traders' minds as illiquid, and it becomes surprisingly difficult to convince anyone to move volume there, ever.

How do exchange designers deal with the risk of launching an unsuccessful market? They will note that trades determine prices, prices determine order flow, and order flow determines trades, which we have seen determine prices. They also need to throw in the psychology of market participants, which is determined by prices, price movements, expectations, and their market positions. The designer can work with trading rules, information availability, and trading costs to achieve an optimal design.

will we deploy them? What benefits will we get? How will other parties attempt to counter, and what resources will we need to block their responses most effectively?

Admittedly, the specific uncertainties addressed above are, by definition, uncertainties, and it is too soon to see how the risks that they produce will play out in the e-commerce arena. Historically, companies that missed out on the initial rounds of e-distribution – airlines that did not launch travel agent reservation systems, such as Eastern Airlines and PanAm – were casualties of this unseen future risk.

In brief, the risk of being blindsided by strategic surprise is perhaps the greatest associated with e-commerce. Scenario analysis coupled with combat economics may be the most powerful response. Scenario analysis breaks us out of our certainty and brings alternative futures to the surface in a predictable and disciplined fashion, while combat economics allows us to develop the necessary range of strategic responses.

There are many forms of risk associated with developing an online strategy. In some cases, specific and detailed computer simulations can assist greatly. Most importantly, however, is the realization that each risk can be managed with techniques that are closely related to strategic management of risks outside the e-commerce environment.

Summary

The striking commercial opportunities of the internet carry significant strategic risks for established companies and dotcoms alike. In this article, **Eric Clemons** identifies four of the most important. Structural risk concerns the alignment of a company's internet plans with the forces of change in industry and consumer behavior. Channel risk refers to the sometimes dangerous transformation of relations between manufacturer, wholesaler, retailer, and customer in a web environment. Another risk – sourcing risk – typically arises from the network of partnerships that e-businesses strike up; start-ups can become fatally dependent on a few crucial suppliers, or find their intellectual property purloined by former friends. More general risks involving strategic uncertainty can be addressed using scenario analysis and fundamental economic analysis.

Branding puts a high value on reputation management

by Bernd Schmitt

Brand protection is often viewed as a legal issue. Names or marks that function to identify a product are used as trademarks to protect the brand. In many countries, trademark and copyright law governs this protection. Legal brand protection creates a monopoly, which is usually unlimited in time as long as the product is sold. Trademark law prohibits another company from using the same or similar names, logos, or marks if these brand identity elements are already in use and if such use would be likely to cause confusion in the marketplace. Legal brand protection is thus an attractive way of securing long-term competitive advantage.

However, a brand is, of course, much more than a name and a logo. Today's brand strategists say brands evoke distinct associations; they ascribe human personality traits to brands; they speak of "long-term relationships with customers," rather than transactional exchanges. Brands carry emotional attachments; brands are your neighbors, your colleagues, and your friends. In short, brands have the potential to provide customers with a variety of pleasant, or unpleasant, experiences.

Given this new complex understanding of the brand, brand protection now has to extend far beyond the legal arena. Brand experiences can be damaged not only via "copycats" or counterfeiters, and simply protecting brands from aggressive competitors is no longer sufficient.

Instead, companies must actively manage the brand–customer "relationship." Brand protection extends to the entire company. It has become a matter of managing the company's reputation in the eyes of its various stakeholders – including its customers, suppliers, trade partners, and employees. Anything a company does or says can add to – or destroy – brand value.

Consider the Italian clothing group Benetton. In January 2000, Benetton launched its Spring/Summer 2000 advertising campaign in Europe, America, and Asia: "We, On Death Row." The campaign was the work of Italian photographer and advertising guru Oliviero Toscani, who for more than two years visited death rows in several US prisons, photographing and interviewing condemned inmates.

The campaign is intended to be an innovative form of corporate communication, in the tradition of earlier Benetton campaigns focussing on war, Aids, discrimination, and racism. A January 7 press release on the company's website (at www.benetton.com) said: "Leaving aside any social, political, judicial or moral consideration, this project aims at showing to the public the reality of capital punishment, so that no one around the world will consider the death penalty either as a distant problem or as news that occasionally appear on TV. Toscani's images aim at giving back a human face to the prisoners on Death Row."

Benetton backfire

Even for Benetton, this was a daring campaign and it appears to have backfired in some markets. In protest, victims' rights activists and family members of crime victims picketted Benetton's New York office. Jerry Della Femina, chairman and creative director of advertising agency Della Femina/Jerry and Partners, wrote a *Wall Street Journal* article on March 20, 2000 criticizing the campaign as tasteless and destructive of brand value. The campaign also caused the US retailer Sears, Roebuck to cancel its contract with Benetton. This hit the company hard: Benetton had designed an exclusive clothing range for Sears intended to boost declining clothing sales in the US.

The consequences of the latest Benetton campaign underscore the need to view brand protection broadly. To be sure, not many companies are as provocative as Benetton. However, all companies are increasingly held accountable and responsible for an assortment of actions by a variety of stakeholder groups. Consumer activism is not limited to advertising messages. More and more, consumers are interested in anything related to the brand: the ingredients of its products; the company's history; the company's attitude and behavior toward environmental issues; its work policy; and its stance on a range of other economic, social, and political issues. Today's companies and their brands are being scrutinized as never before.

Even seemingly benign corporate actions can attract criticism. Nike, the world's biggest sportswear manufacturer, for example, has been supporting basketball culture in China by building and maintaining basketball courts in major cities. The courts themselves are decorated with its ubiquitous logo, so are the clothes worn by coaches and t-shirts, caps and other promotional items.

None of this sounds unusual until one considers that the price of a pair of Nike shoes is far beyond the reach of most Chinese consumers. Are Nike's activities in China really a community service? Do they simply represent an investment in a future market, or are they perhaps a new form of corporate imperialism for manipulating consumers in an emerging market? When such questions are taken together with criticism leveled at Nike for its former alleged use of sweatshop labor in emerging markets, it is easy to see how quickly such an issue can explode into a real threat to a company.

Reputation management is thus a natural extension of brand management. Done well, reputation management can bring considerable benefit to a company. A decent reputation helps to sell goods and services, recruit new talent, and attract desirable business partners. Done poorly, it destroys shareholder value. A bad reputation is an obstacle in selling to outlets and consumers, and in recruiting new talent.

Consequently, reputation management is quickly becoming a popular boardroom analysis and review topic. According to a survey of almost 600 chief executive officers and senior managers conducted by global public relations agency Hill & Knowlton and *Chief Executive* magazine, 43 percent of respondents said that the ability to manage reputation would carry "a great deal of weight" in the choice of a successor.

Reputation management also plays a role in such tactical decisions as recruitment. According to an article in the October 1999 *Journal of Marketing* by Allen Weiss, Erin Anderson, and Deborah MacInnis, many companies try to enhance their reputations by sending the right sales staff into the field. A company's human face can make all the difference in the world to corporate reputation.

Brand reputation management

To practice effective reputation management, managers need to consider five interrelated aspects.

First, reputation management must be broadly conceived. Because almost anything may be viewed as a brand, all companies in all industries must consider reputation management. Over the last decade, the concept of branding has been gradually broadened from its origins in the consumer packaged goods industry into many other forms of commercial – and even non-commercial – offers. Nowadays, everything is viewed as a brand, not just the cereal boxes in the supermarkets and the clothes in the designer boutiques. Examples include universities (Oxford, Harvard, Columbia), museums (the Guggenheim in New York and Bilbao, Spain), medical practices, nursing homes, TV stations, and even people, living or dead (Virgin Group's Richard Branson, the late Princess Diana, British prime minister Tony Blair – even you and me). Consequently, any organization or individual needs to be concerned with reputation.

Furthermore, reputation management is relevant for both old and new brands – older-established brands will be held to the same standards as newer, trendy ones, and if their managers neglect corporate reputation they may find themselves out in the cold.

Second, modern corporations consider brands as intangible assets. Thus, reputation management must be viewed as a way to protect the long-term value of the brand. In many cases, the intangible value of brands exceeds the value of a corporation's tangible assets. Interbrand, the New York-based brand valuation consultancy, has estimated the value of the Coca-Cola brand to be more than 95 percent of all its corporate assets.

To be sure, brand value depends on the nature of the product category and industry: it is higher for luxury goods than for utilities, for instance. Yet Interbrand also found that brand value is growing in practically every single industry. Therefore, brand reputation management must be conceived as an ongoing long-term undertaking; it is not to be confused with short-term crisis management.

Third, branding techniques can be found throughout the corporation. Of course, products are branded, but so are the promotional campaigns related to these products, and so in fact is the corporation as a whole. Indeed, many companies that have traditionally focussed on the branding of their individual products have discovered the corporate brand as an essential new marketing initiative.

For example, the formerly faceless product-driven companies in the pharmaceutical industries have recently emerged with branded personalities as life sciences. The music-to-airlines group Virgin or the online retailer Amazon.com are examples of brands that cut across many different categories.

Because branding can apply to entire organizations, everybody in the organization has a role to play in reputation management. To represent the brand in the right way, all employees need to know the brand and live it. In a wide variety of situations – when meeting customers, when communicating to the public, and at trade shows and conferences, for example – employees are representing the corporate brand, and should thus be prepared to engage in behavior that is consistent with it.

It follows that reputation management cannot be delegated to any single department or function. Inside the organization, reputation management involves marketing, communications, public relations, various information technology functions, and even the chairman's office. Outside, it involves corporate identity companies, PR operations, and advertising agencies. In addition, companies ignore customer service at their peril.

The often-neglected "human interface" between the company and its customers can be enough to undo the best internal efforts at reputation management. It is critical to implement a unified reputation approach that covers all these aspects. Branding succeeds if it is coherent and consistent; the same applies to reputation management.

Finally, markets become real-time exchanges and conversations among consumers on the internet. Brand information – in all different forms and media – is available instantly and globally on the web. The internet empowers consumers, allowing them to post their views about a brand to a worldwide audience. Companies need to be able to deal with this new form of brand scrutiny, protect their brands, and manage their reputation online. This requires effective management of the corporate website and links to other sites; selective presence on other websites; fast and adequate response to electronic inquiries; and the ability to deal with chat rooms and virtual communities.

Moreover, there are now numerous websites (epinions.com, feedbackdirect.com, and eComplaints.com, for example) that organize public concerns and allow customers to express their opinions, make suggestions, and post their complaints online. Neatly sorted into categories we all recognize from the big search engines, these websites allow customers very easily to convey their concerns to a broad audience.

These internet operations promise to help people make better decisions, but they also empower customers to shape corporate reputations. As one such web enterprise declares on its home page, "eComplaints.com is your chance to fight back. It's your chance to be heard by the company at fault and more importantly, by your fellow consumer." In the future, many companies may find it necessary to create and staff positions for online reputation management.

Reputation management is important in protecting the long-term value of a brand. It is not a cosmetic image management device, nor is it a mere strategy to sell more products. Reputation management speaks to the very heart of an organization. Just as it is difficult for an individual to put on a false face without being found out, so it is difficult for a company to espouse values that its actions do not support. On the web, it is easy to find out about a company's true nature.

Therefore, a company that is committed to providing "answers that matter" (the brand slogan of US pharmaceutical company Eli Lilly) needs to involve all its employees in providing relevant and vital answers about its activities. In Eli Lilly's case, medicine, life sciences, and healthcare to all the company's key constituents such as doctors, hospitals, insurers, and regulators.

Similarly, a company that renames itself Clarica (formerly The Mutual Life Insurance Company of Canada), thus promising clarity in communications, needs to align the entire organization and its personnel around such corporate positioning.

From an ethical perspective, reputation management thus requires a consideration of values and competencies that are shared throughout the organization, and is best practiced with reflection and honesty.

Summary

Brands, it seems, can now be lifestyle appendages. In such a world, those who own them had better protect them. In this article, **Bernd Schmitt** urges companies to manage customer/brand relationships and experiences actively. Protection involves defending business reputation to customers, suppliers, trade partners, and employees. In addition, brands are a promising target for consumer advocates. Through exchanges on the internet, they can quickly tackle such issues as brand ingredients, company history, environmental attitudes and behavior, work and economic policy, and so on. Furthermore, the internet has empowered consumers as never before. The author suggests that best practice in reputation management thus requires considerable reflection and honesty. Virtually anything an enterprise does or says will either enhance or destroy brand value. Reputation management has become a natural extension of brand care – good reputations sell goods and services, poorly managed ones destroy shareholder value.

Suggested further reading

Aaker, D.A. and Joachimsthaler, E. (2000) *Brand Leadership*, New York: The Free Press.

Fombrun, C.J. (1996) *Reputation: Realizing Value from the Corporate Image*, Boston, MA: Harvard Business School Press.

Schmitt, B. (1999) *Experiential Marketing: How to Get Customers to Sense, Feel, Think, Act and Relate to Your Company and Brands*, New York: The Free Press.

Weiss, M.A., Anderson, E. and MacInnis, D.J. (1999) "Reputation management as a motivation for sales structure decisions," *Journal of Marketing*, 63(4).

Folly, fantasy, and roguery: a social psychology of finance risk disasters

by Nigel Nicholson and Paul Willman

In 1995, Barings, Britain's oldest merchant bank, went bankrupt because of the derivatives dealing of a single "rogue trader," Nick Leeson. His case, though the subject of several books and a feature film, is not exceptional. It is but one of many similar disasters.

Between 1984 and 1995, Toshihide Iguchi, a former car dealer, lost Daiwa Bank, a Japanese super-regional institution, more than $1bn gambling on the US bond market. Shortly after this, Peter Young, a brilliant and eccentric fund manager with private equity business Deutsche Morgan Grenfell, lost nearly the same amount in unauthorized dealing in unlisted new technology companies.

Even more spectacular is the case of Yasuo Hamanaka, who was one of the most respected longstanding managers at the Japanese trading company Sumitomo Corporation. Hamanaka blew the equivalent of three-quarters of a million dollars a day over a 10-year period, trying single-handedly to manipulate the copper price by cornering the market. Many lesser examples are reported in the press each week, such as Kyriacos Papouis, an options trader at NatWest Capital Markets, the investment banking arm of National Westminster Bank, who lost $150m in 1997 by mispricing derivatives. On January 4, 2000, it was reported that Electrolux, the world's leading maker of white goods, had lost some $11.25m through unauthorized currency trading by an unnamed employee working for its internal bank in Germany.

What is going on here? These cases are all highly individual – each a special blend of folly, fantasy, and roguery. Some are predominantly folly, the result of human error and ignorance and of people losing their grip in highly complex situations. Iguchi, Leeson, and Papouis all show this. Each wandered way out of his depth – especially in the arcane world of derivatives.

The discipline of behavioral finance and its close cousin, behavioral decision theory, are increasingly used to give a more complete explanation and modeling of decision making under uncertainty. They turn out to offer a more realistic alternative to classical economics, with its assumptions of rational decision makers moving markets in the direction of efficiency.

The new science of evolutionary psychology explains how deeply embedded in our design is the crooked thinking to which we are all prey when trying to be rational. It tells us that our brains are nothing like computers in how they operate – not designed for straight-line, rational thinking, but much more for the intuitive leaps that help us adapt to new circumstances and deal with other people. We are naturally poor at statistical reasoning, probabilistic calculus, and logical analysis. This is why trading floors are so full of individuals who have been highly trained in these disciplines, and why investment banks increasingly use computer models that completely bypass the human decision maker.

Fantasy plays a major part in many of the cases illustrated above. Individuals are infected with grandiose delusions about their own power and ability to win against the odds. This inflated confidence is often rewarded in business, but becomes a major hazard when people start to imagine they can control the uncontrollable or predict what in reality is largely random.

Leeson and Hamanaka both became subject to what scholars call "escalating commitment," to the point of believing they could hold up markets by force of will and big spending. The authors' own research with traders illustrates that these fantasies are much more common than is generally known. We found traders to be widely subject to "illusions of control," and those that were most prone turned out to be the worst performers.

Roguery is a term that should strictly be applied to people who engage in willful criminality or deviance. Personality profiles for the cases mentioned do not exist, yet it is clear in accounts of several of them that their thresholds for rule breaking were lower than for most of their colleagues. Leeson had a "jack-the-lad" reputation even before his period of major losses began.

In many cases, deviance begins as a response to something that has gone wrong – the person typically yielding to the temptation to conceal an unexpectedly large loss. Leeson's downfall began in this way, and for someone with his character it was a slippery slope. After he recovered one large tranche of losses, he embarked on a renewed bout of speculative trading, this time illegally falsifying records, inventing fictitious customers, and lying to his bosses. In the world of finance, temptation is never far off. Although the regulatory regimes have tightened greatly in recent years, smart operators can still find ways of subverting the system by insider dealing (illegal use of privileged information), front running (buying a stock and using the company's money to boost its price), and rat trading (waiting to see how trades turn out then booking the best to your account).

Does this mean that finance is especially vulnerable to problems of deviance? It appears so, though in fact there is a greater awareness and prevention of risk in finance than in many other areas of business. We hear more about the problems in finance because of the large sums often involved and their high visibility. With so many decisions being made continually, there is wider scope for things to go wrong. It is also true that decisions in finance are often far more complex than in other fields, and, more than other business worlds, populated by visions of wealth, power, and distinction.

Three key motives

Greed, fear, and ego are three drivers for much of what happens in business. Finance differs mainly in that the stakes tend to be rather higher when large sums of money are involved. These are three motivational themes in human life, hardwired into our evolutionary design over many millennia as a clan-dwelling, hunter-gatherer species clinging tenuously to existence under harsh and unpredictable circumstances.

Greed stands for the essential requirement to do all you can to maximize your status ranking in a pecking order where higher means better odds for survival and reproduction. There is a large literature on the universality of status differentiation in human society and the benefits of advantage, including the Whitehall study, an epidemiological investigation of the UK Civil Service. Health, life satisfaction, and psychological adjustment improve as one's status rises. In business, greed is normal human acquisitiveness. It is what motivates people to work excessively long hours, take promotions they should refuse, do jobs they hate, and sacrifice longer-term interests for short-term gain. In finance, extravagant bonus arrangements, generous share options, and the like often amplify acquisitiveness. Not all the cases we have cited above were motivated by personal gain, though several clearly were.

Fear is the requirement not to lose in a world where losses can be fatal and unrecoverable. Fear takes precedence over all other motives when it is aroused. Research shows that the penalties of low status include harmful biochemical reactions, for humans as for other primates. Work by Zur Shapira of the Stern School of New York on managerial decision making shows that people are not naturally risk averse, but they are certainly loss averse. People's behavior changes in unexpected and unattractive ways when they are threatened.

Thus in finance, where many occupations are high-wire acts, the fear of falling is continually in the background; it sometimes can sweep people along to disastrous acts. This theme emerged clearly in the authors' research: individuals can become gripped by a frantic panic to avoid losses by concealing them, or doubling up their bets like crazed gamblers trying to punt their way out of their mounting debts. In behavioral decision research, it has been found that people will take greater risks to escape losses than to secure gains. This is the classic gambler's trap.

In the two Japanese cases, one can see how the culture values magnified this loss aversion. Where shame is a high-profile negative value, it can turn a respectable lifelong manager such as Hamanaka into an unlikely rogue trader.

Ego is the importance of being well regarded within one's community. Humans might have made egotism a fine art, but we share with other social primates a great concern about where we stand in the pecking order. In the business world it is the leading motive for professionals, for whom reputation counts for more than financial reward, partly because it underwrites longer-term interests.

This is not just about material resources. In highly visible arenas, reputation is a very public good that people care about a great deal. There is an extensive literature on the compelling drive for social regard and recognition, and how people of high self-esteem are often insensitive to warnings of negative feedback and inclined to persist too long with failing projects.

In many areas of finance, such as trading and fund management, egos are very much on the line. Leeson reveled in being king of the Singapore International Monetary Exchange (Simex), and in other cases where there was no obvious payoff, other than the bonuses for achieving star status, notoriety was its own reward. He and other financial adventurers were swept along by the flood of their egos, ignoring warning signs, and failing to cut and run when projects started to fail.

Psychological, and other factors

In many situations, these three motives work to good effect – greed creates wealth, fear prevents disasters, and ego builds success. In balanced proportions, allied with intelligence and a strong skill set, and when linked into a regulated social network, they help to build strong businesses. What throws them out of joint are three sets of factors coming together in combination: individual high-risk profiles, poor management, and a negligent corporate culture.

The high-risk profile involves strong motives to succeed – greed and ego – and little prospect of doing so by conventional means. Typically, low skills, social class, or position restricts them. Add to this a desire for action and excitement, a propensity for rule bending, plus a powerful fear of losing and you have the high-risk profile. The science of behavioral genetics tells us that personality profiles are inherited and stable over the adult lifespan, and many elements of the high-risk profile are inborn. In research on personality and risk taking, the authors identified a high-risk profile that comprises openness, sensation seeking, and tough-mindedness, plus low emotionality and low conscientiousness: in other words, thick-skinned experimenters looking for excitement without hard work.

This profile is much more common in males than in females; indeed, women are rarely the culprits of major folly and malfeasance in business. This is not just because there are fewer women in positions of responsibility, but because they are less subject to excesses of greed and ego, less motivated to be deviant, and less sensation seeking. Studies have found women traders to be less prone to excessive trading than men, and thus potentially better performers. Unfortunately, they generally find the trading environment uncongenial and are more often found in the sales areas of investment banking, where relationships are more valued.

The second element, poor management, does not at first seem borne out by reality. Trading environments look well managed in the sense that they are very "flat" hierarchies with strong self-management in teams. The authors' research, however, finds that poor management usually means reluctant management. This is a problem in a world ruled by greed, fear, and ego. Managers need to be involved at the right level – intervening not interfering, empowering not absent. Managers in the cases described above were either invisible or incompetent: they were unable to get involved because they did not understand what their people were doing.

In most investment banks, this is not a common problem. Managers are ex-traders who have a good understanding of the activities of their charges. Some, especially former "stars," are still running their own books. This gives them credibility, but reduces the time they have for attentive management. Others who have become "pure" managers reserve their attention for high-risk situations, intervening to stop traders chasing their losses. Traders in this environment view a good manager as "someone who leaves me alone." Managers seem to respect this. The result is that traders can develop bad habits undetected. In many institutions, the climate of hands-off management gives scope for errors to escalate into malfeasance.

The third element, cultural negligence, was present in all the cases we have described. Leeson and Iguchi were left to run their own back offices – virtually an open invitation to "creative book-keeping." Almost all other individual cases of rogue trading have been seriously underobserved and unregulated.

In many of the worst cases, such as Barings, companies came new to areas of finance in which they lacked experience and expertise, and were too reliant on individuals who seemed knowledgeable and skilled. Trader mystique is often about intuitive grasp of how to make money by going against the herd. Cultural negligence happens when companies are overly interested in making money and regulators disregard what is really going on.

A big issue here is the extent to which this deviance is a by-product of the "star culture" that exists in many trading environments. This will decline to a degree as the globalization of markets and developments in communications technologies causes margins to be reduced and decisions to become automated. However, stars will continue to shine and be avidly sought by companies – that, too, is human nature at work in a fiercely competitive business where rewards and risks are high.

Remedies and protections

It would be convenient if there were a simple solution to folly, fantasy, and roguery in finance. There is not, but it could be greatly reduced by the following:

- More systematic selection methods to detect the danger signals in traders' psychological profiles.
- More training of traders and their managers in the psychology of risk and decision making.
- More dedicated managers with managerial rather than solely financial skills.
- Reduced emphasis on individual rewards and more value accorded to teamwork in financial decision making.
- More women in trading.
- More leadership to build organizational climates of openness, sharing, and learning from errors.
- Reduced emphasis on "star" cultures.

Can measures such as these make the kinds of cases we have reviewed from the twentieth century unknown in the twenty-first, much as we have nearly eliminated industrial accidents in certain industries, such as textiles, through the prudential application of technologies? The answer is yes in part, but accidents do still happen in newly safe industries.

Wherever individuals are the main agents of decision making, the potential exists for someone to be exceptionally foolish, unwisely creative, or calculatingly corrupt. The finance industry has closed some obvious open doors in regulation, and an increased awareness of the risks has become part of trading-floor culture. However, there still exists a technical orientation to problems of human fallibility. What is needed is a full appreciation of the social psychology of error, boredom, and temptation. Awareness is increasing, and in time this will reduce much of the needless cost of bad judgment. Yet, in a business where the rewards are so great, there will continue to be spectacular disasters and crimes, some of which could be nipped in the bud through a more broad-based intelligence among managers.

Summary

In this article, **Nigel Nicholson** and **Paul Willman** scan the new disciplines of behavioral finance and behavioral decision theory for insights into why some financial traders dice so disastrously with danger. Disturbingly, evolutionary psychology holds that crooked thinking is embedded in the human psyche. The human motives of greed, fear, and ego, which often work to good effect in driving profitable behavior, can become self-destructive when linked with poor management and a negligent corporate culture. The authors suggest that any systematic remedies should incorporate the likely occurrence of error, boredom, and temptation. Tighter supervision is also paramount – proper communication among managers would have thwarted several recent spectacular disasters and crimes in finance.

Suggested further reading

Bazerman, M.H. (1994) *Judgment in Managerial Decision-Making*, Chichester: Wiley.

Nicholson, N. (1998) "How hardwired is human behavior?" *Harvard Business Review*, 76(4): 134–47.

Nicholson, N. (2000) *Managing the Human Animal*, London: Texere.

Nicholson, N., Dow, J., Fenton-O'Creevy, M., Soane, E. and Willman, P. (1999) "Individual and contextual influences on the market behavior of finance professionals," End of grant report, London: Economic and Social Research Council.

North, F., Syme, S.L., Feeney, A., Head, J., Shipley, M.J., and Marmot, M.G. (1993) "Explaining socioeconomic differences in sickness absence: the Whitehall II study," *British Medical Journal*, 306: 361–6.

Shapira, Z. (1995) *Risk Taking: A Managerial Perspective*, New York: Russell Sage Foundation.

Willman, P., Fenton-O'Creevy, M., Nicholson, N., and Soane, E. (2001) "Traders' tales: management behavior and loss aversion in investment banking," *Human Relations*, forthcoming.

Wise words and firm resolve when times get tough

by David Brotzen

Corporate reputation is worth a great deal. Research carried out in 1998 by Citibank and branding consultancy Interbrand showed that the total value of the FTSE 100 companies was £824bn, of which tangible assets accounted for £240bn and goodwill accounted for £584bn. In other words, goodwill – of which reputation is a large part – accounted for 71 percent of total value. Ten years earlier, goodwill accounted for 44 percent of total value.

A recent article in *Fortune* stated: "[As] America's 10 most admired companies ... stand above the rest of corporate America in reputation so do they tower over it in performance ... A 10-year investment [in them] would have yielded nearly triple the shareholder return of S&P 500 stocks." Reputation is now so important that the Turnbull report, which forms part of the UK's corporate governance guidelines, advises companies to treat it in the same way as all other assets. A survey carried out in December 1999 among risk managers in UK companies found that reputation risk was the greatest risk facing their organizations.

Reputation risk can be defined as the set of threats that affect the long-term trust placed in the organization by its stakeholders, which includes its suppliers, customers, staff, and shareholders. It covers risks to products, the company, or the whole industry. Reputation risk involving products was well illustrated in October 1997, when Mercedes-Benz's radical A-class hatchback toppled over during the "moose test," designed to examine handling at high speeds. Fatal reputational damage to a company also occurred when in 1991, the chief executive of the UK jewelry retailer Ratners jokingly described some of the group's merchandise as "crap" in a speech to the UK's Institute of Directors. The share price fell soon after and the executive later resigned. Reputational damage experienced by an entire industry is best illustrated by the loss of trust by consumers of British beef at the time of the crisis over BSE or "mad cow" disease.

In each of these cases senior managers would have experienced the classic symptoms of a crisis:

- a lack of information;
- growing consumer mistrust;

- increased attention from the press and media;
- loss of confidence among stakeholders;
- commercial and/or political pressure to respond;
- internal conflict over what should be done to resolve the situation.

In contrast, those organizations held up as good handlers of crises win plaudits for decisive action and for excellent communications. A good example of this occurred after the 1989 Kegworth air disaster, in which a British Midland Airways Boeing 737-400 twin-engined jet crashed near the UK's East Midlands airport. Sir Michael Bishop, chief executive of the airline, gave convincing and emotional TV interviews that confronted the scale of the disaster and addressed the questions that the public and shareholders were asking. Despite the sensitivity of the public to crash situations, British Midland even saw a short-term increase in sales after the disaster.

The characteristics of successful crisis management include:

- demonstration of decisive remedial action;
- access to the right information;
- high speed in communications;
- a consistent corporate message;
- a full appreciation of the needs of all stakeholders;
- the ability to admit to mistakes;
- a clear recovery strategy.

These characteristics are normally the result of good procedures, comprehensive planning, appropriate training, and good early detection systems, all of which contribute to a reputation protection strategy. So how does a company establish such a strategy?

Protecting reputation

Responsibility for corporate reputation has typically resided with the chief executive or the corporate communications department, whereas traditionally conceived risks such as exchange-rate risk or insurance have been the domain of the risk manager or finance department. Reputation risk falls between the two, cutting across many aspects of the business. It requires a small, cross-functional team to create and implement a protection strategy. This would typically comprise a representative from corporate communications, customer relations, the health and safety department, investor relations, the legal department, operations, public affairs, and risk management, with input from the chief executive or chairman. In setting up a program, they should conduct the following exercises.

Assessing the threats

The organization needs to have a clear understanding of the main threats to its reputation. These might manifest themselves through sustained media coverage, rapid falls in share price, and loss of customer confidence. They can be caused by factors such as the effects of activism, discrimination in the workplace, unethical trading, marketing failures, or more traditional risks such as product failure. This process of listing reputational risks requires honesty and doggedness – perhaps by impartial parties – to cut through corporate defensiveness. In some cases, managers may be unwilling to admit that their fiefdoms could be vulnerable.

Prioritizing reputation risks

Once the risks have been identified, they need to be prioritized in order to help managers determine where to devote effort and resources. This prioritization process should be linked to the organization's existing risk management strategies. The task force might evaluate the reputation risks according to their likelihood and their impact in order to establish a reputation risk ranking. For instance, an organization might feel that the likelihood of an earthquake on a key operation might be relatively low, but if it were to happen such an event would be catastrophic – the risk is therefore defined as small but significant.

Managing reputation risks

Examining reputation risks for their likelihood and impact only shows one side of the coin. The other side requires an assessment of the organization's ability to avoid the risk or respond to it if it occurs. For example, if a company is susceptible to product recall, it needs to assess whether it has a thorough fault detection system and a comprehensive recall plan. Once procedures for managing those risks have been identified, it is possible to map the reputation risks and analyze the gaps.

Monitoring reputation risks

Having mapped important risks, the organization should establish procedures to monitor early warning signs of them occurring or increasing. One of the important listening posts in an organization is the customer services department. This department will often be able to establish early signals of a trend occurring before the issue spills over into the public domain. Consumers recognize the impact of bad publicity and are capable of using it as a negotiating chip. For instance, the producer of one consumer affairs program said she received 10,000 letters each week from viewers who saw her program as a way of getting companies to take their complaints more seriously.

Responding to reputation risks

No organization will be able to avoid or pre-empt all of the risks it faces – neither should it seek to do so, since risk taking is part of a company's *raison d'être*. However, it does need to establish a defensive armory to protect its corporate reputation against the unforeseeable. Such an armory would cover procedures, training, materials, and relationships. For example, procedures would include the establishment of a crisis management team; training would cover aspects such as making skilled communicators available to relate with the media; materials might include policies and background briefs on some of the more complex reputation risks; and relationships might include fostering "credit in the bank" among significant stakeholder groups.

Embedding the reputation risk process

In some respects, reputation risk should be treated in the same way as more traditional risks such as financial or operational risks. It should be included within a company's internal audit procedures to ensure that those to avoid, detect, and respond to reputation risks are being applied and are kept up to date. The Y2K millennium bug illustrates this well. Although in the event most companies survived relatively unscathed, for many the issue only appeared on the reputation radar screen in 1999, despite being an operational risk for a number of years before that.

Perceptions and the internet

Reputation risk management differs from traditional risk management in an important respect: reputation is largely about perception. Many management teams have been criticized for the way they handled a crisis – not because their strategy was ill-conceived or clumsily implemented, but because they failed to tell the outside world what the strategy was. The Exxon Corporation received relatively little comment about its recovery plans after its tanker *Exxon Valdez* ran aground in Prince William Sound, Alaska, but was criticized for its communication with the local community.

The way a company handles a crisis is not only dependent on the quality and timeliness of its decision making but also on how its stakeholders perceive it. This is based on a blend of perceptions, which may pre-date the crisis. If a company has a reputation for putting profit before principle, it will face a tougher battle to protect its reputation. Companies that weather crises of reputation have often accumulated "credit in the bank" with the public and stakeholders.

The internet has opened new areas of reputation risk and caused old ones to proliferate. Corporate websites are bastardized, companies discover pornography on their employees' workstations, and employees can be prosecuted for maligning competitors via email. In addition, complainants can use the cheap, immediate power of the web to mobilize other supporters around the world.

However, the web can act in a company's favor in times of crisis. In a recent air disaster, the airline concerned was able to disseminate sensitive information to different audiences through password-protected websites, one of which provided relatives with information before it was released to the media.

Other organizations create "dormant" websites that can be activated in times of crises. These "hidden sites" can contain the crucial general information that is needed in the early hours of a crisis, and can be updated as further information becomes available. Such prior planning can save vital hours in an emergency and can demonstrate that the organization is in clear control of the situation. It can also ensure that the company is viewed as the best source of information on its own misfortune, thus reducing the need for media pundits to provide speculative and often ill-informed comment on the crisis.

Using the internet proactively enables a company to provide regular updates to all its important stakeholders. This need not only apply to external audiences but can apply internally through the corporate intranet. "Crisis centers" might make information available in real time, assisting those attempting to manage the situation. It can ensure that a single, current position statement is used by representatives in every market in which the company operates, reducing inaccuracy and inconsistency. It can also provide low-cost training and a central facility to capture the lessons learned from past crises.

Senior managers cannot afford to treat one of their most valuable corporate assets in a cavalier manner. Reputation risk should be managed with the same commitment as traditional risks. Generals do not wait until the battle is looming to build their defenses. Chief executives need to be similarly prepared.

Summary

Companies need to treat reputation risk in the same way as they treat risks to other corporate assets, says **David Brotzen**. They should define the risks to reputation, prioritize them, and establish strategies to protect the reputation of the company if they want to avoid a crisis of confidence among stakeholders and the wider public. Though decision-making responsibility for reputation issues resides with the chief executive, this task should be carried out by a company-wide team. In particular, these strategies should capitalize on emerging technologies and the networking power of the internet.

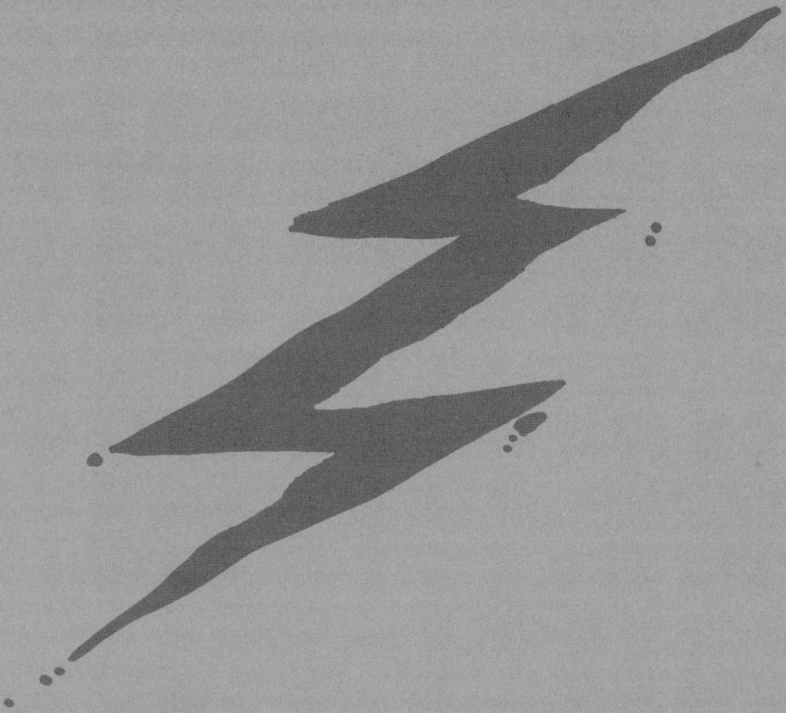

ENVIRONMENTAL RISK AND EXTREME EVENTS

9

Contributors

Forest Reinhardt is an associate professor at Harvard Business School. His research interests are in political economy and business strategy in environmentally salient industries, especially energy and agribusiness.

Rory F. Knight is dean emeritus of Templeton College, University of Oxford. Dr Knight is a director of a number of internet companies.

Howard Kunreuther is the Cecilia Yen Koo Professor of Decision Sciences and Public Policy and Management at the Wharton School of the University of Pennsylvania and co-director of the School's Risk Management and Decision Processes Center.

Deborah J. Pretty is a research fellow at Templeton College, University of Oxford. Dr Pretty specializes in corporate risk management strategy, risk finance, governance, and value.

Ian I. Mitroff is the Harold Quinton Distinguished Professor of Business Policy at the Marshall School of Business, University of Southern California. His research interests include crisis management, strategic thinking, and spirituality in the workplace. He is the author of *Managing Crises Before They Happen* (American Management Association, New York, 2000).

Roland Mann is UK managing director of Guardian iT Group, disaster-recovery and business continuity specialists.

Paul Embrechts is a professor of mathematics at the ETHZ (Swiss Federal Institute of Technology, Zurich), where he teaches insurance and financial mathematics. His current research interests include integrated risk management, securitization of insurance risk (alternative risk transfer), and extreme value analysis.

Contents

Tensions in the environment 255
Forest Reinhardt, Harvard Business School
Government regulators, campaigners, and managers still diverge in their approaches to and understanding of environmental safety.

Seeking succour from the rising costs of catastrophe 260
Howard Kunreuther, Warton School, University of Pennsylvania
Catastrophes wreak havoc on victims and economies in disaster-prone zones. This article suggests ways of extending financial protection via private–public partnership.

The essentials of crisis management 265
Ian I. Mitroff, Marshall School of Business, University of Southern California
Crisis management has implications for corporate operations and reputation. Preparation is critical, while the knock-on effects of a crisis should not be ignored.

Difficult calls in judging risk extremes 269
Paul Embrechts, ETHZ
With extreme events apparently increasing in frequency, extreme value theory can help analyze the unpredictable.

Day of judgment: catastrophe and the share price 275
Rory F. Knight, Templeton College, University of Oxford
Deborah J. Pretty, Templeton College, University of Oxford
Catastrophes offer corporate analysts a number of insights into managerial aptitude and performance. This article shows how the market assesses the way a company reacts after a calamity.

Wise prescriptions for a swift recovery 280
Roland Mann, Guardian iT Group
Disaster-recovery services are a useful kind of insurance against corporate devastation. This article explains how to program for business continuity.

Introduction

Natural catastrophes such as hurricanes, floods, and earthquakes appear to be increasing in frequency and severity around the world. In this section, authors propose robust approaches to prevention and relief: companies and individuals must do everything they can to mitigate the consequences of these events, whether by enhanced prediction, the purchase of insurance, adherence to building codes, or by establishing systematic plans for crisis management and disaster recovery.

Tensions in the environment

by Forest Reinhardt

Pollution of the natural environment carries business risk for corporations. Sometimes this stems directly from the pollution itself – the threat of oil spills is, for example, an obvious risk to cash flows for commercial fishermen or to tour guides in coastal Alaska. More often, however, it is not the environmental damage itself but public concern about the environment that creates the risk to private cash flows and corporate asset values. Managers therefore need to be concerned about public reaction to pollution attributable to their company. From a business perspective, this is the common and intuitive definition of "environmental risk."

Defined in this way, environmental risk encompasses several different but related risks that affect the company through several channels. In the marketplace, a company may lose customers if deficiencies in its environmental performance are publicised. In the courts, "toxic torts" can threaten company balance sheets. In the regulatory arena, government bodies can impose increases in operating costs or, in the extreme, make it impossible for the company to operate at all.

Business managers usually understand environmental risk to mean risk to the company that arises from social concern about the environment. Government regulators and environmental activists commonly mean the risk of damage to ecosystems or to public health arising from some man-made environmental offense. That is, the regulators and activists use "environmental risk" to mean "risk to the environment."

The two interpretations are not the same, and either kind of risk can exist without the other. Companies may impose risk on the environment (that is, increase the sort of risk about which the regulators and environmentalists worry) without imposing financial risks on themselves or other businesses, at least for a time. Conversely, companies can be at risk financially even if the risk they impose on the physical environment is negligible. For example, companies that contributed waste to US facilities later designated as "Superfund" sites can face retroactive cost penalties quite out of keeping with the actual damage to the environment as governments sue to recover often inflated cleanup costs.

Unlike many of the other risks discussed in this book, environmental risk is asymmetric. In contrast, exchange-rate risk has both a downside and an upside – the value of the currency you hold can either fall or rise. Environmental risk resembles security risks such as war and kidnapping, in that it has no short-term upside. Superior management of environmental risk can, however, still be a source of long-term competitive advantage, because better risk management means no more than better management of contingent costs.

Use analytical tools

Because "environmental risk" encompasses so many different but interrelated risks, it is imperative that managers think precisely about the kind of risk they are really trying to manage. Above all, managers need to bring to the job of environmental risk management the same analytical tools they would instinctively and correctly apply to other risk management problems. They need to understand the effects of various possible investments in the management of that risk, whether the investments are

Seeds of destruction?

The agricultural biotechnology industry's recent experience in Europe highlights the difference between risk to the environment and environmental risk to the company. Substantial investments in research enabled companies in that industry to produce seeds for crops that resist insect pests or tolerate herbicides (these companies included Pioneer Hi-Bred, a subsidiary of US chemicals, pharmaceuticals, and agricultural products group DuPont; Monsanto Company of the US; Novartis of Switzerland; and the Franco-German life sciences group Aventis).

Industry economists knew that the genetically engineered seeds offered superior performance from the standpoint of private costs: that is, total costs to the farmer were lower than with traditional weed and pest control. Industry scientists were convinced that the risks to health and environment of the new crops were manageable, especially compared to the well-documented risks to health and environment imposed by conventional pesticides and herbicides.

The verdict of European governments and consumers has sharply contrasted with these optimistic views. Leading food companies, among them Unilever and Nestlé, have scrambled to remove genetically modified organisms from their raw material feedstocks. European Union regulators and EU member governments have withheld regulatory approvals for the cultivation and sale of the crops. US farmers, nervous about their access to export markets, and worried that the backlash against genetically engineered crops will cross the Atlantic, are considering whether they should pass up the cost and yield improvement offered by the new technologies and fall back on traditional pest management approaches. The experience of the agricultural biotechnology companies reflects the fact that low risk to the environment is a necessary condition for low environmental risk to the company, but by no means a sufficient one.

in risk shifting, risk reduction, or risk information. They must also understand how environmental risk management relates to the overall goals of the company.

Many companies manage environmental risk differently from other risks. Often, the task is left to environmental specialists in a separate office, while people elsewhere in the organization manage exchange-rate risk, political risk, and so on. This functional compartmentalization is not accidental, but it may not be appropriate. At the very least, environmental risk managers ought to know how their own activities fit into the company's overall risk management policies.

As with any risk, the job of environmental risk managers is to decide how much of the risk to transfer, how much to invest in risk reduction, and how much risk to carry. Managers also need to decide how much time and effort to invest in better information about these risks.

The appropriate objective will rarely be to "minimize risk," although this catchy slogan may ease communication with outsiders and employees. As with any risk, the benefits of risk reduction must be weighed against the costs of achieving the reduction. Managers who carry risks should do so by conscious choice, not through ignorance; and they should be making sure that they are compensated for the risks they choose to bear.

Reducing environmental risk

There are many ways for a company to shift or reduce environmental risk. It can purchase insurance against some environmental risks, such as the contingent liability arising from waste disposal. It can also use internal command-and-control regulations, spelling out particular procedures that employees must follow when engaged in important but risky activities, in order to reduce environmental risk. It can use "softer" tools, such as the management evaluation and promotion system and even the corporate culture. If the company leadership takes environmental risk management seriously, middle managers will more likely follow suit, particularly if effective management of environmental risk is recognized within the company and is seen to be a necessary condition for managerial advancement.

Few of these tools resemble the kinds of methods that companies use to manage other risks. Forward contracts and options, which play major roles in a company's management of exchange-rate risk and the risk of raw material price changes, are absent from the environmental risk managers' portfolio. Outside purchases of insurance play a smaller role in environmental risk management than in the management of, say, counterparty and political risks.

The choice of tools to manage risk should depend partly on the robustness of the information about the risk. If managers are reasonably secure in their assessment of the underlying probabilities and think it relatively unlikely that new information could change that assessment, they are more likely to want to use price-based tools, such as insurance contracts. On the other hand, because environmental risks are still not very well understood, managers may rightly feel that their assessments of the probabilities and magnitudes of bad events will change substantially as new information arrives. Under those circumstances, it may make sense to rely more heavily on non-price policies, such as command-and-control regulation.

The appropriate tool also depends on the degree to which adverse selection is important. When it is, outside insurance contracts are likely to be especially expensive. This is because when a company seeking insurance knows more about the risks it faces than the insurers do, insurers cannot base premiums on any average risk for a whole group of companies, since only higher-risk companies will want to purchase such insurance. Adverse selection problems are not universal, even for risks that are large and incompletely understood. For example, adverse selection is a relatively small problem in the case of political or counterparty risk; although the risks may be large, the company and its insurers are equally able to assess them. In environmental risk, by contrast, an outside insurer cannot know as much as the company's managers about the risks of their operations, and may not be in a position to price the insurance profitably.

Some tools used within the company to reduce and shift risk closely resemble the ones that government regulators use to reduce the risk of environmental damage. While those who run businesses tend to dislike command-and-control rules when governments use them, they make heavy use of such rules within their own companies. The bulky, constantly updated binder of "Environmental, Health and Safety Procedures" that graces every plant manager's bookshelf is, of course, a book of command-and-control rules. These rules are used within the company for the same reason that they are attractive to government agencies. The benefits of a particular investment in risk reduction are highly uncertain and difficult to quantify, so risk aversion drives regulators – and business managers – toward rules deemed reasonably likely to protect against the largest or most obvious risks, without a careful balancing of costs and benefits for each decision.

Indeed, for many companies the overriding objective of environmental risk management is to reduce the probability of some company-threatening catastrophe, or the company's exposure to such a cataclysm, or both. This is a necessary step to ensure long-term survival, but with investments in better information companies can do more.

Many well-managed companies are investing in better information about environmental risks for precisely this reason. Many of the major oil companies stayed in the oil transportation business even after the 1989 *Exxon Valdez* tanker spill in Alaska, because they wanted to maintain first-hand knowledge of the inside-the-company regulatory controls that would reduce the likelihood of future spills. More recently, the US oil company Chevron Corporation conducted a comprehensive inventory of the sites at which its onetime agricultural chemicals subsidiary sold pesticides and fertilizers, looking for spills and contaminated soil.

Environmental risk is likely to become more complicated in the future as economic output increases worldwide. Increasingly affluent societies will demand higher environmental standards. At the same time, the increased consumption that accompanies affluence will place more stress on unpriced environmental resources. This will lead to more frequent, and more serious, direct effects of environmental change on companies' operations. Climate change, and the concomitant possible increase in the severity of storms, will directly affect real-estate owners and their insurers. Agricultural producers (and their suppliers and customers) will also face greater direct environmental risks from global warming and its impact on precipitation patterns.

As information about environmental risks improves, managers will be able to compare those risks directly against other risks with which the company has to contend. They will also be able to compare the payoffs to investments in environmental risk reduction with the payoffs to other investments in risk management, so that environmental risk management is integrated into the overall risk management policies for the company. Companies that excel at this sort of integration will have lower long-term costs than their competitors.

Incentives for risk management

It is not enough, of course, to choose overall company-level risk management objectives; managers in large organizations also need to design incentives for lower-level managers so that environmental risk is managed in ways consistent with those objectives. In most US and UK companies, where managerial performance evaluations are based largely on business-unit profits, managers have strong incentives to pay close attention to costs, especially if those costs do not contribute to short-term gains. This, of course, is why senior managers impose command-and-control regulations: to ensure that their subordinates will not buy less risk reduction than the senior managers would like.

Other institutions may also blunt managers' short-term proclivity to underinvest in environmental risk reduction. In the US, violation of environmental laws can lead to individual civil or criminal liability; and managers everywhere may wish to reduce risk to the environment in order to enhance their own status in the community or their own feelings of self-worth. Still, in the absence of formal rules and an explicit role for environmental risk management in the evaluation and promotions process, the short-term focus is likely to prevail.

In the short term, corporate actions that reduce risk to the environment may increase the environmental risk to the company. The Endangered Species Act in the US, for example, makes it illegal to kill plants and animals that belong to threatened species, or to destroy the habitats on which these organisms depend.

If a forest products company makes a thorough inventory of the species living on its lands, this is valuable from a social perspective, but it might reduce profits if the timber company is unlucky enough to find endangered species. The opposite strategy – "shoot, shovel, and shut up" – may reduce short-term environmental risk to the company at the expense of long-term, and irreversible, damage to the environment.

This tension between risk to the environment and environmental risk to the company is, however, not universal, even in the short term. In the Chevron pesticide example, when managers decided that cleanups were advisable, the firm could conduct them before any expensive, litigious regulatory proceedings ensued. "We could do voluntary cleanup if that was warranted, which involves much less red tape and allows us to do what makes common sense," said an environmental manager at Chevron's chemical arm.

In other words, by reducing the transaction costs of the cleanup, the company could both deliver more environmental quality to the residents near the sites and reduce environmental risk to its shareholders.

In the long term, regulatory and social pressures will tend to make the reduction of risk to the environment and the reduction of financial risk to the company complementary rather than competing objectives. In the short term, as we have seen, reducing risk to the environment rarely translates directly into reducing the environmental risk to the company. In the long term, however, the only reliable way to reduce environmental risk to the company is to reduce risk to the environment.

I have benefitted from conversations with colleagues Tom McCraw, David Moss, Peter Tufano, and Lou Wells, and from the advice of Susan McCraw. Remaining errors are mine.

Summary

Since environmental risk means different things to different people, **Forest Reinhardt** suggests that managers need to be very clear about what it is they seek to manage. The author cites the controversy over genetically engineered seeds to show how definitions of environmental risk diverge for industry and individual farmers. In addition, business managers, government regulators, and environmental activists all have individual perceptions of environmental risk. Environmental risk management needs to deploy some of the analytical tools used in other risk management problems. Its primary concern is to reduce the likelihood of catastrophes that might threaten corporate survival. In the short term, corporate actions that do cut risk to the environment may, perversely, increase financial risk to the company. Here the impact of legislation has been especially important, an example being the US Endangered Species Act.

Suggested further reading

Milgrom P. and Roberts, J. (1992) *Economics, Organization and Management*, Englewood Cliffs, NJ: Prentice Hall.

Reinhardt, F.L. (2000) *Down to Earth: Applying Business Principles to Environmental Management*, Boston, MA: Harvard Business School Press.

Seeking succour from the rising costs of catastrophe

by Howard Kunreuther

The financial costs of natural disasters are increasing in size and public profile. Until now, they have received relatively little notice except in the immediate aftermath of a catastrophic event. Yet catastrophes cost the world $100bn in 1999, with the global insurance industry covering $28.6bn of the losses. The biggest single loss to the insurance market in 1999 came from the Christmas storms in western Europe, which cost insurers $6.7bn.

Emerging economies have suffered from natural disasters much more than the developed world because the losses have been a much larger proportion of their gross domestic product. Developing nations take longer to recover and can often suffer severe internal damage.

For example, when Hurricane Mitch struck Honduras in October 1998, it caused damage estimated at 70 percent of GDP. In addition, many more lives are lost in developing economies because of poorly constructed property. Flooding and mudslides in Venezuela in December 1999 took the lives of 50,000 people; more than 19,000 died in earthquakes in Turkey in August the same year; and 15,000 in a cyclone in India in October. Many of these fatalities could have been avoided had building codes been enforced in hazard-prone areas.

The costs from natural catastrophes have risen steadily in the past 30 years, not because of global warming, but rather because of increased property development in hazardous areas. The global challenge we face is how to reduce the losses from future natural disasters through the adoption of cost-effective loss-prevention or loss-reduction measures, while at the same time providing adequate financial protection following a disaster. These two goals complement each other. The adoption of mitigation measures reduces aggregate losses from future disasters and hence the costs of financial protection after the event.

When the evidence is presented on the magnitude of damage and loss of lives from disasters, it would appear relatively easy to encourage residents and businesses in hazard-prone areas to take steps to reduce their losses.

The empirical evidence suggests that this is not nearly as easy as it appears to be. In fact, there is limited adoption of cost-effective measures even when they are relatively inexpensive. For example, it costs less than $75 to have someone strap down a water heater in a residential home in California to prevent it from toppling over after an earthquake and perhaps causing a major fire. Indeed, if one did it oneself the cost would be less than $5. Yet few homeowners in earthquake-prone areas of the state have voluntarily adopted the measure. It has therefore become a legal requirement.

Attitudes toward protection

There are a number of reasons why homes and businesses do not undertake cost-effective loss-prevention measures. Probably the most important one is that there is a human tendency to believe "it will not happen to me." This problem is particularly acute for low-probability events such as natural disasters – people have limited personal experience of the event and thus do not regard it as an important possibility.

Furthermore, until recently it was difficult to obtain risk estimates. In addition, there are always more pressing matters demanding attention. As a result, natural disasters may not even be considered until after the event occurs, when protective measures may be too late.

Another reason for the reluctance to adopt protective measures is that it requires an expenditure in advance without any guaranteed return. In the case of insurance coverage, one pays a premium each year to protect oneself against an event that may not happen. Those who do not collect on their policy after a few years are likely to cancel it because they feel it is not a good investment and that their premiums are wasted. It is difficult for people to appreciate that the best return on an insurance policy is no return at all.

Some mitigation measures, such as reinforcing the foundation of a property to make the structure more resistant to earthquake or flood, may require large up-front investment costs that can yield long-term benefits over the life of the property. However, if one has relatively short time horizons and does not take into account the potential benefits for more than the next two or three years, the mitigation investment will look unattractive. Budget constraints exacerbate the situation.

Developments in assessing risks

Fortunately, new developments in information technology (IT) and risk assessment form the basis for developing new strategies for reducing losses from natural disasters. These developments can persuade property and business owners to take mitigation measures against events they would normally perceive as not worth worrying about.

On the IT side, the development of faster and more powerful computers enables people to examine extremely complex phenomena in ways that were impossible 10 years ago. With respect to risk assessment, scientists and engineers have developed more sophisticated models for estimating the risks associated with earthquakes, hurricanes, and other disasters.

Companies specializing in mathematical modeling have taken advantage of these new advances to develop user-friendly software for estimating the impact of disasters under a variety of different scenarios. For example, companies can now provide estimates of the losses to a commercial structure in an earthquake-prone area from disasters of different magnitudes when the property is well designed and when it is not. They can also specify upper and lower bounds on these loss estimates that reflect the degree of uncertainty surrounding the scientists' and engineers' models.

The development of more sophisticated models of physical damage from disasters is only part of the story. There has also been a new appreciation of the importance of broadening cost–benefit analysis to include the indirect effects of a disaster on the affected property.

Consider the case of a commercial operation subject to the risks of flooding. If a severe flood occurs, one needs to take into account not only the damage to physical property but also the indirect losses to the affected population such as business interruption to firms.

The story becomes more complicated when one considers the interdependencies between companies and the providers of their raw materials and services. Loss of electrical power and other infrastructure, such as water supply and highways, will affect companies that have not even received any physical damage. Supply chain interruptions will disrupt the production process. These linkages between units provide an even more compelling reason for designing safer structures and operations in hazard-prone areas. A governmental policy of investing in better infrastructure, for example, can pay dividends far beyond the reduction in physical damage to the facility itself.

When one takes into account both the direct and indirect losses from disasters, the challenges of providing financial resources to aid the recovery process become even more complicated. The standard policy tool for dealing with financial losses is insurance. As mentioned above, there is limited interest in voluntarily purchasing insurance against these disasters until after the event. Given the recent spate of disasters, there has been more interest in protection by residents and business in hazard-prone areas. Insurers, on the other hand, are now more concerned with the possibility of catastrophic losses and hence are limiting the number of policies they write. In other words, they see themselves playing a more limited role in covering the financial impacts of disasters than in the past.

Financial protection

To avoid the possibility of insolvency or a significant loss of surplus, insurers have traditionally used reinsurance contracts as a source of protection. Reinsurance does for the insurance company what primary insurance does for the policyholder or property owner – that is, it provides a way to protect against unforeseen or extraordinary losses. For all but the largest insurance companies, reinsurance is almost a prerequisite for offering insurance against hazards where there is potential for large claim payments. In a reinsurance contract, one insurance company (the reinsurer, or assuming insurer) charges a premium to indemnify another insurance company (the ceding insurer) against all or part of the loss it may sustain under its portfolio of policies against certain types of risks such as property damage.

While the reinsurance market is a critical source of funding for primary insurers, the magnitude of recent catastrophic losses makes it implausible for them adequately to finance future large-scale disasters. Though total insurance capital was slightly more than $400bn in 1999, researchers on the Managing Catastrophic Risk project at Wharton find that the capacity of the insurance and reinsurance industry to bear a large catastrophic loss is actually much more limited than the aggregate statistics would suggest.

In the past few years, investment banks and brokerage companies have shown interest in developing new financial instruments, such as Act of God bonds, for providing funds to insurers, reinsurers, and businesses following a catastrophic disaster. Their objective is to find ways of making investors comfortable trading new securitized instruments covering catastrophic exposures, just like the securities of any other asset class. In other words, catastrophe exposures would be treated as a new asset class.

This appears to be a promising solution, given the fact that the US capital market (worth $26tr) is more than 75 times larger than the property/casualty industry. Thus, the capital markets clearly have the potential to enhance the risk-bearing capacity of the insurance industry and allow them to spread risks more efficiently on a broader level. Though the market for risk-linked securities is still in its infancy, insurers and reinsurers had, as of November 1999, successfully transferred more than \$3bn of catastrophe risk.

Private–public partnerships

There is an opportunity to combine a set of risk management tools for both reducing losses and providing financial protection following a disaster. The private sector cannot do it alone, nor should it be left to public agencies to manage the risk if one feels that those residing in hazard-prone areas bear some responsibility for the risks they face. It is the combination of the two that is likely to work.

Turning first to the private sector, there are opportunities for providing economic incentives to manage the risks by bringing together insurers and financial institutions. Consider the following example. Suppose that a manufacturing company had designed its plant to be more earthquake proof so it would save \$100,000 in property damage should a future severe quake occur in the area. The chance of such an event happening next year is estimated to be 1/50. Hence, the reduction in expected annual loss from undertaking this measure is \$2,000 (that is, 1/50 × \$100,000). How could one encourage the managers of the plant to invest in this measure if it required an advance expenditure of \$15,000?

The most direct and obvious way to do this is to reduce the insurance premium to reflect the lower loss that would have to be made in claims. For this example, if insurance rates were based on risk, the reduction in the company's premium would be in the order of \$2,000. If the managers made their investment decisions so that they required a payback period of between two and five years, then with any positive discount rate they would not want to incur this up-front cost.

On the other hand, if the \$15,000 protective measure was financed as a 20-year loan at an annual interest rate of 10 percent, the annual payment would be \$1,700 a year. This is \$300 less than the \$2,000 reduction in the annual insurance premium from undertaking this measure. Thus there would be no question that the manufacturing industry in question would want to invest in mitigation.

In addition to financial incentives, such as insurance premium reductions and loans, there should be well-enforced building codes that require the adoption of cost-effective mitigation measures. One of the principal reasons for having such codes is that when a building collapses, it may have negative effects in the form of economic dislocations and other social effects that go beyond the economic loss suffered by the owners. These costs are not reflected in the insurance premiums charged to the particular piece of property.

Suppose the manufacturing plant topples off its foundation after an earthquake. The building could break a pipeline and cause a major fire that would damage other property not affected by the earthquake in the first place – these losses would not be covered by the company's insurance policy. All financial institutions and insurers which are responsible for these other properties at risk would favor building codes to protect their investments. The success of such a program requires the support of the building industry and a cadre of qualified inspectors to provide accurate information on whether existing codes and standards are being met.

Building codes applied to a large number of properties have an additional advantage. They are likely to reduce the costs to insurers and reinsurers of protecting themselves against catastrophic losses and hence make coverage more widespread than it is today. Suppose that an Act of God bond were offered to insurers to cover their losses above some upper limit, say \$1bn, from a major disaster. If all property in the hazard-prone area were designed according to a strict building code, then the damage would be much less from the disaster than it would be without the code in place. This translates into a lower cost for an Act of God bond, thus making it more attractive. Insurers would be more likely to purchase these bonds and thus have more capacity available to provide coverage to homes and businesses in the hazard-prone area.

It should now be clear why it is so important to have some type of private–public partnership for dealing with future losses from natural disasters. Only by recognizing the limitations that people face in processing information and their constraints on time, attention, and budget can we develop risk management policies for addressing events with low probabilities and severe consequences.

Such a policy will require a combination of market-based incentives such as long-term loans and lower insurance premiums. Well-enforced building codes are also needed to address the losses not directly affecting the property at risk. In addition, the aggregate reduction in damage will make catastrophe risk instruments more attractive. A private–public partnership is likely both to reduce future disaster losses and to provide more funds for recovery than are available today. Whether these policies will be implemented remains an open question. Let us hope that we are not forced to wait until the next major earthquake, flood, or hurricane wreaks damage in some part of the world before action is taken.

Summary

The increasing cost of catastrophic events poses a challenge to the world's governments, insurance companies, and financial institutions. How can they both fund measures that reduce the impact of catastrophes and provide financial protection to communities and businesses after the event? **Howard Kunreuther** notes that truly devastating events are so rare that people are often unwilling to insure or take simple precautions against them. Advances in risk assessment technology may combat this, since they will highlight the risks of extreme events. Likewise, new economic research demonstrates the fragility of neighboring or associated businesses when disaster strikes. Those who seek financial protection for such events are now turning away from traditional insurance markets toward financial instruments such as Act of God bonds. Ultimately, the best solution may lie in a combination of private and public initiatives, for example economic incentives for risk management and strongly enforced building codes.

Suggested further reading

Froot, K. (ed.) (1999) *The Financing of Property/Casualty Risks*, Chicago: University of Chicago Press.

H. John Heinz III Center (2000) *The Hidden Costs of Coastal Hazards*, Washington, DC: Island Press.

Insurance Services Office (1999) *Financing Catastrophe Risk: Capital Market Solutions*, New York: Insurance Services Office.

Kunreuther, H. and Roth, R., Sr. (eds) (1998) *Paying the Price: The Status and Role of Insurance against Natural Disasters in the United States*, Washington, DC: Joseph Henry Press.

The essentials of crisis management

by Ian I. Mitroff

For over 20 years, my colleagues and I have studied a wide range of human-caused crises and have worked with a large number of organizations to improve their crisis management capabilities. We have found that there is a general framework for managing major crises. We have also found that unless an organization understands the principles behind this framework and uses it to guide its crisis preparations, it will not be able to develop the capabilities it needs to survive a major crisis.

The framework has four components: crisis types, crisis mechanisms, crisis systems, and crisis stakeholders. These must be managed before, during, and after a major crisis. The framework is a composite of "best practices" and serves as a benchmark against which all companies can measure their current crisis management capabilities.

Crisis types

Crises fall into distinct categories, types or "families." Within a particular family, each kind of crisis shares strong similarities with the other kinds. At the same time, there are sharp differences between the families. For instance, there are economic, informational, physical, human resource, reputational, psychopathic, and natural (disaster) crises.

Very few organizations plan for a broad set of crises across a wide array of families. Most organizations, if they plan for crises at all, do so mainly for natural disasters. This is not only because natural disasters are always occurring, but because they strike all organizations equally. Consequently, they pose less threat to the "collective psyche" of organizations.

Consider earthquakes, which threaten all companies in the Los Angeles region. Their effects may be made less devastating by proper building regulations, but since one can neither predict nor prevent them, their occurrence does not encourage the assignation of blame that arises with other types of crises. A crisis of workplace violence, for instance, calls for human vigilance and mitigation.

Once a company moves beyond planning solely for natural disasters, its attention will likely turn to "core crises" within its particular industry. For example, companies in the chemical industry naturally prepare for toxic spills and fires, since these threats are part of their everyday operating experience. Likewise, fast-food companies need little encouragement to establish procedures to avoid food contamination, since such procedures are a natural accompaniment of their business.

On the other hand, organizations need strong and persistent encouragement to prepare for crises outside their direct operating experience. Research into crisis management has shown that, with very few exceptions, all types of crises can happen to all organizations in all industries – the only thing one cannot predict is the exact form a particular crisis will assume.

Consider this example. In 1990, Larousse, the world's leading publisher of French dictionaries, recalled 180,000 volumes of the 1990 color edition of its Petit Larousse dictionary, after a miscaptioned photograph labeled a deadly mushroom "harmless" and a harmless one "deadly." It was not made clear at the time whether the mislabeling was intentional or just human error. However, since the French are avid gatherers and consumers of mushrooms, the error represented a major crisis for the publisher – particularly since it was unexpected and the company had no crisis plan to cope with the problem.

Those organizations that prepare best for crises attempt to prepare for at least one crisis in each of the various families. Why? Because any type of crisis is capable of sparking another type and in turn being caused by it. That is, every conceivable crisis is capable of being both the cause and the effect of any other.

The best-prepared companies do not look at individual crises in isolation, but attempt to view each crisis as related to all others in an overall system. Paradoxically, they may not be concerned with the details of crisis management plans. Instead, they concentrate primarily on developing crisis capabilities. It matters little if an organization has the best plans in the world if it is incapable of executing them.

Crisis mechanisms

Research has found that a small number of mechanisms are extremely important in responding to crises before, during, and after their occurrence. The fact that these mechanisms apply before, during, and after a major crisis shows why effective crisis management is not merely a case of responding or reacting to a major crisis after it has occurred. Effective crisis management is proactive, not reactive. The best form of crisis management is preparation for a major crisis before it has occurred – afterwards is clearly too late.

These mechanisms enable companies to anticipate, sense, react to, contain, learn from, and redesign effective organizational procedures for handling major crises. For instance, far in advance of their occurrence, all (human-caused) crises send out a trail of early warning signals. If these signals can be picked up and acted on before the actual occurrence of a crisis, then a crisis can usually be prevented.

"Signal-detection mechanisms" need to be in place and operating long before the white heat of a crisis impairs their function. For example, the increase in graffiti on factory walls and absenteeism may indicate employee unrest and potential workplace violence; a steep rise in accident rates is often a signal of impending industrial explosions. Furthermore, without proper signal-detection mechanisms, an organization not only makes a major crisis more likely but also reduces its chances of bringing it under control.

Even the best signal-detection mechanisms cannot prevent all crises from occurring. Hence, one of the most important aspects of crisis management is damage containment. This prevents the unwanted effects of a crisis spreading and affecting uncontaminated parts of an organization. On a more physical level, in, for example, the oil industry, damage-containment mechanisms such as baffles in ships, oil skimmers, and firewalls are common. While not perfectly effective, given the varying size and the nature of particular oil spills, such mechanisms are under constant design and improvement to prevent spills from spreading and hence enabling a crisis to be contained.

Two of the most important mechanisms reveal why the vast majority of crisis management programs are ineffective. These concern post-crisis learning and the redesign of systems and mechanisms to improve future crisis management performance. Few organizations conduct postmortems of crises and near misses, and those that do often fail to perform them correctly or learn their proper lessons. Postmortems should form part of an ongoing crisis audit that examines the strengths and weaknesses of an organization on each of the four crisis factors.

Crisis systems

Five components are basic to understanding any complex organization: technology, organizational structure, human factors, culture, and the psychology of senior management.

Modern organizations contain a variety of complex technologies. These range from computers crunching information to the larger plants and processes that manufacture products. Companies in services industries also use sophisticated technologies.

Technology neither exists nor functions in a vacuum – it is run by all-too-human beings, who are prone to error. Whether we like it or not, human beings get tired, suffer from stress, and become irritated, all of which contribute to intentional and unintentional errors. The field of human factors is precisely that area that assesses the causes of human errors and seeks to design systems that decrease or, where possible, eliminate the effects of human errors.

Consider the cockpit of a modern jet aeroplane. To the uninitiated, an aeroplane's cockpit is an exercise in chaos. The controls are so bewildering and laid out in such a fashion that an amateur literally cannot make sense of them, let alone operate them. Nonetheless, human factors engineers have studied the controls and the process of piloting an aeroplane and laid them out so that pilots, who often have to operate under stressful conditions, can minimize the chances of catastrophic error.

In addition, literally hours of training are required so that their safe operation is not left to chance. The same considerations are obviously just as critical, if not more so, in the operation of chemical and nuclear power plants, not to mention hospital operating rooms.

Technology also introduces different kinds of errors when it is embedded in complex organizations. One reason is that communications have to travel across many different layers in such organizations. Another is that reward systems favor certain kinds of behavior and attempt to extinguish other kinds. Such factors can both help and hinder in ensuring that the right information reaches the right people in a timely fashion so the right decisions can be made. In the case of the 1989 *Exxon Valdez* oil spill off Alaska, critical time was lost in getting the right people to the scene of the crisis in order to deal with it in a timely and appropriate manner. Indeed, precious time was lost because the information necessary to activate Exxon's response had to travel up and down innumerable layers of a Byzantine corporate bureaucracy.

The culture and psychology of the management team are the most critical determinants of an organization's crisis management performance. The management team that functions best will be the one that is relatively free of denial, grandiosity, and so on. In contrast, a dysfunctional team will not only fail to manage crises effectively, but will probably cause them and amplify their worst aspects, thus prolonging a crisis.

One of the first and the most important discoveries that research into crisis management shows is that organizations, like individuals, use Freudian defense mechanisms to deny their vulnerability to major crises. Such mechanisms help them justify low levels of expenditure on resources and planning for crisis management.

Crisis stakeholders

Good crisis management involves those internal and external individuals, organizations, and institutions that have to co-operate with the company's managers, share crisis plans, and participate in crisis training programs. These stakeholders can include employees, police departments, the Red Cross, fire departments, and so on, all of whom may be called on to help in a major crisis. Important stakeholder relationships must be nurtured over the course of years if a company is to have the capabilities that are required in the heat of a major crisis. For instance, a company that builds a track record with the media for honesty and integrity, especially when things have gone wrong in the past, will be much more likely to be believed in future.

Conclusion

While the media do not use exactly the same words as I have in describing a crisis management framework, even the most cursory review of any major crisis reveals that the same ideas are at work. In other words, how well an organization does on each of these factors constitutes the "scorecard" that the media will use to evaluate an organization's crisis management performance.

Moreover, this framework is not only characteristic of crisis management. It is characteristic of all the new business and management functions that have emerged as a result of the global information economy. Thus, total quality management, environmentalism, and issues management are systemic and pertain to the organization as a whole. As a result, they share many of the detailed factors described above.

The best form of crisis management combines total quality management, environmentalism, and other forms of risk management. Crisis management will not succeed if it is regarded as just another separate, stand-alone program. It must be part of the integral design of an organization.

In sum, crisis management must be conceived of and practiced systemically and systematically, or it will be part of the problem, not the solution.

Summary

Crisis management has several different aspects, all of which are interlinked and all of which companies must master if they are to avoid the worst effects of a catastrophe, writes **Ian Mitroff**. In this article, he presents a framework for managing human-caused crises, which consists of four crucial components: companies must examine systematically a broad range of crisis types, and not just natural disasters, if they are to be prepared; crisis mechanisms can signal dangers early on; crisis systems can minimize the problems stemming from technological and organizational complexity; and companies should work with crisis stakeholders such as employees, the emergency services, and governmental bodies to forestall problems when a crisis does occur.

Difficult calls in judging risk extremes

by Paul Embrechts

On February 1, 1953, a severe westerly storm battered the Flemish and Dutch coasts. The Dutch provinces of Holland and Zeeland were particularly badly hit and more than 1,800 people died after several dykes collapsed. The flooding represented a surge of 3.85m above normal sea level, which came close to the 4m surge of November 1, 1570, known as the *Allerheiligenvloed*. In the aftermath of the 1953 disaster, the Dutch government asked a group of scientists, statisticians, and engineers to estimate the minimum height of new dykes that would be sufficient to withstand a once-in-10,000-year event. The height requirement would have to ensure that the probability of an overflow in any year would be very small – 0.0001 in the above case.

The committee of experts was faced with calculating a risk measure (the dyke height) to safeguard against a rare event (in this case a surge expected to occur once every 10,000 years) based on sparsely available data. After making their calculations, they estimated that the dykes should be at least 5m tall. The statistical techniques that they used belong to the domain of extreme value theory (EVT), which is the subject of this article.

Rare events

According to the Zurich-based Swiss Reinsurance Company (Swiss Re), catastrophes in 1999 resulted in more than 105,000 dead and $28.6bn of insured losses, representing the second-heaviest loss burden ever for insurers. The main causes were five storms and two earthquakes, which alone cost the insurance industry $15.9bn. Loss ratios (losses over premiums) for earthquake insurance in California are shown in Table 1.

Except for 1989, these Californian losses fluctuate within a comfortable range for the insurer. Basing their calculations on such data, who then would have predicted a 1994 loss ratio of 2,272.7? In the wake of events such as hurricanes Andrew and Northridge, one often hears fears expressed about the "possibility" of a large-scale catastrophe. Given the estimated $300bn in total net assets in the area this is perhaps to be expected – indeed, the property/casualty insurance industry has reasons for concern.

On January 17, 1995, the Hanshin earthquake struck Kobe, Japan, killing 6,425

Table 1: California earthquake insurance, loss ratios 1971–1993

1971	17.4	1977	0.7	1983	2.9	1989	129.8
1972	0	1978	1.5	1984	5.0	1990	47.0
1973	0.6	1979	2.2	1985	1.3	1991	17.2
1974	3.4	1980	9.2	1986	9.3	1992	12.8
1975	0	1981	0.9	1987	22.8	1993	3.2
1976	0	1982	0	1988	11.5		

people and causing insured losses of $2.716bn. As a result, Barings trader Nick Leeson faced serious problems. In his role as a writer of so-called straddles (a derivatives product) on the Nikkei 225 index, he had been speculating that the index would not move significantly out of its trading range. If the financial security underlying a straddle position either decreases or increases significantly (an extreme move), the writer of the straddle loses money. The earthquake resulted in the Nikkei 225 shedding 11 percent and the consequences for Leeson are well known: on February 26, 1995, Barings, the UK's oldest merchant banking group, was placed into administration.

Financial markets have witnessed numerous declines, among them that of 1929 that presaged the Great Depression and the October 1987 Black Monday crash. More recently, in a single one-day drop on April 5, 2000, the Nasdaq dipped more than 13 percent as investors reacted to a highly overvalued, technology-driven bull market. This had been preceded by a 7.64 percent decline the day before, and 7.86 percent a week earlier. Clearly, this barometer of the new economy is prone to extreme swings. Despite these glitches, the Nasdaq gained 85 percent overall in 1999.

Catastrophic events in insurance and finance can now be handled by alternative investment vehicles, called alternative risk transfer (ART) products. These claim to offer the holder of a catastrophic risk portfolio additional protection. They also attract investors who are less risk averse with promises of a high yield in securities that are only vaguely correlated to standard financial markets.

Among such products are the following:

- *Catastrophe bonds.* Here, the coupon payment is contingent on a well-defined catastrophic event. When this happens within a clearly specified time period, the investor stands to lose all or part of the coupon payment and, in some cases, part of the face value also.
- *Catastrophe options.* These are financial derivatives written on an underlying index strongly correlated to the type of catastrophic loss that, typically, the option issuer is bearing.
- *Options triggered by extreme moves in financial markets*, such as a daily decline in the price of a specific financial index exceeding 10 percent.

Such products must be created and calculated to match a well-defined extreme event. Besides establishing such ART markets – which involves engineering the products, finding buyers and sellers, and framing the regulatory environment – pricing and hedging involve an assessment of the probability of the trigger for the extreme event.

In need of a theory

An important difficulty in understanding the meaning of the word "extreme" is finding a yardstick for measuring and distinguishing between "normal" and "extreme." For a start, one is hampered by the language used daily in describing odds. Statements such as "this is normal" or "this is to be expected" take on a meaning of their own – one which can sometimes be misleading. The yardstick constructed by mathematicians to measure the likelihood of random events is probability theory. The data that links this to the day-to-day world comes from statistics. Together, these areas of mathematics (referred to as stochastics) yield powerful tools employed not only in many fields of science but also in insurance and finance. EVT is a subset of tools from stochastics that has been specially developed to describe rare events. Major areas of application include reliability engineering, medical statistics, environmental science, geology and meteorology.

The need for a risk management theory for extreme events has long been recognized. Speaking in 1995, Alan Greenspan, chairman of the Federal Reserve, told the Joint Central Bank Research Conference:

> *A natural consequence of the existence of a lender of last resort is that there will be some sort of allocation of burden of risk of extreme outcomes. Thus, central banks are led to provide what essentially amounts to catastrophic insurance coverage . . . From the point of view of the risk manager, inappropriate use of the normal distribution can lead to an understatement of risk, which must be balanced against the significant advantage of simplification. From the central bank's corner, the consequences are even more serious because we often need to concentrate on the left tail of the distribution in formulating lender-of-last-resort policies. Improving the characterization of the distribution of extreme values is of paramount importance.*

Events surrounding Long-Term Capital Management (LTCM), the US hedge fund that failed spectacularly in 1998, laid further stress on the importance of such a research program. *Business Week* said in September 1998:

> *Extreme, synchronized rises and falls in financial markets occur infrequently but they do occur. The problem with the models is that they did not assign a high enough chance of occurrence to the scenario in which many things go wrong at the same time – the "perfect storm" scenario.*

The Economist commented in October 1998 after the LTCM rescue:

> *Regulators have criticized LTCM and banks for not "stress testing" risk models against extreme market movements . . . The markets have been through the financial equivalent of several Hurricane Andrews hitting Florida all at once. Is the appropriate response to accept that it was mere bad luck to run into such a rare event – or to get new forecasting models that assume more storms in the future?*

In the *Wall Street Journal* on October 21, 2000, the former Chief of LTCM, John Meriwether, commented in general on some of the flawed LTCM tactics and in particular on the tactics of his new investment company, JWM Partners:

> *With globalization increasing, you'll see more crises. Our whole focus is on the extremes now – what's the worse that can happen to you in any situation – because we never want to go through that again.*

Clearly, we have to calibrate our models more carefully with respect to extreme movements. Financial risk managers have already adopted more stringent procedures at the pricing and hedging stages. The current quantitative tool for financial risk management is Value at Risk (VaR). Unfortunately, VaR is often loosely defined as the maximum expected loss of a portfolio over a specific time horizon at a certain confidence.

From an academic point of view, this "definition" is nonsensical. From an applied point of view, it is dangerous. It may give the non-expert the false belief that we are indeed talking about a maximum loss; this same non-expert will no doubt have difficulties with the terms "expected" and "confidence." Instead, the definition

Technical section: a primer on extreme value theory

Consider the normal distribution – the Bell Curve – that is commonly used to calculate scientific and financial probabilities. It is nicely symmetrical and has very thin tails with convenient properties; the tail events can be calculated by multiplying a volatility and time-scaling, resulting in a square-root law. Unfortunately, financial reality cannot be forced into this bell-shaped straitjacket. For risk management purposes, such as estimating VaR and beyond, EVT offers better tools.

Suppose $X_1, \ldots, X_n$ denotes n successive losses to a portfolio, with the total loss denoted by $S_n = X_1 + \ldots + X_n$. The normal distribution offers a reasonable first approximation to the statistical properties of S_n. As risk managers, however, we are more interested in the largest loss, that is, in $M_n = \max(X_1, \ldots, X_n)$, where max stands for maximum. Here, the bell curve is the wrong tool. A very different class of models (typically skewed or non-symmetrical) should be used instead, called Fréchet, Weibull, and Gumbel models. These have been studied in detail by statisticians and are now widely applied throughout the finance and insurance industry.

These models lead to a theory that allows for the estimation of rare events (tail events) and conditional losses. In other words, given that a high loss occurred, the theory can estimate the size of this (conditional) loss. These methods fit better with calculations involving the tails of the data; standard tools can be used for the central part of the curve.

As in any statistical analysis, good estimates require good data. A first step consists in determining which data we want to use. One has to decide from which loss level onward we want to fit the data. This means that somewhere in the procedure one has to decide which (upper) portion of the data will be used in estimating the tail region. One does not want "smaller" events to have a stronger than proportionate impact on the modeling of the "larger" events. This method of fitting data above a certain, chosen threshold (far in the tail) is akin to actuarial pricing mechanisms for excess-of-loss reinsurance treaties.

A simplified example from the realm of insurance should give a first impression of the use of EVT methodology. Figure 1 shows 2,493 losses due to large fires in Denmark between 1980 and 1993. The losses are in millions of Danish krone (1985 prices). The largest loss stands at DK263.3m. Suppose we want to estimate a 1-in-100 event (a 99 percent quantile), denoted by u, and the conditional expected loss above this quantile, denoted by $\hat{e}(u)$.

An application of EVT is summarized in Figure 2. The figure contains, on a so-called log–log scale, the data (the black dots), an EVT fit to the tail (the solid downward-sloping line), estimates of u and $e(u)$, together with confidence intervals (measures of estimation uncertainty) shown through the parabola-like curves. The results are summarized in Table 2.

Hence the probability of a future loss exceeding DK27.3m is 1 percent, whereas our uncertainty about

Figure 1: Danish fire insurance data

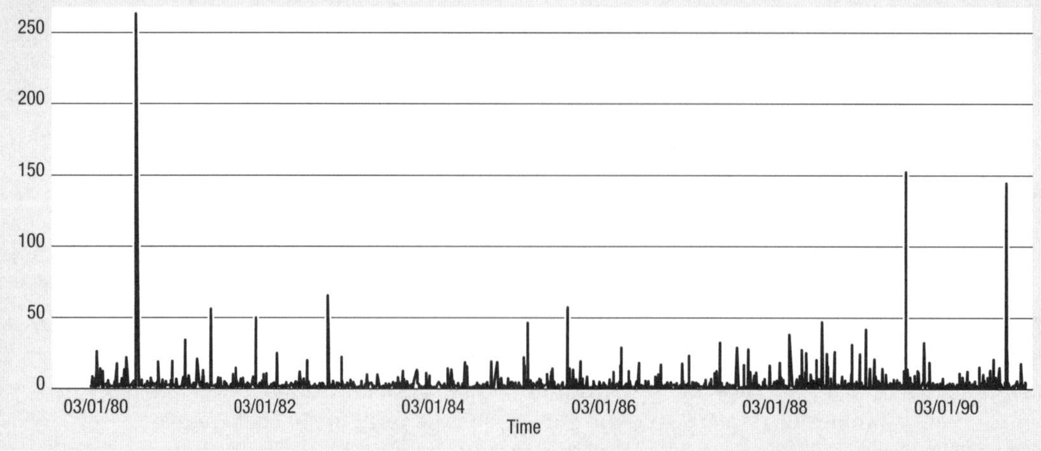

Figure 2: An EVT analysis of the Danish fire insurance data

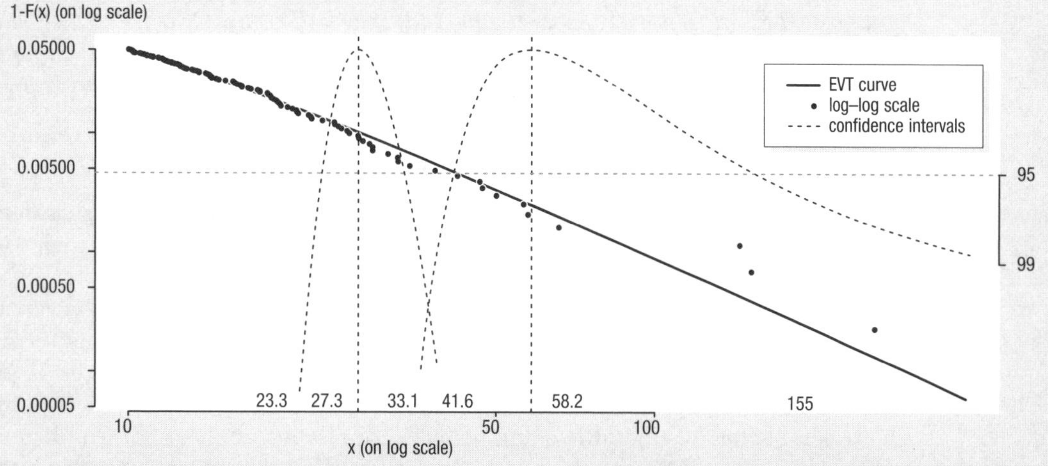

Table 2: Estimates $\hat{u}$, $\hat{e}(u)$ for the Danish fire insurance data, together with 95% confidence intervals (CI)

$\hat{u}$	27.3
95% CI for $\hat{u}$	(23.3, 33.1)
$\hat{e}(u)$	58.2
95% CI for $\hat{e}(u)$	(41.6, 154.7)

this estimate is that, with a probability of 95 percent, the interval DK23.3m–DK33.1m contains this (unknown) 1-in-100 event *u*. Given a 1-in-100 event (that is, a loss above 27.3 occurs), we expect that loss to be DK58.2m, with a similar uncertainty measure of 95 percent given for this estimate of between DK41.6m and DK154.7m. Besides the intrinsic values of these estimates, the full analysis (especially the confidence intervals) can be used to set stress scenarios.

The above example clearly shows the advantages of EVT, that is, fitting tails of distributions based essentially on data far out in that tail. This typically leads to more conservative (larger) values and, indeed, wide confidence intervals. From a statistical point of view, these estimates are "correct" or "better" than most of the *ad hoc* methods used, but they also raise the problem of cost. In the finance context, higher VaR values lead to higher values for regulatory capital, something most institutions will not accept.

The inadequacy of the usual methodology is captured by its use of a stress factor *k* between three and five. EVT calls into question this range for *k*. Whether in finance or insurance, the best approach is to say that estimates of EVT (for, say, premiums) are technically correct, but should be discussed further before being quoted. Obviously, this point warrants elaboration; it is also linked to the ever-recurring discussion on the balance between regulation and disclosure.

should be stated as follows: VaR is a statistical estimate of a portfolio loss, a characteristic of which is that, within a given (small) probability, we stand to incur that loss or more over a given (typically short) holding period.

In the latter VaR definition, EVT not only enters into statistical estimates of VaR but more importantly yields a methodology for estimating the size of "or more." Neglecting this while optimizing a portfolio under VaR constraints can lead to dangerous situations.

As *The Economist* noted in June 1999:

> *The financial systems have weathered storms so freakish they should never have happened at all. It seems inconceivable that they will recur. Or is it? In fact, such shocks are becoming both more likely and bigger. Financial markets' attempts to measure and price risk, and the models that they use to do so, may actually be making markets riskier.*

The difficulty of extremes

The modeling of extremes is a difficult subject: by definition, data is sparse on an extreme event, and often predictions or estimates have to be made at the edge of or even beyond the available data.

EVT does not offer a magical way out of these problems. It does, however, give better results than other approaches, many of which lack a theoretical justification. EVT has developed into a useful toolkit for the integrated-risk manager; it gives that manager a pair of spectacles through which to view extreme events more objectively. It has been and is being tested in numerous applications and has been extended in many different directions. In future, EVT should be as much a part of risk managers' everyday work as are the extreme events it seeks to analyze.

Summary

In this article, **Paul Embrechts** outlines the natural difficulties facing those who wish to judge the risk of extreme events – which are by nature rare and about which there is relatively little data. He begins by citing the 1953 flood in the Netherlands, which took the lives of 1,800 people. Subsequently, the authorities had to determine precisely the height of new dykes that would protect against future extreme flooding. More recently, a rash of both natural and financial catastrophes seems to suggest that extreme events are becoming more frequent and calls into question the reliability of forecasting models. To deal with insurance and finance catastrophes, the industry has designed substitute investment vehicles known as alternative risk transfer (ART) products, which are designed to be attractive to less risk-averse investors through the promise of a high yield. The author suggests that, for now, extreme value theory (EVT) offers the best option for risk managers grappling with the problems of extremes.

Suggested further reading

There is an extensive literature on EVT and its applications. For a review of the theory with finance applications in mind, *see* Embrechts, P., Klüppelberg, C. and Mikosch, T. (1997) *Modelling Extremal Events for Insurance and Finance*, Berlin: Springer. This reference also has more on the Danish fire insurance data, together with a considerable list of references for further reading.

Many relevant examples, related papers, EVT software, and further links are to be found at www.math.ethz.ch/finance.

A compilation of finance and insurance-relevant EVT papers is Embrechts, P. (ed.) (2000) *Extremes and Integrated Risk Management*, London: Risk Publications.

Day of judgment: catastrophe and the share price

by Rory F. Knight and Deborah J. Pretty

Catastrophes happen. It could be a human tragedy beyond comprehension, such as the 1984 Bhopal gas tragedy in India or the loss of life in the 1988 fire on the Piper Alpha North Sea oil platform. It may be an environmental calamity, such as the 11m gallons of crude oil spilt by *Exxon Valdez* into Prince William Sound, Alaska in 1989, or the massive Rhine pollution that followed Sandoz's 1986 Schweizerhalle fire. The financial consequences may also prove harsh for the company concerned – consider Perrier's recall of 160m bottles from 120 countries worldwide following benzene contamination in 1990.

In some cases, the corporate disaster is driven by public perception rather than reality. Prime recent examples are Royal Dutch/Shell's 1995 plan to dump the Brent Spar offshore platform at sea, halted by an environmentalist outcry, and the Coca-Cola health scare and recall in northern Europe in 1999. The extreme and severe consequences from all these events are beyond doubt.

However, catastrophes also provide us with a unique opportunity to evaluate how financial markets respond when major risks become reality. In formulating risk management strategies, corporate managers have to evaluate alternative strategies against the criterion of shareholder value maximization. Therefore, a decision to hedge against specific types of risk depends on whether the value of the company is higher or lower under hedging. A deeper insight is required into how catastrophes affect shareholder value and what factors influence this impact.

This article considers the traditional approach to catastrophic loss analysis, introduces an alternative approach, describing the results of research into the value impact of 15 corporate catastrophes, and draws some conclusions for practicing managers.

Analyzing losses

Conventional financial analyses of loss tend to focus solely on accounting statements. Analysts consider the impact of loss on the company's earnings statement, or the value of the asset lost, or the dent in annual profitability. This type of loss analysis, while useful, overlooks a company's longer-term ability to generate cash flow.

We know that modern finance theory assumes that the prevailing corporate objective is to maximize shareholder value. We also know that a company's share price represents an unbiased estimate of the present value of a company's long-term future cash flow.

Against a background of accounting-based analyses, and with our knowledge of shareholder value, the question then is: how does a catastrophic corporate event affect the fundamental drivers of value?

The cash-flow approach to valuation relies on those management expectations of company performance that have already been formed. These expectations will be revised as new information is received. A catastrophic event affecting a corporation will embody considerable information for all its stakeholders. However, the sheer complexity and volume of such information will confuse the value-estimation process. It is likely that it will also result in the capital markets receiving distorted signals. The extent to which a corporate catastrophe might, for example, affect free cash flow, investment rates, or risk ratings is not obvious.

The information asymmetries that exist between management and shareholders result in each attempting to "second guess" true value. The stock market as a whole, however, will form a collective opinion as to the impact of a corporate catastrophe on the shareholders' claim on assets. This opinion will then be reflected in the share prices of companies suffering the aftermath of catastrophes.

When catastrophe strikes

The research presented below identifies the value impact of catastrophes by focussing on 15 major corporate disasters and tracing their impact on stock returns and trading volume.

The selection of catastrophes is based on four criteria: the disasters are man-made as opposed to natural, each involves a publicly quoted company, each has received headline coverage in world news, and each has occurred since 1980.

The selection of catastrophes is also consistent with the systems approach of North American crisis management experts Thierry Pauchant and Ian Mitroff, where a crisis is defined as meeting at least two conditions: an organization must be affected on a symbolic level as well as on a physical level. This symbolic impact must be on the entire organization and not limited to a self-contained unit. Table 1 provides a chronological list of the catastrophes analyzed.

Six of the disasters profiled are in the oil/petrochemical/chemical industries and six are product-related incidents. Overall, four events are attributable to deliberate acts of tampering or terrorism and, in a further two, sabotage was suspected. Eight are US companies and the remaining six are European – British, Dutch, French, and Swiss. Thus, the catastrophe portfolio is international and constitutes a representative sample across industries and the major classes of loss.

Previous research has focussed largely on the impact of earnings and dividend announcements on share price. One problem with such research is that it is impossible to determine how much of the information has leaked to the market and been absorbed by the share price before the announcement. A study of catastrophes overcomes this issue of anticipation and captures a clean measurement of impact, since it is reasonable to assume that nobody expects a disaster to strike when it does.

The research results show that the market revises its expectations of future cash flow quickly and efficiently. As would be expected, in all cases the catastrophe was found to have had a significant negative initial impact on stock returns. However, after such a sharp reaction – amounting to almost 8 percent of stock value – there is on average an apparent full recovery in just over 50 trading days. This suggests that the net impact on stock returns is negligible. As will be demonstrated, however, the ability to recover the lost shareholder value over the long term varies considerably between companies.

Catastrophes are also shown to have a significant impact on the level of trading in shares. In the immediate aftermath of a catastrophe, trading in shares of these corporations is more than four times its normal level. On average, trading settles down about a month afterwards.

Table 1: Catastrophe portfolio

Date	Company name	Catastrophe	Type of catastrophe
30/09/82	Johnson & Johnson	Tylenol	Product tamper & recall
03/12/84	Union Carbide	Bhopal	Liability
11/02/86	Johnson & Johnson	Tylenol	Product tamper & recall
01/11/86	Sandoz	Rhine	Fire & pollution
06/03/87	P&O	Zeebrugge	Liability
05/05/88	Shell Oil	Norco	Explosion & fire
06/07/88	Occidental	Piper Alpha	Fire & explosions
21/12/88	PanAm	Lockerbie	Terrorism
24/03/89	Exxon	Valdez	Pollution
19/09/89	Upjohn	Halcion	Liability
23/10/89	Phillips Petroleum	Pasadena	Explosion & fire
10/02/90	Source Perrier	Benzene	Product recall
17/07/90	Eli Lilly	Prozac	Liability
10/04/92	Commercial Union	Baltic Exchange	Terrorism
25/08/93	Heineken	Glass	Product recall

Thus, the immediate and negative impact on value not surprisingly coincides with abnormally high levels of trading activity. By contrast, the drift back in stock value occurs at a normal level of trading activity.

Companies affected by catastrophes fall into two relatively distinct groups, recoverers and non-recoverers. These terms relate exclusively to the companies' post-loss share price recovery patterns, rather than whether or not the company ultimately went bankrupt because of the disaster. The initial loss of stock value is approximately 5 percent on average for recoverers and about 11 percent for non-recoverers. Figure 1 shows that by the 50th trading day, the average cumulative impact on stock returns for the recoverers was at least 5 percent. Therefore, the net impact on stock returns by this stage was actually positive.

The non-recoverers remained more or less unchanged between the 5th and the 50th day, but suffered a net negative cumulative impact of almost 15 percent up to one year after the catastrophe. Abnormally high trading is prevalent among the non-recoverers. Thus, an absence of frenetic trading around the time of a catastrophe is usually associated with a subsequent recovery in stock price.

Figure 1: Recoverers' and non-recoverers' abnormal returns

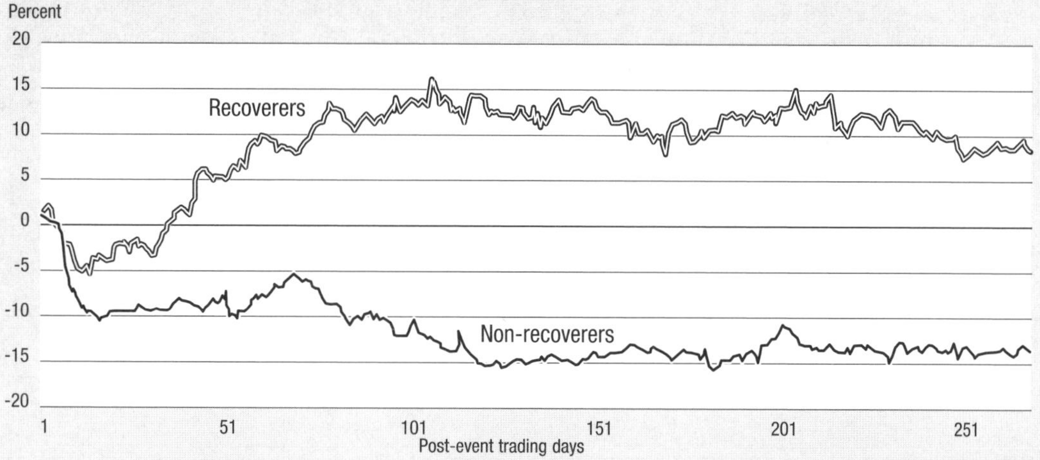

Stock market judgment

More specific results were discovered after further analysis. For the first six calendar months, the stock market appears to judge the company primarily on the impact of the financial loss on its average market capitalization. This judgment is reinforced by the number of deaths arising as an immediate consequence of the catastrophe; the greater the number of fatalities, the more severe the market judgment.

This is seen clearly in the gas leak in Bhopal, India, in which 3,000 people lost their lives. The market made its judgment and Union Carbide shed a third of its market value in the first two weeks of trading.

Beyond six months, the market pays increasingly less attention to the human and financial costs, and begins to judge the company much more on whether it was held responsible for the disaster. Investors' perceptions of managerial responsibility come to the fore in guiding their expectations of future cash flow.

For example, the markets accused Occidental Petroleum, operator of the Piper Alpha North Sea platform where fire and explosion claimed 167 lives, of failing to incorporate critical safety procedures. These procedures had been recommended by experts and accepted by Occidental over the years but had not become operating practice.

There are thus two elements to the catastrophic impact. The first is the immediate estimate of the associated economic loss. Although the cash-flow impact is not known with certainty at the time of the catastrophe, the stock market will form a collective opinion and adjust price accordingly. These direct factors usually will have a negative impact on stock returns, but such impact will be cushioned by the extent to which insurance recoveries reduce the cash outflows.

The second element of the catastrophe's impact hinges on senior managers' ability to deal with the aftermath. Although all catastrophes have an initial negative impact on price, they do, paradoxically, offer an opportunity for managers to demonstrate their talent in dealing with difficult circumstances.

A re-evaluation of management by the stock market is likely to result in a reassessment of the company's future cash flows in terms of both magnitude and confidence. This, in turn, has large potential implications for stock returns.

During Perrier's benzene contamination crisis, the company's efforts to respond through communication and worldwide co-ordination appeared to have broken down at various stages. Despite Perrier's original and emphatic denial that contamination had not spread beyond the US, 160m bottles of mineral water were eventually recalled from 120 countries worldwide and destroyed. The market judgment was straightforward: Perrier lost up to 40 percent in market value and was taken over by Nestlé.

Effective management of the consequences of catastrophes would appear to be a more significant factor than whether catastrophe insurance hedges the economic impact of the catastrophe. Additional anecdotal evidence suggests that managers' immediate, honest and efficient disclosure of relevant information to all parties helps secure share price recovery.

Conclusion

The lessons for managers are clear. They must do all that is reasonably possible to prevent catastrophes from happening. They must also, however, mitigate the effects of catastrophes that do happen and openly demonstrate that all critical actions were taken. There is a fundamental financial value in effective communication and honesty that extends to the practice of sending relevant and timely information regularly to all stakeholders. Ultimately, managers should be able to use these opportunities to show investors their talent for dealing with challenging circumstances. Success here builds investor confidence in a manager's ability to manage risk and create value for shareholders.

Summary

Despite their horrifying human toll and environmental consequence, catastrophes do offer a unique moment for measuring market impact, corporate resilience, and managerial competence, suggest **Rory F. Knight** and **Deborah J. Pretty**. Conventional financial analysis focusses on the impact of loss on earnings, asset base, and profitability. However, by focussing on accounting statements, these analyses are backward looking and overlook a company's longer-term ability to generate cash flow, captured by a shareholder value analysis. The authors look at the effect on stock returns and trading volume in the aftermath of 15 major corporate disasters. Critical to share price recovery is a responsible and fast managerial reaction. In addition, fundamental financial value can be gained from honest, regular, and effective disclosure of information.

Suggested further reading

Pauchant, T.C. and Mitroff, I.I. (1992) *Transforming the Crisis-prone Organization: Preventing Individual, Organizational, and Environmental Tragedies*, San Francisco, CA: Jossey Bass.

Research for this article has been sponsored by Marsh Limited. Copies of the full research report are available from enquiries@templeton.oxford.ac.uk

Wise prescriptions for a swift recovery

by Roland Mann

On April 5, 2000 the computer system of the London Stock Exchange was disabled for nearly eight hours, causing widespread disruption for markets and investors. The crash came at a particularly bad time for retail investors, who traditionally take advantage of annual capital gains tax changes at the end of the UK tax year.

The fact that a seemingly random computer failure had temporarily brought down Europe's largest stock exchange (on total turnover) hammers home the point that no organization, not even the most eminent, is immune to disastrous systems failures. Further, it shows that even the most detailed business continuity plans can come unstuck when the unexpected occurs. Though the exchange had a data backup system and a sophisticated disaster-recovery plan, the backup data was unusable.

Some general lessons can be drawn from this story about the requirements of a business continuity plan. Managers need to consider the following questions: How well does the plan fit the company's operations? How often and thoroughly is it tested in disaster-simulated conditions? Are staff properly briefed as to the steps that best mitigate the effects of a disaster when it occurs?

Business risk encompasses a range of issues, from systems and equipment failures, natural disasters such as fire or flood, to sabotage, terrorism, and theft. However, figures from a 1997 report jointly authored by Contingency Planning Research and Dataquest show that more than 90 percent of corporate disasters result from IT failures. Further, the more sophisticated a company's operations become, the more it exposes itself to different types of risk. Now that many businesses have websites, use email and conduct e-commerce, they also find themselves vulnerable to computer viruses and hackers. With increased networking, enterprise-wide systems, and integrated supply chains, a disaster occurring in a single location can strike many different businesses. During outages (periods of systems failure), companies can suffer enormous losses. The amounts differ according to the size, value, and nature of the business involved, but the same 1997 report places the average company cost for lost time at £52,000 per hour.

Regulation and planning

All companies – not simply e-businesses – should protect themselves from disaster or discontinuity. This may not be a matter of choice. A disaster that occurs within a single company or financial institution can cause a domino effect throughout an entire industry. Thus government and industry regulators often put in place rules for managing the risk of such disasters.

In the US, the Federal Reserve Board insists that financial companies must have a valid business continuity plan in place. In the UK, the Financial Services Authority not only insists that financial companies should have a plan in place but it also carries out inspections of these plans. The Turnbull report on corporate governance makes it a requirement for all listed companies to identify the risk

Disaster definitions

The terms "disaster recovery" and "business continuity" are often substituted for each other. They are not strictly interchangeable:

- Business continuity services are a combination of disaster-recovery services, backup services, and contingency planning or consulting.
- Disaster recovery is the range of service elements that keep a business running in the event of a critical incident that temporarily puts its operations out of action.
- A backup service is the transfer of company data from a live to a protected medium in case of a corruption of the original medium. This process can be internal (the backup is transferred and stored in-house), external (the backup is in-house and the medium is stored at an off-site location), or remote (the backup is conducted electronically to another location).

Source: IDC

factors they face and then show evidence of steps taken to mitigate these risks or evidence of a business continuity plan.

Different businesses need different levels of protection and companies in different sectors need to prioritize different business functions. Assessing the degree of protection that a business needs involves a process called business impact analysis (BIA). Broadly speaking, this involves mapping out the way a business works, and how its constituent processes and functions interact with each other. It then examines what would happen if one of those processes or functions were knocked out and asks how the rest of the business would fare. BIAs help managers assess which parts of their business need the most protection and the level of overall protection that is required.

Going through the process of business impact analysis can reap a number of benefits. It helps those at the helm take a view of the way their company is structured and gives them a clearer picture of which functions are critical to the company. It also fixes the idea of being risk aware within the decision-making process. A BIA might, for instance, ask whether it makes sense to rationalize IT systems and place them in a single building. Depending on the business case for such an outcome, the BIA can help to assess the degree of protection that combined IT systems would need should disaster strike within the building.

Interestingly, the effort companies made in combating the Y2K problem acted as a surrogate BIA. Many companies did not even know how many PCs they owned; by going through the audit and compliance process, executives now have greater knowledge of the way their businesses work and are better placed to introduce innovations and streamline operations.

Managers should ask themselves certain questions as part of a BIA, such as: "How much information can you afford to lose?" and "How much time can you afford to lose getting your systems up and running again?" Some businesses, such as financial institutions, may need fully mirrored services, so that in the event of a disaster they can switch seamlessly from one site to another. Others can get by with a daily or a weekly backup of information, which limits their potential information losses.

Once minimum recovery times have been assessed, a recovery strategy can be constructed that meets these deadlines. The greater the number of business functions that need to be recovered in a short time, the greater the level of sophistication that is required from a business continuity plan.

Business impact analysis

- To identify essential business functions within the company's operations, their priority and required continuity period (the period for which the business continuity plan needs to run in order for the business to return to normal).
- To quantify the impact that a disruption of these business functions will have on the organization.
- To identify and prioritize the basic business assets and applications that the business functions require for continued operation.
- To identify risks to the business and technology operations and recommend countermeasures that can be employed to reduce risk.
- To identify and document the impact and risks to the business as a whole.
- To recommend strategies that can be employed to meet business continuity requirements.
- To develop and agree a business continuity framework for business and support functions.
- To assist in the data population (the day-to-day information essential to business operations such as supplier, employee, and client lists) of continuity plans.
- To provide business continuity planning awareness and crisis management training.
- To organize and facilitate regular and thorough testing of the business continuity plan.

From plan to action

The most sophisticated plan in the world will be useless unless it is well documented, tested regularly, and updated. Above all, those implementing the plan within the company and outside must fully be appraised of its details.

More broadly, employees must know why testing takes place – it is not to evaluate their performance, but to evaluate a plan. Many companies experience a drop in morale from employees during testing, because they feel that disaster-recovery plans prioritize certain functions over others, or they do not want to appear inept in the process of testing.

How should employees handle problems with the recovery plan? If, during a simulated disaster, the plan tells employees, say, to attach server X to server Y via port Z, they should attempt to do exactly that. If, in fact, server X does not exist or cannot be physically connected, they should explicitly point out the flaw in the recovery plan – rather than pick up the phone, call the IT department and try to find an alternative method.

In general, companies and their staff are becoming more alert to risk and its management. There is far greater emphasis on disaster recovery and business continuity in the business world. In addition, small and medium-sized companies are far more aware of the same benefits. Their size leaves them short of technical resources, but they still feel the need to protect their operations.

There has also been a growing trend among organizations that have had business continuity plans in place for a number of years to extend coverage to more areas of their business. For instance, a company that may have originally had a business continuity plan to cover its core IT function is likely to extend coverage to its call centers, dealing rooms, or other critical business functions.

The most telling change perhaps lies in the fact that more businesses, including banking and technology, are prepared to discuss the existence of disaster-recovery plans for their operations. In the past, such an admission would have been tantamount to conceding vulnerability. Nowadays, disaster-recovery and business continuity strategies are becoming part of an organization's sales and marketing armory.

Business continuity services

There is a range of flexible business continuity services available on the marketplace, but they can be broadly categorized as follows:

- *Static restart facilities* – fully equipped sites for disaster recovery and the rehearsal of recovery plans.
- *Mobile restart facilities* – self-contained mobile units, which can be delivered to a nominated site.
- *Relocatable restart services* – hardware systems, which can be relocated to a nominated site.
- *LAN restart* – enabling PC LAN users to incorporate client/server functionality into the IT recovery plan.
- *Workplace, dealing room, and call center recovery* – in the event of serious disruption to an organization's workplace, the organization can relocate to an alternative location, fully configured with desks, chairs, PCs, phone and fax facilities, dealer boards, automatic call distribution (ACD) systems and market information services.
- *Computer data backup* – data is a vital business commodity. Services are available to allow businesses to automatically back up and archive their data, with immediate online access to their information should it be lost or corrupted at their site.
- *High availability systems* – including system resilience, facilities management, remote disk mirroring, and network management.

This is partly due to the fact that companies with just-in-time processes, such as large car manufacturers, are beginning to insist that their suppliers have contingency plans in place to ensure their own output is not halted by a hiccup further up the chain. Other companies even use the fact that they have come through a disaster smoothly to show clients and potential customers how effective their operations are. It may be misleading to say that companies are now in a position to master risk, yet the fact that they are willing to talk about it indicates that they are increasingly confident about their ability to manage it.

Summary

Disaster-recovery and business continuity planning is becoming an increasingly sophisticated activity, says **Roland Mann**. However, managers' failure to ask searching questions about the appropriateness of a particular plan or its integration with operations can cause potential problems during a crisis. For most companies, disaster recovery is about recovering data and protecting IT capabilities. There is a range of options to choose from in ensuring that a company can keep its IT operations running smoothly in times of trouble – but the final decision will depend on the priorities that managers set when figuring out the primary needs of the business.

10

RISK 21C

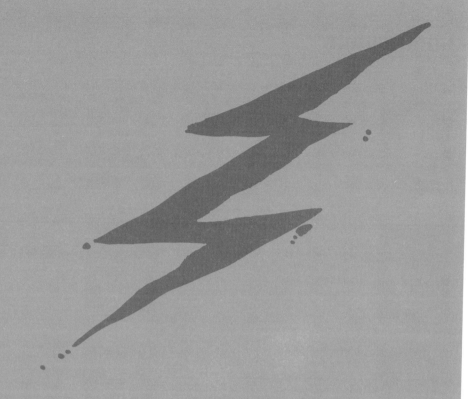

Contributors

Ben Hunt was editor of *Risk Financier* from September 1997 to March 2000. He was previously a director of research agency Brightwater Research & Editing.

Richard Reddaway is insurance manager, group risk at the international pharmaceutical group Glaxo Wellcome.

René Stulz holds the Everett D. Reese Chair of Banking and Monetary Economics at the Fisher College of Business, Ohio State University. He was editor of the *Journal of Finance* for 12 years.

Rory F. Knight is dean emeritus of Templeton College, University of Oxford. Dr Knight is a director of a number of internet companies.

Stephen G. Thieke recently retired as a managing director at J.P. Morgan. His role included being head of the bank's corporate risk management function and chairman of the risk management committee. Mr Thieke is a member of the board of the UK's Financial Services Authority and chairman of the RiskMetrics Group, a company that specializes in developing risk management methodologies and software.

Deborah J. Pretty is a research fellow at Templeton College, University of Oxford. Dr Pretty specializes in corporate risk management strategy, risk finance, governance, and value.

Contents

Issue of the moment: the rise and rise of risk management 289
Ben Hunt
Commercial risk is as old as trade. What are the forces compelling today's risk managers to devise an institutional framework to deal with the issue?

Why risk management is not rocket science 294
René Stulz, Fisher College of Business, Ohio State University
The Russian debt default of 1998 shocked global financiers and undermined a dazzling performance by hedge funds such as that run by Long-Term Capital Management. This article assesses the fallout for risk managers.

Reflections of a risk manager 301
Stephen G. Thieke, RiskMetrics Group
This personal overview describes a discipline the author believes has considerable potential to boost shareholder value. But regulators must avoid stifling innovation.

The devil in the details: attaining coverage for the global corporation 306
Richard Reddaway, Glaxo Wellcome
The daily pursuits of an insurance risk manager offer insights into how the job is linking with that of operational risk management.

Philosophies of risk, shareholder value and the CEO 311
Rory F. Knight, Templeton College, University of Oxford
Deborah J. Pretty, Templeton College, University of Oxford
The chief executive is paid to take risks. The authors suggest this burden could be mitigated by an articulate risk management philosophy.

Introduction

Mastering Risk concludes with a series of articles that offer several viewpoints of risk management: that of the global corporation, the investment bank, the financial risk manager, the insurance manager, and the chief executive. What are the underlying forces that led managers to call for more sophisticated ways of managing risk? What lessons can be learned from the 1998 hedge fund crisis of Long-Term Capital Management? How can financial institutions and corporations see the benefits of risk management without being stifled by the regulations it demands? How does the modern-day insurance manager respond to changes in his or her field? And finally, what role should the chief executive play in the formulation and execution of risk management policy?

Issue of the moment: the rise and rise of risk management

by Ben Hunt

Some time around the mid-1990s, board members of leading global corporations began to take personal responsibility for "risks that kept them awake at night." Once risks were identified, each member would be responsible for reporting back on what they were each doing personally to reduce one significant risk, under an agreed plan. For a large pharmaceuticals company based perhaps in the US or Europe, the biggest risk areas would include product design and recall, supply chain risk, fraud, environmental risk, and treasury exposure. For the first time, senior managers were beginning to formalize a commitment to managing risks that could threaten the continuity and existence of the corporations they were leading.

It is easy to forget, however, that the rapid elevation and widespread adoption of risk assessment and risk control practices in global corporations are a very recent phenomenon. Even 10 years ago, risk management tended to be equated with loss prevention through insurance buying, or hedging financial risk with derivatives. As such, its role was peripheral for companies in most industry sectors.

Today, it is not an exaggeration to say that risk assessment has become central to all forms of management decision making. Risk control is viewed as essential to maintaining stability and continuity in the running of corporations. Regardless of specific risks, events, and industry sectors, risk management is now seen as highly relevant to all corporate functions and processes. The clearest evidence is the "integration" of the management of risk in areas such as commercial strategy, operational management, financial management, and relationships with stakeholders. Today, it is almost as if managers feel they cannot manage without full knowledge of the business risks they face.

Although there are many possible reasons to explain the elevated profile of risk management, most accounts tend to identify globalization, the higher status of shareholder value, or a recent rise in corporate failures. However, such explanations tend to miss what has really changed in corporate life over the past 10 years, at the expense of understanding some wider, and crucial, developments in business management. This article will argue that risk management can be properly evaluated only by understanding changes that affect wider values and attitudes to risk, and the decision-making process.

The evolution of risk management

Before we examine more recent developments in risk management, it is worth giving a wider historical overview, rather than relying on static definitions (in general, a useful definition of risk management is "living with the possibility that a future event may cause harm").

One of the earliest references to the term "risk management" was in 1956 in the US, when it was used in a *Harvard Business Review* article. It was suggested that someone could be employed as a risk manager on a full-time basis to minimize business losses. This was essentially an extension of the position of insurance manager that dated back to a much earlier period.

More generally, various discussions of risk sprung up in the 1950s, but they tended to be highly mathematical in nature. Often, probability theory was applied to try to predict how businesses would fare in volatile markets. However, it was not until the early 1970s that risk management began to gain a wider purchase in business, particularly in the US. The more volatile economic climate created by the end of the Bretton Woods agreement and the oil crisis of 1973 spawned the practice of risk assessment. Risk rating and risk assessment consulting services began, mostly concentrating on "country risk" – how economic volatility in overseas countries could affect western corporations.

The term "risk management" began to gain more currency in the 1970s. The first educational qualifications in risk management were provided in 1973 in the US. The US Professional Insurance Buyers Association changed its name to the Risk and Insurance Management Society (RIMS) in 1975. Non-financial corporations began to buy financial derivatives (initially foreign currency futures) in the early 1970s. Indeed, the development of the corporate treasury in the 1970s was motivated in part by the greater need to hedge exposure to volatile financial markets.

However, it is interesting to note that non-financial corporations did not develop risk management departments, or institutionalize risk management practices, as a response to these developments. A study of non-financial corporations in 1973 found that fewer than 25 percent claimed to have established an in-house risk assessment capability, and only around 10 percent of respondents used outside risk consultants. Another survey in 1975 found that "few multinational corporations have developed systematic approaches for determining the political fortunes of their overseas markets." Banks, by contrast, were more advanced. Chase Manhattan set up a "country risk committee" in the US in 1975, for example.

In fact, in the 1970s, risk management was not really a term in common use. For advice on risk issues, executives would consult widely with a number of different constituencies, including public officials, diplomats, and academics. Nevertheless, even this was done on an *ad hoc* basis. For non-financial companies, the move to formalize risk management practices and manage risk in a centralized, systematic way had to wait until two decades later.

A similar point is that more intensive risk management practices tended to be confined to particular industries, such as large-scale industry and infrastructure, energy, nuclear power, and transport – or particular projects such as oil exploration or space travel. In these areas, the need for extra management supervision of risk stemmed from operational complexities and safety requirements particular to those institutions and projects.

After the 1970s

In the 1980s, attention turned to the issue of political risk. A main catalyst was the overthrow of the Shah in Iran in 1979 and the loss of an estimated $1bn in corporate assets through the Iranian revolution. According to some reports, around 75 percent of multinationals lost all but a small percentage of their Iran-based assets. Anti-western sentiment was also commonplace in many other areas of the developing world. At that point, some began to argue that multinationals should establish in-house political risk divisions. Sections of the insurance industry started to become more proactive in offering risk assessment services in addition to policy cover.

By the end of the 1980s and the fall of the Berlin Wall, it was looking as if many longstanding political conflicts around the world were winding down. Commentators at the time noted that many corporations were closing their political risk departments. As a practice and a discipline that could have wider business application, risk management was far from being institutionalized in very large corporations.

Even the establishment of risk management departments toward the end of the 1980s and early in the 1990s did not herald a more strategic approach to risk and its management. The author's research suggests that the formation of risk management departments within corporations had more to do with applying internal cost-cutting principles to insurance departments. More proactive loss prevention would have had the effect of lowering insurance premiums (because companies were showing greater responsibility for managing risk) and would have removed the need for buying insurance in the first place.

In this sense, non-financial risk management remained framed within the discipline of insurance purchasing. The spectrum of risks that corporations wanted to manage still tended to be "insurable" – physical hazards, liability risks and so on. "Risk" at that point was still interpreted fairly technically, the probability of hazards having an impact on a company.

For example, in the US, a global electronics company changed the insurance department's name to risk management in 1988. The new objective was to minimize resources given to the area of insurance management, to cut back on staff, and to outsource insurance affairs to third parties. A French IT and telecoms company set up a risk management department in 1990, merging its environmental protection and loss-control functions. The main rationale was to cut costs and further self-insure (that is, cut back on insurance purchase and establish an internal provision for loss). One of the largest European pharmaceuticals companies established a formal risk management department in 1991. The main rationale was to improve the efficiency of the company's insurance buying, improve relationships with brokers, understand risk on a global basis, and bring down the cost of insurance purchase.

What began to happen in the early to mid-1990s was qualitatively different, however. In essence, the rationale for assessing risk was shifting. The starting point was no longer minimizing damage from an external hazard affecting a company. Rather, managers (especially those in leadership positions) began to require greater assurances about the unexpected consequences of decisions. Managers began to feel that they needed more information about risk in order to make crucial decisions.

A shift in philosophy

Institutional changes reflected this development. In the mid-1990s, a leading European car manufacturer established a "risk task force" to quantify those risks large enough to trouble the company. They began to examine financial market risk, the prospect of misvaluing investments and acquisitions, and business interruption in the supply chain. A global US diversified consumer products company set up a "risk working group" in 1996 to combine risk management disciplines in the area of insurance, currency risk, credit risk, the risk of fluctuations in the company pension fund, and the impact of earnings volatility on the balance sheet.

Risk management departments themselves began to change to address the new needs of senior management. Managing insurance policies and insurance market relationships was becoming less and less important. It became common to find risk management departments in the US and Europe developing into internal risk consulting practices. In 1998, the department of a prominent European telecommunications company, for example, changed its name from "Group Risk and Insurance" to "Risk and Insurance Solutions," and issued a revised mission statement to raise its profile.

The department began to promote itself as a center of excellence to spread risk evaluation procedures throughout the company and create a more risk-aware culture. Individual project managers were encouraged to call on the center for risk mitigation procedures. At the same time, the department attempted to co-ordinate itself better with the human resources, health and safety, security, internal audit, environmental, and legal departments. Rather than dealing with passive risk (such as hazards affecting a company), risk management began to be oriented toward "business risk management" – to evaluate the risks from greater competition in the marketplace and to aid the expansion and growth of the company.

Other risk managers were finding they were spending more time assessing the risks of critical business decisions. The risk manager of a US technology company, for example, spent most of his time in the late 1990s assessing the risks of new investments and divestitures, as his company entered into strategic repositioning in the marketplace. This was a common experience in many other industry sectors.

My research of risk management practices in 14 large global corporations reveals that by the end of the 1990s the range of risks that companies feel they need to manage has vastly expanded, and continues to do so. Indeed, "risk" has become shorthand for any corporate activity. One of the newest growth areas for risk management is e-business, for example, and nearly all operational tasks and processes are now viewed through the prism of risk.

Concern with the gravity of risk has changed. Corporations are far more concerned with risks that could lead to corporate collapse, in addition to more traditional "high frequency, low severity" risks. Surveys also confirm this trend. The UK Biennial Risk Financing & Insurance Surveys, carried out by Chicago-based Aon Risk Services, show that in 1999, 70 percent of companies surveyed consciously plan to prevent critical disaster, a figure that has increased progressively from 1991, when only 26 percent of companies conducted such a plan. More generally, we see that crisis management has gained in profile over this same period.

The types of risk that most concern corporations have changed. Today, we see increased interest in managing intangible, commercial, and operational risks, while managing traditional, insurable perils seems less important.

Risk management has been institutionalized. Among the main changes are:

- the creation of internal risk controls;
- the establishment of sophisticated risk management frameworks, which include information flows and lines of reporting from board level to business unit;
- the merging of internal auditing with risk management practices;
- the attempt to raise awareness of risk throughout company culture;
- the attempt to reorient the risk management department into an internal consulting practice;
- the increasing representation of risk management directly on the board – some companies have established the position of chief risk officer;

- the attempt to integrate risk assessment and risk control procedures into corporate finance, commercial strategies and operations.

The rise in risk management

Explaining why these changes have taken place is obviously complicated. One task is to separate underlying drivers from expressions of those drivers. For example, there is no doubt that corporate governance requirements have acted to raise the profile of risk management. They have also served to expand the scope for risk management practice. In the UK, for instance, the Turnbull guidance stipulates that boards should manage business risks in their entirety, and should review on a regular basis the effectiveness of risk evaluation and control processes. The Cadbury report of the early 1990s defined risk management more narrowly as financial controls.

At a deeper level, however, any account of the rising profile of risk management must take into consideration both changing definitions of risk and changing definitions of management, over the past 10 years. In these respective areas, the following are arguable:

- Looked at dispassionately, managerial risk taking is more easily equated with recklessness. This is reflected in both changing relationships between business and society more broadly (the requirement for corporations to behave responsibly), and internally to business itself (reflected in the corporate governance codes of conduct for the boardroom and the rise of business ethics). Risk management introduces greater responsibility into the risk-taking process.
- Managers today feel they have a narrower margin for error in their decision making. The idea that managers are constantly "walking a fine line between success and failure" is commonplace. There is both more pressure to avoid things going wrong and more pressure to get things right, to improve corporate performance and shareholder value. It is arguable that "uncertainty" has become incorporated into the worldview of senior managers everywhere.

If these points seem abstract, take the issue of reputation risk management. "Loss of reputation" has become a fear that haunts company boards. Safeguarding brands – holding on to market share and customer loyalty, and ensuring socially responsible behavior – is now of considerable interest.

Why has risk management gravitated into this area – and why now? Clearly, social attitudes to risk play a part. Consumers are increasingly likely to view business as reckless in its behavior, in some shape or form. Nearly all industries have been redefined as destructive in some way, in harming either the environment or people's health. At the same time, in its social interactions business is keen to tread more carefully. Thus, at the level of decision making, managers are more eager to incorporate risk assessment into a range of additional areas, from the extraction of raw materials, to operations, to the final labeling of the product on the shopfloor.

From this perspective, the drivers of risk management institutionalization are not so much globalization, regulation, shareholder value, new technologies, or even the pace of change (though these are undoubtedly important), but changing responsibilities, values, and expectations among managers. Because of shifting attitudes to risk – and added pressures in decision making – managers feel they need fresh assurances about the upside or downside of their decisions. Risk management then acts as a progressive system of assurances and control, and can lead to favorable business outcomes. Institutionalizing risk management is essentially a response to the latest trends.

Summary
Only in the last 10 years has risk management become a top boardroom issue for non-financial corporations. Its initial importance among corporate concerns began to increase mainly in response to new economic and political developments. In this article, **Ben Hunt** argues that it is essential to be clear about the forces that underlie this institutionalization of the concept. Systematic approaches to risk assessment and risk control became prominent in the 1990s because of changing attitudes to risk, contemporary pressures in managerial decision making, and the demands of corporate governance. The increased significance of risk management among non-financial corporations can best be understood as a function of changing managerial values and responsibilities.

Why risk management is not rocket science

by René Stulz

The collapse of the hedge fund managed by Long-Term Capital Management (LTCM) in 1998 was a stunning event. Roughly half the LTCM partners had finance doctorates, most of them from the Massachusetts Institute of Technology (MIT). Two of its partners, Robert Merton and Myron Scholes, had won the Nobel prize for research of which the cornerstone was a technique to hedge the risk of derivatives. LTCM also included a group of traders with considerable experience in the markets and the leader of this dream team was a trader with an awesome reputation. Yet in a matter of months the fund lost more than $4bn and LTCM was accused of seriously endangering the world financial system. Many have argued that this collapse demonstrates that modern financial risk management techniques do not work. Before turning to this issue, it is useful to review the history of LTCM up to and including the collapse.

Where did LTCM come from?

In the 1980s and early 1990s, Salomon Brothers made billions of dollars through its proprietary trading. Most of those profits came from its bond arbitrage group, led by John Meriwether. This group was created to take advantage of misvaluations of securities with correlated risks by taking a short position in the overpriced security and a long position in the underpriced one, hedging those risks that could be hedged (*see* box).

The long and the short

A long position in a security is a position that benefits from price increases in that security (an investor who buys a stock has a long position, but an equivalent long position can also be established with derivatives).

A short position benefits from price decreases in the security. A short position is often established through a short-sale. To sell a security short, one borrows the security and sells it. When one unwinds the short-sale, one has to buy the security back in the markets to return it to the lender. One then benefits from the short-sale if the security's price is lower when one buys it back than it was when one sold it.

To understand this approach, suppose the group decided that the yield on a particular US agency bond was too high compared with US Treasury bonds. Certain agency bonds benefit from various guarantees from the US government. Yet such bonds trade at a higher yield than comparable government bonds. The group would purchase the agency bond and sell short government bonds, with the view that eventually the yields would converge – hence the term "convergence trade" to denote such a position.

Because of government guarantees, the main risk of the bonds is interest-rate risk, but the position would have little interest rate risk because of the offsetting bond positions. The position would generate cash because of the difference between the coupon received and the coupon to be paid on the short position. Further, any narrowing of the spread between the yields of the agency bonds and the Treasury bonds would create a capital gain.

Eventually, Salomon Brothers was embroiled in a scandal when an employee was charged with manipulating auctions for Treasury bonds. Several senior managers at Salomon left the institution in 1991, including Meriwether. Two years later, Meriwether founded Long-Term Capital Management (LTCM) to manage a hedge fund, the Long-Term Capital Portfolio. Hedge funds are unregulated, managed pools of money. LTCM was organized to pursue the strategies that the arbitrage group at Salomon Brothers had implemented, and very quickly several members of this group joined LTCM, along with future Nobel Laureates Robert Merton and Myron Scholes.

A short history of LTCM

The fund began trading in February 1994 and had stellar returns in its first two years – its investors earned 43 percent in 1995 and 41 percent in 1996. In 1997, the fund did substantially less well, earning 17 percent. By December 1997, its equity had grown to more than \$7bn. LTCM decided that it did not need so much equity in the fund and returned \$2.7bn to its investors.

At the beginning of 1998, the fund had capital of about \$4.7bn. Each dollar of capital was used to borrow funds, which brought the total assets of the fund to roughly \$125bn. The fund had derivatives positions in excess of \$1,250bn of notional value. These positions were artificially high because LTCM's strategy was to get out of certain derivatives positions by taking new, offsetting positions rather than by terminating the existing contracts before maturity. In the summer of 1998, the fund had positions in a wide variety of markets: Danish mortgages, US Treasury bonds, Russian bonds, US stocks, mortgage bonds, Latin American bonds, UK bonds, and US swaps. Under normal circumstances, these positions were mostly uncorrelated –

the fund took advantage of diversification to reduce its risk in addition to hedging positions.

LTCM wanted the volatility of the fund to be roughly 20 percent on an annualized basis. Before April 1998, its volatility was consistently below its target, averaging 11.5 percent; the fund's volatility was very stable. After the fund's capital was reduced, its volatility was still substantially lower than 20 percent. With capital of $4.7bn, a monthly Value at Risk (VaR) of 5 percent corresponding to a volatility of 20 percent is $448m. In other words, the fund was expected to lose in excess of $448m in one month out of twenty at its target volatility.

On August 17, Russia defaulted on its domestic debt. This started a period of dramatic markets movements that led to large losses for the fund. On August 21, 1998, it lost $551m, mostly in positions that had nothing to do with Russia, but many were adversely affected by it indirectly, as discussed below. The loss on August 21 was more than 10 times the target daily volatility of the fund – computer spreadsheets return a probability of zero for such an event if returns follow the normal distribution.

By early September, the fund's investors had seen their investments reduced to half their January levels, and the fund was running out of capital. Meeting under the auspices of the Federal Reserve Bank of New York on September 23, the heads of 14 leading banks and investment houses decided to invest $3.65bn in the fund and obtained a 90 percent stake in LTCM. This was not a public money bailout, since no public money was used. Rather, it was the equivalent of pre-packaged bankruptcy: the fund was restructured to avoid default.

In December 1999, the fund was dissolved. The above-mentioned banks and investment banks made a profit of 10 percent on their investment. The fund had about 100 investors who were not part of the management company. Out of these 100 investors, 88 made a profit on their investment. The typical investor's average annual return was 18 percent.

The limits of financial engineering

The entire strategy of LTCM had been based on its ability to manage risk. It had shown until 1998 that it was masterful at doing so. Until then, it had never made a loss two months in a row and its worst monthly loss was 3.85 percent. Its ability to manage risk enabled the fund to economize on equity capital, so that investors could earn more. It looked like a money machine. Yet, despite the considerable successes of modern finance, the partners knew that risks cannot be measured exactly and controlled perfectly, and were well aware of the limitations of the models they were using.

LTCM was full of individuals who had made contributions to the pricing of derivatives – some of them path breaking. Models developed in financial economics are tremendously useful but, like models in any science, they also have limitations. For instance, any trader mechanically applying the Black–Scholes formula for the pricing of options would quickly lose his shirt. Practitioners and academics have developed many adjustments to the Black–Scholes formula. However, adjustments that work well for a period of time may suddenly fail. For example, the mistakes one would have made using the Black–Scholes formula changed after the crash of 1987.

Most of the time and for most applications, the limitations of these models are not consequential. Nevertheless, problems that have little impact on an institution with limited leverage can become dramatically magnified in a highly levered institution.

Imperfections in pricing models could, for example, lead a trader to conclude that there are profit opportunities in the markets when there are none.

Consider the yield spread between debt-rated Baa bonds (bonds with some speculative characteristics) and Treasury bonds. Since 1926, Baa spreads have ranged from roughly 50 basis points to almost 800 basis points. Finance academics have found it difficult to explain spreads of several hundred basis points for Baa debt using characteristics of issuing companies. One way of looking at such large spreads is to say that they represent mispricing that can be exploited to create almost risk-free profits. Another way is to say that the models are missing something important – in other words, part or all of these spreads is more akin to an insurance premium that compensates holders of bonds for the risk they take.

Investors who believe in the mispricing theory may make large profits from exploiting large spreads for a while, even if the mispricing theory is false. Eventually, though, if investors are being compensated for taking risks, their bets will make losses. This is no different from a business that makes its profits by selling earthquake insurance as long as there are no earthquakes. If the bets are highly levered, losses can be crippling. What looked like a free lunch can become a very expensive banquet.

Too much faith in black boxes?

Although LTCM's problems have received most of the attention, the loss in equity value of large banks over the last two weeks of August 1998 make its losses look less dramatic. On August 21, when LTCM lost half a billion dollars, Citicorp's equity fell by more than $2bn. From August 26 to September 4, the market value of the equity of Bankers Trust, Chase Manhattan, Citicorp, and J.P. Morgan fell by a combined $43bn or 29 percent. Clearly, LTCM's risk management systems were not the only ones that had problems on these days. It is, however, important to be clear about where the systems went wrong.

Systems did not fail to predict that large losses were possible. A daily VaR that measures the maximum loss at the confidence level of 99 percent will be exceeded one day out of 100 on average if it is estimated accurately. Risk managers knew that there was some possibility of devaluation in Russia or of capital outflows in Brazil.

However, the systems did not anticipate and were not prepared for the vicious circle of losses that developed as positions could not be unwound without creating further losses, which themselves forced further unwinding of positions. This vicious circle had two critical consequences. First, it made one-day VaR measures irrelevant, because these measures are based on the presumption that positions can be undone rapidly at low cost. Second, as losses forced the unwinding of positions, the crisis spread to unrelated positions, thereby making the returns of unrelated positions highly correlated.

Any risk management system relies on forecasts of the distribution of returns of the portfolio or institution whose risk is managed. In normal times, forecasting the distribution of returns is much easier – the world just keeps repeating itself with no dramatic surprises. Crisis periods are different – the past becomes much less useful in forecasting the future, volatility often grows dramatically, and correlations become much closer to one.

All this happened in August 1998. LTCM's previously uncorrelated positions suddenly became highly correlated. By the time models based on the past adjust to these changes, it is no longer possible to reduce risk cheaply. The fundamental assumption of many risk management models is that bad draws occur randomly – the fact that there was a large loss today means nothing about the probability of a large loss tomorrow. Unfortunately, in August 1998, events that risk models said had an infinitesimal probability of happening were happening several times a week.

Wrong assumptions?

Between the time LTCM was created and 1998, the financial world changed dramatically, partly due to LTCM, partly due to regulatory actions. These changes explain much of what happened to LTCM.

LTCM was a spectacular financial innovation. The way it was structured was a marvel of financial engineering. Unfortunately for the partners, the world is a competitive place. It is hard to keep good ideas hidden. The enormous profits LTCM made early focussed the attention of the financial sector on it. This adversely affected LTCM for three reasons. First, it created a large number of imitators. Second, it put pressure on it to keep having high profits in an environment where this was no longer possible, leading it to create positions in which outsiders would not think it had a competitive advantage. Third, it made markets less liquid for LTCM.

Consider the impact of imitators on LTCM's strategies. Suppose that it finds that yields are too high on a security. It goes and buys the security, while hedging the risk. When imitators do the same, the price of the security rises, eliminating the profit opportunity LTCM had first identified. This effect both reduced the size of the trades that LTCM could make and decreased the profits on those trades.

In 1997, the fund's investors earned 17 percent, less than half what they had earned the year before. Traditional positions exploiting yield spreads were becoming less profitable. To increase returns, LTCM reduced the fund's capital and went into areas that seem questionable: it took positions in Russian bonds; made volatility bets; and took positions in takeover stocks. The partners may have had sound reasons for these positions. However, they seem a long way from fixed-income strategies exploiting apparently excessive spreads. For these new positions, one could find lots of other investors whose skills and training were at least equal to those of the LTCM partners. (For example, LTCM partners had many academic publications, but not a single one dealt with the takeover market.)

LTCM thus took new positions whose outcomes were more dependent on chance than its earlier positions. Nevertheless, it is important to note that the more traditional, fixed-income positions of LTCM explain the bulk of the August and September losses of 1998.

As far as it is possible to tell, however, the risk management systems of LTCM's counterparties failed to notice these changes until well into 1998. LTCM's cost of funds should have increased in early 1998, but there is no evidence that it did. This shows that financial institutions, thinking that the past successes of LTCM would keep repeating themselves, had too few safeguards in place when the markets changed against it.

Imitators had another impact on LTCM. They changed the nature of the markets in which it was trading. Rather than acting in splendid isolation, LTCM became the lead steer of a herd. As it moved, all imitators moved. Thus the fund faced poor market conditions when it had to move out of positions because it did not do so alone. LTCM partly recognized this in its risk measurement by using correlations that were greater than historical correlations. This also meant that the value of the fund's positions was at the mercy of its imitators pulling out of their positions. In the summer of 1998, Salomon did just that – it closed its bond arbitrage department, leading to losses for LTCM.

Modern finance traditionally assumes that there is enough competition in markets for investors or companies to take prices as given and simply react to them. The foundational work of Merton and Scholes is grounded in this assumption, as is virtually all subsequent research in derivatives pricing. Yet in 1998, the prices at which LTCM could trade depended on what the market thought LTCM would or could do. Traditional risk measures, which assume that one can trade out of positions without affecting prices, thus become much less useful. LTCM's short-term risk measures took some of these effects into account, but the extent to which prices depended on its positions and actions took the fund's managers by surprise. The problem became critical after the impact of the market events of August 1998 on the fund became known.

Regulation and the crisis

LTCM's problems were compounded by regulations that required banks to use risk management models to set capital. This virtually guaranteed that a volatility spike would lead financial institutions to shrink their trading portfolios. The regulatory effect was worsened by the fact that many proprietary strategies were complex, leading top management to pull back in the face of greater macro-economic uncertainty. As a result, financial institutions had turned from stabilizing to destabilizing forces.

Financial intermediaries make money out of providing liquidity. As investors want to get out of positions, financial intermediaries receive a liquidity premium to take on those positions. One would therefore have expected that in August 1998, financial intermediaries would make profits by scooping up positions that investors had to abandon. However, because their capital requirements increased with volatility, financial institutions had to dump positions themselves. Instead of being providers of liquidity, financial intermediaries became consumers of liquidity, forced to do so because of the regulatory environment. As a result, losses in Russia forced them to sell securities in other markets, propagating financial contagion.

Providing liquidity in August 1998 had to be hugely profitable, but market participants who should have been the liquidity providers stayed on the sidelines. Failure to be able to take advantage of such profit opportunities is itself a failure of risk management.

Marking to market

At its founding, LTCM had an extremely conservative approach. To minimize the risk that its financing would be pulled, it funded itself with term contracts. Without term financing, the crisis would have been more dramatic and more compressed in time. To minimize counterparty risk, it chose derivatives contracts that were marked to market daily. In other words, no counterparty would be indebted to LTCM for large amounts, because daily gains and losses on derivatives would be settled as they occurred.

In August 1998, as spreads widened, LTCM was making marked-to-market losses – the securities in which it was long were losing value, while those in which it was short were gaining value. If LTCM was right about convergence, this was a temporary problem that did not in any way reduce the profitability of its strategies –

the securities it had bought were mispriced and it was capturing a mispricing that would disappear at maturity of these securities or earlier.

Yet, LTCM's method of marking to market, combined with a decrease in the market value of its positions, caused it to run out of cash (though it never missed a margin call). Although LTCM correctly wanted its investors to commit money for the long term to enable it to take advantage of convergence strategies, it put itself in a position where it could fail before convergence was reached. It may well be that LTCM was right to choose marked-to-market contracts, but, once more, a strategy based on hedging failed because the hedger could no longer cope with its cash requirements.

How to do better

In many ways, the events of August and September 1998 showed that risks can be managed. Despite dramatic changes in markets, no investment bank or bank in a developed country collapsed. Derivatives played a significant role in helping many of these institutions hedge their risks. None of the reasons that justified the award of Nobel prizes to Merton and Scholes was affected by these events.

Yet, at the same time, they showed brutally that risk management is part of the social sciences. What makes social sciences different is that their object of study changes continuously, in this case partly as a result of financial innovation. Understanding these changes and how they influence risk is critical in times of great uncertainty. Risk management is not rocket science – it cannot be, since the past does not repeat itself on a sufficiently reliable basis. Future risks cannot be understood without examining the economic forces that shape them, a skill that is not taught in physics departments or engineering schools. However, understanding risks makes sense only if that understanding is used to create value. This means that risk management cannot be done independently of an understanding of the profits that come from taking risks. Regulation that forces financial institutions to disregard profit opportunities in the name of risk control only ends up making the financial system less stable.

Summary

In 1996 and 1997, the hedge fund run by Long-Term Capital Management (LTCM) had an unbroken run of success and established an unrivaled reputation in managing financial risk, says **René Stulz**. In August 1998, however, Russia defaulted on its debt, setting off a chain of unheard-of market movements that proved disastrous for LTCM. Some say the moral of the story is that risk management is flawed, since the fund's partners were experts in the discipline on Wall Street and in academia. Here, the author offers a much less simplistic interpretation of events.

Suggested further reading

Jorion, P. "Risk management lessons from Long-Term Capital Management," available online at www.SSRN.com

Lee, D., Kho B.-C. and Stulz, R. (2000) "US banks, crises, and bailouts: from Mexico to LTCM," *American Economic Review*, May, version available online at www.SSRN.com.

MacKenzie, D. (2000) "Fear in the markets," *London Review of Books*, April 13.

Pérold, A. (1999) "Long-term capital management," L.P. (A-D), Harvard Business School.

Scholes, M. (2000) "Crisis and risk management," *American Economic Review*, May.

Reflections of a risk manager

by Stephen G. Thieke

In the immediate aftermath of the market disruption provoked by the Russian default in August 1998, I was asked by the Federal Reserve Board to address two sets of issues in a private seminar: the origins and evolution of the market turmoil and the adequacy of risk management systems.

For me, this was yet another indication that the discipline of risk management might well challenge economics for the designation "the dismal science." At first glance, there may be something in this. Risk management professionals seem to spend a disproportionate amount of time reflecting on the dimensions of very low-probability negative outcomes, and are most often called to account (as I was) when those extreme outcomes manifest themselves to the consternation of risk takers and the seeming delight of risk commentators.

There are, however, at least two reasons that I would resist labeling risk management as "the dismal science." For one, I regard the discipline as a blend of art and science, even more so than economics or the other social sciences. Second is that a preoccupation with the "defensive" aspects of risk management ignores the importance of the role of senior risk managers as promoters of the effective use of a company's risk capacity; indeed, in many cases as the allocaters of that capacity.

The ultimate test of the value of a risk management effort is whether it enhances shareholder value. From my experience, full and proactive use of the tools of risk management significantly enhances value – not only those tools that help identify and evaluate risks, but also those that better inform management decisions as to which risks to hedge or mitigate, which to transfer or sell, and which to retain and capitalize.

In a world in which these are increasingly a matter of management choice, not just a passive consequence of customer activity, this dynamic and proactive role is anything but "dismal." It entails robust offensive as well as defensive elements.

Sound risk management

In reflecting on the second question posed to me by the Federal Reserve Bank, it is worth noting that, at least in its current incarnation, the discipline of risk management is still in a stage of development that lies between adolescence and young adulthood. In other words, there is a great deal more to learn and we know less than we think we do.

That is good news for practitioners, since there are many frontiers to explore, and it means there is substance to the adage that this is a discipline in which continuous improvement is necessary. It is also a cautionary reminder to managers and regulators whose instincts are often to prescribe, codify, and standardize risk management techniques. Experimentation, flexibility, and diversity of methods are more in line with the current development stage of this discipline.

If I have personally learned one thing about risk management in my days in the financial markets, it is that there is much more to risk management than just risk measurement. A disproportionate amount of public debate – both within the industry and with the regulators – has been around the nuances, complexities, and apparent precision of various risk measurement tools.

The rules of risk management

- *There is no return without risk.* Rewards go to those who take risk. Intelligent risk taking is to be encouraged by managers, not stifled.
- *Be transparent.* Risks need to be fully understood. A risk that is not understood is a risk that should be avoided.
- *Seek experience.* Risk is measured and managed by people, not mathematical models. No new model is ever worth the sound judgment of an experienced risk manager.
- *Know what you do not know.* Every model is filled with assumptions. Know those assumptions, and actively question them.
- *Communicate.* Risk needs to be discussed openly. A culture where people speak about their risks will be more successful than one that discourages an open risk dialog.
- *Diversify.* Multiple risks will produce rewards that are more consistent. Organizations get into trouble when one risk dwarfs all the other exposures they are taking on.
- *Show discipline.* A consistent and rigorous approach will beat a constantly changing strategy. The temptation to change your goals as the markets change must be avoided.
- *Use common sense.* It is better to be approximately right than precisely wrong. Do not spend your resources on improving the minutiae; concentrate on those issues that make the biggest difference.
- *Get a RiskGrade.* Return is only half the equation. Make sure you have an accurate measure of the risks you are taking to assess accurately the true returns of your business.

Source: RiskMetrics Group (www.riskmetrics.com)

However, from the outset of the corporate risk effort at J.P. Morgan in 1992, we have stressed that an analytically rigorous approach to risk measurement is but one of the important attributes of a strong internal risk management effort. The other features we have emphasized include: the degree of transparency of risk; the timeliness and quality of information; the effectiveness of internal risk policies and controls; the degree of line management and independent oversight; the extent to which we achieve diversification and avoid risk concentrations; and, ultimately, the judgment and experience of our people to know what models and reports cannot tell you about market dynamics (*see* box).

If one were to look back to the risk problems in the market disruptions of 1998, what distinguished financial institutions that fared relatively well from those that experienced greater problems was not the sophistication of their risk measurement models; rather, it was meaningful differences in other aspects of their risk management and related business strategies.

Extreme events

This leads to my next observation: risk measurement has become binary. By this I mean that there is a divergence between the techniques used to measure and aggregate risks under "normal" circumstances and the methods used to evaluate risks driven by extreme events. Gone are the days when organizations relied on a single VaR (Value at Risk) measure of their market risk, as all have become acutely aware of the limitations of such measures (even though they are still the single best way to aggregate and compare risks). While it has become accepted practice to supplement VaR estimates with various forms of stress testing, there is, I sense, more awareness and agreement on how to do stress testing than there is on how to use it.

There are a number of commonsense explanations for this. The most compelling is that it is irrational to evaluate the tradeoff between risk and return when extreme, low-probability outcomes such as those stipulated in stress tests are assigned almost equal likelihood of occurring as mean events.

Stress-testing techniques are not best used to evaluate the merits of a risk position or its performance, either hypothetically or in hindsight. Nor are they best employed to construct regular measures of aggregate risk. Rather, stress testing helps practitioners judge their comfort with the size of risk positions – in effect, to better inform and supplement limit-setting and capital-attribution decisions. This is especially true for risk portfolios that have significant non-linear and/or potential illiquidity characteristics. (Such portfolios contain a large number of options, structured products, and/or non-traditional markets.)

This, of course, is not limited to market risk portfolios. In the aftermath of the Long-Term Capital Management crisis in the fall of 1998, the report of the Counterparty Risk Management Policy Group (June 1999) emphasized the importance of performing stress test market liquidity estimates of both the potential size of counterparty credit exposures and the realizable values of supporting collateral.

This underscores my next observation: there is a greatly heightened sensitivity to the value of liquidity and its fragility, but no simple way to factor that enhanced value into risk measurement methodologies.

In many ways, what risk managers are trying to estimate when they perform stress tests is the potential cost of illiquidity if they have to modify or dispose of their risks in disrupted markets. Implicit in this is a degree of understandable discomfort with using traditional, time-scaled VaR measures as indirect proxies for the risk of illiquidity. That discomfort lies in the assumption of normal market volatility, just extended over a longer liquidation period.

What experience has shown is that when confronting significant market shocks (or the sudden failure of a large counterparty), market price moves become quite abnormal, market liquidity dries up, and, in some cases, almost entirely disappears. These conditions are not at all like normal, time-scaled market VaRs, but crudely comparable to stress test assumptions.

We are, I believe, at the most elementary of stages of development for estimating the risks associated with liquidity. This is thus a very promising area for further research and development. In the meantime, since business and risk taking goes on, a series of "second-best" corrective reactions are in use. These include frowning on "oversized" positions (both internally and at trading clients); reshaping the definitions of "oversized;" raising internal transfer price differentials between the costs of funding liquid versus illiquid assets; raising the costs of internal balance sheet charges; and raising the costs of external client leverage by scaling their limits and collateral requirements to reflect the size and liquidity of positions, not just normal market volatility estimates of the relevant assets.

Knowing when to say "no"

Let me shift back for a moment to my earlier comments about the "defensive" aspects of the role of senior risk managers – the term I used at J.P. Morgan to describe this was guardian of the organization's risk capacity. Performing that facet of the role means at least occasionally saying no, even in a company in which the core business is brokering risks on behalf of clients. What matters most when you say no is that you have clear and understandable reasons to view a risk as inappropriate or excessive. (Since these are matters of judgment, rather than fact, there will usually be differences of opinion.)

As a rule of thumb, I would try to distinguish between three generic reasons for viewing a particular risk as bad, each of which would offer different potential remedies.

The first is a risk for which there is no or grossly inadequate compensation. Why would anyone in business want to take such a risk? Quite often, it is a combination of how the business is done and to facilitate possibly attractive future business. Examples include counterparty settlement risk in foreign exchange markets and many other forms of counterparty credit risk. In these cases, it is not a question of saying yes or no to a risk. It is more a case of insisting that the risk be acknowledged and priced properly internally and the costs of the risk reflected against appropriate profits and losses.

Once that is done, one has both better decision making for short-term business risk/return and real long-term incentives to pursue changes in how business is done so as to reduce or eliminate the need to take unpaid risks.

The second type of reason relates to one's judgment on a particular business unit's capacity to manage a risk. This involves several factors: the state of development of its internal risk control infrastructure; the degree to which the business enjoys a market leadership position; its familiarity and track record with managing similar risks; and its capacity to absorb mistakes, not in terms of its capital, but in its ability to hold to its business plan, keep people in place, and make new investments should it get the risk-taking decision wrong.

Many of these are familiar elements of new product review and control strategies. However, the cases are not limited to new products. In these cases, the issue is not one of pricing risk in new products. Nor is it one of yes or no. It is rather to what extent, how soon, and how quickly one can take corrective actions.

The third type of reason relates to judgments on the organization's appetite and capacity to absorb risks. These are extremely complex judgments to make. They entail evaluation not just of economic capital capacity, but also liquidity considerations, tolerance for earnings volatility, creditor and shareholder awareness of and tolerance for risk taking, management capacity to maintain business investment plans, and even, on occasion, regulatory acceptance. Not only are these complex variables but, in my experience, few if any of them are static. That is why I have always viewed the process of setting company-wide risk limits as an exercise in setting markers to trigger senior management discussion, rather than as hard-and-fast barriers beyond which you would never travel.

The next phase

The last of my observations is that internal economic capital management processes are becoming further divorced from short-term measures of risk, and increasingly linked to forward-looking views of longer-term market-to-market earnings volatility and downside vulnerability.

As I ended my time at J.P. Morgan and was asked by my chairman and my successor to pinpoint our most significant risk management issue and opportunity, I suggested that it was to develop an integrated longer-term view of risks that would be easily understood by our creditors and shareholders and could be linked more closely to capital structure and performance management.

As much as we and other leading financial institutions had invested in our risk methodologies and in developing our economic capital measures, I still regard these as only first-generation tools. In the case of VaR measures, these are better suited to controlling short-term trading-driven earnings volatility than as a metric for relating risk to performance for our shareholders and risk to capital for our creditors.

In the context of economic capital evaluation, once EVA measures have been constructed on the basis of longer-term earnings volatility rather than short-term VaR measures, the issues will begin to change. Discussion will turn to such areas as forward versus historic views, identifying useful external benchmarks, and how to find the right balance between business managers' desire to have highly variable capital allocations and practical market realities about capital structure management.

There are no simple answers here, but I am confident that, in time, the next generation of risk and capital measures that my colleagues develop will represent a significant advance over those established these past several years.

The author would like to thank Ethan Berman, director, RiskMetrics Group, for his assistance and useful advice.

Summary

The turmoil of the Russian default in 1998 left risk managers a worried breed. In this first-person view of the challenges facing the discipline, **Stephen Thieke** suggests that an emphasis on "defensive" risk management detracts from the corporation's capacity to profit from risk-taking. After all, the ultimate test of the risk management effort is whether it enhances shareholder value. With much to learn and many frontiers to explore, risk management today is just emerging from adolescence. We should thus be cautious of over-regulation, instead promoting experimentation and flexibility in risk management. The real opportunity for this youthful discipline is to develop a longer-term view that is easily grasped by creditors and shareholders and is more closely linked to capital structure and performance management.

The devil in the details: attaining coverage for the global corporation

by Richard Reddaway

Why have an operational risk management department? Why can't different managers across the company, applying a "commonsense" approach to risk management, achieve the same ends? One answer is that past experience has shown that a comprehensive, company-wide strategy toward risk cannot be achieved in this way.

Risk managers have developed new ways of working in response to the need for a visible methodology for risk assessment, reduction, and elimination. This includes the establishment of corporate risk committees and risk profiling or mapping, which highlights the potential threats and opportunities facing a business. There is also a new emphasis on the formal reporting not only of financial but also non-financial matters that might have a material impact on the organization.

The operational risk management department at Glaxo Wellcome includes professionals dealing with occupational health and hygiene, safety, environment, and loss prevention as well as insurance and loss provision specialists. In practical terms, there are two sides to the work of an operational risk manager: risk management and insurance and loss provision (ideally, the former should ease the need for the latter). Though the disciplines may not always be found within a single unit, they are increasingly linked within organizations.

In this article I analyze the role of the insurance risk manager within a large global corporation, using Glaxo Wellcome as an illustration of important changes where appropriate. Such an analysis highlights the areas of continuity and change in insurance risk management and its intricate relations with operational risk management.

Physical assets

The traditional role of the insurance manager begins with the protection of physical assets. There are several aspects to this activity.

Insurance valuations. Valuations of physical assets are used for insurance calculations, but they also assist in business continuity planning. Can an existing machine be replaced or will it be necessary to look for the nearest equivalent? How long would it take to order a replacement? Is the existing supplier still in business? Will fluctuations in the currency of the country of origin affect the valuation? In addition, changes in local authority or national regulations can oblige companies to raise standards for replacement and associated costs. These can be insured against using a local authority clause.

Remediation. How will the company handle a loss such as a chemical spill? What expertise is available locally or immediately, and what support may be required from elsewhere? What are the potential costs associated with a loss?

Loss prevention. In recent years at Glaxo Wellcome, we have extended our loss-prevention program from standard ongoing surveys related to fire hazard into the area of earthquake risk. Working with earthquake consultants who provide seismic, wind engineering, and standard design services, we have assessed the probability and potential loss exposure associated with earthquakes in such places as California, Egypt, Japan, and Indonesia. We have also proposed and adopted specific risk mitigation measures, from which the company has already benefitted. In 1999 alone, Glaxo Wellcome companies in Turkey, Greece, and Taiwan experienced earthquakes. No insurance claims resulted.

Earnings

The most dramatic changes to exposures over the last 10 or 20 years have been in the earnings derived from assets. Broadly speaking, companies are making their assets work harder – advances in manufacturing technology and supply chain management have greatly increased the efficiency of the production process. Risk managers are now far more attentive to gross profit analysis and the potential interruption periods that could occur if an item of equipment or a critical facility were damaged or destroyed.

Gross profit analysis. By examining the production process from the stage of raw materials to the point of sale, risk managers can identify the profit streams of the business. This is an important part of the role and a never-ending review. This is particularly true for pharmaceuticals companies, where the introduction of new products is integral to a research-based industry facing limited patent periods.

Working with Highly Protected Risk (HPR) specialist insurers, the operational risk department at Glaxo Wellcome estimates the company's financial dependency on vital buildings and suppliers and contract manufacturers. HPR analysis involves the assessment of potential maximum loss scenarios, the cost of introducing controls through fire protection to buildings, the installation of sprinklers to critical areas, and the likely loss expectancies once these measures are in place. Loss-control measures can be quantified against inherent hazards of the business using residual risk quality graphs (*see* Figure 1). The resulting score is used in negotiations with insurers over the total insurance amounts for the components of gross profit. Such graphs may also highlight potential areas of weakness in the supply chain to those involved in purchasing.

Figure 1: Residual risk quality – all sites

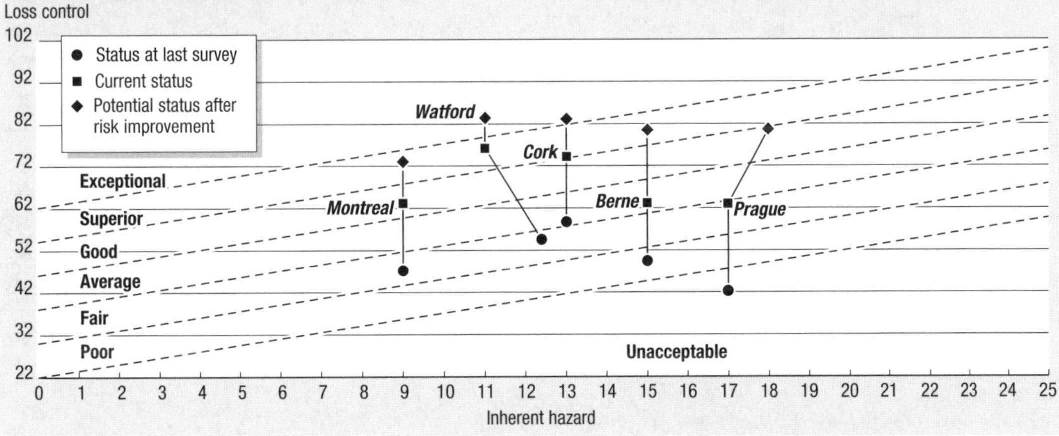

Interruption periods. Proper emergency planning and long-term business continuity planning will greatly reduce potential interruption periods to the business. There are several considerations here:

- Business continuity plans should be drawn up for each department within the company. Such plans will focus on areas of existing vulnerability, disaster-avoidance and prevention procedures, and a usable plan that enables an appropriate reaction in the event of a disaster.
- A "hot site" facility must be made available for instant backup in case a strategic office building is shut down unexpectedly. A risk assessment will determine whether this backup can be provided internally within the organization. If not, specialist companies can provide an instant communications center, computer systems, a backup generator, and other required facilities.
- Global companies should appoint global loss adjusters. In the event of a loss in one country or one that affects supply to several countries, a multinational can therefore work efficiently with a single organization to quantify the loss. Preliminary reports can help the backup effort prevent the consequences of interrupting product supply in the final market.

People

As often stated, an organization's most important asset is its employees. This has important implications for operational risk management.

Away from the workplace. Risks in the workplace can be assessed and controlled, yet this is less true for travel. In most large companies, operational risk managers will work with group security to shape and implement a corporate travel policy. At Glaxo Wellcome, we ensure that travelers are aware of the 24-hour emergency contact numbers. Corporate mobile phones have greatly helped in this, since they enable employees to alert the emergency services immediately an accident occurs.

Motor vehicles. Our experience has shown that the highest potential risk of accident to employees occurs during travel in motor vehicles. Safety videos can highlight the need to use seatbelts (often a contentious cultural issue even where their usage is compulsory by law) or the specific safety features one should look for in a car. Companies can also reduce accident rates through benchmarking, training, defensive driving, and penalty/reward systems.

Life pooling. When someone takes out a life insurance policy, their payments are taken by the insurance company, which will only pay out a claim in the event of death. For large corporations, however, insurance companies can offer policies that pay back corporations based on their pooled experience of accident or illness. Thirty-seven Glaxo Wellcome companies are linked through three life networks, Generali-Aetna, Insurope, and Swiss Life. In the past 10 years, this has returned £4m to the company.

Glaxo Wellcome also uses life pooling to capture data on the health of its employees. It highlights the fact that successful disability rehabilitation not only restores a potentially impaired life, but also brings direct financial benefit. A claims reserve can be reduced or eliminated, and the money pumped back into the company as a dividend.

Transit

Goods-in-transit is another area of responsibility for operational risk managers.

Theft. Global companies will sometimes operate in areas where hijacking and theft are serious problems. In Glaxo Wellcome's case, liaison between the group security manager, insurers, and specialist consultants based, for example, in eastern Europe and Latin America brings invaluable advice.

Accumulation risks. When shipping goods, accumulation risks occur when batches of goods or containers come together in one place, say, while awaiting transportation in a vessel, in the vessel itself, or at a customs warehouse. Risk managers should pay careful attention to the accumulation exposure as well as the loss-prevention standards at temporary transit warehouses.

Recoveries. When accidents occur in transit, international regulations can stipulate that compensation should be made according to the weight of the cargo, rather than the real commercial value of the goods. Risk managers should seek immediate legal and technical advice to demonstrate negligence of the carrier and press for a settlement based on actual commercial value as opposed to weight.

Financial risks

While financial risks are primarily the focus of treasury departments, there will be areas of involvement for operational risk management. These links might include the following.

Fidelity losses. Discussions as to where fraud can occur and encouraging "blanket cover" for all employees (rather than traditional insurance for named individuals or positions) moves attention from the usually minor risk of cash misappropriation and theft. A shift in focus can bring other areas of potential fraud risk to the fore, such as isolated projects in which the company does not have particular expertise. External pension/provident funds and the risk protected by directors' and officers' trustee liability cover need to be regularly audited.

External fraud. Computers and electronic funds transfer open up new possibilities for fraud. Again, third-party computer crime is a standard extension to fidelity insurance policies.

Liabilities

A final area of my involvement with operational risk management, which touches increasingly on insurance, is that of liabilities.

Employer's liability/workmen's compensation. In the UK, Glaxo Wellcome works closely with its insurer, Iron Trades, to keep it abreast of emerging and potential future litigation, such as the implications of the Woolf reforms on civil justice. These reforms aim to introduce new rules and protocols to achieve quicker legal settlements and disposal of issues. In insurance terms, this leads to a better organization of the claims process.

Scope of cover. Especially overseas, it is necessary to understand who can sue. For instance, can directors sue themselves as representatives of the company? Likewise, it is vital to know where responsibility lies, say, for the risk of going to and from work. Are claims linked to basic pay or do they include bonuses and allowance payments? The difference can be substantial.

Public/product liability. It is crucial for insurance managers to examine the contractual terms that limit or define the company's responsibilities in respect of public or product liability. Experts within the company on packaging, tamper-proof devices, quality assurance, and security may be useful sources of advice here.

Directors' and officers' liability. Close liaison with the company secretary will ensure that adequate protection is in place and that coverage issues are properly understood. For example, should cover be extended to protect the corporation? Could it reduce the limits available to individual directors and officers?

Insurance

The integration of insurance with operational risk management is clear from the above examples. It is necessary to know and understand the organization as well as the insurance market to ensure that the company's insurance protection is relevant and that risk is properly managed. To do this, in my opinion, there are certain significant requirements. They would include the following.

Travel. An insurance risk manager needs to investigate all aspects of the business. In my case, for instance, I visit 10 to 15 countries a year, spending one or two days in each meeting with colleagues and partners. These partners may include non-life and life assurance companies, loss adjusters, valuation companies, and consultants.

Loss-provision tools. At its most simple, loss provision can mean paying baggage claims from petty cash if baggage cannot be recovered from airlines, hotels, or insurance provided by Executive Club schemes. At a more sophisticated level, it means running a captive insurance company. The advantages of a captive are many; in particular, it ensures that losses within a subsidiary are not regarded as just a matter for an external insurance company. Instead, losses are an internal matter. This encourages proactive risk management.

Benchmarking. Risk managers can benchmark their practices by reading industry-specific and related journals or by attending commercial or professional conferences. In the US, membership of RIMS (the Risk and Insurance Management Society) provides an important network for risk professionals. In the UK, AIRMIC (the Association of Insurance and Risk Managers) provides a similar source of informed feedback and advice.

Conclusion

Better risk focus facilitates better risk reduction or elimination. This can identify or create competitive advantages that allow the business to progress with greater confidence in its future. The challenge of risk management is never routine or dull. It adds value to a corporation and ensures that a culture of risk awareness is firmly embedded in the organization.

Summary

Global companies face a spectrum of risks, from traditional threats to physical assets to the risks associated with computer-associated fraud. The insurance risk manager has to find ways of preventing or insuring against these risks, writes **Richard Reddaway**. In the past, corporate risk managers may have dealt purely with the calculation of insurance. Today, they are more likely to mix insurance analysis with operational risk control and liaison with senior managers, the finance department, business continuity specialists, the group security department, and the company's legal team.

Philosophies of risk, shareholder value and the CEO

by Rory F. Knight and Deborah J. Pretty

Risk has had a bad press in recent times. The human tragedies of Bhopal and Piper Alpha, the financial demise of Long-Term Capital Management hedge fund and Barings Bank, the latent dangers of asbestos, tobacco, and environmental liabilities, and the extensive product recalls of Perrier and Coca-Cola, illustrate the negative. Such cases propel risk aversion to the very top of the CEO's agenda. The bad news for CEOs is that despite a great expansion in the technologies and instrumentation of risk management, risk by its nature cannot be eliminated. The good news is that you, the CEO, are not expected to remove risk – you are paid to take it.

Removing risk is potentially costly, witness Metallgesellschaft and Ashanti, but, more importantly, getting rid of risk stifles the source of value creation and upside potential. In fact, it may be in shareholders' interests to encourage more risk taking by CEOs. Since they are paid to take risks, they should not timidly look for ways to continuously pass them on to others.

Ultimate responsibility for risk lies with the chief executive officer; it should therefore be part and parcel of his or her agenda at all times, not just when disaster strikes. This article proposes that the CEO needs first to develop a clear philosophy of risk, and then formulate clear corporate policies to guide the management of risk. Such a discussion necessarily begins with the core elements of corporate value.

The components of enterprise value

The core value of a quoted company could be thought of as having three components, tangible value, premium value, and latent value. Tangible value reflects the bedrock of the real and tangible assets, which will sustain the firm's value in times of crisis. It is usually measured as book value. In recent times, tangible value has been degraded as the market valuations of dotcom "clicks and mortar" companies – with little book value but promises of great wealth – have outshone their "bricks and mortar" counterparts.

Premium value represents the value in excess of book value at which the firm trades in the open market. This element of value is the source of a firm's competitive advantage. The value drivers here include, for example, the firm's reputation, its brands, intellectual property, innovation, potential growth, global reach, managerial expertise, and the skills and experience of the workforce. These intangible assets are a source of sustainable competitive advantage for a firm and enhance shareholder value.

Latent value represents the potential or "hidden" value within a firm. Sources of hidden value might include operating efficiencies yet to be realized, underpromoted brands, an unmotivated workforce, innovation without patents, or managers in the wrong jobs. It is by realizing this source of value that the CEO can flourish.

Risk management is all about ensuring that enterprise value is enhanced and protected in a cost-effective manner and that latent value is realized. The biggest risk a CEO faces is that value is not created. The CEO must provide the leadership to face risk. This requires a personal philosophy of risk that is reflected in a clearly stated corporate policy. An event that could seriously damage enterprise value or prevent the realization of latent value should be identified, assessed, profiled, quantified, and considered for avoidance, containment, or retention.

Enterprise risk and value

Firms face a whole variety of different risk exposures. Each company will have a different risk landscape according to its business, objectives, financial structure, competitive position, and operational spread.

Enterprise risk implies a view of risk in aggregate – that is, after the offsetting effects of individual risk factors. However, risk is generally not presented as an opportunity. In order to develop a sound philosophy of risk, the CEO must take a position on (1) what the purpose of enterprise risk management is, and (2) how much risk the firm is prepared to take in the pursuit of opportunity.

Figure 1 illustrates a convenient classification scheme of enterprise risk factors and the three elements of enterprise value. The value equation below illustrates the connection between risk and value.

$$\text{Enterprise value} = \underbrace{\frac{\text{Future cash flows}}{\text{Cost of capital}}}_{\text{[Tangible value]}} + \underbrace{\text{Growth opportunities}}_{\text{[Premium value]}} + \underbrace{\text{Latent value}}_{\text{[Latent value]}}$$

The various risk types are capable of affecting each element of the value equation. Risk policy needs to be grounded in an understanding of the way in which the key value drivers are affected by risk and the magnitude of the impact. This is intended to stand the Value at Risk (VAR) approach on its head. Ask not what value will be protected by removing risk, but what value will be created by retaining risk.

The CEO of the modern corporation is squeezed by the doctrinaire approach of risk avoiders and the apparently scientific approach of risk managers – hence the

Figure 1: Enterprise risk

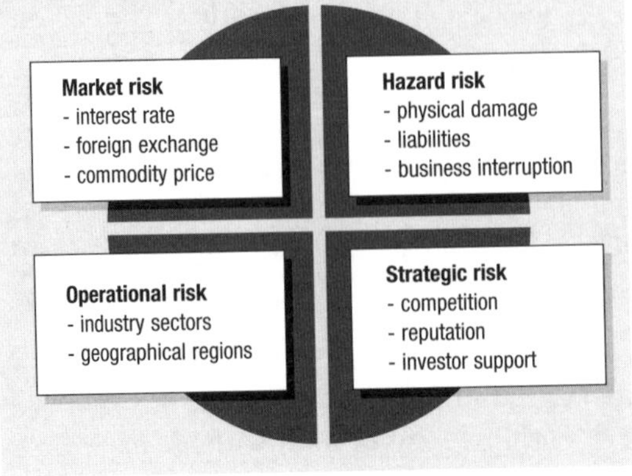

need for a philosophy of risk management. In short, the CEO needs to decide where to position the firm's risk policy: in a performance context or in an avoidance context.

Developing a risk policy

Regardless of which philosophy of risk is adopted, a risk policy is crucial. The risk policy should deal in general terms with the objectives of risk management and the locus of responsibility.

The CEO should consider insurability as the critical factor in assigning responsibility for risk management. All insurable risks can be transferred to the markets in the form of insurance or derivatives instruments. If a risk is not insurable, it is not "delegatable" and remains the CEO's responsibility – it forms part of strategic risk management.

Market risk management represents the management of currency, commodity, and interest-rate risks, which all are capable of being hedged in the short term. Hazard risk management deals with traditional and emerging event risks. Operational risk management deals with business structure approaches to containing risk. The hedging decision in each case will carry different risk and value implications for the firm.

Strategic risk

Significant parts of strategic risk cannot be diversified away. It is the responsibility of the CEO to manage this risk to the shareholders' best advantage by exposing the upside and enhancing value. Exposures here include, for example, the risk to the firm's reputation, the risks of managing investors' perceptions and expectations, the risks of strong competition and erosion of competitive advantage, the risk of losing touch with customers, and the risk of losing (either entirely or the potential of) the firm's skilled staff.

One of the myths surrounding the use of derivatives is that once you've identified the risk and insured it, you no longer have to worry about it. This is severely myopic. Most derivatives markets only deal with risks over a one-year period and thus risks associated with these markets beyond that horizon are uninsurable and, thus, strategic. Consequently, the CEO must continuously consider the strategic implications of events in those markets.

Market risk

The corporate hedging policy plays an essential role in the broader risk policy. If a goldmining company, for example, were to hedge all its gold price risk, in effect it would remove all the downside risk and all the upside potential in one stroke. Investment in the fully hedged firm becomes akin to that in a bond. However, if the firm were battling for survival, and we assume for now that it has a responsibility to survive, then hedging might become a sensible strategy.

Placer Dome and Homestake do hedge, whereas Newmont of the US and Goldfields of South Africa do not fully hedge. These firms cannot all be right or wrong in their hedging strategies. Rather, it is that the hedging decision is not binary: to hedge or not to hedge. There will be circumstances where a degree of hedging makes sense from a value perspective, and other situations where hedging would destroy value. Analogous arguments can be made for interest-rate hedging and currency hedging.

A reason often given for hedging is that it reduces uncertainty and the volatility of cash flows, but, from the shareholders' perspective, this volatility is acceptable (indeed, desired) and the price paid for hedging may produce a net result of value destruction. Alternatively, hedging might reduce the cost of capital, but where investors hold diversified portfolios and the firm encounters a stream of cash flows over many years, this argument equally is made redundant.

Hazard risk

Hazard risks present some key differences from market risks. Generally, hazard risks are not tradable, their insurance operates by the principle of indemnity, and these contracts may be exposed to "moral hazard," where the insured may affect directly the nature of the risk.

However, the hedging rationale remains consistent with that for market risks. The premium paid for an insurance contract may be considered equivalent to the price paid for a levered security, or option. For the same reasons, hedging, or insurance purchase, can make sense for catastrophic risk, but otherwise is questionable from a value perspective. Even in cases of catastrophe, evidence of insurance coverage may be necessary, but is not sufficient to protect the firm's share price from falling. (This subject is considered in our article in Module 9.)

Operational risk

Corporations may diversify operational risks by conducting business across many different industry segments and geographical regions. The authors' research (presented in Module 3) demonstrated that investors favor business focus over conglomeration, yet global spread over domesticity. These results are consistent with the idea that shareholders can diversify away industry risk more cheaply and easily than can managers, but still rely partially on managers to spread geographical risk, given the limited liquidity of some of the world's stock markets.

The emerging role of the chief risk officer (CRO)

A corporate view of risk must be defined before the firm's portfolio of exposures can be managed effectively. In reaching this definition, questions may be raised regarding the interplay of the exposures we have discussed. To what extent do they correlate with and compensate for each other? How does this classification help manage these inter-relationships?

The delineation of responsibility for individual risks across the organization is the role of a chief risk officer. The chief risk officer should co-ordinate risk-related decisions and prioritize and communicate them to the CEO as a way of assisting with the formulation of risk policy. Figure 2 illustrates the role of the CEO in risk management and the way in which responsibility for risk management can be delegated. In addition, it shows how insurable risks should be organized around the markets to which the risks can be transferred.

Risk policy guidelines

Having assigned responsibility, the risk policy needs to deal with a number of issues and provide the parameters within which risk management is to be executed. The CEO's risk policy requires guidelines in the following areas:

- statement of objectives of risk management (philosophy of risk);
- definition of risk classes;
- assignment of responsibility for risk management;

Figure 2: Assignment of risk responsibilities

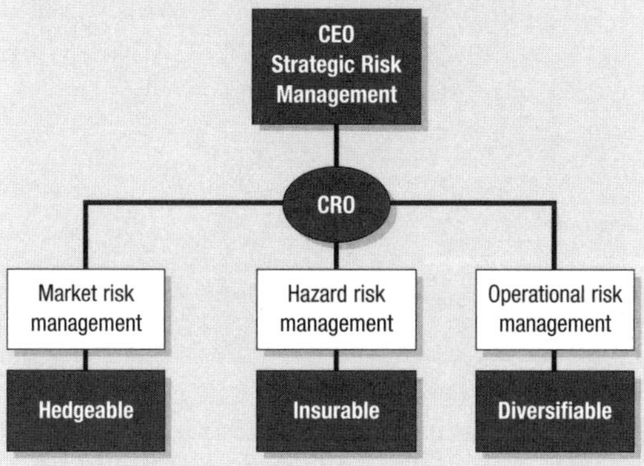

- hedging, insurance and diversification strategies;
- use of instruments: proscribed instruments and financial limits;
- risk reporting, including definition of financial limits, frequency, and critical event reporting.

Risk management for the CEO is about two decisions: whether to retain or hedge/transfer the risk; and whether to provide or not for the retained risk. Provision for the retained risk is used here to indicate a state of mind, rather than an accounting provision. The issue is about the extent to which the exposure should be allowed to affect the CEO's other decisions: financing, investment, dividend policy. Where exposures are provided for in an accounting sense, either explicitly on the balance sheet or implicitly by affecting other decisions, there often is a high opportunity cost of diverted capital. This, by its nature, destroys value. There is no perfect result of any risk analysis, but the CEO needs to know what the "default position" is so that any deviation is informed and understood in value terms.

Developing a risk policy for the chief executive is not a depressing task, full of reticence, warning and pessimism. It should be a creative initiative, exposing exciting opportunities for value growth and innovative handling of risk. The policy is not about compliance and disclosure, important as these may be. It is about developing a strategic approach to enterprise risks that releases value to shareholders. In the absence of such a policy, a company will be, at best, value-neutral; at worst, value-destroying. The risk policy provides the chief executive with the impetus for sustainable value creation.

Summary

Risk is often viewed as a bad thing, yet shareholders pay companies to take risks in the hope of reaping benefits. **Rory F. Knight** and **Deborah J. Pretty** urge chief executives to formulate a philosophy of risk that considers both the traditional aversion to risk and the scientific approach of the risk manager. Such a philosophy will enable the CEO, alongside the chief risk officer, to map out and implement specific risk policies in relevant areas of the business, and clarify the ways in which the company can best use risk to enhance shareholder value.

Subject index

abandonment of projects 147–9
acquisitions 14, 76
Act of God bonds 262, 263–4
adverse selection 196
advertising expenditure 89–90
aggregating risks 70–1
agricultural biotechnology industry 256
Algeria 184–5
alliances 74–9
  and e-commerce 232
  international joint ventures 82–4
  public–private partnerships 263–4
  relationship risks 78
  strategies for 78–9
  and transition costs 76–7
alternative risk transfer (ART) 197–200, 270
Asian crisis 17, 82, 126, 129
assessing risk 54, 55, 261–2
  see also Value at Risk
asset substitution 116, 117
asset valuation 305, 306–7
auditors 22

bankruptcy code 126–7
bankruptcy costs 16–17, 107, 114, 115, 117–18
banks
  capital requirements 203–4, 205–6, 213–18
  central banks 203
  failures 205
  operational risks 22
  runs on banks 202
Basle Accord 110, 121, 123, 203, 205–6, 213–18
batching orders 143–4
Bayes's Theorem 36
benchmarking 310
biases 27–8
bonds 110, 111, 126, 294–5
  Act of God bonds 262, 263–4
  catastrophe bonds 117, 270
  duration measures 110
  yield spreads 297
bottom-up risk profiling 55–6
brands 230–1, 236–40
Bretton Woods 101
bribery 187–90
BSE 167
bullwhip effect 143
business continuity planning 280–3
business impact analysis (BIA) 281–2
business risk 120
business segment diversification 94–5

C2 Principles 190
Cadbury Code 13, 293
capital requirements 203–4, 205–6, 213–18
capital structure 69–70, 93, 114–15
  cost of capital 197
  debt finance 18, 69, 116–18, 126
  equity capital 69–70
  project finance 218–23
captive insurance companies 195–6
cash flow 15–16, 19, 94
  discounted cash flow 47, 147
catastrophe bonds 117, 270
catastrophe options 270
catastrophe risk 260–4, 269–74
  continuity planning 280–3
  disaster recovery 280–3
  finance risk disasters 241–5
  and share prices 275–8
  stress testing 209–10, 302–3
central banks 203
channel risk 90, 230–2
chief executives 23, 311–15
CJD 167
cognitive biases 27–8
commodity derivatives 104
communication 13
  reporting lines 23–4
compensation schemes 57–61
  contest-based 59–61
  managerial incentives 18
  quota-based 58–9
competitor analysis 87–8
compliance management 166–7
computer data backup 283
confidence levels 109
confirmation bias 27–8
conglomerates 92, 95–6
consequential loss insurance 195
consolidating risk 54, 55
construction risk 219–20
Consumer Protection Act (1987) 157
content-related risk 173
contest-based compensation schemes 59–61
contingency management 22
contingent financing 118
continuity planning 280–3
contractual risk 171–2
control beliefs 28
control charts 142
control systems 10–14, 166
corporate governance *see* Turnbull Report
corporate structure 72
correlation of markets 113, 212, 297
corruption 187–90
cost of capital 197
  see also capital structure

costs of risk 15–18, 24, 114–18
counterparty risk 299, 304
credit ratings 19, 126
credit risk 120, 125–9
  management of 128–9
  reduced form models 128
  structural model 127–8
credit-linked notes 117
crime 185–6, 309
crisis management 22, 246–7, 249, 265–8
cultural negligence 244
currencies *see* foreign exchange
customers
  behavior analysis 87
  loyalty 88, 229
  new customer acquisition 89
  ranking 88

data backup 283
data protection 170
debt finance 18, 69, 116–18, 126
  forgivable debt 117–18
  recovery rates on loans 125–6
  reverse convertible debt (RCN) 118
  see also bonds; capital structure; credit risk
debt ratings 19, 126
decision making 8–9, 27–8, 115–16
decision tree analysis 48–52
defamatory emails 173
default risk *see* credit risk
defective products 156–60
delay strategies 144
Denmark 272–3
deposit insurance 202, 205
derivatives 68–9, 101–8
  commodity derivatives 104
  currency hedging 103–4, 105
  and financial risk 106–7
  forward contracts 19–20
  insurance derivatives 198–9
  interest rate swaps 104, 105
  non-delivery forward exchange-rate contracts (NDF) 221
  swaptions 104
  underlying assets 102
  warrants 102
  weather derivatives 199
  see also options
development risk 219–20
disaster recovery 280–3
discounted cash flow 47, 147
distress costs 16–17, 107, 114, 115, 117–18
  bankruptcy code 126–7
distribution channels 90, 230–2
diversification 7, 15–16, 53–7, 92–6
  business segment 94–5
  geographical 94–5
  portfolio theory 53–7, 92–3
  and shareholder value 94–5
diversification discount 19
duration measures 110
dynamic financial analysis 56

e-commerce 229–36
  and alliances 232
  and branding 230–1, 236–40
  channel risk 230–2
  and customer loyalty 229
  and liquidity 235
  outages 280
  scenario analysis 234–5
  sourcing risk 232–3
  strategic drivers 233–5
  structural risk 229–30
  see also Internet
earnings 307–8
earthquakes *see* catastrophe risk
economic risk 106
economies of scope 93
ego 243
Electronic Commerce Bill 171
emails 173
embedded control systems 12–13
employees 90–1, 308
employer's liability 309
employment risk 93
Endangered Species Act 258
enterprise risk management 67–73, 123
enterprise value 311–13
environmental risk 255–9
  analytical tools 255–6
  incentives for 258–9
  reduction techniques 256–8
equity capital 69–70
  see also capital structure
escalating commitment 242
eurodollar loans 122–3
evaluating risks 11–12
event risks 120, 121
evolutionary psychology 241
excess kurtosis 111–12
exchange rates *see* foreign exchange
extreme events *see* catastrophe risk
extreme value theory (EVT) 209, 269–74
Exxon Valdez 249, 258, 267, 275

fantasy 242
"fat tails" 208
fear 26, 243
fidelity losses 309
financial instruments *see* derivatives
financial risk 106–7, 120
  disasters 241–5
finite risk insurance 197–8
focus groups 56
force majeure risks 222
foreign exchange
  Bretton Woods era 101
  currency crises 210
  risk management 19–20, 103–4, 106–7
forgivable debt 117–18
forward contracts 19–20
fraud 309
fund raising 17

game theory 7, 8–9
gaming the system 121–2
geographical diversification 94–5
goods-in-transit 309
goodwill 246

governments
  deposit insurance 202, 205
  as lender of last resort 202–3
greed 242–3
gross profit analysis 307
gross risk 12
group insurance 195

hazard risks 314
health and safety 152–6
hedging 114, 294–5, 313–14
  currency hedging 103–4, 105
  and project finance 220–1
history of risk 5–10
Honduras 260
Huber Report 44–5
hurricanes *see* catastrophe risk

identifying market trends 86–8
identifying risks 11–12, 54, 55
idiosyncratic risk 15
illusion of control 29
improvement options in projects 148, 149–50
Industrial Dynamics 143
information technology (IT) outsourcing 135–41
  contract length 138
  losses from 136–8
  market size 135
  post-contract management 139–40
  skills requirements 139
  success in 139, 140
innocent assistance risk 173–4
insurance 7, 22, 71, 118, 195–201
  adverse selection 196
  alternative risk transfer (ART) 197–200, 270
  captive insurance companies 195–6
  consequential loss 195
  and cost of capital 197
  deposit insurance 202
  finite risk insurance 197–8
  group insurance 195
  and legislation 196
  liability insurance 159, 195
  life pooling 308
  limitations of 196–7
  moral hazard 196, 203–5
  product range 195
  reinsurance market 262
  securitization products 199–200
  and taxation 196
  valuation of assets 305, 306–7
insurance derivatives 198–9
insurance risk managers 306–10
integrated risk management 67–73, 123
intellectual property rights 173
interest rate risk 101, 104
interest rate swaps 104, 105
internal control 10–14, 166
Internet 44, 169–75
  content-related risk 173
  contractual risk 171–2
  and crisis management 249
  and data protection 170
  defamatory emails 173
  innocent assistance risk 173–4
  intellectual property rights 173
  jurisdictional risk 172
  and legal harmonization 169–71
  see also e-commerce
investment decisions 115–16
ISO 9000 158
Israel 221
IT *see* information technology (IT) outsourcing

Japan 205
joint ventures *see* alliances
jurisdictional risk 172
just-in-time delivery 144

kidnapping 182–3
Kobe earthquake 269–70

LAN restart 283
latent value 311–12
Law of Large Numbers 7
legal harmonization 169–71
legal risk 221–2
lender of last resort 202–3
Leverage Irrelevance Proposition 16
liabilities 156–60, 195, 309–10
life pooling 308
lines of credit 118
liquidity 120–1, 122, 235, 299
loss prevention programs 306–7
loyalty of customers 88, 229

maintenance risks 220
managerial incentives 18
mapping risk 53–7
market contagion 210
market correlation 113, 212, 297
market risk 120, 313–14
market trends 86–8
market volatility 112, 208, 209
marking to market 299–300
mean regression 6–7, 40
mental maps 44–5
Mexico 205, 207, 210, 221
mispricing theory 297
mobile restart facilities 283
Monte Carlo simulation 38, 47–8, 54
moral hazard 196, 203–5
motor vehicles 308
MTBE 145–6

natural disasters *see* catastrophe risk
net present value (NPV) 115–16
new customer acquisition 89
non-delivery forward exchange-rate contracts (NDF) 221
non-linear portfolios 112
normal distribution 7, 207
  see also standard model
Norway 188

operating efficiency 93–4
operations risk 67–8, 121, 141–6, 220, 306–10, 314
  batching orders 143–4
  bullwhip effect 143
  continuity planning 280–3
  control charts 142

delay strategies 144
and employees 308
goods-in-transit 309
gross profit analysis 307
health and safety 152–6
just-in-time delivery 144
liabilities 156–60, 309–10
macro-risks 145–6
micro-risks 141–5
process improvement 142
total quality management 143
valuation of assets 306–7
variability in processes 143–4
opportunity capture 150–1
options
catastrophe options 270
financial options 79–81
implied volatility 209
and joint ventures/alliances 77
real options 52, 79–85
valuation models 7, 103, 112, 296
writing options 110
outages 280
outsourcing 135–41

partnerships 263–4
see also alliances
perception of risk 25–9
personal injury claims 152–3, 157
personality 28, 241–4
pharmaceutical companies 48–9, 77–8
policy development 313–15
political risk 145–6, 176–81, 221–2, 290–1
definition 177
external drivers 178
framework 177–80
interaction drivers 178–9
internal drivers 179–80
systematic approach 180
pollution *see* environmental risk
portfolio theory 53–7, 92–3
post-loss investments 116–17
PrecisionTree 49
premium value 311
pricing 90
principal-agent costs 116
prioritizing risks 12, 248
private–public partnerships 263–4
probability theory 5–10, 35–6
process improvement 142
product liability 156–60, 309–10
product recalls 158–9
project management
abandonment options 147–9
development and construction risk 219–20
finance 218–23
force majeure risks 222
hedging 220–1
improvement options 148, 149–50
legal and political risk 221–2
operation and maintenance risks 220
opportunity capture 150–1
selection of projects 116
specification freeze 149
turnkey contracts 219–20

Prospect Theory 26–7
public liability 309–10
public relations 90
public–private partnerships 263–4

qualifications of risk managers 22–3, 290
quantifying risk 54
quota-based compensation schemes 58–9

ranking customers 88
rare events *see* catastrophe risk
RAROC (risk-adjusted return on capital) 121, 122
RCN (reverse convertible debt) 118
real options 52, 79–85
international joint ventures 82–4
multinational networks 82
recession strategies 86–91
advertising expenditure 89–90
competitor analysis 87–8
customer behavior analysis 87
customer loyalty 88
distribution channels 90
and employees 90–1
identifying market trends 86–8
and new customer acquisition 89
and pricing 90
and products/services 89
public relations 90
ranking customers 88
supplier relationships 90
recovery rates on loans 125–6
regression to the mean 6–7, 40
regulation 113, 165–8
compliance management 166–7
self-regulation 165
state regulation 165
and systemic risk 203–5
reinsurance market 262
relationship risks 78
relocatable restart facilities 283
remediation 306
reporting lines 23–4
reputation management 11, 26, 189–90, 236–40, 246–50
restart facilities 283
retrieveability 27
reverse convertible debt (RCN) 118
risk databases 13
risk management 289–94, 301–5
evolution of 289–91
and foreign exchange 19–20, 103–4, 106–7
integrated risk management 67–73, 123
rules of 302
risk managers 21–5
insurance risk managers 306–10
qualifications 22–3, 290
reporting lines 23–4
skills requirements 23
risk mapping 53–7
risk policy development 313–15
risk-adjusted return on capital (RAROC) 121, 122
roguery 242
runs on banks 202
Russia 185, 296
Rutteman Report 13

sampling 7
savings and loan institutions 204
scenario planning 37, 42–6, 210, 234–5
  mental maps 44–5
  subjective assessment 43
Sea Empress 166–7
securitization of insurance products 199–200
security risks 181–6
  crime 185–6
  kidnapping 182–3
  terrorism 183–5
self-regulation 165
sensation seeking 28
share prices 275–8
shareholder value 15–20, 18, 94–5
six-sigma system 143
skills of risk managers 23
sourcing risk 232–3
South Africa 185
South Korea 188
specification freeze 149
stakeholders 17–18, 268
standard deviation 7, 110
standard model 207–12
  correlation breakdown 212, 297
  extreme value theory (EVT) 209, 269–74
  "fat tails" 208
  market contagion 210
  volatility clustering 208
star culture 244
state regulation 165
static restart facilities 283
stochastic modeling 38, 270
stock market risk 37–40
strategic risk 313
stress testing 209–10, 302–3
structured debt 117
subjective assessment 43
supplier relationships 90
swaps 104, 105
swaptions 104
systemic risk 15, 202–6, 203–5
systems failure 280

tactical risk management 72–3
tangible value 311
taxation 67, 196
Telecommunications Decency Act (1997) 174
Tequila Effect 210
terrorism 183–5
theft *see* crime
top-down risk profiling 54–5
total quality management 143
transferring risk 13
transition costs 76–7
travel agents 231
travel policies 308
Treasury bonds *see* bonds
Turkey 188, 260
Turnbull Report 10–14, 23, 166, 280–1, 293
turnkey contracts 219–20

undiversified shareholders 18
Unfair Contract Terms Act 172
utility theory 40, 50–1
  history of 6–9

valuation of assets 305, 306–7
valuation model of companies 114–15
valuation of options 7, 103, 112, 296
Value at Risk 47, 109–14, 119–24, 207, 271–3
  confidence levels 109
  and correlation of markets 113, 297
  definition 109
  and excess kurtosis 111–12
  gaming the system 121–2
  history of 110–11
  and market volatility 112
  and non-linear portfolios 112
  and regulatory requirements 113
  stress testing 209–10, 302–3
variability in processes 143–4
Venezuela 260
volatility 112, 208
  option-implied 209
  standard deviation 7, 110
volatility clustering 208

warrants 102
weather derivatives 199
websites *see* Internet
women traders 244
workplace health and safety 152–6
workshops 56
writing options 110

X-bar control charts 142
yield spreads 297

Organization index

ABB (Asea Brown Boveri) 82
Abbott Laboratories 77–8
Air France 90
Amazon.com 229, 234, 239
American Airlines 90
American International Group (AIM) 71
AOL 45, 174
Aon 56, 118, 292
Argos 172
Ashanti Goldfields 19, 311
Association of Insurance and Risk Managers (AIRMIC) 21, 22, 23
AT&T 44–5, 76–7, 92
Aventis 256

Bank of Scotland 95
Bankers Trust 121, 122, 297
Barings Bank 121, 204, 241, 270
Basle Accord 110, 121, 123, 203, 205–6, 213–18
Benetton 140, 237
BMW 88
BP Amoco 136, 138, 139, 140
British Aerospace 139
British Airways 90, 230
British Gas 140, 173
British Midland Airways 247
British Nuclear Fuels 152
British Railways 167
British Safety Council 153–4
British Telecommunications 90, 149

Caderyta 221
Capital One 138, 234
CargoLifter 149
Carrefour 230
Catastrophe Risk Exchange (CATWX) 198
Caterpillar 90, 144–5
Chase Manhattan 297
Chevron 258, 259
Chicago Board of Trade (CBOT) 198
Chrysler 17, 76
Ciba-Geigy 84
Cisco Systems 45, 140
Citibank 234
Citicorp 297
Clarica 240
Coca-Cola 238, 275
Comcast 76
Commonwealth Bank of Australia 138
Continental Airlines 90
Continental Illinois National Bank 203
Contingency Planning Research 280
Coopers & Lybrand 166
Corning Glass 76, 77, 84
COSO (Committee of Sponsoring Organizations) 166
Cross Israel 221
Crossair 150
CSC 139

Daimler-Benz 76
Daiwa Bank 241
Dataquest 280
Delta Air Lines 90
Demon Internet 173–4
Deutsche Morgan Grenfell 241
DHL 89
Disney 68, 69
DuPont 140, 256

East India Company 75
East Midlands Electricity 138
Eastern Airlines 17, 235
eComplaints.com 239
EDS 137, 138, 139
Electriciti de France 88
Eli Lilly 240
Enron 69
Environment Agency 167
Exxon Corporation 249, 258, 267, 275

Federal Reserve Board 203, 280
Financial Services Authority 165, 280
First Union Bank 88
Fitch IBCA 126

General Electric 96, 155, 220
General Motors 143
Glasgow Caledonian University 22–3
Glaxo Wellcome 306–10
Global Association of Risk Professionals (GARP) 22
Goldfields of South Africa 313
Goldman Sachs 203
Granada 92
Group of Thirty 119

Hanson 92
Hershey 88
Hewlett-Packard 144
Hill & Knowlton 238
Home Depot 231
Homestake 313
Honda 145
Honeywell 71
Hyundai 91

IBM 42, 138
IMF 203
Industrial Dynamics 143
ING 118
Inland Revenue 139
Institute of Risk Management 22
Intel 155

Interbrand 238, 246
International Business Machines (IBM) 42, 138
International Monetary Fund (IMF) 203
Iridium 75
Iron Trades 309
ITT 92

John Deere 142
Johnson and Johnson 155
J.P. Morgan 47, 110, 119, 297, 302
JWM Partners 271

Kidder Peabody 203
KPMG 56

Larousse 266
Lend Lease 138
Levi-Strauss 155
LG Group 91
Lockheed Martin 187
London School of Economics 23
London Stock Exchange 280
Long-Term Capital Management 42, 122, 203, 271, 294–300
Lufthansa 145
LVMH 53

McDonald's 89
Manpower 86–7
Mars 89
Mercedes-Benz 246
Metallgesellschaft 19, 311
Microsoft 68, 69, 76, 104, 111
Milford Haven Port Authority 166–7
Molex 143
Monsanto 256
Moody's 126
Motorola 75, 143, 190

National Audit Office (NAO) 21
National Science Foundation (NSF) 44
NatWest 95, 121, 241
NCR 76–7
Nestli 256
New Zealand Telecom 174
Newmont 313
Nextel Communications 76
Nike 237
Nintendo 174
Norwich Union 173
Novartis 256

Occidental Petroleum 278
OCS Cleaning 153
On-Line Organization 174
Oriflame 89
Origin 139
Overseas Private Investment Corporation (OPIC) 221

PanAm 235
Pemex 221
Perot Systems 137, 138
Perrier 275, 278
Philip Morris 111
Philips Electronics 139, 140
Pioneer Hi-Bred 256
Placer Dome 313
Pokémon 87
Powergen 138
Procter & Gamble 19, 88, 104, 122, 144
Prodigy 42
PwC 55

Ranks Hovis McDougall 92
Ratners 246
Resolution Trust Corporation 116
Reuters 110
Risk and Insurance Management Society (RIMS) 21, 290
RiskMetrics 110–11
RJR Nabisco 72
Royal Bank of Scotland 95
Royal Dutch 275

Sainsbury 230
Salomon Brothers 71–2, 294–5
Samsung 91
Sandoz 275
Sea Empress 166–7
Sears Roebuck 42, 135
Sega 174
Shell 275
Siecor 77
Siemens 77
Special Steel of Attercliffe 152–3
Standard & Poor's 126
Stern School of New York 243
Sumitomo 241
Sutton Bridge 219–20
Swiss Re 269

Takeda Chemical Industries 77–8
TAP Pharmaceuticals 77–8
Taylor Nelson Sofres 89
Teledesic 75
Telefonica del Peru 222
TermoEmcali 219, 222
Tesco 230
Texaco 190
Tomkins 92
Toronto Star 174
Toyota 144
Transparency International 187–8
Treadway Commission 166
Trident 221–2

Unilever 90, 230, 256
Union Carbide 278
United Airlines 90
UOP 145, 146

Virgin 169, 239

Wal-Mart 144, 230, 233
Walt Disney 68, 69
Weyerhaeuser 86

Xerox 76, 137

Yahoo! 45, 174

Zurich International 54–5

Name index

Anderson, Erin 238

Bachelier, Louis 207
Bayes, Thomas 36
Bell, Philip 132, 156–60
Berger, Lisa 155
Bernoulli, Daniel 6, 7
Bernoulli, Jacob 7
Bernstein, Peter L. 2, 5–10
Bishop, Sir Michael 247
Black, Fischer 7, 103
Broadbent, Marianne 136
Brotzen, David 226, 246–50
Brown, Gregory W. 98, 101–8
Browne, Sir John 136
Butterworth, Mark 2, 21–5

Carey, Anthony 2, 10–14
Clemons, Eric K. 226, 229–36
Copeland, Thomas 47
Cox, Sue 154
Cram, Tony 64, 86–91
Cross, John 138

Deep, Akash 192, 218–23
Della Femina, Jerry 237
Deming, W. Edwards 143
Dickinson, Gerry 192, 195–201
Doherty, Neil A. 98, 114–18
Dunfee, Thomas 190

Embrechts, Paul 252, 269–74
Eppen, Gary D. 132, 141–6

Feeny, David 139
Fenton-O'Creevy, Mark 2, 25–9
Fermat, Pierre de 6, 7
Finger, Christopher C. 192, 207–12
Forrester, Jay 143

Gaba, Anil 32, 57–61
Galton, Francis 6–7
Galvin, Robert 143
Gates, Bill 75, 76
Glasserman, Paul 98, 109–14
Godfrey, Dr Laurence 173–4
Gomes-Casseres, Benjamin 64, 74–9
Gore, Al 187
Graunt, John 7
Greenspan, Alan 203, 271

Halley, Edmund 7
Hamanaka, Yasuo 241, 242
Hanley, Mike 32, 53–7
Hanson, Lord 92

Heidelberger, Philip 112
Hertz, David 48
Hess, David 190
Huchzermeier, Arnd 132, 147–51
Hunt, Ben 286, 289–94
Hutter, Bridget 162, 165–8

Iguchi, Toshihide 241

John, Gareth 132, 152–6
Jorion, Philippe 98, 119–24
Juran, Joseph M. 143

Kahneman, Daniel 26
Kalra, Ajay 58
Kaplan, Robert 89, 155
Keenan, Phillip 47
Knight, Rory F. 64, 86, 92–6, 252, 275–9, 311–15
Kunreuther, Howard 252, 260–4

Leeson, Nick 121, 241, 242, 243, 270
Leiblein, Michael J. 64, 79–85
Lewin, Chris 32, 35–41
Lloyd, Edward 7
Loch, Christoph H. 132, 147–51

McCaw, Craig 75
MacInnis, Deborah 238
Malz, Allan M. 192, 207–12
Mann, Roland 252, 280–3
Markowitz, Harry 7, 48, 92
Mauro, Paolo 189
Maxwell, Robert 165
Meriwether, John 271, 294–5
Merton, Robert 294
Meulbroek, Lisa 64, 67–73
Miller, Merton 16
Mishkin, Frederic S. 192, 202–6
Mitroff, Ian 252, 265–8, 276
Modigliani, Franco 16
Moivre, Abraham de 7
Morgenstern, Oskar 7, 8–9
Morris, Nigel 137

Naím, Moisés 187
Netanyahu, Benjamin 187
Nichols, Philip M. 162, 187–90
Nicholson, Nigel 226, 241–6
Norton, David 89, 155

Papouis, Kyriacos 121, 241
Pascal, Blaise 6, 7–8
Pauchant, Thierry 276
Power, Michael 162, 165–8
Pretty, Deborah J. 64, 92–6, 252, 275–9, 286, 311–15

Randall, Julian 162, 169–75
Reddaway, Richard 286, 306–10
Reinhardt, Forest 252, 255–9
Reur, Jeffrey J. 64, 79–85
Robinson, Andrew 132, 152–6
Robinson, Gerry 92
Rosen, Robert 155

Sauer, Chris 132, 135–41
Schmitt, Bernd 226, 236–40
Scholes, Myron 7, 103, 294
Schwartz, Peter 32, 42–6
Shahabuddin, Perwez 112
Shapira, Zur 243
Shepheard-Walwyn, Tim 192, 213–18
Shewhart, Walter A. 142
Slovic, Paul 26
Smallman, Clive 132, 152–6
Soane, Emma 2, 25–9
Stone, Martin 162, 181–6
Stulz, Reni 2, 15–20, 94, 286, 294–300
Suharto, President 189
Sundaresan, Suresh M. 98, 125–9

Tait, Robin 154
Thieke, Stephen G. 286, 301–5
Treacy, Bridget 162, 169–75
Trigeorgis, Lenos 47
Turnbull, Nigel 2, 10–14
Tversky, Amos 26

Vlahos, Kiriakos 32, 47–52
von Neumann, John 7, 8–9

Ward, Stephen 23–4
Wei, Shang-Jin 189
Weill, Peter 136
Weiss, Allen 238
Welch, Jack 96
White, Lord 92
Wilkin, Sam 162, 176–81
Willcocks, Leslie 132, 135–41
Willman, Paul 226, 241–6
Wolfensohn, James 187

Yard, John 139
Young, Peter 241

Zonis, Marvin 162, 176–81